"With rare exceptions, such as the courts headed by John Marshall and Earl Warren, it was not common until recently to explain the work-product of constitutional courts by focusing on their leadership. Now, however, a number of writers have begun to emphasize the importance of the chief justice in guiding courts to be bold or cautious, expansive or restrictive, in their constitutional decisions. With his extensive knowledge and with great judiciousness, Stefanus Hendrianto has examined the important role of chief justices of the Constitutional Court of Indonesia. He shows convincingly that leadership can indeed make a major difference in the emergence of constitutional doctrine, as he examines the work of the Court and compares it to similar courts elsewhere. This is an important work of comparative constitutional law and politics that will repay careful study."

Donald L. Horowitz, Duke University, USA and author of Constitutional Change and Democracy in Indonesia

"This book is a major contribution to comparative constitutional studies. It provides a crisp and authoritative account of the early jurisprudence of the Indonesian Constitutional Court, a highly active and creative court operating in one of the world's largest democracies. It also offers a fascinating account of the role of Chief Justice Jimly Asshiddiqie as the leader of that court, and in doing so makes an important contribution to broader debates about the role of constitutional judges—and different styles of constitutional judging—in the consolidation of constitutional democracy."

Rosalind Dixon, UNSW Sydney, Australia

"This fascinating study of the Indonesian Constitutional Court introduces an entirely new concept for understanding judicial power: the judge as a heroic figure. Providing an exhaustive account of the Court's successes and failures, Hendrianto makes a powerful case for the role of judicial leadership in new democracies."

Tom Ginsburg, University of Chicago, USA

"This book provides a welcome and valuable contribution to the literature of comparative constitutional law and judicial politics. It broadens our comparative horizons by making the important example of the Indonesian Constitutional Court, with its distinctive history and model of constitutional review, more familiar and accessible to us; and at the same time it explores innovatively the connections between judicial leadership and the institutional legitimacy and effectiveness of constitutional courts. Throughout, Hendrianto creatively combines a rich and helpful contextualization of Indonesian judicial politics with a theorization of judicial virtues in an Aristotelian frame."

Paolo G. Carozza, University of Notre Dame, USA

Law and Politics of Constitutional Courts

This book critically evaluates different models of judicial leadership in Indonesia to examine the impact that individual chief justices can have on the development of constitutional courts. It explores the importance of this leadership as a factor explaining the dynamic of judicial power. Drawing on an Aristotelean model of heroism and the established idea of judicial heroes to explore the types of leadership that judges can exercise, it illustrates how Indonesia's recent experience offers a stark contrast between the different models. First, a prudential-minimalist heroic chief justice who knows how to enhance the Court's authority while fortifying the Court's status by playing a minimalist role in policy areas. Second, a bold and aggressive heroic chief justice, employing an ambitious constitutional interpretation. The third model is a soldier-type chief justice, who portrays himself as a subordinate of the Executive and Legislature. Contrary perhaps to expectations, the book's findings show a more cautious initial approach to be the most effective. The experience of Indonesia clearly illustrates the importance of heroic judicial leadership and how the approach chosen by a court can have serious consequences for its success. This book will be a valuable resource for those interested in the law and politics of Indonesia, comparative constitutional law, and comparative judicial politics.

Stefanus Hendrianto is a Jesuit and legal scholar. In recent years, he served as a visiting professor at Santa Clara University School of Law and a guest scholar at the Kellogg Institute for International Studies at the University of Notre Dame. Currently, he is a scholar at Boston College, School of Theology and Ministry. He holds a PhD degree from the University of Washington School of Law in Seattle and an LLM from Utrecht University in the Netherlands, in addition to his LLB degree from Gadjah Mada University, Indonesia.

Comparative Constitutionalism in Muslim Majority States

Series Editor: *Javaid Rehman*

This series encourages research into all aspects of comparative constitutionalism within the Muslim-Majority States of South Asia and the Middle East. Key areas of investigation include the post 9-11 implications on constitutionalism and the consequences of the Arab Spring. The studies within the series span across all aspects of constitutionalism, including constitutional rights, constitutional practices, rule of law issues, human rights, sexual rights and minorities. While the focus of the series is upon the Muslim-Majority States within the South Asia and Middle East region, the comparative critical assessment will engage a global analysis of constitutionalism and application of constitutional rights. Amidst the many cases of failed constitutionalism, there are a number of positives: this series also aims to explore and identify key successes from within the region.

States of Emergency and the Law
The Experience of Bangladesh
M. Ehteshamul Bari

Law and Politics of Constitutional Courts

Indonesia and the Search for Judicial Heroes

Stefanus Hendrianto

Routledge
Taylor & Francis Group
LONDON AND NEW YORK

First published 2018
by Routledge

2 Park Square, Milton Park, Abingdon, Oxfordshire OX14 4RN
52 Vanderbilt Avenue, New York, NY 10017

Routledge is an imprint of the Taylor & Francis Group, an informa business

First issued in paperback 2020

British Library Cataloguing-in-Publication Data
A catalogue record for this book is available from the British Library

Library of Congress Cataloging-in-Publication Data
Names: Hendrianto, Stefanus, author.
Title: Law and politics of constitutional courts: Indonesia and the search for judicial heroes / Stefanus Hendrianto.
Description: Abingdon, Oxon [UK]; New York, NY: Routledge, 2018. |
Series: Islamic law in context | Includes bibliographical references and index.
Identifiers: LCCN 2017054405 | ISBN 9781138296428 (hardback)
Subjects: LCSH: Constitutional courts—Indonesia. | Constitutional law (Islamic law)–Indonesia. | Political questions and judicial power—Indonesia.
Classification: LCC KNW2620 .H46 2018 | DDC 347.598/035—dc23
LC record available at https://lccn.loc.gov/2017054405

ISBN: 978-1-138-29642-8 (hbk)
ISBN: 978-0-367-59174-8 (pbk)

Typeset in Galliard
by Deanta Global Publishing Services, Chennai, India

For the many great Jesuits who have taught me how to build an intellectual and virtuous life, especially Fr. James V. Schall, SJ and Fr. Robert A. Araujo, SJ

Contents

Tables

Cited cases

The Indonesian Constitutional Court Decisions

The Constitutional Court Decision No. 001-021-022/PUU-I/2003 (the *Electricity Law* case)

The Constitutional Court Decision No. 002/PUU-I/2003 (the *Oil and Gas Law I* case)

The Constitutional Court Decision No. 003/PUU-I/2003 (the *Government Securities Law* case)

The Constitutional Court Decision No. 004/PUU-I/2003 (the *Supreme Court Law I* case)

The Constitutional Court Decision No. 005/PUU-I/2003 (the *Broadcasting Law* case)

The Constitutional Court Decision No. 011-017/PUU-I/2003 (the *Communist Party* case)

The Constitutional Court Decision No. 013/PUU-I/2003 (the *Bali Bombing* case)

The Constitutional Court Decision No. 014/PUU-I/2003 (the *Susduk Law* case)

The Constitutional Court Decision No: 018/PUU-I/2003 (the *West Papuan* case)

The Constitutional Court Decision No. 058-059-060-063/PUU-II/2004 (the *Water Resources Law I* case)

The Constitutional Court Decision No. 066/PUU-II/2004 (the *Chamber of Commerce Law* case)

The Constitutional Court Decision No. 067/PUU-II/2004 (the *Supreme Court Law II* case)

The Constitutional Court Decision No. 069/PUU-II/2004 (the *Bram Manoppo* case)

The Constitutional Court Decision No. 072- 073 /PUU-II/2004 (the *KPUD* case)

The Constitutional Court Decision No. 003/PUU-III/2005 (the *Open Pit Mining* case)

The Constitutional Court Decision No. 006/PUU-III/2005 (the *Pemda Law III* case)

The Constitutional Court Decision No. 011/PUU-III/2005 (the *National Education System Law* case)

The Constitutional Court Decision No. 026/PUU-III/2005 (the *Education Budget II* case)
The Constitutional Court Decision No. 003/PUU-IV/2006 (the *Dawud Djatmiko* case)
The Constitutional Court Decision No. 005/PUU-IV/2006 (the *Judicial Commission* case)
The Constitutional Court Decision No. 006/PUU-IV/2006 (the *Truth and Reconciliation Commission Law* case)
The Constitutional Court Decision No. 008/PUU-IV/2006 (the *Right to Recall* case)
The Constitutional Court Decision No. 012-016-019/PUU-IV/2006 (the *Mulyana Kusumah* case)
The Constitutional Court Decision No. 013-022/PUU-IV/2006 (the *Lèse Majesté* case)
The Constitutional Court Decision No. 024/PUU-IV/2006 (the *Military Voting Right* case)
The Constitutional Court Decision No. 026/PUU-IV/2006 (the *Education Budget III* case)
The Constitutional Court Decision No. 2-3/PUU-V/2007 (the *Death Penalty* case)
The Constitutional Court Decision No. 05/PUU-V/2007 (the *Independent Candidate* case)
The Constitutional Court Decision No. 6/PUU-V/2007 (the *Spreading Hatred* case)
The Constitutional Court Decision No. 12/PUU-V/2007 (the *Polygamy* case)
The Constitutional Court Decision No. 29/PUU-V/2007 (the *Film Censorship* case)
The Constitutional Court Decision No. 14-17/PUU-V/2007 (the *Political Crime I* case)
The Constitutional Court Decision No. 024/PUU-V/2007 (the *Education Budget IV* case)
The Constitutional Court Decision No. 15/PUU-VI/2008 (the *Political Crime II* case)
The Constitutional Court Decision No. 10/PUU-VI/2008 (the *DPD Residence* case)
The Constitutional Court Decision No. 13/PUU-VI/2008 (the *Education Budget V* case)
The Constitutional Court Decision No. 14/PUU-VI/2008 (the *Wijaya & Lubis* case)
The Constitutional Court Decision No. 22-24/PUU-VI/2008 (the *Mohammad Sholeh* case)
The Constitutional Court Decision No. 50/PUU-VI/2008 (the *Bloggers I* case)
The Constitutional Court Decision No. 54/PUU-VI/2008 (the *Tobacco Excise Tax* case)
The Constitutional Court Decision No. 2/PUU-VII/2009 (the *Bloggers II* case)

The Constitutional Court Decision No. 10-17-23/PUU-VII/2009 (the *Pornography Law* Case)

The Constitutional Court Decision No. 102/PUU-VII/2009 (the *ID Card* Case)

The Constitutional Court Decision No. 110-111-112-113/PUU-VII/2009 (the *Leftover Votes* case).

The Constitutional Court Decision No.133/PUU-VII/2009 (the *Hamzah & Riyanto* case)

The Constitutional Court Decision No. 137/PUU-VII/2009 (the *Animal Health and Husbandry I* case).

The Constitutional Court Decision No. 138/PUU-VII/2009 (the *PERPU* case)

The Constitutional Court Decision No. 140/PUU-VII/2009 (the *Blasphemy Law* Case)

The Constitutional Court Decision No. 149/PUU-VII/2009 (the *Electricity Law II* case)

The Constitutional Court Decision No. 3/PUU-VIII/2010 (the *Coastal and Remote Islands Law* case)

The Constitutional Court Decision No. 6-13-20/PUU-VIII/2010 (the *Book Banning* case)

The Constitutional Court Decision No. 25/PUU-VIII/2010 (the *Tin Mining* case)

The Constitutional Court Decision No. 49/PUU-VIII/2010 (the *Attorney General* case)

The Constitutional Court Decision No. 50/PUU-VIII/2010 (the *SJSN II* case)

The Constitutional Court Decision No. 48/PUU-IX/2011 (the *2011 Amendment Law I* case)

The Constitutional Court Decision No. 49/PUU-IX/2011 (the *2011 Amendment Law II* case)

The Constitutional Court Decision No. 51/PUU-IX/2011 (the *SJSN III* case)

The Constitutional Court Decision No. 70/PUU-IX/2011 (the *SJSN IV* case)

The Constitutional Court Decision No. 5/PUU-X/2012 (the *International School* case)

The Constitutional Court Decision No. 35/PUU-X/2012 (the *Indigenous Forest I* case)

The Constitutional Court Decision No. 36/PUU-X/2012 (the *Oil and Gas III* case)

The Constitutional Court Decision No. 82/PUU-X/2012 (the *SJSN V* case)

The Constitutional Court Decision No. 84/PUU-X/2012 (the *Blasphemy II* case)

The Constitutional Court Decision No. 87 /PUU-XI/2012 (the *Farmers' Protection and Empowerment* case)

The Constitutional Court Decision No. 93/PUU-X/2012 (the *Sharia Banking* case)

The Constitutional Court Decision No. 99/PUU-X/2012 (the *Plant Cultivation System Law* case).

The Constitutional Court Decision No. 14/PUU-XI/2013 (the *General Election Schedule* case)
The Constitutional Court Decision No. 38/PUU-XI/2013 (the *Private Hospital* case)
The Constitutional Court Decision No. 52/PUU-XI/2013 (the *Twitter* case)
The Constitutional Court Decision No. 82/PUU-XI/2013 (the *Ormas* case)
The Constitutional Court Decision No. 85/PUU-XI/2013 (the *Water Resources Law II* case)
The Constitutional Court Decision No. 97/PUU-XI/2013, (the *Regional Election* case)
The Constitutional Court Decision No. 108/PUU-XI/2013 (the *Presidential Threshold* case)
The Constitutional Court Decision No. 18/PUU-XII/2014 (the *Chevron Pacific* case)
The Constitutional Court Decision No. 22/PUU-XII/2014 (the *Armed Forces Voting Right* case)
The Constitutional Court Decision No. 30-74/PUU-XII/2014 (the *Marriageable Age* case)
The Constitutional Court Decision No. 50/PUU-XII/2014 (the *Presidential Candidate* Case)
The Constitutional Court Decision No. 68/PUU-XII/2014 (the *Interfaith Marriage* case)
The Constitutional Court Decision No. 95/PUU-XII/2014 (the *Forestry and P3H Law* case)
The Constitutional Court Decision No. 33/PUU-XIII/2015 (the *Political Dynasty* case)
The Constitutional Court Decision No. 43/PUU-XIII/2015 (the *IKAHI* case)
The Constitutional Court Decision No. 111/PUU-XIII/2015 (the *Electricity III* case)
The Constitutional Court Decision No. 129/PUU-XIII/2015 (the *Animal Health and Husbandry Law II* case)
The Constitutional Court Decision No. 57/PUU-XIV/2016 (the *Tax Amnesty Law I* case)
The Constitutional Court Decision No. 58/PUU-XIV/2016 (the *Tax Amnesty Law II* case)
The Constitutional Court Decision No. 59/PUU-XIV/2016 (the *Tax Amnesty Law III* case)
The Constitutional Court Decision No. 63/PUU-XIV/2016 (the *Tax Amnesty IV* case)

Abbreviations

BPUPKI	*Badan Penyelidik Usaha Persiapan Kemerdekaan Indonesia*—Investigating Committee for the Preparation of Independence
BPHN	*Badan Pembinaan Hukum Nasional*—National Law Development Agency
BP-MIGAS	*Badan Pelaksana Kegiatan Usaha Hulu Minyak dan Gas Bumi*—Upstream Oil and Gas Regulatory Agency
BPP	*Bilangan Pembagi Pemilih*—Voting Division Number
DPD	*Dewan Perwakilan Daerah*—Regional Representative Council
DPR	*Dewan Perwakilan Rakyat*—People's Representative Assembly
DPRD	*Dewan Perwakilan Rakyat Daerah*—Regional People's Representative Council
DPT	*Daftar Pemilih Tetap*—Final Electoral Roll
GERINDRA	*Partai Gerakan Indonesia Raya*—Greater Indonesian Movement Party
GOLKAR	*Golongan Karya* (literally "Functional Group"—a political vehicle of General Soeharto)
HP3	*Hak Pengusahaan Perairan Pesisir*—Coast Water Concessions Right
KPK	*Komisi Pemberantasan Korupsi*—Anti-Corruption Commission
KPU	*Komisi Pemilihan Umum*—General Election Commission
KPUD	*Komisi Pemilihan Umum Daerah*—Regional Election Commission
MK	*Mahkmah Konstitusi*—Constitutional Court
MPR	*Majelis Permusyawaratan Rakyat*—People's Consultative Assembly
PAN	*Partai Amanat Nasional*—National Mandate Party
PBB	*Partai Bulan Bintang*—Crescent Star Party
PDI-P	*Partai Demokrasi Indonesia Perjuangan*—Indonesian Democratic Party of Struggle
PEMDA	*Pemerintahan Daerah*—Regional Government
PERPU	*Peraturan Pemerintah Pengganti Undang*—Undang—Government Regulation in lieu of Law
PERTAMINA	*Perusahaan Pertambangan Minyak dan Gas Bumi Negara*—State Oil and Natural Gas Mining Company
PILKADA	*Pemilihan Kepala Daerah*—Regional Election Head

PKB	*Partai Kebangkitan Bangsa*—National Awakening Party
PKI	Partai Komunis Indonesia—Indonesian Communist Party
PKS	*Partai Keadilan Sejahtera*—Prosperous Justice Party
PLN	*Perusahaan Listrik Negara*—State Electricity Company
PP	*Peraturan Pemerintah*—Government Regulation
PPP	*Partai Persatuan Pembangunan*—United Development Party
PRD	*Partai Rakyat Demokratik*—People's Democratic Party
SJSN	*Sistem Jaminan Sosial Nasional*—National Social Security System
UGM	*Universitas Gadjah Mada*—Gadjah Mada University
YLBHI	Yayasan Lembaga Bantuan Hukum Indonesia—Indonesian Legal Aid Institute Foundation

Acknowledgments

This book was born out of my academic journeys in several places: my graduate studies at the University of Washington School of Law, my visiting post at Santa Clara University, my sojourn at the University of Notre Dame, and my current academic home at Boston College. In an admittedly brief way, I would like to acknowledge many people who have contributed to the book directly and indirectly. I will be forever grateful to those people who not only helped me to finish this book but also made me a better person.

First, this book grew out of my doctoral work at the Asian Law Center at the University of Washington School of Law, and thus, sincere thanks are owed to my dissertation committee: Veronica Taylor, Clark Lombardi, Stewart Jay, and Mark Cammack. I would also like to thank Rachel Chikowski, who served as the external reader, especially for sharing some important tips on preparing a book proposal. I owe so much also to the late Daniel S. Lev, who brought me to the University of Washington. I would not be where I am today without his advocacy. Special thanks to Patricia "Patti" Goedde, who took me under her wing when I began to make my way into the doctoral program and for her enduring friendship.

Upon the completion of my doctoral studies, I abruptly left legal academia and joined a religious order, the Society of Jesus. Having finished the novitiate and philosophy studies, I joined Santa Clara Law School as visiting faculty. I must thank the Santa Clara University president, Mike Engh, SJ; and the dean of the Law School, Lisa Kloppenberg, for giving me an opportunity to resume my academic endeavors. I am extremely grateful to Santa Clara University Jesuit Community, especially to the then rector, Michael Zampelli, SJ, for his tremendous support in the production of this book. At the Jesuit community, I received constant support from Paul Mariani, SJ; the late Ted Rynes, SJ; the late Jerry McKevich, SJ; John Rose, SJ; Sam Conedera, SJ; and Peter Rozic, SJ.

In the academic year of 2015–2016, I resided at "Our Lady University" in Notre Dame, where I was privileged to spend time writing and researching. At the Kellogg Institute for International Studies at the University of Notre Dame, I am grateful to Paulo Carozza for providing me with an intellectual home as a guest scholar. Henri de Lubac Jesuit House provided me both with a spiritual and physical home during my sojourn at Notre Dame. I thank my local superior,

Michael Magree, SJ, who patiently listened to my struggles in finishing this book. I am also grateful to some individuals that I met at Notre Dame, many of whom have become good friends: Clara Minieri, Mary Mangan, Laura Wolk, Kelly Anderson, and Audrey Rabenberg.

I arrived in Boston in fall 2016, and the final phase of writing took place at Boston College. I am grateful to my rector, Jim Gartland, SJ, who allowed me to continue working on the book while completing my main mission at Boston College. In particular, I would like to thank my fellow Jesuits at St. Peter Faber community: Kevin Embach, SJ; Stephen Wolfe, SJ; Jason Lalonde, SJ; Henry Shea, SJ; and Vince Strand, SJ for their companionship.

I am grateful to certain individuals who gave their genuine support to me in my mad rush to finish the book. I am immensely thankful to Rosalind Dixon, who renewed my confidence in this book. Ros generously provided me with theoretical and practical insight into the production process of this book. Very special thanks to Kristine Kalanges for her prayers and support during my difficult transition in Boston. In the midst of my struggle to finish the book, Kristine repeatedly reminded me about my true vocation. Susan Brusky suddenly appeared at a juncture in my life and has become a good friend in life and school. My deep appreciation goes to Susan for her constant enthusiasm to hear about my political past life in Indonesia.

This project could not have been completed without the support of my "two families." I thank my biological family: my sister Linda, and my parents Iswara and Meina. Through the years, they struggled to understand why I have chosen the road less traveled. Most of all, I find myself grateful for the support of my Jesuit family, especially the Society of Jesus, USA West Province (the Jesuit West). I am proud to dedicate this book to many great Jesuits who have taught me to how to build an intellectual and virtuous life, especially Fr. James V. Schall, SJ; and the late Fr. Robert J. Araujo, SJ.

Finally, my utmost thanks go to the Author of Life, who writes the book of my life and provides me with the abundant love, hope, and faith that helped me to complete this book. *Ad Majorem Dei Gloriam.*

S. Hendrianto
Boston, USA

Part I

Foundations

Introduction

One of the driving forces behind the resurgence of comparative constitutional law studies of the last two decades is the establishment of constitutional courts as the key feature of constitutional reforms in new democracies.[1] Within the growing literature on the court and judicial review, the idea of "judicial heroes" may be something out of the ordinary because it seems overly emotive and not very scholarly. But the heroic persona is nothing new. One of the major functions of judicial review is individual rights' protection, which requires the role of a judge to defend the individual from the mighty state apparatus.[2] The image here is of the judge as a hero who fights for the rights and liberties of the poor and oppressed. Moreover, the legal community has long equated the term "heroic" with the term "activist," in the sense that heroic judges are those who are willing to use the constitution to strike down acts of parliament.[3] Furthermore, the legal community has inducted "activist" judges as "judicial heroes" in the pantheon of heroic courts.[4]

While currently there are few legal scholars and political scientists attempting to explain judicial empowerment in new democracies from the perspective of judicial heroes, we can find evidence that the role of judicial heroes is part of the larger theme of the study of constitutional courts and judicial review. A lot of scholarly works on the first-generation constitutional courts of new democracies, such as those in South Africa[5] and Eastern Europe,[6] point out the contribution of judicial heroes in shaping the role of the courts in judicial politics.

The Indonesian Constitutional Court is the world's 78th Constitutional Court and the first to have been established in the twenty-first century. Within studies of the Indonesian Constitutional Court to date, many scholars have acknowledged the heroic leadership and dedication of the founding chief justice, Jimly Asshiddiqie, in establishing the Court's institutional legitimacy.[7] Nevertheless, since Asshiddiqie's departure from the Court in 2008, his successors have all either been disgraced or put in prison. Moreover, the second and third-generation Court has become less robust and less innovative than the first. As the Court has undergone this transition from a heroic court to one that is less so, one open question is the impact that individual chief justices can have on the Court's performance. Thus, it is important to undertake a critical evaluation of the different chief justices, who had different leadership styles, at the Indonesian Constitutional Court from its inception to present day.

I wrote this book in order to illuminate the unique heroism of the first-generation Indonesian Constitutional Court and to critically examine what happened next—after the heroic Chief Justice Asshiddiqie left the scene.[8] Studies of the Indonesian Constitutional Court suggest, in my view, an overly simplistic explanation that the first-generation Court was an "activist Court."[9] Moreover, Asshiddiqie's leadership has received a great deal of criticism from some scholars who believe that Asshiddiqie simply exploited the political space provided by the post-authoritarian moment, and that he forcefully asserted the Court's role without any compelling legal justification.[10] While these scholars might find significance in applying the notion of "judicial activism" to the Indonesian Constitutional Court, the debate over judicial empowerment has moved far beyond the distinction between judicial activism and judicial restraint.[11] Furthermore, the label of "activism" does not adequately describe Asshiddiqie's leadership as he led the Court to issue many decisions that were palatable to the legislature. In many instances, the Court refused to invalidate the statute, but nonetheless issued directives for the government to follow. A scholar described this phenomenon as "hidden activism,"[12] in the sense that the Court's "activism" is somewhat different from the standard model of judicial activism found in a liberal democracy.

Aggressive-bold versus prudential-minimalist heroes

The missing piece of the puzzle regarding Asshiddiqie's leadership points to a discussion on different varieties of judicial heroism. In my theoretical approach, I rely on the Aristotelean notion of heroism, in which Aristotle discusses heroism in the context of the first two virtues, *andreia* (courage or manliness) and *sophrosune* (temperance).[13] Here, Aristotle makes a classical comparison between the characters of two Homeric heroes: Achilles of the *Iliad* and Odysseus of the *Odyssey*.[14] Achilles is the exemplar of *andreia* and Odysseus is of *sophrosune*, and Aristotle praises them both because they embody different models of heroic virtue.

The defining characteristic of judicial heroes as vigorous and bold judges is the representation of an Achilles type of judicial hero. But there is an Odysseus type of judicial hero, who does not fit the description of everyday robust and bold judicial heroes. An Odysseus type of judicial hero is the one who knows how to enhance the court's authority while also fortifying the court against the executive and legislative branches by playing a minimalist role in some policy areas.

Based on Aristotelian heroism, the book offers a theory of Chief Justice Asshiddiqie as a "prudential-minimalist hero"—a judicial hero who relies on practical intelligence and reason to access possible strategies, and whose approach sometimes involves taking seemingly unheroic actions to achieve his ultimate goals. A prudential-minimalist hero must know when to move one step forward with ambitious constitutional interpretation and when to move two steps back by deferring to the political judgments of other branches of government. In other words, a prudential-minimalist type of judicial hero must be equipped with the prudential judgment to recognize when he needs to be cautious in deferring to the government, or when to be bold in breaking new legal ground.

The unique heroism of the first-generation court

The book argues that the founding chief justice of the Indonesian Constitutional Court, Jimly Asshiddiqie, was a prudential-minimalist type of judicial hero. The main feature of Asshiddiqie's judicial heroism was his reliance on a combination of maximalist and minimalist strategies. Led by Asshiddiqie, the Court struck down many governmental policies, but at the same time the Court sometimes delayed the implementation of its decisions, or it allowed the government to make practical adjustments to its policies.

Under the chairmanship of Jimly Asshiddiqie, the Court employed techniques that I would like to call "quasi-weak-form review." The concept of weak-form judicial review first emerged in Mark Tushnet's early articles on an alternative model of judicial review,[15] which he refined in his 2008 book *Weak Court's Strong Rights*.[16] The weak-form judicial review has also come to be known by several other names, such as the "dialogic judicial review model"[17] or the "new Commonwealth model."[18] Weak-form judicial review stands for the idea that constitutional limitations can be enforced without designating a final and exclusive role for the judiciary. Under weak-form judicial review, a court's interpretations merit great respect and have great weight, but its decisions can at times be overridden or rejected by legislatures.

In the Indonesian constitutional system, there is no formal feature that allows political branches to examine any judicial ruling and to override the Court's decision by ordinary majority vote or otherwise. The Court, therefore, still has the exclusive power of constitutional review. Nevertheless, led by Chief Justice Asshiddiqie, the Court adopted several techniques that can be considered to represent a quasi-weak-form review. First, the Court issued "conditionally constitutional" rulings, in which it allowed the laws in question to remain valid as long as they were applied or implemented in the way the Court interpreted them.[19] In some instances, the Court asked the government to interpret the statute in a certain way or prescribed directives to help the government implement the statute. Second, the Court issued weak remedies in different forms, such as "suspended declarations," which hold the decision of invalidity for a certain period during which the government must adopt a new plan to replace the law; "progressive realizations," which allow the state to take incremental steps to achieve the full realization of the constitutional rights; and "prospective overrulings," in which the Court decision would only apply to future cases.

In different instances, Asshiddiqie also led the Court to issue decisions that bear a resemblance to John Marshall's *Marbury* strategy. In the historic decision of *Marbury v. Madison*,[20] Justice Marshall broadened the power of the judiciary by establishing judicial review, yet at the same time, he sided with the Executive by not issuing a mandamus as a remedy to Marbury on the grounds that the legislation granting the Court this authority (the Judiciary Act of 1789) was unconstitutional. Similarly, Asshiddiqie's quasi-weak-form review shows a willingness to yield to the will of other branches of government, while at the same time creating space for the Court to provide constitutional interpretation on actions taken by other branches of government. In other words, the Court retained the exclusive power of constitutional review while also frequently issuing resolutions to renounce or delay the use of its power to invalidate statutes.

Another feature of Asshiddiqie's heroic leadership was his social leadership within the Court. Although Asshiddiqie was instrumental in setting the Court's agenda, he did not have complete dominion over his fellow justices. But one of the most remarkable influences ascribed to Asshiddiqie can be traced to his skill as a consensus builder in unifying the justices to follow the agenda he set. Moreover, Asshiddiqie successfully promoted a culture of collegiality, in which the justices did not disagree too strongly with their brethren. Asshiddiqie successfully persuaded his brethren to take a slow approach in expressing their disagreement with each other. Instead of frequently issuing dissenting opinions, Asshiddiqie persuaded the Justices to keep their disagreements internal matters of the Court.

In sum, this book argues that the key success of the first generation of the Indonesian Constitutional Court stems from the atypical heroic leadership of Chief Justice Asshiddiqie, who was willing to take a go-slow approach with perseverance and a willingness to strategically retreat in order to achieve the Court's ultimate goals. The key takeaway is that a new court like the Indonesian Constitutional Court needs a heroic "judicial captain" like Jimly Asshiddiqie. Asshiddiqie served as a strategic-minded chief justice who combined ambitious interpretations of the Constitution with the quasi-weak-form review, which included the willingness to recognize the merits of deferring to political judgments about the Constitution. Through this strategy, Asshiddiqie successfully strengthened the Court's authority while simultaneously fortifying the Court against the Executive and Legislative branches of government.

The second-generation decline

On August 20, 2008, the Court held an election for chief justice, and a new associate justice, Mohammad Mahfud, defeated Chief Justice Asshiddiqie by one vote. Initially, Asshiddiqie remained as an associate justice; however, on October 8, 2008, he submitted his resignation from the Constitutional Court. The departure of Asshiddiqie raised a critical question as to whether the next generation of the Constitutional Court would be able to maintain the legacy of the first-generation Court.

Comparative constitutional scholars have devoted much attention to highlighting the success of first-generation constitutional courts in new democracies,[21] like the Indonesian Constitutional Court. But the optimism over the global success of constitutional courts has been clouded by the pessimism that arises when many observe the signs of decline found in second-generation constitutional courts. Many scholars have attributed the decline of second-generation courts to a political backlash to the bold and aggressive approach of the first-generation court in checking other governmental branches' power.[22] The governments in new democracies, particularly those recovering from an authoritarian regime, tend to push back against the first-generation courts that challenge their authority. Consequently, the second-generation judges either retreat under pressure or try to avoid confrontation with the government. In the context of Indonesia, there is an argument that the government's attempts in 2011 and again in 2013 to reduce the Court's jurisdiction and powers were the driving forces that led the second-generation Court to its subsequent decline.[23] For instance, the Court's series of decisions on the judicial review of the electoral process in 2014 demonstrated greater judicial restraint.[24]

Apart from the political attack by governments on constitutional courts, there is also an argument that the second-generation decline was due to the success of democratic consolidation. This argument is based on the assumption that the first-generation Court has a mission to liberally defend constitutionalism and to foster democratic consolidation.[25] As the first-generation Court had done the work of advancing democracy and liberal constitutionalism, the second-generation Court needed to intervene less frequently.[26]

The government's attempts in 2011 and again in 2013 to reduce the Indonesian Constitutional Court's authority have been described as a direct political attack on the Court. But none of these is particularly treacherous when compared to a series of direct political attacks by governments on constitutional courts and judiciaries in several new or less mature democracies, such as in Russia, where President Yeltsin shelled the Parliament's building and suspended the Russian Constitutional Court in 1993.[27]

Moreover, the argument on the success of democratic consolidation is not persuasive either. It is not always easy to identify and define the success of democratic consolidation. At what point can we determine that the democratic transition was successful and at what point can the Court shift its role? The democratic transition as embodied by the establishment of a new constitutional identity is almost never encompassed in one event—and in the case of Indonesia, it may span decades in the form of power struggles and a political consolidation process.[28] Consequently, there is still a large gap to be filled by the second and even third-generation Court. For instance, many complex cases that involved judicial review of the electoral process in Indonesia arose in the second-generation Court.[29] Thus, the connection between second-generation decline and democratic consolidation does not appear to apply to the case of Indonesia.

This book argues that the change of judicial leadership was the most important factor that influenced the performance of the Indonesian Constitutional Court. Chief Justice Jimly Asshiddiqie, with his atypical heroic leadership, is almost by definition an extraordinary heroic figure, while his successors were more ordinary and employed different styles of leadership. At the same time, later chief justices steered the Court away from the legacy of the first-generation Court.

Asshiddiqie's immediate successor, Mohammad Mahfud (2008–2013), displayed a bold, aggressive type of judicial leadership. During his tenure, Mahfud displayed arrogance and a combative approach toward the elected branches of government. Mahfud transformed quasi-weak-form review into a tool to issue strong remedies without giving substantial deference to the legislature. In the name of substantive justice, Mahfud led the Court to bypass many procedural rules in the Court. Moreover, Mahfud proclaimed the Court as a pro-social justice court with a mission to provide benefits for poor and disadvantaged people. This aggressive leadership style, however, did not serve the Court in the long run because it proved hard to maintain the Court's longevity under such a bold, aggressive approach. Mahfud's leadership style was one of the contributing factors that provoked the direct attack on the Court by the elected branches of government in 2011.

The last three chief justices, Akil Mochtar (2013), Hamdan Zoelva (2013–2015), and Arief Hidayat (2015–present) by definition are more ordinary chief justices. Mochtar immediately defined himself as a villain instead of a hero when he was charged and convicted for bribery. Zoelva and Hidayat are typical soldier chief justices, who see the role of the Court as following the orders of the Constitution and the political branches of government.[30] Zoelva appeared to pursue a path of retreat, underscoring the Court's weakness in relation to other branches of government. The Court under the chairmanship of Hamdan Zoelva did not issue many bold decisions on the merit of the case, but rather it jumped directly to the declaration of "conditionally unconstitutional."[31] In other words, the Court played safe through the issuance of conditionally unconstitutional decisions minus bold rulings. Under the chairmanship of Arief Hidayat, the Court has retreated even further from the position of the first-generation court. In most cases, the Court chose the retreat position without any backlash or political pressure. Instead of relying on the quasi-weak-form review to temper the Court's bold decisions, the Court simply refused to issue bold decisions that challenged the Executive and Legislative branches of government.

In sum, this book argues that the second-generation and the third-generation Courts are less heroic than the first because of the break in judicial leadership at the Court. The key success of the first-generation Court can be found in the prudential-minimalist leadership of the founding chief justice, Jimly Asshiddiqie. His successors displayed different leadership styles that failed to maintain the continuity of the first-generation Court's success. Mahfud's bold-aggressive style failed to fortify the Court's interests, and, furthermore, it became one of the contributing factors that triggered the political attacks against the Court in 2011. The president and Executive, however, did not have to apply extra pressure or launch more vicious attacks after that, however, as the last two chief justices can be described as typical judicial soldiers. Instead of retreating under pressure, the soldier chief justices like Zoelva and Hidayat voluntary chose not to challenge the political branches of government.

Plan of the book

This book aims to answer two main questions: (1) What is the impact that individual chief justices can have on the development of judicial authority?

(2) How do we evaluate different models of judicial leadership in the Indonesian Constitutional Court? To answer these questions, this book is divided into four parts. The first part lays out the theoretical foundation of the relationship between judicial leadership and judicial heroism. Chapter 1 begins with a theoretical analysis to outline the basic concept of judicial heroes by relying on the Aristotelian concept of heroism. This chapter presents the notion of prudential-minimalist judicial heroes, which was not defined by courage alone but rather by a combination of prudence and other virtues.

The second part of the book explores the first-generation court under the chairmanship of Asshiddiqie. Chapter 2 presents a historical account of the creation of the Indonesian Constitutional Court. Although politicians equipped the Court with wide-ranging authority—including judicial review—they nonetheless intended to create a weak institution. The weak institutional design, however, paved the way for the emergence of a heroic chief justice who quickly transformed the Court into a functioning institution. Chapter 3 explores the intellectual leadership of Chief Justice Asshiddiqie, in which he led his brethren to invoke an ambitious understanding of the Constitution and to embark on significant projects for social and economic change. At the same time, however, Asshiddiqie led his brethren to minimize the impact of the Court's decisions. Chapter 4 presents the atypical character of Asshiddiqie's leadership through the application of quasi-weak-form review. The quasi-weak-form review allows the Court to issue constitutional interpretations while simultaneously yielding to the will of other branches of government. While Chapter 3 presents the significance of intellectual leadership at the Court, Chapter 5 argues that a chief justice also needs to possess the skill of social leadership. Although Chief Justice Asshiddiqie was instrumental in determining the direction of the Court, he had to deal with dissenting voices against his ways of thinking. Nevertheless, Asshiddiqie showed brilliant social leadership as a consensus builder, in which he managed to persuade his fellow justices to follow his direction.

In Part III, the book moves on to describe what happened after the heroic chief justice left the scene. Chapter 6 examines the development of the Constitutional Court under the presidency of Mohammad Mahfud. The departure of Jimly Asshiddiqie did not automatically bring an end to the "conundrum" of a heroic chief justice. The leadership of Chief Justice Mahfud, for the most part, was the embodiment of a bold, aggressive type of heroism. Chapter 7 analyzes the short tenures of Akil Mochtar (May 2013–October 2013) and Hamdan Zoelva (Nov 2013–December 2014). In this period, we begin to see the trend of "decline" in many different forms. Mochtar was forced to leave the Court in disgrace due to a bribery scandal. Zoelva chose to retreat and defer to the judgment of other branches of the government in many different cases. Chapter 8 continues to explore the "decline" by analyzing the leadership of the current chief justice, Arief Hidayat. Hidayat can be described as being out of his depth in politics and prefers to portray himself as subordinate of the president. Moreover, the Court has also begun to reverse many liberal democratic accomplishments of the last decade.

In Part IV, the book concludes with a comparative analysis of the unique leadership of the first-generation Court and the second-generation decline. The evidence in the Indonesian Constitutional Court suggests that, contrary to popular expectation, the prudential-minimalist leadership that employs a more cautious approach is in fact more effective than a bold, aggressive approach. The examination of the development of judicial power in Indonesia can also help us to understand whether there is a trend of second-generation decline. The first-generation judges are, as will be shown, extraordinary heroic figures, but these extraordinary heroic judges might only come once in Indonesian history. Therefore, their successors could very well be more ordinary figures. From this perspective, what needs to be explained is not the decline of the second-generation Court, but rather the atypical heroic nature of the first-generation Court.[32]

Ultimately, judicial leadership is one of the most crucial factors shaping judicial development in newer democracies. Courts in newer democracies often need heroic chief justices, who can make the strategic calculations that are critical to navigating the courts through the "deep seas" of politics. But often, the disadvantages of bold and aggressive heroic chief justices come to outweigh the advantages. The bold, aggressive heroic leadership is more likely to put the judiciary under stress because it has a tendency to result in the politicization of the courts. Shall we abandon the bold, aggressive heroic model? This book posits the answer that it is wiser for chief justices to move into less traditionally heroic stances and to exercise prudential-minimalist leadership, which includes the willingness to recognize the merits of deferring to political judgments about the Constitution.

Notes

1 Some scholars have noted that it was not until roughly 1999 that the resurgence of comparative constitutional law began. See David Fontana. "The Rise and Fall of Comparative Constitutional Law in the Postwar Era," 36 *Yale J. Int'l L.* 1 (2011); Mark Tushnet. "The Possibilities of Comparative Constitutional Law," 108 *Yale L.J.* 1225 (1999). The global wave of constitution-making, however, had taken a place a decade earlier; during this period, many Eastern Europe countries moved to establish constitutional courts after the fall of Soviet Union in 1989.

2 See Tom Ginsburg and Zachary Elkins. "Designing a Judiciary: Ancillary Powers of Constitutional Courts," 87 *Tex. L. Rev.* 1431, 1436 (June 2009).

3 Cass Sunstein. *Constitutional Personae*, (New York, NY: Oxford University Press, 2015), 6–7.

4 Roy Schotland. "Remembering a Constitutional Hero," 43 *N.Y.L. SCH. L. REV.* 13, 27 (1999); John Philip Reid. "Beneath the Titans," 70 *N.Y.U. L. Rev.* 653 (1995); Sarah Barringer Gordon. "The Creation of a Usable Judicial Past: Max Lerner, Class Conflict, and the Propagation of Judicial Titans," 70 *N.Y.U. L. REV.* 622, 623 (1995); Bernard Schwartz. "The Judicial Ten: America's Greatest Justices," 4 *S. ILL. U. L.J.* 405 (1979).

5 Theunis Roux. *The Politics of Principle: The First South African Constitutional Court, 1995–2005* (Cambridge: Cambridge University Press, 2013).

6 Kim Lane Scheppele. "Guardians of the Constitution: Constitutional Court Presidents and the Struggle for the Rule of Law in Post-Soviet Europe," 154 *U. Pa. L. Rev.* 1757 (2006).

7 Simon Butt. *The Constitutional Court and Democracy in Indonesia* (Leiden, the Netherlands: Brill, Nijhoff, 2015); See also Haig Patapan. "Leadership, Law and Legitimacy: Reflections on the Changing Nature of Judicial Politics in Asia." In *The Judicialization of Politics in Asia*, edited by Bjorn Dressel (Routledge, 2012); and Marcus Mietzner. "Political Conflict Resolution and Democratic Consolidation in Indonesia: The Role of the Constitutional Court," 10(3) *Journal of East Asian Studies* 397 (2010).

8 My earlier attempt to explain the heroism of the first-generation court and what happened next can be found in Stefanus Hendrianto. "The Rise and Fall of Heroic Chief Justices: Constitutional Politics and Judicial Leadership in Indonesia," 25 *Washington International Law Journal*, 489–563 (June, 2016).

9 See Simon Butt. *Judicial Review in Indonesia: Between Civil Law and Accountability? A Study of Constitutional Court Decisions 2003–2005* (December 2006) (unpublished PhD dissertation, University of Melbourne) (on file with author); Simon Butt. "Indonesia's Constitutional Court: Conservative Activist or Strategic Operator?" In *The Judicialization of Politics in Asia*, edited by Bjorn Dressel (Routledge, 2012); See also Marcus Mietzner. "Political Conflict Resolution and Democratic Consolidation in Indonesia: The Role of the Constitutional Court" 10(3) *Journal of East Asian Studies* 397 (2010).

10 Theunis Roux. "American Ideas Abroad: Comparative Implications of US Supreme Court Decision-Making Models," 13(1) *Int J Constitutional Law* 90 (2015).

11 See David Landau. "A Dynamic Theory of Judicial Role," 55 *B.C. L. Rev.* 1501 (2014) (noting the gap in bodies of scholarship, which has focused heavily on the activism of courts in the fragile democracies of the "Global South."); David Law. "Judicial Comparativism and Judicial Diplomacy," 163 *U. Pa. L. Rev.* 927 (2015) (noting that it is questionable whether comparativism actually leads to judicial activism in the form of more frequent invalidation of laws).

12 See Butt. *Conservative Activist or Strategic Operator?*

13 Aristotle. "Nichomachean Ethics." In *The Basic Works of Aristotle*, edited by Richard Mckeon (New York: Random House, 1941), 3.6.1115a6; 3.9.1117b24; for an excellence analysis of Aristotelian heroism, please see Donald Henry D'Amour. *Aristotle on Heroes*, (unpublished PhD dissertation, University of Notre Dame, 1971).

14 Patrick J. Deneen has made an excellent comparison between the heroism of Odysseus and Achilles. See Patrick J. Deneen. *The Odyssey of Political Theory: The Politics of Departure and Return* (Lanham: Rowman & Littlefield Publishers, 2000).

15 Mark Tushnet. "New Forms of Judicial Review and the Persistence of Rights- and Democracy-Based Worries," 38 *Wake Forest L. Rev.* 813, 814 (2003); Mark Tushnet. "Alternative Forms of Judicial Review," 101 *Mich. L. Rev.* 2781 (2003).

16 Mark Tushnet. *Weak Courts, Strong Rights Judicial Review and Social Welfare Rights in Comparative Constitutional Law* (Princeton, NJ: Princeton University Press, 2008).

17 Yap Po Jen. *Constitutional Dialogue in Common Law Asia* (Oxford, United Kingdom: Oxford University Press, 2015).

18 Stephen Gardbaum. *The New Commonwealth Model of Constitutionalism: Theory and Practice.* (Cambridge: Cambridge University Press, 2013).

19 Simon Butt and Tim Lindsey. *The Constitution of Indonesia: A Contextual Analysis* (Hart Publishing, 2012), 138.

20 *Marbury v. Madison*, 5 U.S. 137 (1803). Private conversation with Jimly Asshiddiqie, chief justice of the Indonesian Constitutional Court, in Jakarta, Indonesia (July 31, 2006).

21 See, for example, Theunis Roux. *The Politics of Principle.* In *Constitutional Judiciary in a New Democracy: The Hungarian Constitutional Court*, edited by

Laszlo Solyom and Georg Brunner. (Ann Arbor, MI: University of Michigan Press, 2000).

22 The second generation of the Hungarian, Russian, and South African Constitutional Courts are examples of courts that are viewed as being less heroic than they once were. For an analysis of the decline of the Hungarian Constitutional Court, please see Kim Lane Scheppele. "Not your Father's Authoritarianism: The Creation of the 'Frankenstate'," *American Political Science Association European Politics & Society Newsletter* 5 (2013); for the development of the Russian Constitutional Court, please see Carla Thorson. *Politics, Judicial Review and the Russian Constitutional Court* (Basingstoke: Palgrave Macmillan, 2012), 55; see also Alexei Trochev. *Judging Russia: Constitutional Court in Russian Politics, 1990–2006* (Cambridge: Cambridge University Press, 2008); for the decline of the South African Constitutional Court, please see Heinz Klug. "Constitutional Authority and Judicial Pragmatism: Politics and Law in the Evolution of South Africa Constitutional Court." In *Consequential Courts: Judicial Roles in Global Perspective, edited by Diana Kapiszewski, Gordon Silverstein, and Robert A. Kagan.* (New York: Cambridge University Press, 2013).

23 Fritz Edward Siregar. *Indonesian Constitutional Politics, 2003–2013* (unpublished SJD thesis, University of New South Wales, 2016).

24 Stefanus Hendrianto. "The Indonesian General Election and the 'Weak' Constitutional Court, *I-CONnect: Blog of the Int'l J. Const. L.* (June 4, 2014). http://www.iconnectblog.com/2014/06/the-indonesian-general-election-and-the-weak-constitutional-court.

25 Chien-Chih Lin. "Pace of Constitutional Transition Matters: The Judicialization of Politics in Indonesia and Korea," 20 *UCLA J Int'L & For. Aff.* 275 (Fall, 2016); Simon Butt. *The Constitutional Court and Democracy in Indonesia* (Leiden, the Netherlands: Brill, Nijhoff, 2015); Mietzner, *Political Conflict Resolution and Democratic Consolidation in Indonesia.*

26 Theunis Roux and Fritz Siregar. "Trajectories of Curial Power: The Rise, Fall and Partial Rehabilitation of the Indonesian Constitutional Court," 16(2) *Australian Journal of Asian Law* article 2 (2016).

27 Trochev. *Judging Russia*, 74–75.

28 See Donald L. Horowitz. *Constitutional Change and Democracy in Indonesia* (Cambridge: Cambridge University Press, 2013), 2.

29 For a detailed analysis of judicial review of electoral process in Indonesia, please see Stefanus Hendrianto. "A Curious Case of Weak-Form Review: On Judicial Review of Electoral Process in Indonesia." In *Judicial Review of Elections in Asia*, edited by Yap Po Je (London: Routledge, 2016).

30 It was Cass Sunstein who coined the term "judicial soldier"; see Cass Sunstein. *Constitutional Personae.*

31 This issue will be discussed in more detail in Chapter 7of the book.

32 This argument was originally developed by Mark Tushnet in "Studying Second-Generation Constitutional Courts: After the Heroes Have Left," a presentation at the Annual Meeting of Law and Society Association, New Orleans, June 2–5, 2016.

1 Theorizing judicial heroes

Through his play *A Man for All Seasons*,[1] Robert Bolt created an excellent study of the heroism of Sir Thomas More. More was a former Lord Chancellor of England who refused to endorse King Henry VIII's decision to challenge the authority of the Pope after he divorced his wife, Catherine of Aragon, so that he could marry Anne Boleyn. But Bolt was an agnostic, which makes it puzzling that he would choose a Catholic saint as the hero in his play. As Bolt put it, "Why do I take as my hero a man who brings about his death because he can't put his hand on an old black book [the Bible] and tell an ordinary lie?"[2] For Bolt, the answer to that question lay in More's notion of self and the idea of what he would and would not do. In other words, Bolt treated Sir Thomas More as a hero of selfhood.[3] Thus, the agnostic Bolt admired More not for how he died as a martyr of faith, but for how he lived as a public servant.[4]

I recalled the story of Saint Thomas More when I began my research on the idea of judicial heroism. Does this story have anything to do with comparative constitutional law? I believe so. In constitutional law studies in general, we usually focus on the professional achievements of a "great justice," setting aside most considerations of their personal lives, especially as to how they died.[5] Similarly, many students and scholars of comparative constitutional law adore heroic justices because of their great contributions and achievements. Notably, heroic figures such as Laszlo Solyom (Hungary), Manuel Cepeda (Colombia), and Albie Sachs (South Africa) dominated the constitutional courts in new democracies.

No one will dispute that judges, at whatever level, can achieve hero status, but there are many interpretations and definitions of judicial heroism. Before proceeding further, it is thus necessary to consider that the concept of judicial hero is well-established in the literature of constitutional law in general and in comparative constitutional law in particular. This chapter will start by addressing some basic concepts. What is a judicial hero? What must a judicial hero do to achieve his heroic status? Is a judicial hero needed? What kind of judicial heroes are in the realm of judicial politics?

Conceptual frameworks for judicial heroes

The first issue to clarify is whether a judicial hero is similar to a military hero, whose heroic acts usually involve physical courage; or a political hero, whose heroism means bold or charismatic leadership. When we speak about military heroes, we often assume the idea of a conqueror, while political heroes are identified as founders or rulers.[6] George Washington was a military hero who became a political hero as the first president of the United States. Some political heroes, however, do not possess a heroic military character. Mahatma Gandhi was a charismatic political hero who liberated his people without military force but who continues to hold heroic status in the eyes of his people.

A judge is a neither a founder nor a ruler, but the notion of political heroism still seeps into the legal community. Chief Justice John Marshall was recognized by many as the original American judicial hero,[7] especially for establishing the institution of judicial review in the case of *Marbury v. Madison*.[8] In the twentieth century, Chief Justice Earl Warren was the iconic judicial hero, and some compare his heroism to that of Chief Justice John Marshall.[9] One author went so far as to say that Chief Justice Warren "looked like a larger-than-life heroic figure."[10] Warren's heroic status was related to the transformative work of his Court, which established many important rights for the less fortunate.[11] Both Marshall and Warren earned their heroic status as charismatic leaders and founders: Marshall established the foundation of judicial review, and Warren cemented the notion of judicial review through his Court's achievement of correcting many perceived social wrongs.

One definition of a heroic judge is those who "boldly discover rights, refuse to be bound by out-of-date precedents and replace strict rules with flexible standards based on their notions of reasonableness, fairness, and efficiency."[12] An apt example is Chief Justice Laszlo Solyom of the Hungarian Constitutional Court (1990–1998), who established the notion of "invisible constitution."[13] For instance, one could find the right to life and human dignity in Article 54(1) of the 1990 Constitution. Nevertheless, Chief Justice Solyom explained that these rights are foundational principles of Hungarian constitutional law and therefore would exist even without a reference in the constitutional text.[14] Similarly, Chief Justice Awad al-Murr of the Supreme Constitutional Court of Egypt took enormous pride in developing ambitious jurisprudence based on an expansive reading of rights provisions and using international human rights standards to anchor the Court's rulings.[15]

Another definition of a heroic judge is one who is motivated by the mission to reconstruct social institutions and to help remake the bureaucracy and its institutional arrangements into an expression of justice.[16] Jennifer Widner, in her study of emerging constitutionalism in southern and eastern Africa, revealed the heroism of Francis Nyalali, the former chief justice of Tanzania (1976–1999), who tried to reconstruct the judicial institutions in the country.[17] Widner sketches how Nyalali spent his time lobbying for judicial independence and democratic reform at every level.[18] As part of his judicial heroism, Nyalali attempted to educate members of the legal profession and society on matters of constitutional interpretation by periodically contributing columns on legal issues to newspapers and participating in other law-related educational initiatives on the radio and television.[19]

The modern world is less concerned with the idea of conquests, but we still consider the virtue of courage as a primary quality of a heroic figure. Similarly, the legal community has produced heroic figures in the shape of its courageous judges. Chief Justice Ifthikar Muhammad Chaudhry of Pakistan was the exemplar of courage and bravery when he stood up against the military executive General Pervez Musharraf.[20] In 2007, Musharraf asked Chaudhry to resign, but he refused, and the conflict between the two led to the latter's suspension and house arrest. The chief justice's refusal unleashed an unprecedented revolt led by Pakistani lawyers in support of judicial independence. Chief Justice Chaudhry was later reinstated and remained in office until his retirement on December 11, 2013. In short, although judicial heroism does not require physical courage like military heroism, to be heroic, a judge must be courageous.

A heroic judge also has to play the role of a savior of society from social wrongs. Again, Chief Justice Solyom is an exemplary heroic chief justice who tried to save post-communist Hungarian society from social wrongs. Under Solyom's leadership, the Court struck down many laws related to economic issues such as property rights, entrepreneurship, contracts, and social security benefits.[21] A telling example of Solyom's courage occurred when he declared that the government's economic plan violated the principle of legal security in the Constitution because it did not give the citizens adequate time to adjust themselves to the welfare cuts.[22]

A heroic judge can also achieve such status by playing the role of an arbiter of social and political conflicts. The Russian Constitutional Court under the leadership of Chief Justice Valery Zorkin is an example of a heroic court as political arbiter. In his early tenure (1991–1993), Zorkin led the Court to become an influential political actor by taking virtually every politically sensitive case concerning issues of jurisdiction and competencies, both within and between branches of the federal government.[23] Overall, the Zorkin Court favored accepting political challenges filed by political actors over civil rights challenges filed by individual citizens.[24]

In sum, a judicial hero achieves such status through courageous and ambitious interpretation of the constitution, which amounts to a judge participating in economic, social, and political governance. A judicial hero has to play the role of the savior of society from social wrongs by discovering rights in the law and challenging the status quo.

But Cass Sunstein offers a fresh way of thinking about judicial heroes, beyond the standard norm of bold and courageous judges. In his recent book, *Constitutional Personae*,[25] Sunstein tries to describe different types of justice and federal judge that transcend politics and ideology and that span the history of the U.S. Supreme Court. Sunstein divides judges into four groups: the hero, the soldier, the minimalist, and the mute. Sunstein acknowledges that judicial heroes usually take bold and courageous steps. Heroic judges believe in a transformative role for the judiciary and are willing to use judicial power to achieve desired results.[26] Nonetheless, Sunstein warns his readers that *judicial heroism* is a tricky term because, within the categories of heroes, we can find significant differences of degree, from relatively modest heroes to super-ambitious heroes.[27]

Some heroes are willing to strike down statutory regulations without having major agenda reform. But there are some superheroes who have great ambitions and are willing to embark on significant endeavors toward social change.

According to Sunstein, judicial heroes may be both liberals and conservatives. While liberal judges like Earl Warren, William Brennan, and Thurgood Marshall represent the most sustained academic example of the heroic judges, Sunstein argues that conservative judges, such as Antonin Scalia and Clarence Thomas, are heroic as well.[28] From this argument, Sunstein begins to draw a link between judicial heroes and soldiers. Sunstein posits that judicial soldiers are those who are willing to defer to the choices of the elected, political branches of government.[29] Judicial soldiers see the role of the court more narrowly, following the orders of the constitution and the political branches.

Sunstein made a distinction between first-order soldiers, who defer to the judgments of the elected political branches, and second-order soldiers, who can be described as hero-soldiers, as they are willing to trump their soldierly role to uphold the constitution.[30] Justice Scalia and Justice Thomas were judicial soldiers whenever they sought to follow the will of the elected political branches of government. But they were also willing to invalidate the actions of the federal government or the states in some cases. Justice Scalia's willingness to overturn gun laws in *District of Columbia v. Heller*[31] falls on the heroic side, but on the other hand, when he relied on textualism and originalism to justify his decision by following the language of the Second Amendment, his opinion was more soldierly. Likewise, Scalia and Thomas could be both heroes and soldiers at the same time.

Along the same line as Sunstein's hero-soldiers, Daniel Suhr introduced "Judge Cincinnati" as a model of a hero-soldier.[32] The idea of "Judge Cincinnati" derived from the character of a Roman statesman, Cincinnatus. In 458 BCE, when the Roman Republic was under attack, the Senate turned to a former general, Lucius Cincinnatus, and vested him with emergency powers as a dictator for six months.[33] He accepted the power, gathered an army, and led them in a tough battle against the enemy of the state and vanquished them. After securing the victory, he disbanded his troops and returned home to tend his farms. Based on Cincinnatus' character, Suhr introduced the character of "Judge Cincinnati," who is consistent in applying originalism that appropriately reflects the limits of a humble servant of justice. In the character of "Judge Cincinnati," he would apply an originalist methodology to all cases before him. Based on the principle's originalism, "Judge Cincinnati" would, from time to time, rule against what one would expect to be his personal policy preference in a given case. For Suhr, Justice Antonin Scalia is an exemplar "Judge Cincinnati," a humble judicial hero who follows an originalist methodology, even when it conflicts with his expected policy preferences.[34]

Returning to Sunstein's *Constitutional Personae*, in the next category, he postulates a concept of judicial minimalists who are in favor of incremental steps and believe in a humble role for the judiciary.[35] Sunstein holds up the eighteenth-century political theorist Edmund Burke as the source of inspiration for a minimalist approach, in which judges should take small steps, respecting tradition and experience in their judgments.[36] Sunstein hails Justice Felix Frankfurter as an iconic judicial minimalist because of his enthusiasm for tradition, his commitment to case-by-case judgment, and his skepticism about large-scale theories.[37]

Nevertheless, one can count some minimalists as heroes, in that they initiate an incremental step toward a heroic decision. Or some heroes can present themselves as minimalists, in that they are committed to the transformative role of the judiciary but reject revolutionary change and instead advocate for incrementalism. Sunstein praises Justice Anthony Kennedy as a hero-minimalist in *Lawrence v. Texas*,[38] in which he proceeded in a relatively minimalist fashion to strike down the ban on same-sex sodomy.[39] In short, like judicial heroes and soldiers, judicial minimalists come in different shapes and sizes, and within the category of judicial minimalist, we can also find hero-minimalists.[40]

Sunstein's *Constitutional Personae* is among the finest works in recent constitutional theory on heroism.[41] The book discusses the notion of heroism within the context of U.S. constitutional law. Nevertheless, it is also relevant for comparative constitutional theorists who often embraced the image of the judicial hero as bold and courageous. Sunstein's theory may help comparative theorists to understand better that there are many variations of judicial heroes beyond bold and courageous judges.

Is a judicial hero needed?

The theory of judicial heroes raised a critical question: Is it necessary for a court to have a judicial hero? To answer this question, I turn to Jon Elster, who has successfully attracted scholarly imagination and analytic interest by using Homer's *Odyssey* as a primary source of legal and political thought.[42] Elster's earlier work created tremendous interest in the notion of constitutions as exercises of self-binding—referring to a metaphor of Odysseus having himself bound to the mast to hear the Sirens safely.[43] Specifically, Odysseus is unwilling to forgo the opportunity to hear the Sirens' song; therefore, he instructs his crew to tie him to the mast of the boat before they meet the Sirens.[44] He also gave his crew beeswax to plug their ears and instructed them further to lash him more tightly to the mast if he protested.[45]

But having received some critical comments that "in politics, people never try to bind themselves, only to bind others," Elster took a fresh look at his theory.[46] In his survey on democratic transitions in Eastern Europe, Elster argues that:

> [T]he question of the moment was not "What is to be done" but is there anyone who might be able to do anything – including defining what needs to be done?[47]

With his new argument, Elster concedes that the act of binding may not occur if there is no-one who is capable of imposing chains on Odysseus. In other words, the democratic transition requires a heroic figure capable of defining what needs to be done.

Apart from the metaphor of Odysseus and the Sirens, the necessity of having a heroic figure in democratic transition periods is often expressed by a different metaphor: Constitutions are chains imposed by Peter when sober, on Peter when drunk,[48] "Peter" being a metaphor crafted by Justice David Brewer in a presentation to the New York Bar Association in 1893,[49] although other sources trace it to Francis Bacon.[50] But in reality, constitutional provisions tend to be enacted at times not of sober rationality, but of high political feeling.[51] Thus, instead of "Peter sober" legislating for "Peter drunk," we seem to find "Peter drunk" legislating for "Peter sober."[52]

The idea of "Peter drunk" legislating for "Peter sober" does not only take place during the constitutional drafting process. Many legislatures, in developing countries or in new democracies still recovering from an authoritarian regime, could be a "Peter drunk" trying to formulate policies as part of their daily operations. It is common in a democratic transition period that politicians with ties to a former regime sit in legislatures. Also, many legislatures in new democracies or the developing world are plagued by dysfunctional party systems that are often highly fragmented. Under a dysfunctional party system and ineffective legislature, a robust and independent constitutional court does appear to be possible.[53] Nathan Brown, in his analysis of the establishment of limited government in Arab worlds, argues that genuine democratic accountability in Arab states must be brought by pressure from within, through strengthening Arab political institutions such as constitutional courts.[54] In sum, a constitutional court is a possible "Peter sober" who can help the country to move toward a fully constitutionalist regime.

Both the analogies of Odysseus and the Sirens and "Peter sober" or "Peter drunk" are closely tied to the issue of self-realization.[55] Odysseus first realized that he would be unable to resist temptation, and therefore he asked his crew to tie him to the mast. Similarly, "Peter drunk" must first realize that he has developed alcohol problems and that his life has become unmanageable. In other words, "Peter drunk" must begin with an admission of alcoholism before he seeks help from others.

Constitutional identity is a significant step toward addressing the issue of self-realization. The identity of a constitution, according to Mary Ann Glendon, tells stories about the culture that helped shape it and which it, in turn, contributes to shaping stories about who we are, where we came from, and where are we going.[56] Thus, constitutional culture is closely related to the realization of who we are. Nevertheless, in most countries that are recovering from an authoritarian regime, a robust constitutional culture that is attuned to constitutional values often does not exist. It is more common for political elites and citizens to ignore their constitution rather than to take it seriously.[57] Under these circumstances, it is unlikely that politicians and citizens would realize they need help to bind themselves. The constitution would therefore not likely be taken seriously unless there is a judicial hero—one who is willing to lead the constitutional courts to nurture a new constitutional culture.

The need for heroes in times of transition has deep roots in ancient Greece. In *Book III* of the *Politics*, Aristotle deals with the question of whether the *polis*[58] is the same *polis* or a different one after the revolution.[59] Aristotle suggests that location and human inhabitants do not constitute the identity of a *polis*.[60] Instead, what determines the identity of the *polis* is the human character of the inhabitants. Aristotle argues that a change in the character of the people in the *polis* will cause a change in the *polis*'s ultimate identity. Aristotle's chain of argument begins with the premise that a *polis* is a type of community (*koinonia*) and that the *polis* is a community (*koinonia*) of citizens in a regime or "constitution" (*politeia*).[61] Thus, the logic of this argument is that if the character of the citizens changes, the regime will change; if the regime changes, one could assume that the *polis* will also change.

Based on the premise that a change in the character of the citizen in the *polis* will cause a change in the regime, Aristotle posits the idea of "the excellence of the citizen." He begins with the analogy of a sailor on a ship. Although certain sailors have a particular function, they are all working together to operate the ship with the shared goal of preserving the ship during its voyage.[62] Similarly, although citizens are dissimilar, preservation of the community (*koinonia*) is the common task of all citizens; hence, the excellence of the citizen is necessary for the salvation of the *polis* of which he is a member.[63]

Is the excellent citizen similar to the aforementioned "hero"? In explaining the excellent citizen, Aristotle does not speak about the good (*agathos* or *kalos*) citizen, but rather he speaks about the serious (*spoudaios*) citizen.[64] Thus, he speaks of excellence in relation to serious citizens and the serious man. The serious man (*spoudaios*) is the man who possesses the various virtues, including magnanimity; the politically just man; and the man who concentrates on contemplation and the development of various intellectual virtues.[65] He is the model of human perfection that sees and values the real and not just the apparent good. It is he who sees the truth in practical matters.[66] Aristotle further specified the character of the *spoudaios* as the man of practical wisdom (*phronimos*).[67] The *spoudaios-phronimos* is the ideal type of hero who can operate in the best regimes.[68] The *spoudaios-phronimos* is the hero who will determine the identity of the *polis*, especially after times of political revolution or crisis. In sum, Aristotle provided valuable insight for democratic transition periods, namely, that there is a need for a heroic figure, the *spoudaios-phronimos*. This hero can work together with all on board to operate the ship with a common purpose of its preservation during the voyage through a possible turbulent transition.

Judicial heroes and existing theories

Having reviewed the basic concepts and definition of judicial heroes, I will now review the notion of judicial heroes within the existing theories of comparative judicial politics. In the past decades, there has been a growing body of robust literature in constitutional courts that sought to answer the question of why powerful politicians would restrict their future political choices by giving power to unelected judges through constitutional review.[69] Social scientists who were doing comparative law in the 1980s and 1990s argued that constitutional review arose to respond to the rise of the modern bills of rights, which demand protracted state action for their implementation.[70] Included in these earlier theoretical accounts was the idea of constitutional review as a response to problems of governance, such as federalism or the need to patrol the boundary between the parliament and presidency.[71]

At the beginning of the twenty-first century, a new generation of comparative judicial scholars came out with different theories, including constitutional review as an insurance mechanism[72] or hegemonic preservation strategy adopted by elites who foresee losing power.[73] Under a different genre, there is also a theory of political insurances by ruling elites who foresee constitutional review as a tool to keep the foreign investor at ease, in which property rights would be protected through an independent process of judicial review.[74] One scholar tried to advance insurance theories by arguing that constitutional review needs some trigger, not only related to the strategic calculation of the incumbents but also an aversive response rooted in past negative political experience.[75]

The second important issue addressed by these bodies of scholarship is the process by which courts and judges come to make policy or to increasingly dominate the public policy-making process that was previously only conducted by other governmental branches. Political and legal theorists have offered plausible explanations for the expansion of judicial powers such as political liberalization[76] or the institutional context of courts and the courts' interaction with various political actors.[77] The division of power may sometimes pull courts into the political fray as independent arbiters.[78] Some theorists look into different factors of the expansion of judicial power, such as a push by special-interest groups to use the courts for the achievement of their objectives;[79] or the influence of legal culture, which includes legal language, the cluster of attitudes, ideas, and values that people hold concerning the legal systems and institutions.[80]

All of these theories point out important aspects of the origin and expansion of judicial review, but none is entirely persuasive in and of itself. For this reason, some scholars begin to employ a combined approach to explaining both the creation and subsequent strengthening of constitutional courts. In a comparative study on the Argentinian and Brazilian high courts, Diana Kapiszewski postulates the court's "character" theory as the product of naming procedures and other institutional features that, over time, foster a particular manner of working together among judges and inserting themselves into the political realm.[81] Kapiszewski posits that a court's character comprises several features: a court's stability, the professional profile of appointees, and institutional cohesion, which include the presence of recognized leadership of either formal (chief justice) or informal leaders in the court.[82]

Kapiszewski further developed her theories by describing the development of judicial power as a ship sailing on high seas.[83] In *Consequential Courts*, Kapiszewski and her colleagues, Gordon Silverstein and Robert A. Kagan, argue that several interacting forces and factors influence change in judicial politics. The first factor is the ocean and its current, which represents broad structural dynamics, the type of regime that built each particular ship, and the constitutional and international context in which judicial ships sail.[84] The second factor comprises opportunities and challenges for ships navigating these waters, which include the winds of demand for greater judicial participation in politics and policy and winds of resistance that slow or prevent a change in judicial direction.[85] The third factor is the capability of judicial captains (chief justices) and their crews (fellow justices) to make critical strategic calculations in navigating the ships through high seas.[86]

Kapiszewski's judicial ship metaphor reminds us that judicial leadership is arguably one of the most crucial factors contributing to the development of constitutional review. Calm seas and favorable winds are not enough to explain the roles that courts play, because courts in democratic transition usually sail in the most turbulent seas, where wind and storms can arise without warning, causing the sea lanes to become dangerous. Consequently, the journey of a judicial ship depends on upon a skillful judicial captain who must constantly consider how he will react to unexpected political storms and sometimes maneuver his less-stable judicial ships through stormy seas.[87] Kapiszewski suggests further that strategic timing and skilled crafting of rulings can make it possible for a judicial captain to navigate the judicial ship through dangerous seas, emerging with a powerful grip on new roles, powers, and responsibilities.[88] According to Kapiszewski, under the leadership of a skillful judicial captain, "judicial ships could emerge from a storm with torn sails … having added the ballast of increased legitimacy, enabling them to carry even more cargo in the future, taking on more and greater roles in governance."[89]

In sum, the journey of a "judicial ship" depends heavily on the heroic leadership of judicial captains, especially the navigational skills and communication techniques that they employ. As a judicial captain, a chief justice must make critical strategic calculations regarding the course of his ship, and he must be able to persuade his crew whether they should change course, wait out the storm, press forward into potentially stormy seas, or drop anchor. Thus, this book is about the heroic role of judicial captains in leading their ships into the constitutional journey of the deep sea.

Judicial leadership theories revisited

As this book is about judicial leadership, a theoretical overview of judicial leadership is necessary. A systematic study of leadership in the constitutional courts in new democracies is a relatively recent phenomenon.[90] Nevertheless, scholars of law and politics in the United States have produced numerous theories on judicial leadership to explain the significance of leadership in the U.S. Supreme Court. Some prominent theories focus on the chief justice's authority to assign majority opinion,[91] the interplay between factual circumstances of the case, internal norms and political forces from outside the Court,[92] and the role of chief justice as manager.[93] More recent works have begun to focus on historical-institutionalist dimensions of judicial leadership[94] and the role of informal leaders (associate justices) in the Court.[95]

There is no need to repeat the pros and cons of these theories here because this book is not comparing the Indonesian Constitutional Court and the U.S.

Supreme Court. Nevertheless, David Danelski's classic work can be considered part of the theoretical framework for this book. Fifty-five years ago, Danelski published his pioneering work, using concepts of social (group cohesion) and task (intellectual) leadership to examine the role played by chief justices during the Taft, Hughes, and Stone Chief Justiceships. Although many scholars have moved beyond Danelski's work, his theory still proves useful in analyzing the leadership of the current chief justice, John Roberts, and that of his predecessor, William Rehnquist.[96] This book, at some level, employs Danelski's analysis of how a chief justice exercises his intellectual and social leadership.

This book will rely primarily on theoretical analysis of judicial leadership in new democracies. One significant study that is highly relevant to this book is the work of Kim Lane Scheppele, in which she focused on two first chief justices of constitutional courts in Eastern Europe in the early 1990s: Laszlo Solyom of the Hungarian Constitutional Court and Valery Zorkin of the Russian Constitutional Court.[97] Scheppele's key argument is that both the Hungarian Constitutional Court and the Russian Constitutional Court became aggressive constitutional guardians because of the leadership of their chief justices.

Scheppele's work is important because she explains the nature of the office of the chief justice under a constitutional court system. Scheppele argues that there are some significant institutional differences between constitutional court models and the U.S. Supreme Court model, which contribute to different roles for the chief justices. First, the jurisdiction of constitutional courts is limited to constitutional matters, and therefore, constitutional court chief justices only preside over the development of constitutional law, and not any other branch of law.[98] In other words, constitutional courts' chief justices do not have administrative responsibility for courts outside their own, giving them a different role than the U.S. Chief Justice, who is responsible for lower federal courts.

Given that the jurisdiction of constitutional courts is limited to constitutional matters, which tend to have a high political impact, constitutional courts cannot avoid political engagement. If a constitutional question falls within the jurisdiction of the court, the court must answer it.[99] Moreover, constitutional courts have neither formally recognized discretionary powers to choose which cases they will decide, nor a political questions doctrine for avoiding tough political issues.[100] As a result, it is common in constitutional court systems to find that chief justices are considered the most prominent political figures and are expected to play a role in the public debate over constitutional issues.

The political context of the creation of constitutional courts also contributes to the uniqueness of the office of the chief justice of the constitutional court system. As mentioned earlier, many governments that are recovering from an authoritarian regime want to designate their constitutional court as the "guardian of the constitution."[101] A constitutional court's chief justice is the public personification of the guardian of the constitution. As the public embodiment of the court, the chief justice projects himself as the voice of the constitution itself, which gives him a much bigger and more important role than that possessed by the chief justice of the United States, for example.[102]

In many constitutional courts, the judges themselves select their chief justices, who serve for substantially shorter terms than their overall terms of office.[103] For instance, while the judges might serve for 5 years, the chief justice may only serve 2.5 years. Under these arrangements, a chief justice has to consider how liked he would be by his fellow judges if he wants to win re-election. In other words, constitutional courts' chief justices must have the ongoing support of their colleagues to stay on the job. By contrast, in the United States, the president appoints the chief justice for life, and he can be the least popular person in the court or even an outsider.

Scheppele's analysis is important for this book because her assessment is highly relevant to the office of chief justice in the Indonesian Constitutional Court. The Indonesian Constitutional Court chief justice has a 2.5-year term, renewable once, and his fellow associate justices elect him in an internal election. The Court also has particular and narrow functions but is politically crucial in the context of democratic politics. The Court is regularly engaged in the review of government action, and consequently, the chief justice is someone who is always in the midst of political controversy.

Two models of Aristotelian heroes

The heroic judicial leadership described above shows that most of the chief justices in newer democracies are courageous and bold. This phenomenon begs for an answer to another question—namely, whether there is a competing model of heroic judicial leadership.

To answer this question, I will turn back to the Aristotelian's notion of heroism. As explained earlier, Aristotle postulates the concept of a hero as a serious man (*spoudaios*) with practical wisdom (*phronimos*). Aristotle elaborates further the concept of the hero in *Nichomachean Ethics*, in which he discusses the first two virtues: *andreia* (courage or manliness) and *sophrosune* (temperance).[104] For Aristotle, courage and temperance are ideally found together in the virtuous soul. Heroism must, therefore, be discussed concerning courage and temperance. Here Aristotle makes a classical comparison between the characters of two Homeric heroes: Achilles of the *Iliad* and Odysseus of the *Odyssey*.[105] Achilles is the exemplar of *andreia* and Odysseus of *sophrosune*, and Aristotle praises them both because they embody different models of heroic virtue.

In *Nichomechean Ethics*, Aristotle explains that many actions of the serious (*spoudaios*) man are done in the interest of his friends and his homeland, and that if there is a need for it, he will lay down his life for them.[106] This passage appears to represent Achilles's heroic deed of dying on the battlefield more than Odysseus's struggle for survival. But remember that Aristotle celebrated the distinct heroism of both Achilles and Odysseus. In other words, it can be heroic to die on the battlefield, but it can also be equally heroic to survive like Odysseus.

Indeed, Odysseus does not fit the description of a hero in Greek mythology, or one who prizes honor and glory above their life and dies on the battlefield in the prime of life.[107] When the typical Greek hero found someone who blocked his path, he would fight against the obstacle until something broke.[108] But Odysseus looks for another path around, instead of battering his head against the obstacle. One of the critical episodes in Homer's *Odyssey* is when Polyphemus, a vicious one-eyed giant known as a cyclops, traps Odysseus and his men in a cave.[109] Polyphemus eats two of Odysseus's men and falls asleep. Initially, Odysseus was planning to stab Polyphemus, but the difficulty was that Odysseus and his men would not be able to escape after killing Polyphemus because they could never move the stone door that blocked the cave's entrance. So Odysseus and his crew wait until they can trick Polyphemus into moving the stone door from the mouth of the cave and allow them to pass unharmed. Odysseus then comes up with a cunning plan: He lies that his name is "Nobody" and he blinds Polyphemus. If Odysseus had not cleverly lied about his name, the other cyclopses would come to help Polyphemus when he cried for help after he was blinded. Finally, Odysseus and his crew escaped the cave under cover of the sheep put out to graze.[110] A typical Greek hero would have chosen to kill Polyphemus, instead of lying that his name was "Nobody" and leaving the cave by hanging onto a ram's belly.

Odysseus is also untypical of a Greek hero *par excellence* because he is the only Homeric hero who bears the epithet of *polutlas*, or "much-enduring," described as the one who is always exposed to long suffering and humiliation.[111] Odysseus's suffering is not merely about being away from home and family for 20 years or experiencing shipwrecks that took the lives of his entire crew, but also the destruction of his name and reputation.[112] One of the outstanding examples of Odysseus's distinct suffering occurred when he landed home in Ithaca and disguised himself as a beggar to sneak into the city. Not only did he disfigure himself, but he threw on rags like a household slave. Other Greek heroes, such as Achilles, would never have been willing to make Odysseus's choice of disguising himself as a beggar.[113] But the disguise helps Odysseus sneak into his palace and prepare a strategy to fight against the large number (118) of overbearing men who are wooing his wife and consuming the goods of his household. With the help of his wife, Odysseus then set a plot to vanquish the overbearing suitors. In short, Odysseus embodies a different kind of heroism, which relies on practical intelligence and reason to access possible strategies and sometimes involves employing seemingly unheroic actions to achieve his ultimate goals.

Above all, Odysseus's heroism is a manifestation of prudence. The term *prudence*, which originally comes from the Latin *prudentia*, is contracted from the term *providentia*, which means limited human attempts to look ahead (*providere*) and anticipate events relying on signs.[114] In many ways, Odysseus had the patience to undergo voluntary submission that suspends the impulse to respond. Odysseus's patience is the manifestation of prudence. His patience is not a passive submission to his fate, but a strategic move of holding back for the right moment to move forward. As W. B. Stanford argues, Odysseus's prudence is a "gift for anticipating dangers and his readiness to avoid them when it best served his purpose."[115] In other words, Odysseus's prudence involves the strength to endure certain sufferings for the sake of achieving something good.

Based on two models of Aristotelian heroism, I would like to coin two concepts of heroic judicial leadership. The first I will call the "bold-aggressive hero."

In legal academia, Ronald Dworkin's "Judge Hercules" is the most sustained academic elaboration of the bold, aggressive, heroic judge.[116] Dworkin described "Judge Hercules" as one who aggressively interprets the constitution. With his skills of reasoning, a herculean judge would be ready to judge a case with entire theories of law available to justify any particular decision. As the antithesis of the bold, aggressive, judicial leadership model, I would like to introduce "prudential-minimalist heroes."[117] Prudential-minimalist heroes are willing to take a go-slow, persevering, willing-to-strategically-retreat approach in achieving their ultimate goals. Prudential-minimalist heroes also understand their role within the legal system and respect the sources of authority that constrain and guide their behavior. Nevertheless, prudential-minimalist heroes also know the right time to be bold in issuing a robust constitutional interpretation.

Among newer democracies, there was a judicial hero who embraced the prudential-minimalist approach: Chief Justice Arthur Chaskalson of the Constitutional Court of South Africa (CCSA). Theunis Roux, in his work on the CCSA, examined the heroism of Chief Justice Chaskalson.[118] Roux traced the journey of Chaskalson back to the apartheid era, when Chaskalson sublimated his opposition to apartheid into his role as a human-rights lawyer.[119] Chaskalson built a powerful litigation firm, the Legal Resources Center (LRC), with a vision of the common law as the repository of principles of freedom and justice. These principles, in turn, could be used by activist lawyers to protect individual rights against state encroachment.[120] In June 1994, President Nelson Mandela appointed Arthur Chaskalson as the president of the CCSA, where he remained until his retirement in 2005.

Roux praises the CCSA as one of the most successful post-Cold War constitutional courts because, under the leadership of Chief Justice Chaskalson, the Court was able to survive without any debilitating attacks on its independence. Roux believes the Chaskalson Court's ability to survive until Chaskalson's retirement is a remarkable achievement.[121] Roux explains that several factors led to the survival of the Chaskalson Court. But one of the keys successes of the Chaskalson Court lay in its ability to find the balance between its ruling as a forum to be a bridge among the competing political forces and its consistent support for a range of constitutional rights.[122]

Chief Justice Chaskalson was a strategic chief justice who knew how to enhance the Court's authority by engaging in rights-based discourse while also fortifying the Court's status by playing a minimalist role in some policy areas. Chaskalson asserted his minimalist strategy as follows:

> I think in the early days it's appropriate not to decide more than you have to decide.... To that extent, then, the Court has indicated that it will endeavor not to decide more than it has to and that constitutional issue ought not to be raised if the matter can deal with on other legal grounds.[123]

Chaskalson, however, took a maximalist view on socio-economic rights. He stated that:

> [T]he socio-economic rights are entrenched in the Bill of Rights. Unless the courts resort to stratagem of declaring disputes concerning socio-economic rights to the political questions and for that reason decline jurisdiction, they must confront and decide the hard cases that arise.[124]

Thus, the Chaskalson Court was able to play an effective role in South African politics by employing a combination of minimalist and maximalist strategies.

In sum, Chief Justice Chaskalson was a judicial hero who knew when to move one step forward with ambitious constitutional interpretation and when to move two steps back by deferring to the political judgments of other branches of government. Chief Justice Chaskalson was a hero whose prudential judgment recognized when he needed to be cautious in deferring to the government, or when to be bold in breaking a new legal ground. With his prudential judgment, Chaskalson successfully led the Court in building a foundation for new constitutionalism in post-apartheid South Africa.

The *Marbury* Strategy and prudential-minimalist heroes

The premise of my argument in this book is that the prudential-minimalist model of judicial leadership is a competing model to the bold, aggressive one. The prudential-minimalist approach, however, is different from judicial self-restraint. In the context of new democracies, Stephen Gardbaum explains that judges often choose to exercise "passive virtues" as a pragmatic response to the need to find a balance between the functions of judicial review and the fragility of judicial independence.[125] The use of "passive virtues" is the manifestation of judicial restraint, and it might include either or both of the following approaches. First, judges make a strategic choice to decide only relatively "safe" or routine cases rather than politically charged cases about which elected politicians care deeply. Second, judges can adopt a general norm of issuing cautious, measured judgments rather than bold, provocative rulings.[126]

The prudential-minimalist approach, however, does not rely on "passive virtues," as it permits courts to engage in risky cases and to issue robust decisions. A focus on prudential-minimalist approach is a court's engagement in judicial deferral. The strategy of judicial "deferral" allows courts to defer to elected political branches of government and minimize the disruption or damage caused by courts' decisions.[127] Rosalind Dixon and Samuel Issacharoff argue that there are two models of judicial deferral.[128] The first model is the ***explicit judicial deferral***,[129] which focuses on ensuring the remedial measures that a judge orders for constitutional violations. The most well-known explicit judicial deferral is in the form of a remedy known as "suspended declaration of invalidity." The 1996 South African Constitution explicitly states that the Constitutional Court has the authority to enact an "order suspending the declaration of invalidity for any period and on any conditions, to allow the competent authority to correct the defect."[130] An apt example of this model is the CCSA's decision *Fourie*,[131] the same-sex marriage case, where Parliament was given one year to enact new legislation to remedy the violation of the right to equality or else the Court would read words permitting same-sex marriage into the 1961 Marriage Act.[132]

Another form of explicit judicial deferral is known as *progressive realization*, in which the state must take incremental steps to achieve the full realization of constitutional rights.[133] A pertinent example of the doctrine of progressive realization is the CCSA's decision in *Grootboom*.[134] The case involved a challenge to the government's failure to fulfill the constitutional guarantee of the right to housing under Section 26 of the Constitution. The Court held that the state was obliged to take positive action to meet the needs of those living in extreme conditions of poverty, homelessness, or intolerable housing.[135] Nevertheless, the Court allowed the state to fulfill the constitutional mandate to provide adequate housing based on available resources and with consideration for the many competing claims for government funding.[136] In other words, the Court preferred an incremental approach based on the notion of reasonable implementation by the government.

Dixon and Issacharoff argue that the United States is the home of an older and more implicit judicial form of deferral, which emerged in the famous case *Marbury v. Madison*.[137] Chief Justice Marshall's opinion first acknowledged the merits of Marbury's claim that he had a valid legal claim to his commission and upheld the general propriety of issuing a writ of mandamus against Madison as the proper form of redress.[138] Furthermore, Marshall proclaimed the authority of the courts to engage in the process of judicial review, including the authority to interpret and enforce constitutional limits on the powers of all three branches of government.[139] But Chief Justice Marshall made a sudden turn by declining jurisdiction on the ground that Section 13 of the Judiciary Act was unconstitutional in purporting to authorize the Supreme Court to issue a mandamus in an original action against federal officials.[140]

The conventional wisdom of *Marbury* is that it is a strong form of judicial review. But Christopher Wolfe's *The Rise of Modern Judicial Review* highlights Marbury as the inception of a moderate form of judicial review.[141] Wolfe provides a careful analysis of Chief Justice Marshall's moderate approach to constitutional interpretation, in which the court would refrain from deciding political questions and defer to legislative decisions except when unconstitutionality was clear.[142] Thus, the remaining issue is whether Marbury is the manifestation of strong or weak form review or a combination of both.[143]

Like the blind men who are seeking to describe the elephant, those who approach Marbury must exercise caution, otherwise their description will depend on what one grabs first. The crux of the matter of *Marbury* is whether the Supreme Court, acting within its original jurisdiction, had the authority to grant the requested writ of mandamus.[144] Section 13 of the Judiciary Act of 1789 authorized the Supreme Court, but not the lower federal courts, to issue writs of mandamus to federal officials (as well as to the lower federal courts).[145] Article III of the U.S. Constitution, however, equips the Supreme Court with both "original" and "appellate" jurisdiction.[146] In Marshall's opinion, cases within the "original" jurisdiction could be initiated in the Supreme Court, but cases within the appellate jurisdiction must be initiated in some other appellate court.[147] Marshall asserted that the writ of mandamus fell under the category of appellate jurisdiction because the case arises under the laws of the United States.[148] But Marbury chose to file his petition directly in the Supreme Court, which according to Marshall, involved the exercise of the Court's original jurisdiction.[149] Considering that the Constitution precluded the exercise of original jurisdiction in *Marbury*, Marshall then concluded that the Court had no authority to entertain Marbury's claim for mandamus as its original jurisdiction.[150]

Marshall's decision in *Marbury* was quite deft; on the one hand, he inserted a new constitutional doctrine that the interpretation and enforcement of the Constitution are the province of the judiciary and, ultimately, the Supreme Court. On the other hand, he avoided a confrontation with the Jefferson administration by refusing to issue the writ of mandamus against Madison.

Dixon and Issacharoff argue that *Marbury*'s strategy is a kind of implicit deferral,[151] in which the Court proclaimed powers of judicial review but deferred the legal and political effect of this reasoning by holding that it lacked jurisdiction to grant an order for mandamus. This kind of implicit deferral is a common feature in the U.S. constitutional realm; on the one hand, the Court issues a maximalist reasoning, but on the other hand, it produces minimalist legal outcomes or remedies.[152] In other words, the implicit judicial deferral takes place in the form of a combination of a "soft" confrontation with the elected branches of government and avoidance or delay of the legal remedies or the effect of a ruling.

Marbury has become an iconic approach to judicial review and decision making around the globe.[153] In the strong form aspect of *Marbury*, based on the evidence of Chief Justice Marshall's statement, "it is emphatically the province and duty of the judicial department to say what the law is,"[154] which has become the model for the constitutional courts adopted by other nations after World War II.[155] The judicial deferral aspect of *Marbury* has also become more apparent in countries where courts have played a central role in the transition to democracy.[156]

One of the resemblances of the *Marbury* strategy in newer democracies is the CCSA's decision in *Minister of Health v. Treatment Action Campaign* (*TAC*).[157] In TAC, the plaintiffs challenged the adequacy of a government program that provided the anti-retroviral drug nevirapine to pregnant mothers, but limited the provision of the drug to a small number of research and training sites and banned the use of it outside of these sites. The most significant aspect of the decision is the specific terms of the Court's order. The Court required the government to take specific action to correct the constitutional defect by extending the provision of nevirapine beyond the pilot sites.[158] But the Court gave the government permission to ignore that directive and adapt "its policy in a manner consistent with the Constitution if equally appropriate or better methods become available for the prevention of mother-to-child transmission of HIV."[159]

The TAC decision is reminiscent of *Marbury* because the Court combined the proclamation of its strong powers with refusal to invoke those powers. In TAC, the Court reaffirmed its power to require the state to revise their policy and to submit the revised policy to the Court, but the Court did not consider it necessary to invoke its power.[160] Instead, the Court stated that the government has always respected and executed orders of the Court and there is no reason to expect a different result in TAC.[161] Moreover, the Court acknowledged that the executive branch has the power to ignore the Court's order regarding implementation: "Government must retain the right to adopt the policy, consistent with its constitutional obligations, should it consider it appropriate to do so."[162] In other words, the Court deferred to the executive branch to interpret the best way to fulfill its obligation under the socio-economic rights provisions in the Constitution.

While any courts can apply the *Marbury* strategy across different cases for a long period, there must be a heroic "judicial captain" who can lead the court to implement the *Marbury* strategy. *Marbury v. Madison* would not have come into fruition without John Marshall, who was a master of strategy and tactics.[163] The *Marbury* decision put the Court in a delicate position; if the Court issued a ruling in Marbury's favor, it might provoke the Jefferson administration to retaliate against the Court. Ruling against Marbury on the merits, however, could appear to be a sign of the Court's submission to a hostile president. Marshall, however, was capable of finding a more moderate course, which fortified the Court's legitimacy and satisfied the Jefferson administration at the same time.[164]

Similarly, the CCSA could not release a decision in TAC without the leadership of Arthur Chaskalson. Theunis Roux explains that initially, TAC was the case in which a decision against the government would expose the Court to a significant political backlash.[165] Nevertheless, right before the Court began its hearing, the government ended its political opposition to the case due to the domestic and international pressure to President Mbeki's policy on HIV.[166] Despite the collapse of the government's opposition, however, the Court continued to play a cautious approach in issuing its decision. Roux argues that the Court did not want to raise the bar too high because Chaskalson was thinking of the Court's longer-term relationship with the African National Congress (ANC) as the ruling party and the need to engage political branches as partners in building constitutionalism in South Africa.[167]

In sum, courts in newer democracies often need prudential-minimalist leaders like Marshall and Chaskalson. Courts in newer democracies need a strategic chief justice who knows how to combine ambitious interpretations of the constitution with the willingness to recognize the merits of deferring to political judgments about the constitution. Through the prudential-minimalist approach, a chief justice will be able to strengthen the court's authority and fortify the court's interest at the same time.

Conclusion

This chapter has explained not only a new theory of judicial heroes but also a relevant theory of judicial review. This chapter reaffirmed the postulate that judicial leadership is one of the most crucial factors contributing to the development of judicial review in newer democracies. The development of a judicial institution depends on upon a skillful chief justice who must constantly consider how he will react to the political climate surrounding the judicial branch and lead the judicial branch vis-à-vis elected governmental branches. Contrary to the stereotype of a bold, aggressive, judicial leadership style, this book offers the theory of prudential-minimalist leadership as an effective leadership model for leading courts through transitional periods. While this theory has certainly contributed to the literature of comparative judicial politics, it also constitutes a rival explanation to the popular expectation that the success of judicial review depends upon robust-bold judicial heroes. This chapter, therefore, provides both an analytic overview and a theoretical reference for the following chapters.

Notes

1 Robert Bolt. *A Man for All Seasons: A Play in Two Acts* (New York: Random House, 1962).
2 Ibid., xiii.
3 Ibid., xiv.
4 Randy Lee. "Legal Ethics for Government Lawyers: Straight Talk For Tough Times: Robert Bolt's *A Man for All Seasons* and the Art of Discerning Integrity," 9 *Widener J. Pub. L.* 305, 335 (2000).
5 See Paul Gewirtz. "A Lawyer's Death," 100 *HARV. L. REV. 2053*, 2055–56 (1987); see also Richard Posner. "Judicial Biography," 70 *N.Y.U. L. REV.* 502, 512 (1995).
6 Todd Lindberg. *The Heroic Heart: Greatness Ancient and Modern* (New York: Encounter Books, 2015), chapter 3.
7 Jean Edward Smith. *John Marshall: Definer of a Nation* (New York: H. Holt & Co., 1996); R. Kent Newmyer. *John Marshall and the Heroic Age of the Supreme Court* (Baton Rouge: LSU Press, 2001).
8 *Marbury v. Madison*, 5 U.S. 137 (1803).
9 Akhil Reed Amar. "Hugo Black and the Hall of Fame," 53 *Ala L. Rev.* 1221 (2002).
10 Michael R. Belknap. "Earl Warren Professorship Acceptance Speech," 39 *Cal W. Int'l L.J.* 366 (2009).
11 Bernard Schwartz. "The Judicial Ten: America's Greatest Justices," 4 *S. ILL. U. L.J.* 405 (1979).
12 John Gava. "The Rise of the Hero Judge," 24 *University of New South Wales Law Journal* 747 (2001).
13 Kim Lane Scheppele. "Guardians of the Constitution: Constitutional Court Presidents and the Struggle for the Rule of Law in Post-Soviet Europe," 154 *U. Pa. L. Rev.* 1757 (June, 2006).
14 For a discussion of the development of the idea of "invisible constitution" in Hungarian case law, see Ethan Klingsberg. "Judicial Review and Hungary's Transition from Communism to Democracy: The Constitutional Court, The Continuity of Law, and the Redefinition of Property Rights," 41 *B.Y.U. L. Rev.* 78–81 (1992).
15 Tamir Moustafa. *The Struggle for Constitutional Power: Law, Politics, and Economic Development in Egypt.* (New York: Cambridge University Press, 2007).
16 Paul Kahn. "Owen Fiss: Heroism in the Law," 58 *U. Miami L. Rev.* 103, 107 (2003).
17 Jennifer A. Widner. *Building the Rule of Law: Francis Nyalali and the Road to Judicial Independence in Africa* (New York: W.W. Norton, 2001).
18 Ibid., 279.
19 Ibid., 322.

20 For a detailed analysis of the role of Chief Justice Ifthikar Muhammad Chaudhry, please see Charles Kennedy. *The Judicialization of Politics in Pakistan*. In *The Judicialization of Politics in Asia*, edited by Bjorn Dressel. (London: Routledge, 2012); Taiyyaba Ahmed Qureshi. "State of Emergency: General Pervez Musharraf's Executive Assault on Judicial Independence in Pakistan," 35 *N.C.J. Int'L. & Com. Reg*. 485 (2010); Shoaib A. Ghias. "Miscarriage of Chief Justice: Judicial Power and the Legal Complex in Pakistan Under Musharraf," 35 *Law & Soc. Inquiry* 985 (2010); Moeen H. Cheema. "The 'Chaudhry Court': Deconstructing the 'Judicialization of Politics' in Pakistan," 25 *Washington International Law Journal* 448 (2016).

21 See Ethan Klingsberg. "Contextualizing the Calculus of Consent: Judicial Review of Legislative Wealth Transfers in a Transition to Democracy and Beyond," 27 *Cornell Int'l L.J.* 303 (1994).

22 See the Constitutional Court of Hungary, Summary Decision No. 43 of 1995 on Social Security Benefit.

23 See Carla Thorson. *Politics, Judicial Review and the Russian Constitutional Court* (Palgrave Macmillan: 2012), 55; See also Alexei Trochev. *Judging Russia: Constitutional Court in Russian Politics, 1990–2006* (Cambridge: Cambridge University Press, 2008).

24 Thorson, ibid., 57–58.

25 Cass Sunstein, *Constitutional Personae* (New York, NY: Oxford University Press, 2015), 5.

26 Ibid.

27 Ibid., 6.

28 Ibid., 8.

29 Ibid., 10–11.

30 Ibid., 15.

31 *District of Columbia v. Heller*, 554 U.S. 570 (2008).

32 Daniel Suhr. "Judicial Cincinnati: The Humble Heroism of Originalist Justices," 5 *FIU L. Rev.* 155 (2009).

33 Pamela Marin. *Blood in the Forum: The Struggle for the Roman Republic* (London: Continuum, 2009).

34 See Suhr. *Judicial Cincinnati*, 169–170.

35 See Sunstein. *Constitutional Personae*, 16.

36 In his original law review article, Sunstein used the term *Burkean Judges* instead of Minimalist Judges, please see Cass Sunstein. "Constitutional Personae"; 2013 *Sup. Ct. Rev.* 433, 443 (2013).

37 See Sunstein. *Constitutional Personae*, 18.

38 *Lawrence v. Texas*, 539 U.S. 558 (2003).

39 Sunstein. *Constitutional Personae*, 17–18.

40 The final category of Sunstein's constitutional personae is the judicial mute, who prefers to say nothing at all and has zero interest in engaging in the political drama. But I will not discuss the notion of judicial mute; it is irrelevant for this book because Sunstein does not posit any link between judicial hero and judicial mute.

41 One of the most recent works on the idea of heroism is Owen Fiss. *Pillars of Justice: Lawyers and the Liberal Tradition* (Cambridge, Massachusetts: Harvard University Press, 2017). In this book, Fiss explores the heroic accounts of 13 lawyers who shaped the legal world during the past half century. These heroes are American lawyers, with the exception of two foreign lawyers: Chief Justice Aharon Barak of Israel, who was credited with defending and advancing liberal values in Israel; and Carlos Nino of Argentina, who received high praise as the most important legal philosopher ever to come from Latin America.

42 A fall 2017 Lexis-Nexis search in the Journals and Law Reviews database using a search term like "Jon Elster" w/p "Ulysses" would generate around 482 hits; a search term like "Ulysses" w/p "the sirens" would make around 655 hits. A further search of that database for discussion of the idea of pre-commitment turned up around 698 hits.

43 Jon Elster. *Ulysses and the Sirens: Studies in Rationality and Irrationality* (Cambridge: Cambridge University Press, 1979).

44 *The Odyssey of Homer* (Martin Hammond trans., Duckworth ed., 2000), Book 12, 160–170

45 Ibid. Book 12, 178–180.

46 Jon Elster. *Ulysses Unbound: Studies in Rationality, Precommitment, and Constraints* (Cambridge: Cambridge University Press, 2000), ix.

47 Jon Elster, Claus Offe, and Ulrich Klaus Preuss. *Institutional Design in Post-Communist Societies: Rebuilding the Ship at Sea* (Cambridge: Cambridge University Press, 1998), 25.

48 For a detailed analysis on the origin of the image of "Peter sober" and "Peter drunk," please see Samuel Issacharoff. "The Enabling Role of Democratic Constitutionalism: Fixed Rules and Some Implications for Contested Presidential Elections," 81 *Tex. L. Rev.* 1985 n. 13 (2002).

49 Jeffrey Rosen. "Class Legislation, Public Choice, and the Structural Constitution," 21 *Harv. J.L. & Pub. Pol'Y* 179, 182 (1997).

50 Frank I. Michelman. "Foreword: Traces of Self-Government," 100 *Harv. L. Rev.* 4, 61 n. 320 (1986). Michelman, however, noted that Bacon used the image of "Philip sober" and "Philip drunk."

51 Jed Rubenfeld. *Freedom and Time: A Theory of Constitutional Self-Government.* (New Haven: Yale University Press, 2001), 129–130.

52 Ibid., 129–130.

53 David Landau. "Political Institutions and Judicial Role in Comparative Constitutional Law," 51 *Harv. Int'l L.J.* 319, 329 (Summer, 2010).

54 Nathan J. Brown. *Constitutions in a Nonconstitutional World: Arab Basic Laws and the Prospects for Accountable Government* (Albany, NY: State University of New York, 2002); See also Nathan J. Brown. *The Rule of Law in the Arab World: Courts in Egypt and the Gulf* (Cambridge: Cambridge University Press, 1997).

55 Some scholars argue that these analogies are related to a theory of human behavior that establishes a separation between reason and emotion, with calm, deliberative reason offered as a superior alternative to the destructive effects of emotion. See Nathan J. Brown. "Reason, Interest, Rationality, and Passion in Constitution Drafting," 6(4) *Perspectives on Politics* 675–689 (2008); Jon Elster. "Don't Burn Your Bridge Before You Come to It: Some Ambiguities and Complexities of Precommitment," 81 *Tex. L. Rev.* 1751 (2003).

56 Mary Ann Glendon. *Abortion and Divorce in Western Law* (Cambridge, MA: Harvard University Press, 1987), 8.

57 H. W. O. Okoth-Ogendo. "Constitutions Without Constitutionalism: Reflections on an African Political Paradox." In *Constitutionalism and Democracy: Transitions in the Contemporary World*, edited by Douglas Greenberg et al. (New York: Oxford Univ. Press 1993), 65–80.

58 Polis means both "state" and "city."

59 Aristotle. "Politics." In *The Basic Works of Aristotle*, edited by Richard Mckeon. New York: Random House, 1941), Book III; 1276, 20.

60 Ibid., 1276, 25.

61 Ibid., 1276b, 1–4.

62 Ibid., 1276b, 20.

63 Ibid., 1276b, 28–30.

64 Ibid., 1276b, 17.

65 See Donald Henry D'Amour. *Aristotle on Heroes* (Unpublished PhD Dissertation, University of Notre Dame, 1971).
66 Aristotle. "Nicomachean Ethics." In *The Basic Works of Aristotle*, (edited by Richard Mckeon, New York: Random House, 1941), 1113a30, 1166a10–15, 1170a13, 1176a15.
67 The discussion of *phronimos* appears in *Nicomachean Ethics*, Book VI chapter 5, 7, 8, 10–13.
68 D'Amour. *Aristotle on Heroes*, 209.
69 For an overview of the body of scholarship on the creation of the constitutional court, please see Tom Ginsburg and Mila Versteeg. "Why Do Countries Adopt Constitutional Review?" 30(3) *The Journal of Law, Economics, and Organization* 587–622 (2013).
70 Mauro Cappelletti. *The Judicial Process in Comparative Perspective* (Oxford: Clarendon Press, 1989).
71 For an overview, see Martin Shapiro. "The Success of Judicial Review." In *Constitutional Dialogues in Comparative Perspective*, edited by Sally J. Kenney, William M. Reisinger, and John C. Reitz. (New York, NY: St. Martin's Press, 1999), 193–207.
72 See Tom Ginsburg. *Judicial Review in New Democracies: Constitutional Courts in Asian Cases* (Cambridge: Cambridge University Press, 2003); Jodi Finkel. *Judicial Reform as Political Insurance: Argentina, Peru, and Mexico in the 1990s* (Notre Dame, IN: University of Notre Dame Press, 2008); Matthew C. Stephenson. "'When the Devil Turns …': The Political Foundation of Independent Judicial Review," 32 *J. Leg. Stud.* 59 (2003).
73 Ran Hirschl. *Towards Juristocracy: The Origins and Consequences of the New Constitutionalism* (Cambridge, MA: Harvard University Press, 2004).
74 Tamir Moustafa. *The Struggle for Constitutional Power.*
75 David Oliver Erdos. *Delegating Rights Protection: The Rise of Bills of Rights in the Westminster World.* (Oxford: Oxford University Press, 2010), 43.
76 C. Neal Tate. "Why the Expansion of Judicial Power?" In *The Global Expansion of Judicial Power*, edited by C. Neal Tate and Torbjörn Vallinder. (New York: New York University Press, 1995), 28–30.
77 See Alec Stone Sweet. *Governing with Judges: Constitutional Politics in Europe* (Oxford: Oxford University Press, 2000).
78 See Björn Dressel. "Towards a Framework of Analysis." In *The Judicialization of Politics in Asia*, edited by Bjorn Dressel, 10–11; Rachel Sieder et al. ibid. 15–16.
79 Rachel Sieder, Line Schjolden, and Alan Angell. "Introduction." In *The Judicialization of Politics in Latin America* (New York: Palgrave Macmillan, 2005), 5; Tate. *Why the Expansion of Judicial Power*, 30; Moustafa. *The Struggle for Constitutional Power*, 110.
80 Javier Couso, Alexandra Huneeus, and Rachel Sieder. *Cultures of Legality Judicialization and Political Activism in Latin America* (Cambridge: Cambridge University Press, 2010), 6–8; Rachel Sieder et al. *The Judicialization of Politics in Latin America*, 12–13.
81 Diana Kapiszewski. *High Courts and Economic Governance in Argentina and Brazil* (Cambridge: Cambridge University Press, 2012).
82 Ibid., 27–28.
83 Diana Kapiszewski, Gordon Silverstein, and Robert A. Kagan. "On Judicial Ships and Winds of Change." In *Consequential Courts: Judicial Roles in Global Perspective*, edited by Diana Kapiszewski, Gordon Silverstein, and Robert A. Kagan, (New York: Cambridge University Press, 2013), 400.
84 Ibid., 19.
85 Ibid., 19.
86 Ibid., 21.

87 Ibid., 401.
88 Ibid., 401.
89 Kapiszewski et al. *Consequential Courts*, 401.
90 To date, there are not many scholarships on judicial leadership in new democracies; Jennifer Widner's work on the role of judicial leadership in the emerging constitutionalism in southern and eastern Africa is the pioneering work. See Jennifer A. Widner. *Building the Rule of Law*; see also Haig Patapan. "Leadership, Law, and Legitimacy: Reflections on the Changing Nature of Judicial Politics in Asia." In *The Judicialization of Politics in Asia*, edited by Bjorn Dressel. (London: Routledge, 2012).
91 David W. Rohde. "Policy Goals, Strategic, Choice and Majority Opinion Assignments in the US Supreme Court," *Midwest Journal of Political Science* 652–682 (1972); Gregory J. Rathjen. "Policy Goals, Strategic Choice, and Majority Opinion Assignments in the US Supreme Court: A Replication." *American Journal of Political Science* 713–724 (1974); Saul Brenner and Harold J. Spaeth. "Majority Opinion Assignments and the Maintenance of the Original Coalition on the Warren Court," *American Journal of Political Science* 72–81 (1988); Forrest Maltzman and Paul J. Wahlbeck. "May it Please the Chief? Opinion Assignments in the Rehnquist Court," *American Journal of Political Science* 421–443 (1996).
92 Joseph F. Kobylka. "Leadership on the Supreme Court of the United States: Chief Justice Burger and the Establishment Clause," *The Western Political Quarterly* 545–568 (1989); H. W. Perry. *Deciding to Decide: Agenda Setting in the United States Supreme Court* (Cambridge, MA: Harvard University Press, 1991).
93 Judith Resnick. "Managerial Judges," 96 *Harv. L. Rev.* 376 (1982); Carl Tobias. "Warren Burger and the Administration of Justice," 41 *Vill. L. Rev.* 505 (1996); Tracey E. George and Albert H. Yoon. "Chief Judges: The Limits of Attitudinal Theory and Possible Paradox of Managerial Judging," 61 *Vand. L. Rev.* 1 (2008); Catherine Stone. "The Dual Role of a Chief Justice," 45 *St. Mary's L. J.* 553 (2014).
94 Thomas Walker, Lee Epstein, and William J. Dixon. "On the Mysterious Demise of Consensual Norms in the United States Supreme Court," 50(2) *Journal of Politics* 361–389 (1988); Lee Epstein and Thomas G. Walker. "The Role of the Supreme Court in American Society: Playing the Reconstruction Game." In *Contemplating Courts*, edited by Lee Epstein (Washington DC, CQ Press, 1995), 315–346; Jack Knight and Lee Epstein. "On the Struggle for Judicial Supremacy." *Law and Society Review* 87–120 (1996); Sue Davis. "The Chief Justice and Judicial Decision-Making: The Institutional Basis for Leadership on the Supreme Court." In *Supreme Court Decision-Making*, edited by Cornell Clayton and Howard Gillman. (Chicago: The University of Chicago Press, 1999), 135–154.
95 Peter Irons. *Brennan vs. Rehnquist: The Battle for the Constitution*. (New York: Knopf, 1994); Paul H. Edelman and Jim Chen. "The Most Dangerous Justice: The Supreme Court at the Bar of Mathematics," 70 *S. Cal. L. Rev.* 63 (1996); Paul H. Edelman and Jim Chen. "The Most Dangerous Justice Rides Again: Revisiting the Power Pageant of the Justices," 86 *Minn. L. Rev.* 131 (2001); Thomas Merrill. "The Making of the Second Rehnquist Court: A Preliminary Analysis," 47 *St. Louis ULJ* 569 (2003); Nancy Maveety. *Queen's Court: Judicial Power in the Rehnquist Era*. (Lawrence, Kansas: University Press of Kansas, 2008).
96 Joel K. Goldstein. "Leading the Court: Studies in Influence as Chief Justice," 40 *Stetson L. Rev.* 717 (2011).
97 Kim Lane Scheppele. Guardians of the Constitution, (1777 ([2006]).
98 Ibid., 1762.
99 Ibid., 1769–1770.

100 Ibid., 1770.
101 Ibid., 1772.
102 Ibid.
103 Ibid., 1766–1767.
104 Aristotle. *Nichomachean Ethics*, 3.6.1115a6; 3.9.1117b24.
105 Patrick J. Deneen has an excellent comparison between the heroism of Odysseus and Achilles. See Patrick J. Deneen. *The Odyssey of Political Theory: The Politics of Departure and Return* (Lanham: Rowman & Littlefield Publishers, 2000).
106 Aristotle. *Nichomachean Ethics*, 9.8.1169a18–20.
107 J. Griffin. *Homer on Life and Death* (Oxford: Clarendon Press, 1980), 81.
108 William Bedell Stanford. *The Ulysses Theme: A Study in the Adaptability of a Traditional Hero* (Oxford: Blackwell, 1963), 73.
109 *The Odyssey of Homer* (Martin Hammond trans., Duckworth ed., 2000), Book 9: 290.
110 Ibid. Book 9: 360–450.
111 Margalit Finkelberg. "Odysseus and the Genus 'Hero'," *Greece and Rome* (Second Series) 42, no. 01 (1995): 1–14, 2.
112 Ari Kohen. *Untangling Heroism: Classical Philosophy and the Concept of the Hero* (New York: Routledge, 2014), 46.
113 Stanford. *The Ulysses Theme*, 74.
114 Jeffrey Barnouw. *Odysseus, Hero of Practical Intelligence: Deliberation and Signs in Homer's Odyssey*, (Lanham, MD: University Press of America, 2004), 73.
115 Stanford. *The Ulysses Theme*, 73.
116 Judge Hercules emerged in Dworkin's essay on "hard cases," and later he grew up and matured in Dworkin's *Law's Empire*. See Ronald Dworkin. *Law's Empire* (Cambridge, MA: Belknap Press, 1986).
117 Different scholars have provided different models of judicial heroes as the antithesis to bold-aggressive judicial heroes; see J. W. Harris. "Unger's Critique of Formalism in Legal Reasoning: Hero, Hercules, and Humdrum," 52 *Mod. L. Rev.* 42 (1989); R. P. Peerenboom. "A Coup D'Etat in Law's Empire: Dworkin's Hercules Meets Atlas," 9 *Law & Phil.* 95 (1990).
118 Theunis Roux. *The Politics of Principle: The First South African Constitutional Court, 1995–2005* (Cambridge: Cambridge University Press, 2013).
119 Ibid., 221–222.
120 Ibid., 222. Justice Chaskalson founded LRC as the first South Africa's public-interest law firm to fight apartheid, modeling it after the NAACP Legal Defense and Educational Fund. Financing came primarily from three American sources: the Ford Foundation, the Carnegie Corporation of New York and the Rockefeller Brothers Fund. See also Mark S. Kende. *Constitutional Rights in Two Worlds: South Africa and the United States,* (Cambridge [England]: Cambridge University Press, 2009), 32–33; Douglas Martin. "Arthur Chaskalson, Chief South African Jurist, dies at 81," *N.Y. Times*, December 3, 2012, http://www.nytimes.com/2012/12/04/world/africa/arthur-chaskalson-south-african-chief-justice-dies-at-81.html?_r=0.
121 Roux. *The Politics of Principle*, 188.
122 Ibid., 36.
123 Kate Kempton and Malcolm MacLaren. "The Protection of Human Rights in South Africa: A Conversation with Justice Arthur Chaskalson, President of the Constitutional Court of South Africa," 56 *U.T. Fac. L. Rev.* 161 (1998).
124 Arthur Chaskalson. "From Wickedness to Equality: The Moral Transformation of South African Law," 1(4) *Int J Constitutional Law* 590 (2003).
125 Stephen Gardbaum. "Are Strong Constitutional Courts Always a Good Thing for New Democracies?" 53 *Colum. J. Transnat'l L.* 285, 309 (2015).
126 Ibid., 309.

127 For an excellent analysis on the idea of judicial deferral, please see Rosalind Dixon and Tom Ginsburg. "Deciding Not to Decide: Deferral in Constitutional Design," 9 *Int'l J. Const. L.* 636 (2011).
128 See Rosalind Dixon and Samuel Issacharoff. "Living to Fight Another Day: Judicial Deferral in Defense of Democracy," 2016 *Wis. L. Rev.* 683 (2016).
129 Ibid., 696.
130 The 1996 South African Constitution, Art. 172 § 1.b.ii.
131 *Minister of Home Affairs v. Fourie* 2006 (1) SA 524 (CC) (S. Afr.).
132 The deadline set in the case of *Fourie* was November 30, 2006. After long debate and negotiation, Deputy President Phumzile Mlambo-Ngcuka, acting for President Thabo Mbeki, signed the Civil Union Act into law on November 29, 2006, and it became law the following day.
133 The idea has its origins in the International Covenant on Economic, Social and Cultural Rights, which provides that each state party to the covenant must "take steps … to the maximum of its available resources, with a view to achieving progressively the full realization of the rights recognized in the present Covenant by all appropriate means, including particularly the adoption of legislative measures." See Article 2 of the International Covenant on Economic, Social and Cultural Rights.
134 *South Africa v. Grootboom* 2001 (1) SA 46 (CC).
135 Ibid., Para. 35.
136 Ibid., Para. 41–42.
137 See Rosalind Dixon and Samuel Issacharoff. "Living to Fight Another Day: Judicial Deferral in Defense of Democracy," *Wis. L. Rev.* 683 (2016).
138 5 U.S. (1 Cranch) 137 (1803), 152–180.
139 Ibid.
140 Ibid.
141 Christopher Wolfe. *The Rise of Modern Judicial Review: From Constitutional Interpretation to Judge-Made Law* (Lanham, MD: Rowman & Littlefield, 1994).
142 Ibid., 91–113.
143 Mark Tushnet. "Marbury v. Madison Around the World," 71 *Tenn. L. Rev.* 251 (2004) (noting that although Marbury is the likely origin of strong-form review, there has been a long debate on whether the United States had a strong system. Tushnet argues that Marbury did not have to become the origin of the strong-form review as the United States adopted the strong-form system of judicial review no later than 1958 in *Cooper v. Aaron*).
144 Marbury. 5 U.S., 173.
145 See the Judiciary Act of 1789, chapter. 20, 13, *1 Stat. 73,* 80–81.
146 Marbury. 5 U.S., 174.
147 Ibid., 174–175.
148 Ibid., 175.
149 Marbury's decision to file the case directly in the Supreme Court has been the subject of considerable speculation. See Susan Low Bloch. "The Marbury Mystery: Why Did William Marbury Sue in the Supreme Court?" 18 *Const. Commentary* 607 (2001).
150 Marbury. 5 U.S., 176.
151 Dixon and Issacharoff. *Living to Fight Another Day*, 699.
152 Cass R. Sunstein. *One Case at a Time: Judicial Minimalism on the Supreme Court* (Cambridge, MA: Harvard University Press, 1999); Robert Anderson IV. "Measuring Meta-Doctrine: An American Assessment of Judicial Minimalism in the Supreme Court," 32 *Harv. J.L. & Pub. Pol'y* 1045 (Summer, 2009); Diane Sykes. "Minimalism and Its Limits," *Cato Sup. Ct. Rev.* 17 (2014–2015). For discussions of the strategy of judicial deferral by the Roberts court, please see Richard L. Hasen. "Constitutional Avoidance and Anti-Avoidance by the

Roberts Court," *Sup. Ct. Rev.* 181 (2009); Damien Schiff. "Nothing New Under the Sun: The Minimalism of Chief Justice Roberts and the Supreme Court's Recent Environmental Law Jurisprudence," 15 *Mo. Envtl. L. & Pol'y Rev.* 1 (2007); Charles W. "Rocky" Rhodes. "What Conservative Constitutional Revolution? Moderating Five Degrees of Judicial Conservatism After Six Years of the Roberts Court," 64 *Rutgers L. Rev.* 1 (2011).

153 See M. C. Mirrow. "Marbury in Mexico: Judicial Review's Precocious Southern Migration," 35 *Hastings Const. L.Q.* 41 (2007); H. Kwasi Prempeh. "Marbury in Africa: Judicial Review and the Challenge of Constitutionalism in Contemporary Africa," 80 *Tul. L. Rev.* 1239 (2006); Robert J. Morris. "China's Marbury: Qi Yuling v. Chen Xiaoqi—The Once and Future Trial of Both Education & Constitutionalization," 2 *Tsinghua China L. Rev.* 273 (2010).

154 *Marbury v. Madison*, 5 U.S. 137, 177 (1803).

155 See Mark Tushnet. "Judging Judicial Review: Marbury in the Modern Era: Alternative Forms of Judicial Review," 101 *Mich. L. Rev.* 2781 (2003).

156 See Dixon and Issacharoff. *Living to Fight Another Day*, 708 (noting that the German Constitutional Court and the Indian Supreme Court provided the critical jurisprudence on proportionality review with the capacity to protect democracy from threats, yet they enjoyed some degree of success in enforcing their decisions.) Dixon and Issacharoff also note that judicial caution has become apparent in countries like Colombia and Indonesia.

157 *Minister of Health v. Treatment Action Campaign* 2002 (5) SA 721 (CC) (S. Afr.).

158 Ibid., para. 135 § 3.

159 Ibid., para. 135 § 4.

160 Ibid., para. 129.

161 Ibid.

162 Ibid., para. 127.

163 For an excellent analysis of how Marshall was willing to sacrifice methodological consistency for the sake of achieving important political ends, please see Thomas C. Shevory. *John Marshall's Law: Interpretation, Ideology, and Interest* (Westport, CT: Greenwood Press, 1994), 45–53; see also Herbert Alan Johnson. *The Chief Justiceship of John Marshall, 1801–1835* (Columbia, SC: University of South Carolina Press, 1998), 58–60; Newmyer. *John Marshall and the Heroic Age of the Supreme Court*, 157–175.

164 Herbert Alan Johnson. *The Chief Justiceship of John Marshall, 1801–1835.* (Columbia, SC: University of South Carolina Press, 1998), 58 (noting that *Marbury* was the characteristic of Marshall's style, in which the court adroitly avoided a conflict with the executive branch over enforcement).

165 Roux. *The Politics of Principle*, 299.

166 Ibid.

167 Ibid., 303.

Part II

The first-generation court

2 The birth of the Constitutional Court

A joke that turned serious

Introduction

Tom Ginsburg, one of the most distinguished scholars of comparative constitutional law, first published his seminal work *Judicial Review in New Democracies* in 2003.[1] In this book, Ginsburg put Indonesia in the footnote of the list of the Third Wave of Democracies that adopted constitutional review; the footnote says "a constitutional court was proposed for Indonesia in 2001." Indeed, the Indonesian Constitutional Court was only a "footnote" in world constitutional history at the dawn of the twenty-first century. The birth of the Indonesian Constitutional Court, in my view, was a joke that turned into something serious. Other than setting up the Constitutional Court as an "insurance" mechanism to safeguard political power, politicians did not have any intention of creating a robust judiciary. Moreover, the government delayed the establishment of the Court for 2 years after its initial inception.

Scholars of comparative law and politics have been studying judicial power for many decades and have put forth different explanatory theories about the main driving forces for the creation of constitutional courts across the globe. Why would self-interested politicians restrict their future political choices by giving power to unelected judges?[2] This chapter argues that two main causes drove the creation of the Indonesian Constitutional Court in 2001: the ultimate causes and the proximate cause. By *proximate cause*, I mean an event that is closest to, or immediately responsible for causing, some observed result. This exists in contrast to a higher-level *ultimate cause*, which is usually thought of as the "real" reason something occurred.

So defined, there are at least three ultimate causes that contributed to the creation of the Indonesian Constitutional Court. First, from historical and political perspectives, the establishment of a constitutional court was a response to continued demand for judicial review by civil society.[3] Second, the fall of the military government opened the window of democratic reform, which includes the adoption of judicial review. Third, the political diffusion theories, which suggest that the introduction of judicial review is a response to constitutional development in foreign states, might help explain the adoption of the Indonesian Constitutional Court.[4] Based on their international study missions, the members of the Indonesian

People's Consultative Assembly (MPR—*Majelis Permusyawaratan Rakyat*) borrowed the structure and jurisdiction of the South Korean Constitutional Court as a template for the new Indonesian Constitutional Court.[5]

The proximate cause for the creation of the Court is the division of power among the elite. It is hard to maintain a strong presidency under the fragmented political configuration of Indonesia, unless the president establishes a firm base of support in the People's Representative Council (*Dewan Perwakilan Rakyat*—DPR), either through coalition or majority control. Therefore, the winning presidency also needs additional "insurance," like, for example, the impeachment mechanism that was to be supervised by the Constitutional Court. It was under these circumstances that the winning party, PDI-P (*Partai Demokrasi Indonesia Perjuangan*—Indonesian Democratic Party of Struggle), proposed the creation of the Constitutional Court.

When the MPR voted for the adoption of the Constitutional Court on November 9, 2001, they never intended to create a robust and vibrant constitutional court. First, the scope of the Court's jurisdiction is limited so that the Court only has the authority to review the constitutionality of statutes but not of inferior regulations, which results in the Court having little authority over how statutes are implemented through administrative directives and regulations. Second, the length of term of the constitutional court justices is limited to 5 years, renewable once. The shorter term of appointment has a potential to circumscribe judicial independence, because the constitutional court justices will be at risk of being subject to pressure from executive and legislative branch if they want to be re-appointed. Finally, politicians tried in many ways to restrict access to the Court.

Brief account of Indonesian constitutional history

Indonesia was a Dutch colony from the end of the sixteenth century through the beginning of World War II. After the bombing of Hiroshima, which ended a brutal Japanese occupation, Indonesia declared its independence on August 17, 1945. At the time of its declaration of independence, Indonesia did not have a constitution; yet only one day later, the Preparatory Committee for Indonesian Independence (*Panitia Persiapan Kemerdekaan Indonesia*—PPKI) ratified what became known as the 1945 Constitution. When the founding fathers adopted the 1945 Constitution on August 18, 1945, they assumed that it would only be temporary, as the charismatic leader of independent movement Soekarno stated, "this is a constitution made in a flash of lightning."[6] The Constitution itself mandated that the MPR adopt a new constitution within six months of its formation.[7]

Although the 1945 Constitution was meant to be "a lightning Constitution," it has had a long-lasting effect beyond its temporary nature. Two features of the Constitution deserve to be mentioned to better understand its effect. The first is the philosophy of *Pancasila*, which means observing the five principles: Belief in one God, Humanity, the Unity of Indonesia, Democracy and Social Justice. It was Soekarno who coined the term *Pancasila* and later it was included in the preamble of the 1945 Constitution.[8] The second feature is the proposal of Professor Soepomo, who advocated for an "integralist state."[9] Citing the experience of Germany under Adolf Hitler, and of Imperial Japan, Soepomo's "integralist state" advanced the idea that the state was conceived as a family, and that the good of the family must supersede that of its individual members.[10] The subsequent governments would later use both *Pancasila* and the notion of "integralist state" to justify their authoritarian regime.

The 1945 Constitution did not play a significant role in Indonesian constitutional constellation until 1959. From 1949 to 1959, two other constitutions were introduced: the 1949 Indonesian Federal Constitution and the 1950 Constitution. In 1959, President Soekarno reinstated the 1945 Constitution and began his experiment of "Guided Democracy."[11] For Soekarno, the 1945 Constitution had the benefit of strong presidential powers, which enabled him to concentrate all power into his own hands. But the Guided Democracy regime collapsed after a mysterious coup in 1965, when six Army generals were kidnapped and murdered. Following the coup, the military under the command of then-Major General Soeharto seized power through a mixture of force and political maneuvering against the backdrop of international and domestic unrest.[12] Soeharto's "New Order" regime kept the 1945 Constitution for the same reasons Soekarno liked it, that is, in order to equip the president with strong power. During the three decades of Soeharto's reign, the regime treated the 1945 Constitution as sacred and unamendable. The involvement of armed forces as the guardian of *Pancasila* and the 1945 Constitution then became the core elements of the New Order doctrinal concept. Soeharto used *Pancasila* and the 1945 Constitution as an ideological weapon to set boundaries of political contestation until his downfall in 1998.

With regard to the issue of judicial review, the 1945 Constitution simply states that the Supreme Court will run the judiciary according to the law.[13] During the constitutional debate in the Investigating Committee meeting in July 1945, Mohammad Yamin proposed a Supreme Court with powers of judicial review that were drawn from the American model.[14] Soepomo, however, dismissed Yamin's proposal, arguing that Indonesian lawyers had no experience with the system Yamin proposed, and, moreover, he considered it entirely irrelevant in a state based on familial principle (*asas kekeluargaan*).[15] In the end, Yamin's proposal was voted down, and the Constitution did not recognize judicial review. Moreover, after independence, Indonesia inherited the Dutch civil law tradition, in which acts of parliament are qualified as the supreme expression of the democratic will, and consequently, courts were not authorized to question them. Under the Guided Democracy and the New Order regimes, judicial review became impossible at either an ideological or practical level. Moreover, the Indonesian Supreme Court had been progressively weakened by the government. As a result of the executive branch's interference in the Supreme Court, the judiciary was unable to challenge the government and was consistently compliant. It was not until the fall of the New Order regime in 1998 that a new hope for judicial review arose in the Indonesian constitutional milieu.

Why create a new constitutional court?

For more than 32 years, Indonesia was under the authoritarian rule of General Soeharto's military regime. By 1998, General Soeharto was aging and ailing, but he gave no indication that he intended to step down in the near future. In March of 1998, he was sworn in as president for his seventh five-year term, and he appointed his most trusted lieutenant, B. J. Habibie, as his vice president.[16] Soeharto's seventh term in office lasted only two months. He was forced to resign due to mounting popular unrest and a collapsed economy that he was unable to revive. After Soeharto tendered his resignation on May 21, 1998, Habibie was sworn in as the new president on the same day. His presidency marked the beginning of a new era called *Reformasi* (Reform). *Reformasi* brought new hope for institutional change, including opportunities to establish an independent judiciary with judicial review authority.[17] Habibie's administration held parliamentary elections in June of 1999.

Following the parliamentary elections, the MPR held a general assembly to elect a new president. Habibie, however, did not receive sufficient support to run as their next presidential candidate and consequently had to withdraw his bid to recapture the presidency.[18] The assembly instead elected Abdurrahman Wahid as the next president.[19]

Abdurrahman Wahid—usually called by his nickname, Gus Dur—was a prominent critic of the New Order military regime, especially during his 15 years' tenure as the chairman of *Nahdatul Ulama* (NU), a traditional and rural-based Muslim organization. Nevertheless, due to Wahid's ill health, including becoming nearly blind as the result of diabetes and two strokes, he was hardly seen at the forefront of the reformist uprising against the military dictatorship in 1998. Through a combination of political maneuvers, compromises, and support from the alliance of Islamic parties called Central Axis (*Poros Tengah*),[20] Wahid defeated the favorite candidate Megawati Soekarnoputri and became the fourth president of Indonesia. Megawati's defeat angered millions of her supporters, who went on a rampage. It was to pacify her supporters that Wahid agreed to appoint her as the vice president.

Throughout the first year of his presidency, Wahid showed erratic and often provocative behavior, which led to increased animosity toward him from his opponents and even from the political allies who helped him get elected.[21] Meanwhile, two major financial scandals that involved Wahid's inner circle broke out.[22] The scandals provided political ammunition for Wahid's opponents to transform their animosity into open opposition. On July 13, 2001, the MPR called an emergency session (*Sidang Istimewa*) to impeach Wahid. On the following day, the MPR formally impeached Wahid and chose vice president Megawati as his successor.

In the days leading up to Wahid's removal, President Megawati sent PDI-P leaders to ask for guarantees from other party leaders that this would not also happen to her.[23] Although the other party leaders guaranteed that they had no intention of bringing her down, PDI-P did not trust the political blocs in the Parliament based on the experience in the 1999 presidential election, in which the political blocs in the MPR united against Megawati. Therefore, PDI-P tried to propose a mechanism that might prevent, or at least increase the threshold of, impeachment through the involvement of a constitutional court to supervise the process.[24] Based on these facts, a strong argument can be made that the primary purpose of the establishment of the Court was to solve the immediate political crisis circa 2001 instead of creating a robust judiciary with judicial review authority. The founding chief justice of the Indonesian Constitutional Court, Jimly Asshiddiqie, even argued that the Constitutional Court would not have been established without the political crisis that led up to the impeachment of President Abdurrahman Wahid in 2001.[25]

The ultimate cause

While acknowledging that the Wahid impeachment was an important trigger for the establishment of the Indonesian Constitutional Court, many scholars have dismissed the impeachment as being the sole reason behind the creation of the Court, but rather point to many factors at play.[26] Instead of dismissing Wahid's impeachment, I would like to make a distinction between the proximate and ultimate causation of the creation of the Court. Again, by proximate cause, I mean an event that is closest to, or immediately responsible for causing, some observed result. This exists in contrast to an ultimate cause, which is usually thought of as the "real" reason something occurred.

Such distinction will help us to distinguish between what is usually thought to be the "real" reason for the establishment of the Indonesian Constitutional Court and what is the factor that immediately responsible or closest to the establishment of the Court.

Let me now turn to review the ultimate causes. First, from historical and political perspectives, the establishment of a constitutional court was not a new or foreign concept for Indonesia. The establishment of the Constitutional Court was a response to the long absence of judicial review in Indonesia. It was the culmination of the consistent demand made by lawyers, scholars, and non-governmental organizations (NGOs) to adopt judicial review.[27] In the early days of Soeharto's New Order regime, the Judges' Association and the government fought bitterly over the issue of judicial power and constitutional review. Nevertheless, the Judges' Association stood alone and, in the end, did not have sufficient support to bring about such reform.[28] Fast forward to the period after the 1998 fall of the New Order regime; activists and NGOs under the banner of *Koalisi Ornop untuk Konstitusi Baru* (NGOs Coalition for a New Constitution) proposed the establishment a Constitutional Commission, with the hope that the commission would adopt judicial review.[29]

While it was true that judges, lawyers, and NGOs had long pushed for judicial independence and judicial review, these parties were not permitted to play a significant role in the creation of the Constitutional Court. The MPR rejected the NGO's proposal to establish a Constitutional Commission; instead, the MPR formed an expert team to help the constitutional reform process.[30]

The NGOs' coalition, however, dismissed the work of the expert team, arguing that the establishment of the expert team was merely for cosmetic reasons, because most of the team's recommendations were not adopted by the MPR.[31] In the end, the MPR Annual Session reaffirmed their rejection over the proposal of the Constitutional Commission and decided that the Assembly Working Body should again be responsible for preparing further amendments.[32]

In sum, the civil society represented by NGOs had a very minimal role in the establishment of the Constitutional Court. First, their focus was on the establishment of constitutional commission and not on the specific issue of judicial review. Second, by dismissing the work of the expert team, the NGOs' coalition had distanced itself from the MPR in charge of constitutional making and consequently they almost had no influence on the political process in the assembly. In the end, most of the constitutional reform process was in the hands of political elite who controlled the seats in the MPR.

The second ultimate cause was the support for democratic reforms found within the MPR after the fall of Soeharto's military government. Some scholars believe that many elected politicians had a vigorous and genuine desire to defeat authoritarianism,[33] including some noted reformists and former opposition leaders who had pushed for democracy and human rights protection during the Soeharto era.[34] Those members of the MPR who might not have otherwise supported reforms found themselves swallowed by a competitive environment alongside the reform-minded newcomers, and they could not resist calls for democratic reform.[35]

But the irony is that the proposal for judicial review came from a few Islamic-oriented politicians instead of prominent opposition leaders.[36] It was Hamdan Zoelva and Valina Singka Subekti who for the first time raised the issue of judicial review.[37] Zoelva, who later became the chief justice of the Indonesian Constitutional Court, stated that the MPR should discuss the idea of making the Supreme Court into a constitutional court.[38] Subekti, from the Functional Delegates (*Utusan Golongan* or UG), urged the MPR to put a priority on judicial independence and the authority of the Supreme Court to conduct judicial review.[39]

Although the proposal for judicial review came from within the MPR, this does not mean that the majority of the MPR supported the idea. In response to the proposal, the MPR was divided into two groups. The first group was strongly opposed to the adoption of judicial review and wanted to maintain the old system, in which the Supreme Court had limited judicial review over administrative regulations that are inferior to the act of parliament.[40] This group comprised of the military blocs;[41] the PDI-P; the Islamic-oriented Reform blocs;[42] the former ruling party, Golkar; and the New Order–sponsored Islamic-oriented party, PPP (United Development Party). Together they controlled 410 out of 600 seats in the MPR. In a nutshell, this group argued that a court cannot review a statute because a statute is made by the president and the parliament, an argument that is in line with the traditional civil law rationale on the role of the court.[43] Moreover, this group argued that the reform agenda should focus on empowering the

Supreme Court to exercise its limited judicial review authority instead of creating a new institution.

The second group was made up of the political blocs that clearly favored the idea of having a court with the authority to review acts of parliament.[44] The PBB (Crescent and Star Party), the UG (Functional Delegates),[45] and the PKB (National Awakening Party) controlled 129 out of 600 seats in the MPR. Actually, this group did not come up with convincing arguments for their proposal. Their proposal was merely a counterargument to the position of the first group, in which they argued that the old system of limited judicial review of administrative regulations was insufficient to empower the Supreme Court, and therefore there must be a new system that would allow a court to review a statute.[46]

By the end of the General Session on October 13, 1999, the MPR could not reach any consensus over the Supreme Court's authority to conduct judicial review, and the MPR decided to postpone the discussion.[47] In short, the majority of the MPR's members were against the adoption of judicial review. Therefore, the MPR was far from the main driving force for the establishment of a constitutional court.

The third ultimate cause was international influence. There are many different opinions on how the international community influenced the creation of the Indonesian Constitutional Court. One theory suggests that that the international financial institutions, such as the International Monetary Fund (IMF) and the World Bank, put pressure on politicians to establish a new legal order that was based on constitutionalism.[48] But there is no sufficient evidence to suggest that international financial institutions "coerced" the drafters to adopt the Constitutional Court. Although the IMF and the World Bank were involved in the legal reform process in Indonesia after the fall of Soeharto, their concerns were primarily to do with economic law reform and judicial institutions in general.

Donald Horowitz posits that Indonesian politicians wanted to establish internationally legitimate institutions and they believed that conferring the power of judicial review on a new institution was an attractive idea to follow.[49] To suggest that Indonesian politicians were competing with other countries to adopt the standard kit for new democracies is not a convincing argument either. Although by 1998, Indonesia stood out as one of few countries without constitutional review, there was no evidence that drafters were motivated to work toward a gold standard in the world of constitutional review. Even so, there were international study missions that fueled new debate in the MPR on the adoption of the Constitutional Court, to which I now turn. From March to April of 2000, the MPR's Ad Hoc Committee visited 21 countries with an ambitious plan to conduct comparative research on a broad range of issues, from intra-governmental branch relations to civil–military relations.[50] Despite having many critics,[51] these international study missions became one factor contributing to the creation of the new Constitutional Court. After the legislators returned from the study missions, various political blocs came out with proposals for a constitutional court that could review acts of parliament.[52]

When the MPR Annual Session convened on August 7, 2000, the discussion on the proposal for a constitutional court soon turned into a heated debate.[53] The majority of political blocs opposed the proposal and did not want to establish a new institution of the Constitutional Court.[54] It was only small political blocs that explicitly proposed creating a specialized constitutional court: UG, KKI bloc,[55] and a small fraction of PDI-P.[56] By the end of the Annual Session, the MPR did not pass any constitutional amendments regarding judicial review.

Many factors contributed to the establishment of the Constitutional Court. Nevertheless, these ultimate causes are insufficient to explain why in the end the politicians in the MPR adopted the Court. It was true that the idea of judicial review originated from within the MPR, and international study missions fueled the idea of the constitutional tribunal. But even so, as of August 2000, a majority of the members of the MPR still opposed the plan to establish a constitutional court.

The proximate cause

As explained earlier, a few months before the establishment of the Constitutional Court, the MPR had impeached President Wahid and elevated Vice President Megawati as the new president. During the MPR Ad Hoc Committee meeting in September 2001, PDI-P bloc proposed that a constitutional court should supervise a presidential impeachment process.[57] This proposal appeared driven by the experience of Wahid's impeachment in the previous month. President Megawati and her party, PDI-P, feared that the political blocs in the MPR might try to impeach her in the future. PDI-P then proposed a mechanism that might prevent, or at least increase the threshold of, impeachment through the involvement of a constitutional court to supervise the process.

But the PDI-P tried to avoid the impression that they proposed a constitutional court mainly out of the fear that it be used on their party's president.[58] PDI-P tried to justify their proposal by arguing that impeachment contains two elements, namely, the legal and political processes. A constitutional court should examine the motion for impeachment from a legal point of view and decide whether the initiation of the impeachment proceedings was within legal bounds. Then, the decision by a constitutional court would determine whether or not the MPR could move forward and try the impeachment as a political process.[59]

PDI-P's proposal apparently did not face any stiff resistance from the political blocs in the MPR. It seems that most of the political blocs silently reached a consensus that the future Constitutional Court should have the authority to supervise a presidential impeachment process. One possible explanation for this silent consensus was that those political blocs had shifted their focus to preparing for the 2004 elections, in which they expected to win the presidency, and therefore they did not want to hold a weak presidency that could be easily impeached.

In mid-October 2001, a majority of the political blocs agreed to accept PDI-P's proposal that a constitutional court should supervise the impeachment process.[60] The decision was taken in the midst of the discussion of the impeachment clause, which preceded the debate of the judicial clause. As a result, the Constitutional Court was legally referenced for the first time in Article 7 B of the Third Amendment, which provides that:

> Any proposal for the removal of the President and/or the Vice President may be submitted by the People Representative Council (DPR) to the People's Consultative Assembly (MPR) only by first submitting a request to the Constitutional Court to investigate, bring to trial, and issue a decision on, the petition of the DPR either that the President and/or the Vice President has violated the law.[61]

The adoption of Article 7B is like putting the cart before the horse, because the Committee had agreed to assign the Constitutional Court to supervise impeachment before they had even reached an agreement on the primary jurisdiction and structure of the Constitutional Court itself.

When the MPR reconvened on November 1, 2001, there was a substantial change of circumstances. The previous opponents of a constitutional court now agreed on the proposal to establish a constitutional court.[62] One possible explanation for this change was a political compromise between the political blocs that opponents would agree on a constitutional court, but in return, they demanded that the future court have limited jurisdiction. This issue will be explored further in the next section of this chapter. Thus, on November 9, 2001, the MPR unanimously agreed to adopt the Third Amendment on the establishment of the Constitutional Court.

Unusual political insurance and division of power

A different set of theories, *electoral market theories*, grounds the adoption of constitutional review in domestic political logics. The basic premise of electoral market theories is that the establishment of constitutional courts should be understood as an integral part of the larger political setting and cannot be explained independently from it.[63] Based on this set of theories, Tom Ginsburg postulates that whenever the political configuration is divided between political parties that fight for power, no party can have confidence that it is likely to win future elections. When the ruling party cannot count on re-election and may end up as an opposition party, it would be more likely to set up an independent court as political insurance for the outgoing regime to challenge the policies of the future government.[64] Ran Hirschl offers a complementary account to the electoral market theories, which he calls the *hegemonic preservation thesis*. Hirschl argues that constitutionalization of rights and judicial review is the result of a strategic pact led by hegemonic yet increasingly threatened political elites, who seek to insulate their policy preferences against the changing wheel of fortune.[65]

Hirschl and Ginsburg's theories represent the finest work in the theory of the adoption of judicial review. They both rely on electoral uncertainty as the driving force for the adoption of judicial review. The remaining question is whether these theories can be applied universally with regard to the adoption of judicial review in newer democracies. As explained earlier, division of power was indeed an impetus for the establishment of the Indonesian Constitutional Court. Therefore, the Indonesian experience can be a good case to evaluate whether the birth of the Indonesian Constitutional Court validates either, both, or neither of Ginsburg and Hirschl's theories.

Simon Butt has identified several weaknesses in Ginsburg's and Hirschl's theories as applied in the context of the Indonesian experience.[66] Butt argued that Ginsburg's insurance theory requires several conditions not present in Indonesia, such as politicians who have some understanding of the essence and the implications of judicial review; and that it also assumes a conscious choice from the politicians to establish a constitutional court as their political insurance.[67] In Butt's opinion, it is unlikely that the Indonesian politicians would have had any understanding of the concept of judicial review because nothing like it had been practiced before in Indonesia.[68] Moreover, no evidence proves that the Indonesian politicians actively supported the Constitutional Court for the purpose of insuring themselves from future political risks.[69] Similarly, Butt holds that Hirschl's hegemonic preservation theory does not fit in the Indonesian context because, at the time of transition, the surviving elements of the New Order regime were unable to pursue a strategic pact to preserve their interest.[70] The only interest that former New Order officials could probably have expected by supporting a constitutional court was to help maintain their power.[71] But there is little evidence to suggest that the surviving factions of the old political regime could envision a constitutional court as an instrument to safeguard their power. In short, Butt doubted that Soeharto's supporters could have co-opted a newly elected parliament to help them preserve their interest.

In my view, the insurance and hegemonic preservation theories have limited utility in explaining the birth of judicial review in Indonesia because politicians were unlikely to include the judiciary at the top of their reform agenda. Above all, for political actors in the MPR, the center of constitutional reform was focused on the power of the presidency instead of the judiciary.[72] The authoritarian character of the presidencies of both Soekarno and Soeharto created a widespread perception among Indonesian politicians and public that the original 1945 Constitution established a strong presidency, and therefore, the MPR set out to redefine executive–legislative relations, especially in the First Amendment. The First Amendment focused mainly on shifting primary control of the legislative process from the president to the House of Representatives (DPR).[73] The Second Amendment further strengthened the legislative power by granting the DPR the rights of "interpellation," which can be described as a "parliamentary" feature in the Indonesian presidential system, through which the DPR is equipped with a right to call the president before the legislature for questioning and inquiry.[74]

None of the five largest political blocs in the MPR shared the view in 1999 that judicial review was necessary for reconstructing the new Indonesian state.[75] For the losing parties, Golkar and the military, a weak judicial oversight would enhance their ability to avoid accountability for their past abuses. Thus, there was no point for them to support a robust court with judicial review authority.[76] The military blocs consistently opposed the adoption of judicial review and the establishment of the Constitutional Court. As the loser in the 1999 election, Golkar did not see the creation of the Constitutional Court as insurance either. Instead, the Golkar leaders supported constitutional reform that curtailed presidential power. Simply put, Golkar stood for a weaker presidency because it was no longer in control of the presidency. The reduction of presidential power, therefore, served as a tool for Golkar to challenge its political opponents.

The biggest bloc in the MPR, the PDI-P, initially did not consider judicial review as a tool to serve their interest. The primary interest of the PDI-P was in the power of the presidency, with the expectation that the chairwoman, Megawati, would someday become president, and so they did not wish to circumscribe the broad powers granted to the presidency by the original 1945 Constitution.[77] Therefore, at the beginning of the constitutional reform process in 1999, the PDI-P tried to block amendments to the 1945 Constitution. Nevertheless, after Megawati became the president, PDI-P leaders were already aware that in a democratic context, the presidency was a less powerful institution than it had been during the authoritarian period. Therefore, the PDI-P changed its position and supported the establishment of the Constitutional Court, which can serve as political insurance against the threat of impeachment.

The establishment of the Indonesian Constitutional Court shows the type of political insurance that Ginsburg had not considered. Ginsburg's insurance theory suggested that judicial review and constitutional courts may serve as insurance for electoral losers against their political adversaries. The Indonesian Constitutional Court, however, served as insurance in a different way. It was the winning parties, PDI-P and Megawati, who proposed a constitutional court as insurance to safeguard their power. The driving force behind PDI-P's proposal was the division of power between the political forces in the postauthoritarian regime. The constitutional reform process had increased the so-called veto players in Indonesia, from one (General Soeharto) before *Reformasi* to three or four (the president, the MPR, the DPR, and the military) after *Reformasi*.[78] Consequently, it was difficult to maintain a strong presidency under the fragmented political configuration of Indonesia, unless the president established a firm base of support in the DPR, through either coalition or majority control.[79] Therefore, the winning presidency may also need additional insurance like the Constitutional Court. By establishing a constitutional court that has the authority to supervise the impeachment mechanism, the president has secured an extra insurance that might minimize the chances that an over-powerful parliament could successfully oust the president through impeachment proceedings.

Establishing judicial review: Powers and jurisdictions

As explained above, the MPR had agreed to assign the authority to supervise presidential impeachment to a court before having reached an agreement on the court's competence and structure. After the adoption of Article 7B, politicians in the MPR realized that they could not establish a constitutional court with sole jurisdiction to supervise impeachment, and therefore they had to find additional powers to ascribe to the Constitutional Court.[80] After long debates, politicians finally agreed to adopt Article 24C § 1 & 2 of the Third Amendment, which provides that the Court shall have the authority to (1) review the consistency of statutes with the Constitution; (2)resolve disputes over the powers of state institutions; (3) decide the dissolution of a political party; (4) settle disputes over the result of general elections; and (5) review a motion for impeachment of the president. Therefore, the MPR ultimately created a constitutional court with a broad range of jurisdiction beyond merely supervising the presidential impeachment mechanism.

Constitutionality of statutes and jurisdictional cohabitation

An important question to be addressed is what the driving forces were behind the adoption of such a broad range of jurisdiction for the constitutional court. To answer this question, let me turn first to what is supposed to be the primary competence of any constitutional court in general, that is, to review the consistency of statutes with the constitution. Through this authority, the Court possessed abstract review powers to dismiss unconstitutional legislation and practices, and the review of laws takes place in the absence of concrete cases. But this provision does not mean that the right of judicial review was uniformly given to a single court, because the Constitution also provided the Indonesian Supreme Court with the authority to review ordinances and regulations made under any statutes.[81] In other words, the Supreme Court and the Constitutional Court shared a judicial review authority—though different in what they covered—which I would like to call *jurisdictional cohabitation*.

The jurisdictional cohabitation adopted by the MPR in Article 24C signified that principal actors in the MPR were not sensitive to the arguable incompetence of the Supreme Court. For more than three decades, the Supreme Court had failed to exercise the limited judicial review authority that had been vested in the institution.[82] While the Supreme Court during the *Reformasi* period might behave differently than the Supreme Court during the New Order regime, the opportunities for political and institutional changes that *Reformasi* represents have completely missed one of the core institutions in the Indonesian state, namely the judiciary.[83] Despite all of these disconcerting facts, politicians continued to equip the apparently corrupt Supreme Court with authority to conduct judicial review of secondary legislation instead of assigning such power to the new Constitutional Court.

One plausible explanation for the MPR's adoption of jurisdictional cohabitation is constitutional borrowing. Some politicians shared the view that the jurisdictional cohabitation found in Indonesia is based on the South Korean Constitutional Court.[84] The 1987 South Korean Constitution provides two high courts with separate jurisdiction: the Constitutional Court and the Supreme Court. The South Korean Constitution provides that the ordinary courts must request the review of the constitutionality of statutes.[85] In other words, whenever the constitutionality of law is at issue in a trial, the Supreme Court shall request a decision of the Constitutional Court.[86] Also, the South Korean Supreme Court has the power to make a final review of the constitutionality or legality of administrative decrees, regulations, or actions when their constitutionality is at issue in the trial.[87]

But the South Korean Constitutional Court has much more power than the Indonesian Constitutional Court.[88] The South Korean Constitutional Court has the authority to decide the constitutionality of a law that arises in ordinary court proceedings, after receiving a request from the court with original jurisdiction over the case.[89] Unlike its Korean counterpart, the Indonesian Constitutional Court has no such authority to review the constitutionality of a law that arises from ordinary court proceedings. Moreover, there is a significant feature of the South Korean Constitutional Court that is missing from the Indonesian Constitutional Court—that is, a constitutional complaint mechanism. The South Korean Constitutional Court provides two kinds of constitutional complaints. The first is the ordinary constitutional complaint, which is a common procedure for any person who claims that an exercise or nonexercise of governmental power has violated their fundamental rights.[90] The second is a constitutional complaint that is unique to the Korean system, in which an individual may directly file a constitutional complaint whenever an ordinary court denies his or her motion to refer a constitutional question to the Constitutional Court.[91]

Does the Indonesian Constitutional Court provide a constitutional complaint mechanism similar to the one in South Korea? No, because constitutional complaint is essentially a legal mechanism that arises from a concrete dispute in which the parties want to defend their rights against the enforcement of law or action by the state. In the context of the Indonesian legal system, the claimants do not defend their rights against the enforcement of law or action by the state. Instead, the applicant presents an abstract constitutional question before the court. Therefore, the Indonesian system does not include a mechanism of constitutional complaint. The constitutional amendment process also did not show any evidence that Indonesian politicians had any thought about adopting a constitutional complaint mechanism or any concrete review.[92] In sum, Indonesian politicians only copied a portion of the South Korean Constitutional Court's features, and at the same time, the new court they created had much more limited authority than its Korean counterpart.

Ancillary jurisdiction

Apart from representing a central authority to conduct constitutional review of legislation, many constitutional courts around the globe have been granted other powers, ranging from determining whether political parties are unconstitutional to adjudicating electoral disputes.[93] The Indonesian Constitutional Court also follows this trend, as the Court also has ancillary jurisdiction, which includes jurisdiction to preside over the dissolution of political parties, controversies between state institutions, and disputes over the result of general elections.[94]

What were the political motives of the Indonesian politicians in designing such ancillary jurisdiction? One plausible explanation is that ancillary jurisdiction was created solely based on political necessity in the early days of *Reformasi*. By Simon Butt's account, it was clear to those drafting amendments to the Constitution that Indonesia needed an impartial dispute resolution body to deal with the division of powers.[95] Presumably, Butt made this observation based upon the political situation surrounding the impeachment saga of President Wahid in 2001. Apart from the corruption scandal, one other source of confrontation between President Wahid and his opponents was the appointment of the chief justice of the Supreme Court, in which Wahid rejected both candidates proposed by the DPR, citing that both were known to loyal to the New Order regime.[96] Later, President Wahid was also involved in a bitter confrontation with the DPR over the appointment of the national chief of police.[97] Under such circumstances, it is not surprising that Indonesian politicians came to the conclusion that they needed an institution capable of resolving disputes between political branches of government.

Wahid's impeachment saga also led to the dissolution of a political party. In responding to the call of an emergency session (*Sidang Istimewa*) to impeach him, Wahid declared the dissolution of Golkar, the former ruling party, which he considered to be the driving force behind the impeachment threat against him. The dissolution of Golkar was just one in a series of dissolutions of political parties found in Indonesian history.[98] These historical accounts show the necessity for an institution with jurisdiction to preside over the dissolution political parties.[99] Therefore, politicians decided to equip the Indonesian Constitutional Court with the authority to rule on the dissolution of political parties.

Historical accounts also provided justification for Indonesian politicians to assign the Constitutional Court jurisdiction over general elections. During 32 years reign of military government, Golkar always came out as the winner in general elections.[100] Golkar secured these consecutive victories with intimidation, money politics, and manipulation.[101] It is therefore not surprising that Indonesian politicians thought it important to establish an institution to settle general election disputes at the moment that Indonesia was entering a new democratic era.

In sum, the driving force behind the adoption of the ancillary jurisdiction of the Indonesian Constitutional Court was the short-term interests of Indonesian politicians, who wanted to find a solution for the fragmented political architecture in Indonesia, especially in light of the bitter confrontations experienced with President Wahid. Indonesian politicians realized that it would be hard for them to reach a consensus under such fragmented political configuration, and therefore, they needed an institution that could become an arbiter of constitutional disputes.

Institutional design of the Constitutional Court

Appointment of constitutional court justices

Having explained that the jurisdictional design of the Indonesian Constitutional Court reflects the short-term interests of Indonesian politicians, I would like to turn the discussion to the appointment of constitutional court justices.

The 1945 Constitution provides that the Indonesian Constitutional Court shall be composed of nine constitutional court justices, in which the president, the DPR, and the Supreme Court have the power to nominate three judges each.[102] A plausible explanation behind this appointment mechanism is that politicians were simply copying the selection method from different jurisdictions, that is, the South Korean Constitutional Court.[103] By copying the Korean model, in which each political branch has the power to nominate three justices, the political blocs were hoping to minimize political conflict during the appointment process of constitutional court justices.[104] The chief proponent of this mechanism was the PDI-P bloc,[105] which had a big interest in avoiding political conflict during the selection process. President Megawati, who took the presidency in 2001, still needed to maintain political support from different political blocs in the Parliament. Therefore, the PDI-P tried to avoid political conflicts by proposing a selection method that offered equal distribution of appointing power.

Required qualifications of constitutional court justices

Article 24C (5) of the Constitution requires each constitutional justice to be a person who has high levels of integrity; to have a honorable character; to be a statesman who has a comprehensive understanding of the constitutional and administrative law; and not to hold any position as a state official while serving on the Court. The 2003 Constitutional Court Law restated these requirements (Article 15–19). Specifically, Article 16 required a constitutional court justice to have Indonesian citizenship, a law degree, and at least 10 years of legal experience; to be at least 40 years of age; to have never been convicted of a crime carrying a sentence of 5 years or more; and to not be in a stage of bankruptcy.

In 2011, the DPR passed a new law that amended the requirements for a constitutional court justice.[106] The law provided that a candidate must have a doctorate and master's degree, with an undergraduate degree in law; and to be committed to God Almighty, as well as to be a virtuous person. Furthermore, he or she must be between 47 and 65 years of age, with the physical and spiritual capacity to carry out his or her duty; must never have been convicted of any criminal offense; and should have at least 15 years' legal experience or government service.[107] Also, a candidate must provide various documents, such as a statement of interest, curriculum vitae, copies of degrees, wealth reports, and tax registration numbers.[108]

In September 2012, the Court struck down the master's degree requirement.[109] The Court held that a candidate must have a doctorate, but not necessarily a master's degree. The Court explained that there are many law graduates from overseas who hold a doctorate without holding any master's degree.[110] It was not clear what the Court meant by its holding. One plausible explanation is a lack of understanding regarding academic degrees in the American law school system. Presumably, the Court thought that a JD degree is equivalent to a PhD or SJD degree, and a person who holds a JD degree does not necessarily have an LLM degree. Based on a false understanding that a JD degree is equivalent to a doctoral degree in law, the Court is trying to make a JD degree sufficient to meet the requirement.

In 2013, the president passed an Interim Emergency Law (*Peraturan Pemerintah Pengganti Undang—Undang—PERPU*), which added one more criterion for a constitutional court justice—that is, a candidate must not have been a member of a political party within the 7 years before his nomination.[111] Nevertheless, the Constitutional Court invalidated this emergency law within a few months of its promulgation, and, consequently, there is no prohibition for members of political parties to be constitutional court justices.[112] The Court considered that the prohibition for a member of political party to be a constitutional court justice was simply based on the corruption scandal of Akil Mochtar, who happened to be a member of a political party (Golkar).[113] Therefore, the Court opined that the prohibition was based on unfounded fear that every member of a political party must be a corrupt politician. The Court held that the prohibition violated the constitutional guarantee of the freedom of assembly, which enables every citizen to join a political party.[114]

Length of term for constitutional court justices

The Constitutional Court Law provides that constitutional court justices can serve for a five-year term and can then be re-appointed for another 5 years.[115] Initially, the Law stated that a constitutional court justice must retire at the age of 67.[116] The Law also stated that the constitutional court justices elect the chief justice and deputy chief justice for a three-year term.[117] But in 2011, the DPR changed the retirement age to 70 years of age[118] and reduced the term of chief justice and deputy chief justice to 2 years and 6 months.[119]

Why did the Indonesian politicians design a limited term for the justices, and especially limited terms for the chief justice and deputy chief justice? The minutes of the discussion in the House Judiciary Committee indicated that there were two main reasons for the limitation to a five-year term. First, the nature of the Constitutional Court is different from the Supreme Court. The judges in the Supreme Court are career judges who start their career from below and climb to the top, and therefore they can serve for longer terms. The majority of the members of the House Judiciary Committee believed that the Constitutional Court was a kind of ad-hoc court, and, therefore, a constitutional court justice should serve for a more limited term.[120] Second, politicians shared a concern that a constitutional court justice would serve for an extended period and could not be held accountable. Therefore, the limited term was to avoid an unaccountable judge from serving for a long time.[121]

A similar argument applied in the proposal to limit the term of the chief justice. Politicians were eager to limit the term of the chief justice with the motivation of not giving a chief justice too much leverage and privilege. During a parliamentary debate in 2003, a high-ranking leader in the House Judiciary Committee said, "if a chief justice has a one-year term, then he would not demand facilities such as car and housing."[122] In the end, the proponents of limited terms won and set the limited term for a chief justice at 3 years. In 2011, the then minister of justice, Patrialis Akbar, brought back the idea that a chief justice only serves for a one-year term and that each justice should take a turn to become chief justice.[123] But the government could not convince the legislature to accept the proposal, and finally, they settled to reduce the term of the chief justice to 2.5 years.[124]

The term limit indicates that the political leaders were eager to restrict the power of the constitutional court justices, and they did not see length of term as important to the issue of judicial independence. Politicians simply wanted to limit the term based on unfounded arguments, such as the nature of a constitutional court and the enjoyment of housing and car facilities. Length of term is an essential component of judicial independence because a judge with a longer appointment term would likely have more independence in exercising his or her authority.[125] Arguably, term length is one of the weakest points in the design of the Indonesian Constitutional Court. With a short-term limit, justices sit on the bench with insecurity that they might not be re-appointed for a second term if they fail to please the authority that appointed them in the first place.

Selection processes for constitutional court justices

The Constitution and the Constitutional Court Law do not provide guidelines for the selection process, and therefore each political branch conducted the selection process in its own way.[126] Consequently, there is no uniformity between the president, the DPR, and the Supreme Court in how they select constitutional court justices. The Supreme Court has consistently employed a closed internal mechanism. The then chief justice of the Supreme Court, Bagir Manan, clearly stated that he, himself, had the prerogative to choose candidates from his institution.[127] The chief justice argued that he did not see any necessity for public participation because he knew the capabilities of his judges.[128]

The executive, depending on who held the office, employed either a closed internal mechanism or a public selection process for choosing constitutional court justices. In 2003, then President Megawati relied on a private internal mechanism, in which she appointed a small team comprised of several cabinet members to recommend a few candidates for her to pick from.[129] In 2008, President Yudhoyono established a selection committee, which solicited public input on the candidates and then interviewed them.[130] In his second term in office (2009–2014), however, President Yudhoyono simply appointed constitutional court justices without any "fit and proper" test similar to the selection committee process of his first term in office.[131] In 2015, President Jokowi employed a public "fit and proper" test model and established a selection committee to select a constitutional court justice.[132] In 2017, President Jokowi again established a selection committee to find a replacement for Justice Patrialis Akbar.[133]

The DPR tried to establish itself as the most transparent institution in choosing a constitutional court justice by consistently holding public hearings. In 2003, the House Judiciary Committee set up a selection team; then, the team invited each political bloc in the DPR to nominate a maximum of three candidates. After that, the team would listen to suggestions from the public before holding its selection interviews.[134] In 2013, the DPR decided to form a five-member selection team from outside the institution.[135] The selection committee then conducted the initial phase of a "fit and proper" test on the constitutional court justice candidates. Later, the committee handed over a list of names for the House Judiciary Committee to select from.

"Impeachment" of constitutional court justices

The Constitution does not prescribe an impeachment mechanism for a constitutional court justice. Nevertheless, the Constitutional Court Law specifies that justices could receive "honorable" discharges (*pemberhentian dengan hormat*) or "dishonorable" discharges (*pemberhentian dengan tidak hormat*). The grounds for honorable discharge are death, resignation, reaching the mandatory retirement age of 70, reaching term limit, and being unable to perform the judicial duty for three consecutive months because of physical and mental illness.[136] The grounds for dishonorable discharge are being convicted of a crime, for which imprisonment is the punishment; committing inappropriate conduct (*melakukan perbuatan tercela*); missing court proceedings for five consecutive sessions without valid reason; breaching the oath of office; violating the prohibition on working in another profession; and breaching the Code of Ethics and Conduct of Constitutional Court Justices.[137]

The law further states that the president has the authority to remove a justice upon the request of the chief justice.[138] Before the removal, justices shall be given the opportunity to defend themselves before the Constitutional Court Honorary Council (*Majelis Kehormatan Mahkamah Konstitusi*).[139] The Honorary Council was established on an ad hoc basis, and it was composed of a serving constitutional court justice, a former constitutional court justice, a law professor, a community member, and a member of the judicial commission.[140] But it is not clear whether the lawmakers designed the Honorary Council as a system for disciplining justices or as a mechanism to remove them from the Court.

In practice, the Honorary Council can serve both as a system of disciplining judges and "impeachment trial." The first Honorary Council convened to examine the bribery allegation against Justice Arsyad Sanusi.[141] The Honorary Council concluded that Justice Sanusi violated the judiciary code of ethics because he failed to stop his family members from making deals with parties involved in cases being handled by the Court. The Council recommended that Sanusi be given a private warning (*sanksi teguran*).[142] In this case, therefore, the Honorary Council acted to discipline instead of remove the justice who appeared before it.

The arrest of Chief Justice Akil Mochtar in 2013 further illustrated the ambiguity of the Honorary Council's intended role. On October 2, 2003, the Anti-Corruption Commission arrived with a warrant for Mochtar's arrest and confiscated approximately U.S. $260,000 from his residence. The money was allegedly given so that Mochtar would rule on the Gunung Mas regional election dispute in the incumbent's favor.[143] On October 5, 2013, President Yudhoyono announced that he had decided to remove Akil Mochtar temporarily from the position of chief justice.[144] As mentioned earlier, the 2003 Constitutional Court Law states that the president has the authority to remove a constitutional court justice upon the request of the chief justice.[145] Therefore, President Yudhoyono dismissed Akil Mochtar simply based on the request of the acting chief justice, Hamdan Zoelva. After the president had removed Mochtar from his position, the Court established the honorary council to investigate Mochtar. On November 1, 2013, the Council issued a verdict that ordered a dishonorable discharge for Mochtar.

By removing Akil Mochtar from the court, the Honorary Council established itself as an impeachment authority for the Constitutional Court. Mochtar was in fact removed by the Honorary Council from his position as a constitutional court justice in a speedy trial that lasted mere weeks. It was interesting to note that the Council decided to remove Mochtar before his criminal trial began, let alone his conviction. The grounds for his removal was merely a violation of the code of ethics and conduct.

After the arrest of Akil Mochtar and his removal as chief justice, the Constitutional Court moved to establish a permanent body to act as Ethics Council, comprising a former justice of the constitutional court, a law professor, and a community figure.[146] The Ethics Council has the authority to investigate complaints of judicial misconduct and judicial incapacity, and, then to recommend whether to establish an Honorary Council and release a justice from his or her duty temporarily.[147] It would therefore appear that the Constitutional Court would like to assign the role of disciplining judges to the Ethics Council, and allow the ad hoc Honorary Council to play the different role of "impeaching" justices.

The Court also employed this "impeachment" mechanism in the case of Justice Patrialis Akbar. On January 25, 2017, in a sting operation, the Anti-Corruption Commission arrested 11 people, including Justice Patrialis Akbar. Akbar reportedly received U.S. $20,000 and SGD $200,000 (U.S. $140,000) in bribes related to a judicial review of Law No. 41 of 2014 on Animal Health and Husbandry (a detailed analysis of this case will be presented in Chapter 8). The Ethics Council moved immediately to examine the case. In a swift proceeding, the Ethics Council concluded that Akbar's alleged involvement in the graft scandal is a grave offense (*pelanggaran berat*) of the Code of Ethics and Conduct of the Constitutional Court justices.[148] The Ethics Council then recommended the court to relieve Akbar of duty (*pembebasan tugas*), and, furthermore, it recommended the establishment of an honorary council to review his case.[149]

The ethics council announced its decision on January 27, 2017, and, three days later, Akbar submitted his letter of resignation as a constitutional court justice. The Court, however, rejected Akbar's letter of resignation[150] and moved immediately to establish an ad hoc Honorary Council, which consisted of five members.[151] On February 6, 2017, the Honorary Council recommended a temporary dismissal (*pemberhentian sementara*) of Justice Patrialis Akbar.[152] In the meantime, the Honorary Council stated that it would continue its investigation and gather more evidence to reach a conclusive decision.[153] Having heard nine witnesses in a closed-door hearing, the Honorary Council announced its final decision on February 16, 2017, and issued a verdict ordering a dishonorable discharge for Akbar.[154]

It would therefore appear that the Honorary Council has been functioning as an ad hoc "impeachment body" for constitutional court justices. But again, the Honorary Council decided to remove a sitting justice before his criminal trial had even begun. Moreover, during the hearing before the Honorary Council, Akbar challenged the Council by arguing that he had not yet been proven guilty.[155] In other words, the Honorary Council could remove a constitutional court justice based solely on finding of a violation of the code of ethics and conduct instead of a criminal conviction.

Access to the court

Access to the court is one of the most important constitutional features that can reflect the political views of the designers of a constitutional court regarding the role of citizens and opposition vis-à-vis the governmental power. A winning and dominant party will typically seek to limit access to judicial review because, by restricting access to a limited number of parties, the dominant party will be better able to avoid the check on its power from the opposition or citizens.[156] In contrast, the losing political forces will seek to maximize access to legislative minorities and ordinary citizens to create a forum in which they can contest the majority.

When the DPR prepared the bill on the Constitutional Court in late November 2002, it was evident that politicians tried to limit access to the Court. The constitutional court bill proposed by the DPR provided that only the National Ombudsman Commission has the right to file for judicial review on behalf of individual citizens, a group of people, or institutions before the constitutional court.[157] The bill was apparently aimed to minimize the work of the constitutional court.[158] Limited access to the Court via an ombudsman can be seen as a reflection of the political preferences of politicians in the DPR who wanted to see a constitutional court with a limited role.

Nevertheless, the proposal for restricted access via the National Ombudsman faced stiff resistance from inside and outside the Parliament.[159] The DPR finally agreed to drop the proposal,[160] but they insisted that the Parliament should develop a set of criteria for claimants to bring a case before the Constitutional Court.[161]After lengthy discussion and debate, the DPR came up with a final proposal that allowed individual citizens, customary communities, public or private institutions, and state agencies that have a direct interest with the enactment of the statute to bring a case before the Court. The Executive, however, thought that the DPR's proposal was still too broad and moved to modify the proposal by adding a new component that the claimant must be the one who claims that a statute has violated his or her constitutional rights.[162] In the end, the executive and the legislature reached a consensus that access to the Court is open to individuals, private or public institutions, state institutions and customary communities who claim that a statute has violated their constitutional rights.[163]

The Executive, however, did not stop its crusade and came out with a new proposal that the Court could only review statutes that were promulgated after the First Constitutional Amendment (October 19, 1999). There were several arguments behind the proposal. First, there are many statutory regulations that did not rely on the new Constitution as its primary sources.[164] Second, there would be a disastrous impact on legal development policy in Indonesia if the Court could invalidate any statute without limitation, as the invalidation of law creates a legal vacuum.[165] Not surprisingly, a majority of the political blocs in the DPR agreed with the executive branch's proposal.[166] The DPR agreed to adopt the provision that limited the scope of review under Article 50, in which the Court could only review statutes that were promulgated after the adoption of the First Amendment of the 1945 Constitution (October 19, 1999).[167]

In short, the executive and the legislature tried in many ways to limit access to the Constitutional Court. In the first place, they tried to restrict access to the Court via the Ombudsman. After that proposal fell flat, they introduced a device that limits access to the Court based on the date of the statute, namely Article 50. All of these offer proof that Indonesian politicians wanted to have a weak constitutional court. Neither the executive nor the legislature wanted to establish a court that could become an avenue for citizens to challenge governmental policy.

The Constitutional Court decision making

Above, I have presented evidence supporting the argument that Indonesian politicians intentionally designed the Indonesian Constitutional Court to have limited authority. In the last part of this chapter, I would like to explore how politicians in the DPR crafted the Court's decision-making process and whether this also reflects their preference for a weak constitutional court.

Decision-making process

During the parliamentary debate on the adoption of the Constitutional Court, the Ministry of Justice and Legislature spent a lot of energy discussing the Court's procedure.[168] The Executive wanted to limit the Court's scope of operation by establishing a detailed process for how the Court should hear and decide a case. Some parliamentarians, however, believed that the executive had gone too far in its effort to limit the court, and the Court should have authority to make its own procedure instead of one that was drafted by the executive and legislature.[169] But in the end, the government's proposal prevailed, and the DPR approved the provisions regarding constitutional court procedure.

It is interesting to note that Ministry of Justice itself had no concrete proposal for the procedure to be used in the Constitutional Court. High-ranking officials of the Ministry proposed borrowing criminal procedure as the model for constitutional court procedure.[170] This proposal was arguably quite absurd, because if the Executive wanted to adopt procedural law from a different jurisdiction, the administrative court procedure would be a more suitable model than criminal proceedings. Yet it appeared that the Ministry of Justice had no clue about constitutional adjudication process and the DPR ultimately approved the borrowing of some aspects of criminal law procedure. For instance, the law provides that the constitutional court justices shall examine the evidence, which was presented during the hearing,[171] and the Court must reach its decision based on two pieces of evidence.[172] Moreover, the law also states that constitutional court justices should examine witnesses during the court's hearings.

Therefore, even though the adjudication process in the Constitutional Court is inherently different than the adjudication process in the criminal proceeding, lawmakers nonetheless required the justices to apply some aspects of criminal procedure in their hearings. The combination of a desire to limit the Court's authority and a lack of understanding regarding constitutional adjudication led the government and legislature to pass ambiguous provisions on the Constitutional Court's procedure.

In practice, Indonesian Constitutional Court procedure is a combination package of many different elements. Once the court decided to hear a case, attorneys of the claimant present their petition in the court's chamber. As prescribed by law, the applicants bring some witnesses and experts, and the Court usually spends many hours hearing the witness and expert testimonies. The sessions are open to the public and are televised. But this procedure is different than oral arguments in the United States, because the attorney of the other side does not present their case. The Court does not organize its proceedings as a contest between the claimants and the government. Instead, the Court usually summons the executive and legislative branches to come before it to explain the original intent of the challenged statute. It does not, however, summon them as parties involved in adversarial proceedings. Thus, the government's lawyers do not participate in oral arguments.

As the justices sort through numerous legal briefs and the witness and expert testimonies, the justices engage in private debate, argument, and discussion (*Rapat Permusyawaratan Hakim*). Once a relatively clear majority emerges in support of one side or the other in a case, a justice (or justices) writes and circulates "draft" opinions or explanations of the Court's decision. Ultimately, a majority of the Court (five or more justices) decides the outcome of the case, and a final opinion is written and announced to the public.

Structure of judgments and types of opinion

The 2003 Constitutional Court Law provides a structure for the Court's decision. The Court's decisions shall include the summary of the petition (*ringkasan permohonan*), followed by the legal consideration of the facts that were revealed during the court proceeding (*pertimbangan terhadap fakta yang terungkap*). Finally, the judgment should contain some legal basis for the decisions made (*pertimbangan hukum yang menjadi dasar putusan*), and the formal holding (*amar putusan*).[173] In a separate provision, the law made it obligatory for the Court to include all facts in its judgments.[174] Under this structure, the summary of petition and facts comprise the bulk of most constitutional court judgments. The justices typically copy and paste from the original petition by the claimants, written submissions from the DPR, the president, related parties (*pihak terkait*), and any statements from witnesses or experts. For instance, in the *West Papuan* case, the Court spent the first 130 pages repeating the facts of the case, and spent only ten pages on its consideration and holding. Within these ten pages, the Court spent less than five pages on its reasoning. In short, in spite of having a legislatively set structure for court decisions, the Court did not necessarily issue clear decisions; the justices often did not provide extensive reasoning for the Court's holdings, and the Court judgments contained a large amount of arguably unnecessary repetition of the facts that were alleged by the parties.

The 2003 Constitutional Court Law provides that there are three types of court decisions about statutory judicial review. First, in cases where the applicant does not fulfill the standing and timing for review requirements,[175] the application for judicial review shall be denied (*tidak dapat diterima*).[176] Second, the Court may declare that a specified article, subarticle, and/or parts of a statute are unconstitutional, and in this case, the application for judicial review shall be granted (*dikabulkan*).[177] The third type of decision is when the challenged statute remains constitutional—both in a procedural and substantive way; and then the application shall be rejected (*ditolak*).[178] Later, the Court invented a new type of decision, which is known as *conditionally constitutional decision*, and this will be explained in detail in Chapter 4 of this book.

The Indonesian Constitutional Court was the first court that consistently allowed dissenting opinion among the judges. When the DPR enacted the Constitutional Court Law in 2003, it permitted the justices to issue dissenting opinions, which at that time was not common in Indonesia.[179] But dissents appear to do little to enhance judicial accountability, because the disagreement between the majority and minority is almost never mentioned in majority judgments and rarely in the minority.[180] This lack of engagement is probably because the justices are either unaware of the purpose of dissents or reluctant to confront other members of the bench. This issue will be explored in Chapter 5 of this book.

Effects of constitutional court decisions

The decision of the Constitutional Court is final, and therefore it shall not be subject to reversal by the Parliament or general courts.[181] The Court can declare one or more provisions of a statute or an entire statute to be inconsistent with the constitution, and therefore the invalidated provision of the law has no legal binding force.[182] The Constitutional Court Law provides that the effects of the Court's decision only begin on the day of the announcement of the decision.[183] This rule has become one of the most controversial provisions in the Court's history because the justices interpret it to mean that the Court's decisions have only prospective effect. This subject is discussed further in Chapter 4.

In sum, the Constitutional Court's decision-making process also reflects the preference of Indonesian politicians to design a weak court. Although the limitations upon the Court's procedure are less obvious than the limitations upon jurisdiction and access to the Court, nevertheless, politicians tried to limit how the court should hear and decide a case. Their lack of understanding regarding constitutional adjudication and the drive to create a weak court eventually led politicians to design a court procedure that looks like a joke in comparison to the gold standard of judicial review procedure in both newer and older democracies.

Conclusion

The birth of the Indonesian Constitutional Court can be seen as a joke because, from the beginning, politicians in the legislative branch did not have any intention of creating a court capable of exercising a robust model of judicial review. They established the Court as a court to supervise presidential impeachment in the first place, but then they realized that they must endow the Court with more authority than just that. They therefore equipped the Court with additional powers but simultaneously tried to restrict the Court by allowing it to review the constitutionality of statutes but not any ordinances, governmental regulations, or actions. Furthermore, politicians only allowed the Court to review the constitutionality of statutes that were enacted after October 19, 1999, and tried to limit access to the Court. Politicians designed the Court with limited authority, and in so doing, they arguably hoped to prevent the Court from playing a prominent role on the Indonesian political scene.

The joke continued when the Court opened on August 19, 2003. It had no funding, no office, and no support staff. Chief Justice Jimly Asshiddiqie frequently stated that he started the Court with only three pieces of paper: the Constitution, the Constitutional Court Law, and the presidential decree that appointed the constitutional court justices. When the Court did not receive sufficient support from the government to begin its operations, the responsibility for building the Court was left squarely in the hands of its new justices, and especially the chief justice.

Notes

1 Tom Ginsburg. *Judicial Review in New Democracies: Constitutional Courts in Asian Cases* (Cambridge: Cambridge University Press, 2003).

2 For an overview of the body of scholarship on the creation of the Constitutional Court, please see Tom Ginsburg and Mila Versteeg. "Why Do Countries Adopt Constitutional Review?" 30(3) *The Journal of Law, Economics and Organization* 587 (2013).

3 For a historical analysis of the struggle for judicial review in Indonesia during the military dictatorship, please see Daniel S. Lev. *Legal Evolution and Political Authority in Indonesia: Selected Essays* (The Hague: Kluwer Law International, 2000); Sebastian Pompe. *The Indonesian Supreme Court: A Study Of Institutional Collapse* (Ithaca, NY: Southeast Asia Program, Cornell University, 2005); Adriaan Bedner. *Administrative Courts in Indonesia: A Socio Legal Study* (The Hague:

Kluwer Law International, 2001); David K. Linnan, "Indonesian Law Reform, or Once More unto the Breach: A Brief Institutional History," 1 *Australian Journal of Asian Law* 1 (1999); Muhammad Asrun, *Krisis Peradilan: Mahkamah Agung di Bawah Soeharto* [Judiciary in Crisis: the Supreme Court under Soeharto] (Jakarta: ELSAM, 2004).

4 For a detailed analysis of the political diffusion theories, please see Zachary Elkins. "Constitutional Networks." In *Networked Politics: Agency, Power, and Governance*, edited by M. Kahler. (Ithaca, NY: Cornell University Press, 2009); Rosalind Dixon and Eric Posner. "The Limits of Constitutional Convergence," *11 Chi. J. Int'l L.* 399 (2011); David Law. "The Evolution and Ideology of Global Constitutionalism," 99 *Calif. L. Rev.* 1163 (2011).

5 A senior politician in the MPR, in discussion with the author, July 24, 2006; adviser to the ad hoc committee of the MPR, in discussion with the author, August 23, 2006.

6 Muhammad Yamin. *Naskah Persiapan Undang—Undang Dasar 1945* [Notes of Debates in the Making of 1945 Constitution] (Jakarta: Yayasan Prapanca, 1959), 410.

7 See Additional Provisions of the 1945 Constitution, section 2.

8 See the speech of Soekarno in front of the Investigating Committee for the Preparation of Indonesian Independence (*Badan Penyeledik Usaha Persiapan Kemerdekaan Indonesia*), June 1, 1945, in Yamin. *Naskah Persiapan Undang Undang Dasar 1945,* 78.

9 Soepomo used the term "integralistic staatsidee" (Dutch), which was translated in Indonesia as *pandangan negara integralistik.* David Bourchier traced the origin of "integralist state" to the German romantic notion of the state as the spiritual manifestation of the people, especially in the thought of Adam Muller. See David Bourchier. *Illiberal Democracy in Indonesia: The Ideology of the Family-state.* (New York: Routledge, 2015), chapter 2; Marsilam Simandjuntak maintained the primary source of Soepemo's integralism was the ideas of Friedrich Hegel. See Marsilam Simandjuntak. *Pandangan Negara Integralistik: Sumber, Unsur dan Riwayatnya dalam Persiapan UUD 1945* [Integralistic State Philosophy: Its Sources, Elements and History in the Preparation of the 1945 Constitution] (Jakarta, Indonesia: Pustaka Utama Grafiti, 1994).

10 See the speech of Soepomo in front of the Investigating Committee for the Preparation of Indonesian Independence (*Badan Penyeledik Usaha Persiapan Kemerdekaan Indonesia*), June 1, 1945, in Yamin. *Naskah Persiapan Undang Undang Dasar 1945*, 112.

11 For the origin of Guided Democracy, see Daniel S. Lev. *The Transition to Guided Democracy: Indonesian Politics, 1957–1959.* (Ithaca, NY: Modern Indonesia Project, Southeast Asia Program, Dept. of Asian Studies, Cornell University, 1983).

12 For a detailed analysis on how Soeharto exploited the killing of the army generals, please see John Roosa. *Pretext for Mass Murder: The September 30th Movement and Soeharto's Coup D'Etat in Indonesia.* (Madison, WI: University of Wisconsin Press, 2006); Harold A. Crouch. *The Army and Politics in Indonesia.* (Ithaca: Cornell University Press, 1988).

13 The Constitution of Republic of Indonesia 1945, Art. 24–25.

14 Yamin. *Naskah Persiapan*, 33.2

15 Ibid., 341–342

16 See Adam Schwarz. *A Nation in Waiting: Indonesia's Search for Stability* (London: Allen & Unwin, 2000). Prior to his appointment, Habibie had held the post of minister of research and technology for 20 years. During his tenure as technology czar, Habibie presided over the many strategic government projects, ranging from aircraft manufacturing to satellite technology. In the early 1990s, Soeharto extended a mandate to Habibie to become more active in political arenas.

He became the chairperson of the Association of Indonesian Moslem Intellectuals (ICMI—*Ikatan Cendekiawan Muslim Indonesia*), a new center of politico-bureaucratic power within the government.

17 See Benny K. Harman. *Perkembangan Pemikiran Mengenai Perlunya Pengujian UU Terhadap UUD Dalam Sejarah Ketatanegaraan Indonesia, 1945–2004* [The Development of Legal Thought on the Judicial Review of Act Parliament Against the Constitution in the Indonesian Constitutional History, 1945–2004] (May 20, 2006) (unpublished PhD dissertation, University of Indonesia) (on file with author).

18 Bacharuddin Jusuf Habibie. *Decisive Moments: Indonesia's Long Road to Democracy* (Jakarta: Ilthabi Rekatama, 2006), 428.

19 See Yang Razali Kassim. *Transition Politics in Southeast Asia: Dynamics of Leadership Change and Succession in Indonesia and Malaysia* (Singapore: Marshall Cavendish Academic, 2005), 146.

20 Ibid.

Wahid's political party, the National Awakening Party (*Partai Kebangkitan Bangsa*—PKB) only controlled 51 seats. In the meantime, Megawati's party, the Indonesian Democratic Party of Struggle (*Partai Demokrasi Indonesia Perjuangan* – PDI-P) controlled the largest number of seats (154 seats) in the DPR.

The Central Axis (*Poros Tengah*) launched a campaign to suggest that a predominantly Muslim country like Indonesia cannot have a woman as its head of state.

21 In a very short period, Wahid dismissed some of his cabinet members who had helped him get elected. In late November 1999, Wahid sacked the coordinating minister for social welfare, Hamzah Haz, on allegations of corruption. Four months later, on February 14, 2000, Wahid removed retired General Wiranto from his cabinet. On April 24, 2000, Wahid fired two more cabinet ministers, one from PDI-P and one from Golkar, accusing them of corruption.

22 First, a man claiming to be Wahid's masseur, Suwondo, was alleged to have used his name to illegally secure U.S. $4 million worth of funds from the State Logistic Agency, *Bulog*. Second, the disclosure of a new scandal involving U.S. $2 million in donations from the Sultan of Brunei, in which a gift given via President Wahid went missing.

23 Blair King. "Empowering the Presidency: Interest and Perceptions in Indonesia's Constitutional Reforms, 1999–2002," (PhD dissertation, the Ohio State University, 2004), 116.

24 See Minutes of Lobby Meeting, PAH I BP MPR, September 18, 2001, 36

25 Jimly Asshiddiqie. "Setahun Mahkamah Konstitusi: Refleksi, Gagasan Dan Penyelenggaraan, Serta Setangkup Harapan" [The First Year of the Constitutional Court: Reflection, Idea, Action and Hope], In *Menjaga Denyut Konstitusi: Refleksi Satu Tahun Mahkamah Konstitusi*, edited by Refly Harun, Zainal A. M. Husein, and Bisariyadi (Jakarta: Konstitusi Press, 2004), 11.

26 Timothy Lindsey. "Indonesian Constitutional Reform: Muddling Towards Democracy," 6 *Sing. J. Int'l & Comp. L.* 244, 261 (2002); Benny K. Harman. "Perkembangan Pemikiran Mengenai Perlunya Pengujian UU Terhadap UUD Dalam Sejarah Ketatanegaraan Indonesia (1945–2004)" [The Development of Legal Thought on the Judicial Review of Act Parliament Against the Constitution in the Indonesian Constitutional History] (Unpublished PhD dissertation, University of Indonesia, 2006); Simon Butt. *The Constitutional Court and Democracy in Indonesia* (Leiden: Brill Nijhoff, 2015).

27 Lindsey. Ibid., 261–266.

28 See Pompe. *The Indonesian Supreme Court*, 213.

29 Andrew Ellis. "The Indonesian Constitutional Transition: Conservatism or Fundamental Change?" 6 Sing. *J. Int'l & Comp. L.* 116, 143 (2002).

The coalition comprises 17 NGOs chiefly led by the Center for Electoral Reform, the Independent Election Monitoring Committee, Indonesian Corruption Watch, the Indonesian Legal Aid and Human Rights Association, and the Indonesian Forum for the Environment.

30 Denny Indrayana. *Indonesian Constitutional Reform 1999–2002: An Evaluation of Constitutional-Making in Transition* (Jakarta: Kompas Book Publishing, 2008), 191.

See also the *Jakarta Post*. "Assembly Working Group Blasted over Constitutional Amendments," March 22, 2001.

31 Indrayana. ibid., 193.

32 Ibid., 170

33 Donald L. Horowitz. *Constitutional Change and Democracy in Indonesia*. (Cambridge: Cambridge University Press, 2013), 87–88.

34 Butt. *The Constitutional Court and Democracy*, 26.

35 Horowitz. *Constitutional change and democracy in Indonesia*, 49–50.

36 See Minutes of 2nd meeting, BP MPR, October 6, 1999.

37 See Minutes of 2nd meeting, BP MPR, October 6, 1999.

38 See Minutes of 2nd meeting, BP MPR, October 6, 1999.

39 See Minutes of 2nd meeting, BP MPR, October 6, 1999.

40 Harman. *The Development of Legal Thought of Judicial Review*, 274.

41 After the armed forces had come to power, the army took special seats in the DPR, in which they were appointed by the president instead of elected by the people. From 1971 to 1987, the army took 100 seats in the DPR, and from 1987 onward, they took 75 seats. After *Reformasi*, they managed to maintain 38 special seats in the DPR. This system has now been abolished.

42 Reform bloc is composed by two Islamic oriented parties: the National Mandate Party (*Partai Amanat Nasional* or PAN) and the Justice Party (*Partai Keadilan* or PK), a new political party that was established in 1999 by young generation of Islamic political activists.

43 See Minutes of 1st meeting PAH III BP MPR, October 7, 1999, 29–43; and Minutes of 3rd meeting PAH III BP MPR, October 9, 1999, 25–28.

44 Harman. *The Development of Legal Thought of Judicial Review*, 276.

45 Functional delegates composed by representatives of various religious, social and professional organizations. In 1999 there were 65 representatives, which were chosen by the Election Commission.

46 Minutes of 1st meeting PAH III BP MPR, October 7, 1999, 34, 38; Minutes of 3rd meeting PAH III BP MPR, October 9, 1999, 23.

47 Ibid., 281. See also Minutes of 3rd meeting, BP MPR, October 14, 1999.

48 Harman. *The Development of Legal Thought of Judicial Review*, 409.

49 Horowitz. *Constitutional Change, and Democracy in Indonesia*, 28.

50 See Minutes of 5th meeting, BP MPR, March 6, 2000.

The members of the ad hoc committee were divided into nine groups, in which each group visited at least two countries. Group 1 (Iran and Russia); Group 2 (Malaysia, the Philippines, and South Africa); Group 3 (People's Republic of China, Japan, and South Korea); Group 4 (the United States and Canada); Group 5 (Egypt and the United Kingdom); Group 6 (Greece and Germany); Group 7 (Italy and the Netherlands); Group 9 (Spain and France); Group 10 (Denmark, Hungary, and Sweden). See Minutes of 6th meeting, BP MPR, May 23, 2000.

51 See Denny Indrayana. *Indonesian Constitutional Reform*, 209–210.

52 See Minutes of 41st meeting, BP MPR, June 8, 2000.

53 See Minutes of 5th meeting, Commission A, the MPR Annual Session, August 13, 2000.

54 The military, PPP, Reformasi, PDU, PDKB blocs and a small fraction of the PDI-P proposed a constitutional court as a chamber within the supreme court.

The former ruling party, Golkar, PKB, and PDI-P suggested that a constitutional court should be neither part of the supreme court nor a specialized tribunal but part of the People Consultative Assembly (MPR), as the highest state institution in the country.

55 Indonesian National Unity Bloc (*Kesatuan Kebangsaan Indonesia* or KKI) consists of seven nationalist-oriented parties, of which the Party of Justice and Unity (Partai Keadilan dan Persatuan or PKP) won 1 percent of the votes and the other six less than 1 percent each.

56 Harman. the *Development of Legal Thought on Judicial Review*, 304.

57 See Minutes of Lobby Meeting, PAH I BP MPR, September 18, 2001, 36.

58 See Minutes of Plenary Meeting, PAH I BP MPR, October 16–19, 2001.

59 Ibid., 29–32.

60 See Minutes of Plenary Meeting, PAH I BP MPR, October 16–19, 2001.

61 The 1945 Indonesian Constitution, Article 7B.

62 Harman. *The Development of Legal Thought of Judicial Review*, 343.

63 Ginsburg and Versteeg. *Why Do Countries Adopt Constitutional Review*, 594–595.

64 Tom Ginsburg. *Judicial Review in New Democracies*, 25.

65 Hirschl. *Towards Juristocracy: The Origins and Consequences of the New Constitutionalism* (Cambridge, MA: Harvard University Press, 2004), 49.

66 Simon Butt. "Judicial Review in Indonesia: Between Civil Law and Accountability? A Study of Constitutional Court Decisions 2003–2005" (PhD dissertation, University of Melbourne, 2006), 44–48.

67 Ibid.

68 Ibid.

69 Ibid.

70 Butt. *The Constitutional Court and Democracy in Indonesia*, 27.

71 Ibid., 27.

72 King. *Empowering Presidency*, 79.

73 Ibid.

74 Article 20A § 2 of the Second Amendment to the 1945 Constitution.

The right of "interpellation" is a standard feature in a parliamentary system, under which the prime minister may be held accountable to the parliament. The Indonesian Constitution is based on a presidential system. The Second Amendment, however, modified the current presidential system by adding parliamentary features.

75 Pompe. *The Indonesian Supreme Court*, 147.

76 King. *Empowering Presidency*, 109.

77 Ibid., 94.

78 Andrew MacIntyre. *The Power of Institutions: Political Architecture and Governance*, (Ithaca: Cornell University Press, 2003), 153.

79 See R. William Liddle. "Year One of the Yudhoyono–Kalla Duumvirate," 41(3) *Bulletin of Indonesian Economic Studies* 325–340 (2005).

In 2004, President Susilo Bambang Yudhoyono and Vice President Jusuf Kalla, who were elected through the first direct election, had to cope with a fragmented political configuration under which seven political parties are significant players in parliament. In the weeks following their inauguration, the so-called National Coalition that was hostile to Yudhoyono's presidency seriously threatened his government's stability by issuing "interpellation." Therefore, Yudhoyono had to maneuver by assigning his vice president to take control of the leadership of Golkar, which controlled the largest proportion of seats in the parliament, so that they could establish a solid political base in the parliament.

80 Private conversation with a member of the House Judiciary Committee, September 6, 2006.

81 The Indonesian Constitution 1925, Art. 24 A.

82 Since 1972, the supreme court stopped short of examining government regulations, and later it consistently refused to hear cases in which it was asked to quash administrative regulations. See Daniel S. Lev. "Judicial Authority and the Quest for An Indonesian Rechtstaat." In *Legal Evolution and Political Authority in Indonesia: Selected Essays*, edited by Lev (The Hague: Kluwer Law International, 2000), 213.

In the period from 1992 to the end of the military government in 1998, the Indonesian Supreme Court received twelve judicial review cases; two cases were dismissed and two cases were rejected, while the court has never resolved the rest of the cases. See Harun Hasan. "Hak Uji Materiil di Indonesia: Studi Tentang Hak Uji Materiil Mahkamah Agung dan Mahkamah Konstitusi Setelah Perubahan UUD 1945" [Judicial Review in Indonesia: Study on the Judicial Review Authority of the Supreme Court and the Constitutional Court after the Amendment to the 1945 Constitution] (Master Thesis, University of Indonesia, 2002), 132.

83 Sebastian Pompe. "'Absen dari Reformasi': The Indonesian Judiciary in the Face of History," V(1) *Indonesian Law and Administration Review* 74 (1999).

84 Private conversation with a member of the House Judiciary Committee, July 24, 2006.

85 The South Korean Constitution 1987, Art. 111.

86 Ibid., Art. 107 (1).

87 Ibid., Art. 107 (2).

88 For a detailed analysis of the comparison between the structural design of the Indonesian Constitutional Court and the South Korean Constitutional Court, please see Stefanus Hendrianto. "Institutional Choice and the New Indonesian Constitutional Court." In *New Courts in Asia* edited by Andrew Harding and Penelope (Pip) Nicholson (London: Routledge, 2011).

89 The South Korean Constitutional Court Act, Art. 41 (1).

90 Ibid., Art. 68 (1).

91 Ibid., Art. 68 (2).

92 Private conversation with a former member of the MPR, August 9, 2006.

93 Tom Ginsburg and Zachary Elkins. "Designing a Judiciary: Ancillary Powers of Constitutional Courts," 87 *Tex. L. Rev.* 1431 (2009).

94 Law No. 24 of 2003 on the Constitutional Court, Art. 24C (1).

95 Simon Butt. *The Constitutional Court and Democracy in Indonesia*, 16.

96 *Jakarta Post.* "House Seeks a Solution to Chief Justice Snag," March 1, 2001.

In 2001, the DPR proposed two candidates for the position of chief justice of the supreme court, Muladi and Bagir Manan. After months of stalemate, President Wahid finally bowed to the DPR demand and picked Bagir Manan for the position of chief justice.

97 In April 2001, President Wahid issued Presidential Decree No. 54/2001, which abolished the position of deputy police chief. However, in June 2001, Wahid issued a new Presidential Decree, No. 77 /2001, which reinstated the position of deputy chief of police. In early July 2001, President Wahid fired Suroyo Bimantoro, the defiant chief of police, and assigned the deputy chief of police, Chaeruddin Ismail, to carry out all the responsibilities of the national chief of police. The DPR argued that the president should obtain its approval before appointing a new national chief of police. The rivalry between the president and the DPR was resolved in the supreme court, where the supreme court decided to strike down President Wahid's decisions.

98 In 1960, President Soekarno banned two political parties, Masyumi and the Indonesian Socialist Party (PSI), based on the grounds that several leading members and some intellectuals from both parties supported the rebel Revolutionary Government of the Republic of Indonesia (PRRI). Later, in 1966, the military government banned the Indonesian Communist Party (PKI) based on the accusation that the Communist Party initiated an action to kidnap and murder six generals of the armed forces.

99 See Abdul Mukthie Fadjar. *Hukum Konstitusi & Mahkamah Konstitusi* [Constitutional Law and Constitutional Court] (Jakarta: Konstitusi Press; & Yogyakarta: Citra Media, 2006), chapter 14; Abdul Rasyid Thalib. *Wewenang Mahkamah Konstitusi dan Implikasinya Dalam Sistem Ketatanegaraan Republik Indonesia* [The Authority of the Constitutional Court and Its Implication on the Indonesian Constitutional System] (Bandung, Indonesia: Citra Aditya Bakti, 2006), 426–440.
100 Soeharto's New Order regime held the first election in 1971, followed by general elections in 1977, 1982, 1988, 1992, and 1997. In these six general elections, the ruling party, Golkar, always came out as the winner, by garnering about 68 percent of the votes cast on average.
101 See Afan Gaffar. *Javanese Voters: A Case Study of Election under a Hegemonic Party System* (Yogyakarta, Indonesia: Gadjah Mada University Press, 1992).
102 The Indonesian Constitution 1945, Art. 24C § 3.
103 The minutes of plenary meetings clearly recorded that the proposed selection method is modeled after the selection process in the Korean Constitutional Court. See Minutes of Plenary Meeting, PAH I BP MPR, September 25, 2001.
104 Private conversation with a member of the House Judiciary Committee, July 26, 2006.
105 See Minutes of Plenary Meeting, PAH I BP MPR, September 25, 2001.
106 Law No. 8 of 2011 on the Amendment of the 2003 Constitutional Court Law.
107 Ibid., Art. 15 (2).
108 Ibid., Art 15 (3).
109 The Constitutional Court Decision No. 68/PUU-IX/2011 (the *Constitutional Court Justice Requirement* case).
110 Ibid., Para. 3.23.
111 Government Regulation in Lieu of Law No. 1 of 2013, Art. 15 (2) (i).
112 The Constitutional Court Decision No. 1-2/PUU-XII/2014 (hereafter the *2014 Perpu* case).
113 Ibid., 116.
114 Ibid., 118; the Court made reference to Art. 28E (3).
115 Law No. 24 of 2003 on the Constitutional Court, Art. 22.
116 Ibid., Art. 23 (1).
117 Ibid., Art. 4 (3).
118 Law No. 8 of 2011 on the Amendment of the 2003 Constitutional Court Law, Art. 23 (1c).
119 Ibid. Art 4 (3).
120 See the Minutes of the House Meeting, PANJA Mahkamah Konstitusi (the Working Committee on the Constitutional Court bill) July 29, 2003.
121 Ibid.
122 Ibid.
123 *Hukumonline*. "Masa Jabatan Ketua MK Dipersingkat" [Shortening the Term Length of the Chief Justice], June 15, 2011. http://www.hukumonline.com/berita/baca/lt4df8706b5baae/dpr-pangkas-masa-jabatan-ketua-mk.
124 Law No. 8 of 2011 on the Amendment of the 2003 Constitutional Law, Art. 4 (3).
125 Tom Ginsburg. "Economic Analysis and the Design of Constitutional Courts," 3 *Theoretical Inquiries L.*49, 65 (January, 2002).
126 Article 20 of the Constitutional Court Act 2003 provides that the procedure of selection, election, and nomination of the constitutional court justices shall be regulated by each institution authorized to make appointments.
127 *Jakarta Post*. "Recruitment of Judges Must Be Impartial," August 9, 2003.
128 Ibid.

129 *Jakarta Post.* "Government Names Seven Candidates for the New Court," August 13, 2003.The small team comprising the minister of justice, Yusril Ihza Mahendra; Attorney General M. A. Rahman; and coordinating minister for political and security affairs, Susilo Bambang Yudhoyono.

130 *Hukumonline.*, "Pemerintah Baru Memikirkan Mekanisme Seleksi Hakim MK" [The Government Just Thinks About the Selection Mechanism of the Constitutional Court Justice], March 1, 2008. http://www.hukumonline.com/berita/baca/hol18665/pemerintah-baru-memikirkan-mekanisme-seleksi-hakim-mk.

131 The Presidential Decree No. 87 of 2013 on the Appointment of the Constitutional Court Justices.

It was important to note the controversial appointment of Patrialis Akbar as a constitutional court justice in 2013. It was suspected that then President Yudhoyono appointed Patrialis Akbar to the bench to fulfill his promise to provide Akbar with a strategic position after he was fired from his post as minister of justice in October 2011. Two NGOs challenged the validity of the presidential decision in the Jakarta Administrative Court, arguing that the nomination of a constitutional court justice must be transparent and participatory. The Jakarta Administrative Court ruled that the appointment process of Patrialis Akbar did not fulfill the requirement of transparent and participatory principles. On the appeal, however, the High Administrative Court held that the NGOs who brought the case had lacked the standing to challenge the presidential decision. On February 25, 2015, the supreme court affirmed the decision of the High Administrative Court that the claimants have no direct interest that was harmed by the presidential decision.

132 Stefanus Hendrianto. "The Indonesian Constitutional Court in Crisis over the Chief Justice's Term Limit," *Int'l J. Const. L. Blog* (February 5, 2015), at: http://www.iconnectblog.com/2015/02/the-indonesian-constitutional-court-in-crisis-over-the-chief-justices-term-limit/.

133 "Committee to Recommend Three Candidates for New Constitutional Court Justice." *Jakarta Globe*, March 31, 2017. Accessed May 15, 2017. http://eyewitness.thejakartaglobe.com/news/committee-to-recommend-three-candidates-for-new-constitutional-court-justice/.

134 *Jakarta Post.* "House, Govt, Supreme Court Rush to Select New Judges," August 8, 2003.

135 *Jakarta Post.* "House Begins Selection of new Constitutional Court Justice," February 28, 2013, http://www.thejakartapost.com/news/2013/02/28/house-begins-selection-new-constitutional-court-justice.html#sthash.heP8G-RAY.dpuf.

136 Law No. 8 of 2011 on the Amendment of the 2003 Constitutional Court Law, Art. 23 (1).

137 Ibid., Art. 23 (2).

138 Ibid., Art. 23 (4).

139 Ibid., Art. 23 (3).

140 Constitutional Court Regulation No. 2 of 2014.

141 *Jakarta Post.* "MK to Examine Judge Arsyad's Daughter Next Week," December 11, 2010.

In 2009, the court reviewed a dispute over the Head of Regency Election in South Bengkulu. A candidate for the position, Nirwan Mahmud, allegedly bribed both Sanusi's daughter and Arsyad's brother to convince Justice Sanusi to sway the court's decision in Mahmud's favor. Justice Sanusi admitted that his daughter indeed met the candidate; however, he denied that his daughter had introduced the candidate to him.

142 In the end, Arsyad tendered his voluntary resignation and left the court before reaching his mandatory retirement age, but he maintained that he did not commit any crime. Justice Sanusi would arrive at a mandatory retirement age of 67 by April 14, 2011. It was reported that Chief Justice Mahfud persuaded Justice Sanusi to stay on the court until the parliament passed the new mandatory retirement age of 70. But Sanusi tendered his voluntary resignation on December 17, 2010.

143 *Jakarta Post.* "MK Chief Justice, Golkar Lawmaker Arrested for Bribery Charges," October 3, 2013, http://www.thejakartapost.com/news/2013/10/03/mk-chief-justice-golkar-lawmaker-arrested-bribery-charges.html .

144 *SBY Berhentikan Sementara Akil Mochtar* ("President SBY Removed Akil Mochtar Temporarily"), SINDONEWS.COM, http://nasional.sindonews.com/read/791201/13/sby-berhentikan-sementara-akil-mochtar-1380966478.

145 See Constitutional Court Law No. 23 of 2003, Art. 23 (2a) & 23 (4).

146 Constitutional Court Regulation No. 2 of 2014, Art. 15 (1).

147 Constitutional Court Regulation No. 1 of 2014, Art. 4.

148 The Ethics Council Decision No. 16/Info-IV/BAP-DE/2017 (January 27, 2017).

149 Ibid.

150 "Constitutional Court Must Reject Patrialis' Resignation Letter." Gres.news. February 7, 2017. Accessed May 15, 2017. http://gres.news/news/law/112899-constitutional-court-must-reject-patrialisacute-resignation-letter/0/.

151 The members of the honorary council are Justice Anwar Usman of the constitutional court; a former constitutional court justice, Achmad Sodiki; a former chief justice of the supreme court, Bagir Manan; a former deputy chief of the State Intelligence Agency, As'ad Said Ali; and the deputy chief of the Judicial Commission, Sukma Violetta. See Fachrul Sidiq. "Judicial Commission Appoints Vice Chairwoman to join MK Honorary Council." *Jakarta Post*, February 1, 2017. Accessed May 15, 2017. http://www.thejakartapost.com/news/2017/02/01/judicial-commission-appoints-vice-chairwoman-to-join-mk-honorary-council.html.

152 The Honorary Council Decision No. 1/MKMK-SPP/II/2017.

153 Ina Parlina. "Panel to Rule on Patrialis' Alleged Ethics Breach Next Week." *Jakarta Post*, February 3, 2017. Accessed May 15, 2017. http://www.thejakartapost.com/news/2017/02/03/panel-to-rule-on-patrialis-alleged-ethics-breach-next-week.html.

154 The Honorary Council Decision No. 1/MKMK-SPL/II/2017.

155 Ibid., Para. 4.5.

156 Ginsburg. *Judicial Review in New Democracies*, 37–38.

157 Article 55 (1 & 2) of the Constitutional Court Bill.

The bill also stated that the National Ombudsman Commission would scrutinize the request for judicial review before filing the petition to the constitutional court.

158 Private conversation with a member of the House Judiciary Committee, September 6, 2006.

159 *Kompas.* "Antara Keinginan Memonopoli dan Membuka Partisipasi" [Between a Desire to Monopolize and to Open The Participation], Jakarta, June 9, 2003; *Kompas.* "Pembahasan RUU Mahkamah Konstitusi Berlarut: Bingungkan Posisi MA" [The Discussion On The Bill Continued: Confusion Over The Position of the Supreme Court], June 21, 2003.

160 *Koran Tempo.* "Komisi Ombudsman Dicoret dari RUU Mahkamah Konstitusi" [The National Ombudsman Commission is Deleted from the Constitutional Court Bill], Jakarta, June 14, 2003.

161 Private conversation with a member of the House Judiciary Committee, September 6, 2006.

162 See the Minutes of the House Meeting, PANSUS Mahkamah Konstitusi (the Special Committee on the Constitutional Court), August 2, 2003, 14–15.
163 Law No. 24 of 2003 on the Constitutional Court, Art. 51 (1).
164 Ibid.
165 Interview with a high ranking official at the Ministry of Justice, August 1, 2006.
166 The only opposition came from the PDI-P bloc. See J. E. Sahetapy. "Pasal Yang Konyol" [The Ridiculous Article], *Suara Pembaruan*, August 5, 2003; *Kompas*. "Pasal Pengujian UU Belum Disepakati" [No Agreement on the Scope of Review], Jakarta, August 5, 2003.
167 *Koran Tempo*. "DPR dan Pemerintah Setuju RUU Mahkamah Konstitusi Diundangkan" [The House and Government Agreed to Approve Constitutional Court Bill], Jakarta, August 7, 2003.
168 See the Minutes of the House Meeting, PANSUS Mahkamah Konstitusi (the Special Committee on the Constitutional Court), July 30th, 2003.
169 Ibid. It is interesting to note that the chief opponent of the government proposal was Akil Mochtar, who later became the infamous chief justice of the constitutional court. Mochtar raised his concern that if politicians set up a significant hurdle for the court, the newly established institution could do nothing.
170 See the statement of Abdul Gani Abdullah, the director general of Legislation of the Ministry of Justice, at the meeting of PANSUS Mahkamah Konstitusi (the Special Committee on the Constitutional Court), July 30th, 2003.
171 Law No. 24 of 2003 on the Constitutional Court, Art. 41 (1).
172 Law No. 24 of 2003 on the Constitutional Court, Art. 45 (2).
173 Law No. 24 of 2003 on the Constitutional Court, Art. 48 (2).
174 Law No. 24 of 2003 on the Constitutional Court, Art. 45 (3).
175 Article 50 requirement—the statutes that were enacted after 1999.
176 Article 56 (1) of the Constitutional Court Law 2003.
177 Article 56 (2 & 3) of the Constitutional Court Law 2003.
178 Article 56 § 5 of the Constitutional Court Law 2003.
179 The dissenting opinions were first authorized in Indonesia's commercial court. Nevertheless, the 1998 Bankruptcy Law never formally authorized the dissenting opinion; it was the Supreme Court Regulation (Peraturan Mahkamah Agung – PERMA) No. 2 of 2000 on the Appointment of Ad Hoc Judges in the Commercial Court, which allow a judge to issue a dissenting opinion (Art. 9 § 2). In 2004, the government enacted Law No. 4 of 2004 on Basic Judicial Power, which formally permitted the Indonesian courts in general to issue dissenting opinions (see Art. 19 § 5).
180 Butt. *the Constitutional Court and Democracy in Indonesia*, 67.
181 Article 24 C § 1 of the Third Amendment to the 1945 Constitution.
182 Article 57 (1) of the Constitutional Court Law 2003.
183 Article 47 of the Constitutional Court Law 2003.

3 A heroic intellectual leadership

Prelude

Fifty-five years ago, David Danelski published his pioneering work using the concepts of task and social leadership to examine the role played by chief justices during the Taft, Hughes, and Stone chief justiceships.[1] The task leadership focused on the court's work to reach a decision, whereas the social leadership emphasized the need for the members of the institution to remain sufficiently cohesive, socially, to accomplish its work.[2] Danelski suggested that the most important task function of the chief justice is to present the cases to the conference, which allow the chief to frame the issues and steer the discussion in a particular direction.[3]

Inhering in the idea of task leadership are two distinct functions: managerial and intellectual leadership.[4] A chief justice as a managerial leader must maintain a maximum degree of court unity, provide expeditious direction of the judicial conference, and assign opinions thoughtfully and with deliberation.[5] As an intellectual leader, the chief justice's views are a principal source of ideas and doctrine, and furthermore, the chief justice provides tactical and strategic guidance in political dilemmas.[6] A chief justice as intellectual leader usually has a stronger intellectual capacity to influence the direction of the court than his brethren; nonetheless, he needs to present his views persuasively.

In this chapter, I would like to turn to a discussion of the extent to which the intellectual vision and leadership of the chief justice influence court decisions in a few major policy areas. To answer that question, first I will provide a general analysis of the scholarly work and personal vision of the founding chief justice of the Indonesian Constitutional Court, Jimly Asshiddiqie. Later, I will analyze several important and high-profile cases and discuss to what extent the academic work of the chief justice and his personal vision appear to have influenced those Court decisions.

The rise of Jimly Asshiddiqie: From academia to judiciary

Before jumping into the web of Asshiddiqie's intellectual vision and leadership, an important question that needs to be answered is who Jimly Asshiddiqie is. How did he become the first chief justice of the Indonesian Constitutional

Court? How did he become so effective in leading the Court in its early days of operation?

Jimly Asshiddiqie was born in Palembang, South Sumatera, on April 17, 1956. He grew up in a staunch Muslim family and went to Islamic school from his primary education to high school.[7] After finishing high school, he enrolled in the undergraduate law program at the University of Indonesia. Asshiddiqie obtained his bachelor of law degree in 1982 and immediately joined the faculty as a lecturer. In 1984, he went to graduate school at the University of Indonesia and obtained his doctorate in legal studies in 1993. While finishing his dissertation, Asshiddiqie spent some time in Seattle as visiting scholar at the Political Science Department of the University of Washington. Soon after the completion of his doctoral program, he went to Harvard Law School to join a summer course on Legal Theories and Philosophy.

In the early 1990s, he joined the Association of Indonesian Muslim Intellectuals (ICMI), which had emerged as a new political force within the government. The leader of ICMI was General Soeharto's trusted lieutenant, B. J. Habibie. Habibie held the post of minister of research and technology under the Soeharto administration, and his friendship with General Soeharto stretched back to the 1950s. With powerful endorsement from General Soeharto, ICMI grew rapidly, claiming 42,000 members by the mid-1990s, mostly made up of the Islamic middle class. The rise of ICMI was to Asshiddiqie's advantage as the government appointed him as the secretary to the minister of education in 1993.

By 1998, General Soeharto was aging and ailing, but he did not show any indication that he would step down anytime soon. In March 1998, Soeharto and Habibie were sworn in as president and vice president for the 1998–2003 terms. After Habibie had assumed the office of vice president, some ICMI leaders did follow Habibie into positions of power, including Jimly Asshiddiqie, as Vice President Habibie appointed him as his assistant for Social Welfare and Poverty Alleviation.[8]

Soeharto's seventh term in office did not last very long; the mounting of student revolts, economic crisis, and internal conflict within the political elite all contributed to the resignation of Soeharto on May 21, 1998. In a brief ceremony, Soeharto made his resignation speech and handed over the presidency to Habibie. After Habibie became president, he established the Council for Restoration of Security and Legal System (*Dewan Penegakan Keamanan dan Sistem Hukum*) in his attempt to overcome the political crisis in the country.[9] Habibie appointed Jimly Asshiddiqie as secretary for the Council for Restoration. His primary duties included coordinating cabinet ministers and political leaders who sat on the council. On February 24, 1999, Habibie assigned Asshiddiqie to another important position as the coordinator for the Legal and Statutory Reform Team, which reported directly to the president.[10] There was little doubt that Asshiddiqie played a significant role in the legal reform process during the Habibie administration.

The main problem for the Habibie presidency was that he lacked a firm base to maintain his political power. He had neither full political support from the military nor from his party, Golkar. Although he already made some political compromises, he could not satisfy all people. Following the results of the June 1999 election, Habibie was selected as Golkar's next presidential candidate. But some of his party representatives were quite reluctant to support him. During the General Session of the People's Consultative Assembly (MPR) in October 1999, Habibie's accountability speech was rejected, and consequently, Habibie was forced to withdraw from the presidential race, as the rejections signified that Habibie was not capable of leading the country.[11]

After his political patron Habibie lost his presidential bid in 1999, Asshiddiqie went back to academia to teach at the University of Indonesia. He returned to public service for a brief time when the MPR called him to join an expert team on the constitutional reform process.[12] By the time the government established the Constitutional Court in 2003, Asshiddiqie had established a reputation as an expert on constitutional law and a skillful politician. With excellent credentials, he was one of the top choices to lead the new Constitutional Court.

In the previous chapter, I explained that the Constitutional Court Law distributed the appointment power equally between the president, the House of Representatives (DPR) and the Supreme Court. In August 2003, the DPR immediately appointed Jimly Asshiddiqie as a Constitutional Court justice along with the other two justices, Achmad Roestandi and I Gede Palguna.[13] President Yudhoyono appointed three justices, Achmad Natabaya, Abdul Mukthie Fadjar, and Harjono (one name only). The Supreme Court appointed Laica Marzuki, Maruarar Siahaan, and Soedarsono (one name only) to fill the remaining three spots.

Soon after the nine Constitutional Court justices were inaugurated on August 19, 2003, the judges rushed to their first meeting. Since they did not have an office, they had to borrow the Supreme Court chief justice's meeting room.[14] According to Article 4 (3) of the Constitutional Court Law, the chief justice and deputy chief justice are elected by the Constitutional Court justices for a three-year term. Therefore, in the first meeting, the justices discussed the procedure to elect the chief justice and deputy chief justice. None of these new justices had a public profile like Asshiddiqie. With his stellar reputation and political experience, Asshiddiqie was elected by his colleagues as the first chief justice of the Indonesian Constitutional Court.[15]

The court's humble beginnings and its challenges

Having explained the background of Jimly Asshiddiqie, this chapter will go on to discuss how his leadership shaped the Court in its early days of operation. As a newly established institution, the Constitutional Court had no direct connection with the old judicial system, and therefore it did not carry the legacy of being marginalized by the government. Nevertheless, the Court had to face many major challenges that could not be resolved easily.[16]

The main challenge for the Constitutional Court was to build its judicial status. For many years, the authoritarian government in Indonesia put the judges in the civil service apparatus by subjecting them to bureaucratic hierarchies and compulsory membership in the government-sponsored civil service union.[17] Consequently, judges never enjoyed a respected status in Indonesian history. In his first months in office, Chief Justice Asshiddiqie already complained that he was not receiving proper treatment as a high ranking governmental officer and that he did not enjoy any facility that he was supposed to receive.[18] The chief justice believed it was his right to receive a house and a car because another high-ranking official in Indonesia received a house and a car. When he went to see the government to demand a house and a car, the government did not give an immediate response. The chief justice then contacted the deputy cabinet secretary, Erman Rajagukguk, to help him to lobby the government to provide facilities for him. Rajagukguk, a former colleague at the University of Indonesia, decided to seek a legal opinion on the issue from another constitutional expert, Professor Harun Al Rasyid.[19] Professor Al Rasyid then came out with a legal opinion that as the chief justice of the Constitutional Court, Jimly Asshiddiqie deserved a house and a car that equaled those of other high-ranking governmental officers.[20] Based on such a legal opinion, then Erman Rajagukguk went back to the president and convinced the president to grant proper facilities to the chief justice of the Constitutional Court.[21]

The struggle for judicial status seems to have been a common struggle for all the justices in their early days. There were many unpleasant experiences for the justices because the general public did not respect the position of Constitutional Court justices. Once, a Constitutional Court justice was sitting in the VIP room at the airport, and suddenly high-ranking military officers came in and declined to sit in the same room with someone who did not deserve to sit there.[22] On a different occasion, a governor declined to meet with a Constitutional Court justice and delegated one of his inferior officers to meet with the justice.[23] The Constitutional Court justices did not receive a warm welcome on university or college campuses either. There was an incident where a president of a university declined to facilitate for the Constitutional Court justices a public speaking engagement on campus.[24] The university president thought that the Constitutional Court was under the Ministry of Justice; the university was only willing to facilitate a speech by the minister of justice and not his subordinate.

Having realized that the other branches of government did not respect the Court, Chief Justice Asshiddiqie tried to bring the fight for judicial status to a higher level: the fight for recognition that the chief justice has an equal position with the president. For many years, the chief justice of the Supreme Court had been considered a second-class officer in the governmental hierarchical line. The most telling incident in Indonesian judicial history was when the chief justice of the Supreme Court, Wirjono Projodikoro, joined President Soekarno on his 1959 state visit to the United States, and he was seated with senators and congressmen, while the American chief justice, Earl Warren, sat with Soekarno and President Eisenhower.[25] The story, however, is somewhat different during the tenure of Chief Justice Jimly Asshiddiqie. When Asshiddiqie was re-elected as chief justice in summer 2006, he took the oath by himself, and President Soesilo Bambang Yudhoyono stood just behind, watching the chief justice take his oath.[26]

This little incident signified that the chief justice tried to place himself on an equal footing with the president, something that would have been impossible earlier in Indonesian judicial history.

Apart from the struggle for judicial status, the Court had also to deal with the lack of governmental support. When the Constitutional Court started its business on August 19, 2003, it had no funding, no office, and no support staff. Chief Justice Jimly Asshiddiqie frequently stated that he started the Court with only three pieces of paper: the Constitution, the Constitutional Court Law and the Presidential Decree that appointed the Constitutional Court justices.[27] With no office and infrastructure, the Court had to use the chief justice's mobile phone as its first contact number.[28] Chief Justice Asshiddiqie described how awkward the situation was when the Court had to use his cell phone as temporary contact information, "When some people called the Court on my cell phone, they thought I was the assistant of the Chief Justice, and I said yes."[29]

In response to the lack of governmental support, Asshiddiqie then used his political connections to successfully lobby the MPR to let the Court borrow one of the assembly's meeting rooms as a temporary courtroom. Six out of nine Constitutional Court justices were not Jakarta residents, and they did not have a permanent place to stay. Therefore they had to stay temporarily in hotels, and the judges then decided to use the hotel as their meeting place. In October 2003, the minister of finance decided to deliver the so-called contingency plan for the Constitutional Court, of RP 10,6 billion (U.S. $ 10 million).[30] Having obtained funding from the government, the Court decided to rent some office space in Plaza Centris, Jakarta. While the Court had a temporary office address, it continued to use the assembly building as the courtroom. It was not until January 2004 that the Court obtained a permanent office address when the government let the Court use a building that had originally belonged to the minister of communication and information.

When people wonder how the Court was able to lobby the government to provide funding and office space in a relatively short period, the chief justice simply said it was because he knows many people in the government.[31] Indeed, Asshiddiqie's experience in government service enabled him to connect with many people in the government, and his political connections enabled him to lobby the government to provide support for the newly established Court. In fact, Asshiddiqie had a good connection with minister of finance Boediono because they both served under the Habibie administration. Boediono was formerly the minister of planning and national development, and Asshiddiqie was a special assistant to President Habibie. Therefore it was not difficult for Asshiddiqie to lobby the minister of finance to provide contingency funding for the Court. Moreover, the initiative from Asshiddiqie to start the Court—even before the money was ready—was helpful for the Court to lobby the government to provide sufficient funds because the Court was already in operation and badly needed financial support.

Asshiddiqie believed that the Court needed a new and decent building because it would symbolically represent the status of the Court as a new institution.

In Asshiddiqie's view, to get respect from the other branches of government, the Court needed a great office building to symbolize the significance of the institution within the Indonesian governmental system. After having an office in a hotel and renting a temporary office, Chief Justice Jimly Asshiddiqie came up with a plan to build a new office. The Court proposed a budget of RP 191 billion (around U.S. $180 million) for a 16-floor office building.

The DPR, however, opposed the proposal and suggested that the Court use an abandoned governmental office building.[32] The chief justice, however, did not want to take no for an answer, and he rigorously lobbied the House Judiciary Committee and convinced them that the Court desperately needed a permanent office building, and that the idea of using a governmental office did not seem viable because the government still needed those offices. In the end, the DPR approved the Court's proposal, and the government allocated some money for the office building in the national government budget. By the time the Court finished its four-year term, it had a new magnificent office building that combines Greek and dome-style architecture. Before the construction of the building, at least five designs were prepared, and the Court approved none of those designs.[33] Then the Court came up with a proposal to adopt Greek-style architecture. The chief justice argued that many foreign courts have chosen Greek-style architecture because of its impressive image.[34]

When the Court officially opened its new building in August 2007, President Yudhoyono was invited, as were former presidents and political leaders who were involved in the constitutional reform process; these included former President Megawati, former DPR speaker Akbar Tandjung, and former chair of the MPR, Amien Rais.[35] All of these prominent leaders and President Yudhoyono were invited to put the inscription of their signature in the founding monument of the new Constitutional Court. This little incident also signified that Chief Justice Asshiddiqie did not want to give special status to the then President Yudhoyono, but tried to balance the figure of the president with other prominent figures in the country.

Intellectual vision of Jimly Asshiddiqie

After Asshiddiqie was successful in securing infrastructure, personnel, and status for the Court, he moved forward with his next crusade to set the doctrinal foundation of judicial review through his intellectual leadership. This section seeks to identify the central themes in Chief Justice Asshiddiqie's vast body of intellectual work. I would like to start with his 1994 doctoral work, *Gagasan Kedaulatan Rakyat* (The Concept of Popular Sovereignty).[36] In this book, Asshiddiqie emphasizes the doctrinal meaning of Article 33 of the 1945 Constitution.[37] Before jumping further into Asshiddiqie's thinking, it is necessary to provide a quick overview of Article 33. Article 33 provides that (1) the economy shall be structured as a common endeavor based upon the family principle; (2) branches of production that are important to the state, and that affect the common good, are to be controlled by the state; and (3) the earth and water and the natural resources contained within them are to be controlled by the state and used for the greatest prosperity of the people.[38]

Article 33 has survived the sea of changes in Indonesian politics from the left-leaning Soekarno regime to the right-wing Soeharto New Order military rule, and it also continued to survive in the post-authoritarian period. The constitutional reform process in the early 2000s left the original version of Article 33 untouched. Nevertheless, the Fifth Amendment added a new provision: "the organization of the national economy shall be conducted on the basis of economic democracy upholding the principles of togetherness, the efficiency with justice, continuity, environmental perspective, self-sufficiency, and keeping a balance in the progress and unity of the national economy."[39]

In his doctoral dissertation, Asshiddiqie attacked the Indonesian economic policy of the late 1980s and early 1990s. With the collapse of oil prices in the mid-1980s, Indonesia was no longer able to depend on oil revenues and desperately needed to encourage private enterprise to be the engine of the country's economic growth. The government then announced far-ranging economic reforms from the trade sectors to the financial sector.[40] The government deregulated foreign direct investment by removing restrictions that had existed for many years. In the financial sector, the government removed restrictions on bank licenses, and foreign banks were allowed to operate outside Jakarta without restriction.[41] Asshiddiqie argued that the government's economic reforms were not compatible with the constitutional values found within the 1945 Constitution, especially Article 33. Asshiddiqie believed that the government's economic reforms were merely a liberalization process that gave capitalistic economic power the chance to grow stronger and bigger.[42]

Asshiddiqie believed that Article 33 required government intervention to guarantee people's welfare, and therefore he emphasized the role of state-owned enterprises in controlling the sectors of production that affect the common good.[43] Further, Asshiddiqie argued that the Constitution guarantees the existence of private businesses, but that they should have a marginal position in the Indonesian economic arena and are not supposed to be the driving forces of the Indonesian economy.[44] Asshiddiqie argued that the solution for Indonesian economic policy was to find a balance between so-called individualism and collectivism.[45] He considered the privatization of state-owned enterprises as an open option for the Indonesian economy. But he proposed that there should be a systematic evaluation to determine which state enterprises were vital for the country and affected the people's lives; and that the government could privatize those companies that were deemed less important for the country.[46] Furthermore, Asshiddiqie proposed limited privatization of state enterprises that only allow cooperatives (*koperasi*) to become shareholders of state enterprises.[47]

As explained in the previous chapter, after the adoption of the new constitution in 2002, Asshiddiqie had successfully established his reputation as a dominant figure on the issue of constitutional reform. During Indonesia's democratic transition, Asshiddiqie wrote many essays and articles on his ideas and reflections on the constitutional reform process.[48] One of his focuses of study was the scope and meaning of state institutions under the new constitution. When the lawmakers adopted a new constitution in 2002, they created many new institutions within the Indonesian governmental structure. But there was enormous complexity in the scope and function of the newly established institutions. For instance, the creation of many new administrative agencies begs an explanation of whether the regulator is a part of the executive branch or an independent decision-making body that does not follow the direction of any governmental departments.

In his writing, Asshiddiqie attempted to make the complexity of the new Indonesian governance structure more understandable. In his essays *Pembangunan Hukum dan Penegakan Hukum di Indonesia* (Legal Development and Legal Implementation in Indonesia), Asshiddiqie argued that there are two different types of state institutions under the new constitution.[49] The first group is the so-called "upper state institutions" (*Lembaga Tinggi Negara*), which receive a clear constitutional mandate. This category includes some state institutions, such as the MPR, the president, the DPR, the Regional Representative Council (DPD), the National Audit Agency (BPK), the Supreme Court, and the Constitutional Court.[50] The second group is made up of state institutions that have authority from the Constitution but do not fall into the category of "upper state institutions."[51] There are several sub-categories within the second group. First, there are the state agencies that play a role as a supporting organ, such as the Judicial Commission, which supports the Supreme Court. Second, the Constitution assigned a constitutional status to institutions such as the National Armed Forces and National Police. Third, some state institutions obtain their legal authority as an implication of their function, such as the National Election Commission. Finally, some state institutions do not receive a clear constitutional mandate, but the Constitution assigned the lawmaker to specify the authority of such institutions at the statutory level—the Central Bank is one example of a state institution in this category.[52]

Asshiddiqie, however, did not stop with an explanation of the complexity of the new governmental structure in Indonesia. He further envisioned a massive reform during the period of democratic transition. Asshiddiqie revealed his vision on broad reform in his 2004 end-of-year speech. He stated, "Indonesia is in a gradual transition from a centralized, authoritarian and militarized power state towards the era of the rule of law."[53] For that reason, the chief justice believed that there are at least three important agendas during democratic transitions: legal reform (*pembaruan dan penataan sistem hukum*), law enforcement (*pelaksanaan dan penegakan hukum*), and legal education and communication (*pendidikan dan komunikasi hukum*).[54]

Asshiddiqie believed that the Court should play an active role in resolving political and economic catastrophes during Indonesia's transition period. Asshiddiqie explained:

> Our country is in a complete mess. It is supposed to be the domain of the Executive to clean the mess, but the President does not seem to have any

> plan to clean the mess, so the Court has to take the initiative to solve the problems in transition. You can call these actions as judicial activism, and I would say yes, this is a kind of judicial activism.[55]

In sum, Asshiddiqie believed that there should be political and economic reform in the country, and, for that reason, the Court should actively be involved in the reform process. The timing seemed perfect when, in 2003, Asshiddiqie became the chief justice of the Constitutional Court, thereby giving him the chance to apply his ideas to the newly established Court.

Overcoming the legacy of human rights abuses

Because Indonesia is a country in democratic transition, many of its citizens expected the Court to correct past human rights abuses.[56] From the beginning, Chief Justice Asshiddiqie made it clear that the Court has a commitment to "clean the mess left by the military regime" by correcting the past authoritarian practices and recognizing the protection of fundamental liberties.[57]

In the *Communist Party* case,[58] the Court decided its first high-profile civil and political rights case relating to past human rights abuses. The claimants were 35 political activists who filed a petition challenging the constitutionality of the General Election Law.[59] The Law banned a former member of the Indonesian Communist Party (*Partai Komunis Indonesia*—PKI) and its affiliate organizations from becoming a legislator in the national and local parliaments.[60] The ban had existed since the late 1960s after the government accused the PKI of kidnapping and killing six army generals.[61] The Constitutional Court struck down the provision in the General Election Law, and held that "individual members of the Communist Party and its affiliates should be treated equally as citizens without discrimination."[62] Nevertheless, Chief Justice Jimly Asshiddiqie announced that the decision would not have an immediate effect, as it would come into force for the 2009 general elections.[63] I will explain in more detail about the effect of the Court's decision in the next chapter.

One of the legacies of the New Order military regime was the frequent use of the colonial penal code to penalize political dissidents.[64] The regime mostly relied on two parts of the penal code. First, the regime relied on the "spreading hatred" articles (the Criminal Code, Art. 154–157), which criminalize "public expression of hate or insult to the government." Second, the regime frequently used the *Lèse Majesté* articles (the Criminal Code, Art. 134–137), regarding insults directed at the president or the vice president. Also, there are the "lesser" *Lèse Majesté* articles (the Criminal Code, Art. 207 and 208) on insults to government authorities.

After the establishment of the Constitutional Court, citizens had the opportunity to test the constitutionality of these articles. The first test came in the *Lèse Majesté* case.[65] Eggi Sudjana and Pandapotan Lubis were veteran activists who faced criminal charges for insulting President Susilo Bambang Yudhoyono. Both of them asked the Court to nullify the *Lèse Majesté* articles that formed the basis of their criminal charges.[66] The Court majority accepted the petition and with a split decision (7–2), the Court declared that the *Lèse Majesté* articles were unconstitutional. The Court held:

> *Lèse Majesté* articles are irrelevant in a democratic state like Indonesia because they could negate the principle of equality before the law, and moreover, it could harm the freedom of expression, freedom of information, and the principle of legal uncertainty.[67]

The Court's decision signified the end of an era in which the power holders could use the criminal code to silence their political opponents. Nevertheless, the Court held that its decision only applies to future cases. So, despite the judgment of unconstitutionality, the District Court continued the criminal trial proceeding and sentenced the claimants to three months in jail. Again, this issue will be discussed in detail in the next chapter.

The next case is the *Spreading Hatred* case.[68] The claimant, Panji Utomo, was convicted by a district court of violating these "spreading hatred" articles. Utomo was found guilty of criticizing the work of the Aceh and Nias Reconstruction and Rehabilitation Agency. Utomo asked the Court to nullify these articles, claiming they were impeding his right to the freedom of expression.[69] The Court ruled that the potential for abuse of power through these articles is flagrant, as the provisions could be subjectively interpreted based on the government's interests because prosecutors were not even required to prove whether the statement or opinion had resulted in the spread of hatred or hostility among the general public.[70] The Court finally decided that these provisions were unconstitutional because they violated constitutional rights to the freedom of expression.[71] Again, the Court's decision had no effect on the claimant's conviction as he had already served his criminal sentence long before the Court announced its decision.[72]

Obviously, in these cases, Chief Justice Asshiddiqie led the Court to issue bold and provocative decisions. But at the same time, Asshiddiqie also led the Court to temper the remedial measures by suspending the invalidating of the ruling like that in the *Communist Party* case. Moreover, both in the *Lèse Majesté* and the *Spreading Hatred* cases, the Court's remedial measures "fail" to redress the claimants' injury as they did not enjoy the benefit of winning in the Constitutional Court.

Battling against privatization policies and market economy

While the Court did issue some bold decisions related to past human rights abuses, the Court also made a strategic choice to focus on economic-related issues. Before I go on to explain the Court's cases in the economic-related issues, it's important to revisit Asshiddiqie's vision of the Constitution and the economy as his vision might help us to understand the Court's decisions. Asshiddiqie believed that the state should intervene in the economic process in transitional countries like Indonesia. According to Asshiddiqie, the government should draw a road map for economic reform, and he suggested that the government build a secure social infrastructure first before liberalizing markets in the country.[73]

For instance, Asshiddiqie believed that there would be a tremendous social cost if the government let the market determine the oil price.[74] In short, instead of allowing full-speed and unfettered economic liberalization, Asshiddiqie argued for a gradual and planned reform led by the state.

State-led economic reforms were not without issue, however, because Asshiddiqie believed that the Indonesian government relied too much on the support of the World Bank and the International Monetary Fund (IMF) for economic reform.[75] The World Bank and IMF had long thought that the state-owned enterprises such as PLN (the State Power Company) and *Pertamina* (the State Oil Company) had a poor accountability record, and the solution was to privatize those public companies.[76] Thus, already in his first month in office, Chief Justice Jimly Asshiddiqie warned lawmakers on the constitutionality of government economic policy. He stated:

> In the last fifty years, the lawmaker rarely made reference to the Constitution in formulating economic policy. I would like to warn lawmakers that they should not disregard the Constitution. They should be cautious. If the Court reviews a statute that does not refer to the Constitution, then it shall be declared unconstitutional. I should remind them earlier because there are not many people who realize this issue and they continue to make reference to WTO. Beware! Our constitution is not a liberal constitution. These are not my words but the words of our founding fathers since 1945.[77]

Apparently, in the early days of the Court's operation, Asshiddiqie had delivered a signal that the Court should clean up the mess not only related to the past human right abuses but also to economic issues. Moreover, Asshiddiqie made it clear that he was willing to lead the Court to quash the liberal economic agenda.

After the establishment of the Constitutional Court, the opponents of the pro-market reforms had the opportunity to challenge many statutes that mandated the privatization of state enterprises.[78] These claimants usually contested the series of laws on privatization as being contrary to the economic clause in the constitution.[79] With the help of the opponents of pro-market reforms, the Court was able to review many cases related to Article 33.

Article 33 cases

The Court's decision in the *Electricity Law* case was the first instance involving Article 33.[80] The principal claimant was a human rights NGO called the Indonesian Human Rights Lawyers Association (*Assosiasi Penasehat Hukum dan Hak Asasi Manusia Indonesia*—APHI). The claimants attacked the new Electricity Law, which allowed for the establishment of a competitive electricity market with the involvement of private enterprises and an independent regulatory body for oversight of the power sector.[81]

The Court began its judgment by addressing the issue of the meaning of the term "shall be controlled by the state" (*dikuasai oleh negara*) in Article 33 (2).

The Court said that the term "shall be controlled by state" has a broader meaning than private ownership.[82] The Court said further that the concept of state control has a close connection with the principle of popular sovereignty found in the Constitution.[83] The Court then defined the meaning of state control as a mandate to the state to perform a policy-making function (*kebijakan*), administrative function (*pengurusan*), regulative function (*pengaturan*), management function (*pengelolaan*), and supervisory function (*pengawasan*).[84] Nevertheless, the Court ruled that the meaning of state control under Article 33 does not always mean 100 percent ownership. The Court ruled that the state can have an absolute majority control (over 50 percent ownership of shares) or relative majority control (under 50 percent ownership of shares), as long as the government as shareholders may control the decision-making process in the company.[85]

Having defined the meaning of state control, the Court moved on to address the issue of whether electricity is an important sector of the industry that should be controlled by the state. The Court ruled that it is up to the government and legislature to decide what industries are "important" enough to be controlled by the state; they may also choose how long an area of production will fall into the category of an essential industry, and they could change the decision over time.[86] Nevertheless, the Court argued that none of the government officers or members of the legislature had ever objected that electricity is considered an important sector for the country that affects people's lives.[87] Thus, the Court held that electricity is an important industry for the country because it constitutes a common good.[88]

After defining electricity as an important sector of production, the Court then addressed the question of whether free-market competition complies with Article 33. Here, the Court addressed the provision that allowed the government to split the electricity industry into different business units under the management of different business entities (an unbundling system). Furthermore, the Electricity Law also allowed the private sector to manage the electricity business, ranging from operating power plants to becoming power sales agents. The Court considered that unbundling systems in the power industry did not bring any benefit for the people because the private sector would not be interested in providing electricity to underdeveloped areas as they would only focus on the profit that they could gain from the well-developed and densely populated areas.[89] The Court held that unbundling systems "will not guarantee power supply to all sectors of the society," and, therefore, the Court held that the Electricity Law does not comply with Article 33.[90]

The Court finally decided to strike down the entire statute, because the provisions that allowed market competition are the "heart" (*jantung*) of the Electricity Law. Nevertheless, the Court held that the decision should have only "prospective" effect, so that all agreements or contracts signed under the law should remain valid until they expired.[91]

The Court continued to deal with privatization policies in the *Oil and Gas Law I* case.[92] In this case, four human rights-based NGOs, a labor union, and an academic challenged the constitutionality of Law No. 22 of 2002 on Oil and Gas.

The claimant argued that the Law reduced the state control over the oil and gas industry to exploration and exploitation activities only, and the state no longer has control over the process of transportation, storage, and processing for the purpose of the separation and purification of the oil and gas.[93] The Court held that the law did not relinquish state control over oil and gas, considering that the authorities responsible for regulating, administering, managing, and supervising the oil and gas industry remain in the hands of the government.[94] But the Court agreed with the claimant that private business entities shall not be authorized to conduct exploitation and exploration activities because it will deprive the state of control over the oil and gas industry.[95]

The Court also faced two further issues in this case. First, the Court had to decide the constitutionality of the fuel prices regulation, which prescribed that the market mechanism should govern fuel prices. The Court held that the government must regulate the fuel price instead of the market mechanism.[96] Second, the Court had to decide on the constitutionality of the production quota regulation, which mandated private business entities to provide a maximum of 25 percent of their share of crude oil and natural gas production to fulfill domestic demands.[97] The Court held that the law only set the domestic production quota at a maximum of 25 percent, but it never set the minimum quota for private companies to provide for domestic consumption. The Court held that the private business entity could potentially abuse the law by offering the lowest amount of their oil and gas products (for instance 0.1 percent), which would eventually threaten the domestic oil supply. Finally, the Court held that the "fuel price" provision was contrary to Article 33 (3) because the principle of the common good requires sufficient fuel stocks for domestic consumption. Unlike in the *Electricity* case, the Court refused to invalidate *Oil and Gas I* entirely, but it made a strategic choice to invalidate only the "fuel price" provision. In other words, the Court issued a more cautious judgment rather than a bold and provocative one like in the *Electricity* case.

The influence of Chief Justice Jimly Asshiddiqie is evident in the Court's holdings in the cases above.[98] As explained earlier, Asshiddiqie's dissertation heavily emphasized the role of state-owned enterprises in the Indonesian economy. The Court, indeed, adopted a similar approach and held that Article 33 required government intervention to guarantee people's welfare, and state-owned enterprises must play a significant role in achieving this objective. Moreover, his brethren appeared to agree with Asshiddiqie by invoking Article 33 to invalidate the government's economic policies.

Defending the court's decisions

The Court's decisions in cases above raise the question of whether the Court has gone too far in second-guessing the government's economic policies. In a private conversation, Asshiddiqie defended the Court's decisions by stating that the Court should review the privatization policies to fulfill its role in the transitional period. The chief justice expressed his concern that the state, market, and civil society could not reach a consensus on how to solve economic problems in Indonesia's transitional period, and, therefore, the Court should step in to take the initiative to lead those elements of society.[99] Asshiddiqie stated:

> The Court should play a unique function as a conductor that leads three different essential elements in the country (state, market, and civil society) to fulfill the greater collective goal to solve economic problem in transition.[100]

In sum, the chief justice believed that through its decisions, the Court played a role in solving the economic problems in the transition from the state-controlled economy, which concentrated economic resources in the hands of the dominant military, political, and economic powers, into a free market economy.

These cases illustrate that Chief Justice Asshiddiqie was a chief justice who pursued a mission to confront and attempt to solve deeply embedded economic problems found in the country. Nonetheless, Asshiddiqie was aware that he needed to be cautious in dealing with the elected branches of government. In the *Electricity* case, Asshiddiqie stated that although the Court invalidated the entire statute, the decision sent a clear message that the Court is not anti-privatization or globalization because the Court also issued a holding that allowed private involvement in important sectors of production, as long as it does not reduce the scope of state control.[101] Asshiddiqie believes that through its decision, the Court tried to balance the competing interests of state, market, and civil society.[102]

In the aftermath of the *Oil and Gas I* case, Asshiddiqie also had to strike a delicate balance between confronting the government and overseeing the implementation of the Court's decision. As mentioned earlier, in the *Oil and Gas Law I* case, the Court struck down the market price clause in the law and ruled that the government must set the fuel price instead of the market mechanism. Nevertheless, not long after the Court issued its decision, the government issued a Presidential Regulation that set up fuel prices based on the market mechanism.[103] In response, the Court wrote a letter and reminded the president that the Court had invalidated the market price clause in the Oil and Gas Law, and the government should not consider it as the source of law any longer.[104] The president in his formal reply to the Constitutional Court stated that the government's decision corresponded with the Court's holding.[105] The president argued that the Court mandated the Executive branch to set the fuel price, and, therefore, the president chose to set the fuel price based on the market price.[106]

Apparently, the president refused to comply with the Court's decision. But the chief justice was not willing to go the extra mile in facing the government when he saw that the government had ignored the Court's decisions. Chief Justice Asshiddiqie believed that he had successfully delivered the message that the government should consider the Court's decision seriously. The chief justice said, "Now the government is becoming more cautious in preparing government regulations. Without my controversial letter, the government would never have considered the Court's decision."[107]

Restructuring administrative agencies

As discussed earlier in this chapter, Indonesian lawmakers created many different regulatory bodies as part of the constitutional reform process. And yet lawmakers failed to define the functions and roles of these newly established administrative agencies, which created conflict among constitutional stakeholders about what the role of agencies should be. Asshiddiqie had long argued that the government should first draw a road map for administrative reform before letting the legislature create many independent regulatory agencies.[108] As the former head of the Legal Reform Team and an adviser to the MPR for constitutional reform, Asshiddiqie might have had compelling academic and personal reasons to seek to clarify the new complex Indonesian governance structure.

The opportunity for Asshiddiqie to take on the subject matter arose when the Court reviewed many cases related to administrative agencies, which mostly grew out of confusion over the function of newly established regulatory bodies in Indonesia. In this section, I will focus on two high-profile cases that involve constitutional questions on the role and function of administrative agencies, including the General Election Commission and the Judicial Commission.

The KPUD *case*

In the *KPUD* case,[109] the claimants were made up of two main groups: some NGOs driven by the Center for Electoral Reform (CETRO), and 21 Regional Elections Commissions (KPUD—*Komisi Pemilihan Umum Daerah*). The claimants challenged the Regional Governance (*Pemerintah Daerah—Pemda*) Law, which regulates regional elections.[110] First, the claimants challenged the provisions in the *Pemda* Law that allowed the central government to intervene in the regional election process through the issuance of government regulations (*Peraturan Pemerintah*).[111] Secondly, the claimants argued that the *Pemda* Law did not comply with the Constitution because the Constitution provided that the National General Election Commission (KPU) should be in charge of the election process.[112] Instead, the *Pemda* Law provided that the Regional Election Commission (KPUD) should be in charge of regional elections.[113] Finally, the claimants asserted that the KPUD could not maintain its independence because, according to the law, it shall be held accountable to the Regional Parliament (*Dewan Perwakilan Rakyat Daerah*—DPRD).[114]

On the first issue, the Court deferred to lawmakers and held that government intervention through the issuance of a government regulation (*Peraturan Pemerintah*) was lawful because the president has constitutional authority to issue government regulations to implement statutory rules (*undang—undang*).[115] On the second issue, the Court held that the lawmakers have the authority to decide which institution will be in charge of regional elections, and in fact, the lawmakers agreed that KPUD is responsible for regional elections.[116] Nonetheless, the Court concurred with the claimants' concern that KPUD would not be independent if it was held accountable to the Regional Parliament. Therefore, the Court held that the provision on KPUD's accountability to the Regional Parliament be declared unconstitutional.[117]

A few days after the Court announced the *KPUD* decision, Chief Justice Jimly Asshiddiqie explained in an interview with national media that the President and legislature had failed to consider how KPUD fit in within the governmental structure.[118] The chief justice stated further that the KPUD (Regional Election Commission) should be held accountable in five different ways.[119] First, the KPUD (Regional Election Commission) should be held accountable to the KPU (National Election Commission) in administrative matters. Second, the commissioner of the KPUD took an oath before assuming office, and therefore, according to the chief justice, the KPUD as an institution should be held accountable to God. Third, all people who serve in public office should be held answerable to the legal system. Fourth, as an independent administrative agency, the KPUD should be held accountable financially to the National Audit Agency (*Badan Pemeriksa Keuangan*—BPK).

Asshiddiqie explained further to the media that, to maintain its independence, KPUD should be held accountable to the public. According to Asshiddiqie, there are different layers of public accountability. First, KPUD should submit its accountability to the Regional Parliament as a matter of administrative formality instead of responsibility. As an independent institution, the KPUD is not a subordinate of the Regional Parliament, and, consequently, it could not be held accountable to the Regional Parliament.[120] Second, KPUD should publish the accountability report in the mass media. Third, KPUD should provide an annual report. Finally, KPUD should abide by the principle of transparency.[121]

In sum, the Court's decision in the *KPUD* case is very similar to the personal view of the chief justice, who on many different occasions consistently expressed his concern over the mushrooming of administrative agencies.[122] Asshiddiqie once stated, "Nowadays there are too many independent commissions that are not useful in carrying out their functions."[123] Thus, for Asshiddiqie, the function of all administrative agencies must be assessed and systematized within the governance structure.[124]

Despite Asshiddiqie's strong assertive approach, he led the Court to make a strategic choice to strike down only a relatively "safe" issue, that is, the independence of the KPUD. The Court decided to defer to the elected institutions on the issue of the central government's involvement in the regional election process. The central government's involvement in the regional election is a politically charged issue because it is about a tug of war between the central and local government to have control over power in the post-authoritarian regime. The Court made a strategic move by deferring to the elected legislatures to decide who has responsibility to run regional elections.

The Judicial Commission *case*

Asshiddiqie's personal thinking is also evident in the *Judicial Commission* case,[125] which involved the question of what the proper functions of the Judicial

Commission should be. In 2001, the MPR adopted the Third Amendment of the 1945 Constitution, which established a Judicial Commission with the authority to nominate Supreme Court justices and to uphold the dignity of the judge.[126] In 2004, the legislatures enacted the Judicial Commission Law, which equipped the Commission with authority to recommend sanctions for poorly performing judges to the Supreme Court or Constitutional Court.[127] Not long after its establishment, the Judicial Commission engaged in a tug of war with the Supreme Court.[128] The conflict escalated when the Commission later made public the names of 13 justices it called "problematic," and the Commission decided to summon those justices.[129]

The case involved a high-stakes conflict, as the Judicial Commission was going after those at the very top leadership of the Supreme Court, including the Chief Justice Bagir Manan, the deputy Chief Justice Mariana Sutadi, and a senior associate justice, Paulus Effendi Lotulung.[130] Those justices decided to challenge the Judicial Commission Law and asked the Constitutional Court to scrap the Judicial Commission's authority to investigate them.

In their petition, the claimants argued that the Constitution only gives power to the Judicial Commission to supervise lower court judges instead of higher court judges.[131] The claimants argued further that the Judicial Commission is essentially a partner for the Supreme Court to supervise the lower court judges.[132] The claimants asked the Constitutional Court to declare that the Judicial Commission has no authority to supervise higher court judges.[133]

In its judgment, the Constitutional Court first ruled that the supervisory role enumerated in the Judicial Commission Law shall not be construed in the context of "separation of powers" because the Judicial Commission was merely a supporting organ of the Supreme Court.[134] Second, the Court ruled that the supervisory role under the Judicial Commission Law is obscure. The Court explained that the legislature designed the Commission to supervise the judge's behavior, but there was neither a code of ethics nor a code of conduct that governed judges' behavior. Furthermore, it remained unclear who had the authority to formulate such a code of ethics and a code of conduct. The Court ruled that the Judicial Commission Law assigns a supervisory role, but the object of supervision remained unclear.[135] The Court concluded that lack of clarity and details on the Commission's supervisory authority of judges' behavior created unintended consequences, including that the Judicial Commission and the Supreme Court each came out with their interpretation.[136] Finally, the Court held that all provisions in the Judicial Commission Law that relate to its supervisory role should be declared inconsistent with the Constitution and void because it created legal uncertainty.[137] The Court later recommended that the DPR and the president revise the Judicial Commission Law.[138]

In short, the Court under the leadership of Jimly Asshiddiqie believed that the lawmakers had failed to make a proper statutory regulation on the functioning and duties of the Judicial Commission. The Court also found that the Judicial Commission had improperly interpreted the law so as to allow it to evaluate judicial decisions instead of judicial behavior.

The decision in the *Judicial Commission* case was unanimous, but obviously Asshiddiqie was the brain behind the decision. In his treatise on state institutions,[139] Asshiddiqie explained that the Judicial Commission is an auxiliary organ for the judicial institution, and it has the function of upholding a code of ethics among the judicial rank and file.[140] The Court holding in the *Judicial Commission* case delivered precisely the same message as the treatise written by the chief justice—namely, that the Judicial Commission is a supporting organ for the Supreme Court, and it is supposed to uphold codes of ethics rather than evaluate the performance of individual Supreme Court judges. There is no doubt that the ruling in the *Judicial Commission* case amounts to an adaptation of the chief justice's scholarly work into a Court decision.[141]

Many political activists, NGOs, and media outlets condemned the Court's decision in the *Judicial Commission* case, as they believed that the Court had gone too far in declaring the law unconstitutional.[142] Nevertheless, the Court made it clear that its role is just to make a "recommendation," to the president and the DPR to write a new law. The Court acknowledged that it is the role of the legislative branch to pass a new law and that therefore the Court will defer all of the law-making process to the legislatures.[143]

Restructuring new judicial institutions

Apart from having concerns about administrative agencies, the chief justice also had great concern about the proper role of judicial institutions under the new constitutional arrangement. Asshiddiqie believed judicial reform was part of the constitutional reform agenda, but he was skeptical over the creation of many judicial institutions after the fall of Soeharto's authoritarian regime.[144] In his major treatise on "The Principle of Indonesian Constitutional Law in Post *Reformasi*" (*Pokok—Pokok Hukum Tata Negara Indonesia Pasca Reformasi*),[145] Asshiddiqie expressed his great concern over the mushrooming of new special courts in the post-*Reformasi* era.[146]Asshiddiqie asserted that the president and legislature did not act wisely and prudently in establishing many special courts. Furthermore, Asshiddiqie saw the newly formed courts as typically bringing new problems, such as a lack of supporting structure, redundancy (overlap of jurisdiction with another court), inefficiency, and high cost.[147]

In his treatise, Chief Justice Asshiddiqie criticized the government's decision to establish the Fisheries Court.[148] In 2004, the government enacted Law No. 31 of 2004 on Fisheries, which established special Fisheries Courts in Jakarta, Medan, Pontianak, Bitung, and Tual. Nevertheless, not long after the enactment of the law, the president issued an emergency decree that postponed the establishment of the Fisheries Court because of a lack of sufficient resources.[149] The chief justice argued that the president and legislature must not pass the law before conducting any studies on the viability of the Fisheries Court.[150] In other words, Asshiddiqie saw the lack of foresight and planning as evident on the part of the President and legislatures' failure in supporting the creation of special courts.

The Mulyana Kusumah *case*

The Court dealt with the issue of a special court in the *Mulyana Kusumah* case.[151] The case involved a question regarding the proper role of the Anti-Corruption Court. The claimants, Mulayana Kusumah and Nazaruddin Sjamsuddin, were former Commissioners of the National Electoral Commission (*Komisi Pemilihan Umum*—KPU). The Anti-Corruption Court tried Kusumah for his attempt to bribe an auditor from the Supreme Audit Agency (BPK) in an apparent effort to influence audit results.[152] Similarly, the Anti-Corruption Court tried Sjamsuddin because he received a kickback from an insurance firm that was appointed to provide occupational accident coverage for electoral commission staff during the 2004 general election.[153] The Anti-Corruption Court found both Sjamsudddin and Kusumah guilty and sentenced Sjamsuddin to a 7-year prison term, and a term of 1.5 years for Kusumah.

Kusumah and Sjamsuddin then challenged the constitutionality of Law no. 32 of 2002 on the Eradication of Corruption Commission in the Constitutional Court. One of the claimants' key arguments was that the Anti-Corruption Court applied a different procedure than a general court in trying corruption cases. For instance, the Anti-Corruption Court does not recognize the procedure to terminate a case because of a lack of evidence.[154] The claimant also filed a complaint about the absence of a pre-trial hearing in the Anti-Corruption Court procedure, in which the law required a speedy trial within 90 days.[155]

The Court concurred with the claimants that the Eradication of Corruption Commission Law created two competing jurisdictions between a General Court of jurisdiction and the Anti- Corruption Court, in which each court has authority to try corruption cases. The Court accepted the claimant's argument that the existence of two courts created a double standard in the effort to combat corruption effort, in which the Anti-Corruption Court applied a stricter procedure in comparison to a more lenient procedure in the general court of jurisdiction. The Court finally declared the Law on Eradication of Corruption Commission to be contrary to the Constitution because it created a dual judicial system in handling corruption cases.[156]

The Court, however, decided that it should give sufficient time for the lawmakers to create a new law. It gave the DPR a three-year deadline to prepare a new law, and in the meantime, the Anti-Corruption Court could continue to operate.[157] Nevertheless, if the lawmakers failed to do so within that time, then the authority over corruption cases should be handed over to General Courts of jurisdiction.[158] Justice Laica Marzuki filed a dissent, but he did not challenge the majority argument. Specifically, Marzuki's dissent argued that the Court's decision should take effect immediately and that the Anti-Corruption Court should cease to operate.[159]

The Court gave lawmakers a period of 3 years to prepare a new law based on the consideration that they should have sufficient time to study many subjects of the Anti-Corruption Court and to develop an informed opinion about each one before they considered and voted on proposals that might become a new law.[160]

This consideration echoed Asshiddiqie's approach to defer to the lawmaker as he led the Court to issue a decision that aims to correct the lack of foresight and planning on the part of the president and the legislatures by giving them the mandate to take sufficient time to prepare a new law.

An intellectually superior chief justice

The case analyses above signify that Chief Justice Jimly Asshiddiqie had influence over the Court's decisions in a wide range of policy areas. One factor that might explain this phenomenon is the perceived intellectual superiority of Chief Justice Jimly Asshiddiqie. Chief Justice Asshiddiqie was the only justice who held a professorship of constitutional law from a top-tier university, the University of Indonesia Law School. Asshiddiqie was also the only justice who holds a PhD from the University of Indonesia and has overseas education experience as a visiting scholar to the University of Washington in Seattle and the University of Leiden, the Netherlands.

Since the Court's conception, there were many criticisms that the president, the DPR and the Supreme Court did consider some legal scholars from prestigious Law School, and instead, they picked up some mediocre candidates.[161] The president's three appointees were Achmad Syarifuddin Natabaya, a law professor at Sriwidjaya University, Palembang; Mukthie Fadjar, a law professor at Brawijaya University, Malang; and Harjono (one name only), a senior lecturer at Airlangga University, Surabaya. Clearly, it was only Harjono who taught at the first-tier law school in the country, and the rest come from second-tier law schools. Harjono did his master's studies at Southern Methodist University, Dallas, and held a PhD from Airlangga University, but he had not published any major scholarly work before his appointment to the Court. Achmad Natabaya obtained his LLM degree in public international law at Indiana University School of Law and served as an adviser to the minister of justice. Mukthie Fadjar taught constitutional law, but none of his publications suggest that he had done extensive research on constitutional law.[162]

As mentioned earlier, out of the three DPR appointees, only Jimly Asshiddiqie who had a constitutional law background, having some publications on constitutional law and a professorship at the University of Indonesia. The rest of the DPR appointees were I Gede Palguna and Achmad Roestandi. Palguna was a lecturer at Udayana University, Bali. By the time of his appointment in 2003, Palguna held neither a doctorate nor a full professorship.[163] Roestandi graduated from Padjajaran Faculty of Law, Bandung. After finishing his legal education, he joined the Army and had taught within the Army, but he spent most his career representing the Armed Forces in Parliament during the New Order military regime.

The three Supreme Court appointees were Laica Marzuki, Maruarar Siahaan, and Soedarsono. Marzuki held a PhD from the Padjajaran University of Indonesia and spent most of his career as a Professor of Law at a medium-tier law school, Hasanuddin University, South Sulawesi. Marzuki was a respected legal scholar, but he had not published any scholarly work on constitutional law before his appointment to the Court.[164] Siahaan and Soedarsono were career judges from the administrative court, and neither of them had achievements or experience in constitutional law. Soedarsono graduated from a lower-tier law school, August 17 University Law School, and he did enjoy a brief legal training at the Institute of Public Administration in France. Siahaan obtained his Bachelor of Law from the University of Indonesia Law School. As an administrative judge, he established a long record of overseas experience as a visiting scholar at the University of Berkeley School of Law and the University of Texas, and he had participated in legal training in the United States and Australia (Table 3.1).

Obviously, Asshiddiqie was a towering figure among many mediocre judges, especially when we look at the list of his publications. The chief justice had numerous publications in the area of constitutional law, and none of the associate justices could compete with his publication record.[165] For example, Asshiddiqie was the only one who published on comparative judicial review in different countries.[166] With his impressive academic background and experience, one can make an argument that Chief Justice Asshiddiqie had academic superiority over his brethren, and therefore he commanded the decision-making process in the Court.

Table 3.1 Constitutional Court Justices 2003–2008

Names	*Prior position*	*Nominator*	*Education*
S. Natabaya	Professor of law	President	– LLB (Unsri, Indonesia) – LLM (Indiana University School of Law, USA)
A. Mukthie Fadjar	Professor of law	President	– LLB (UGM, Indonesia) – Master of Science (Unair, Indonesia)
Harjono	Senior lecturer in law	President	– LLB (Unair, Indonesia) – Master of Comparative Law (Southern Methodist University, Dallas, USA) – PhD (Unair, Indonesia)
Jimly Asshiddiqie	Professor of law	DPR (House) (Golkar bloc)	– LLB (UI, Indonesia) – Master of Law (UI) – PhD (UI, Indonesia)
Achmad Roestandi	Retired military general	DPR (House) (PPP bloc)	– LLB (Unpad, Indonesia)
I Dewa Gede Palguna	Lecturer of law	DPR (House) (PDI-P bloc)	– LLB (Udayana, Indonesia) – Master of Law (Unpad, Indonesia)
Laica Marzuki	Professor of law	Supreme Court	– LLB (Unhas, Indonesia) – PhD (Unpad, Indonesia)
Soedarsono	Administrative court judge	Supreme Court	– LLB (Untag, Indonesia)
Maruarar Siahaan	Administrative court judge	Supreme Court	– LLB (UI, Indonesia)

Despite his towering intellectual figure, there were some different opinions among associate justices on the intellectual superiority of the chief justice. One of the associate justices at the time stated:

> One of the strengths of Pak Jimly is his intellectual capacity. Although he is relatively young, with his excellent intellectual credentials, he can lead the associate justices who are mostly older than him.[167]

Nevertheless, some associate justices contested the notion that the chief justice had intellectual superiority. A senior associate justice argued that while it was true that Asshiddiqie had impressive credentials as a constitutional law professor, this did not mean that he was knowledgeable on other legal issues.[168] Another senior associate justice cynically said that Asshiddiqie looked intellectually superior because he had better access to foreign literature in the early days of the Court.[169]

This book does not make the claim that Asshiddiqie had total control over the Constitutional Court. Despite his academic credentials and experience, Asshiddiqie apparently did not have complete control over his brethren, a matter explained further in Chapter 5. Nevertheless, with his intellectual rigor, Asshiddiqie managed to exert significant influence over his fellow judges, and, in the process, he was able to move the Court in a particular direction of his choosing.

Conclusion

Chief Justice Jimly Asshiddiqie believed that the Constitutional Court should help to resolve the political and economic problems that the Indonesian government was facing. Therefore, Asshiddiqie led the Court to engage with a broad range of political and economic issues by reviewing cases involving political and economic problems in transition. Moreover, Chief Justice Asshiddiqie managed to apply his personal ideas to the Court's decisions. For example, Asshiddiqie used his scholarly views on Article 33 when the Court had to deal with the issue of the constitutionality of the government's economic program. Furthermore, Asshiddiqie believed that the Court should systematize new governmental structure in Indonesia because the lawmakers had created too many new institutions without careful thinking. Consequently, he led the Court to strike down some of the legislation that established new administrative agencies, such as the Judicial Commission; and special courts, like the Anti-Corruption Court.

Chief Justice Jimly Asshiddiqie appears to be the one who orchestrated some of the Court's major decisions. One plausible explanation for his dominance involves his academic credentials. He was the only full-time professor from an elite university with impressive academic and political experience. As former head of the Legal Reform Team and later the adviser to the MPR, Asshiddiqie was the one who was very knowledgeable about constitutional matters in Indonesia.

Above all, Asshiddiqie acknowledges both the important functions of judicial review and the fragility of judicial independence in new democracies. Therefore, he combined his ambitious constitutional interpretations with a minimalist approach by issuing cautious judgments, and especially by tempering the remedial measures that the Court orders to redress constitutional violations, which will be discussed in detail in the next chapter.

Notes

1 David J. Danelski. "The Influence of the Chief Justice in the Decisional Process." In *Courts, Judges, & Politics: An Introduction to the Judicial Process*, edited by Walter F. Murphy, C. Herman Pritchett, and Lee Epstein. (Boston: McGraw-Hill, 5th ed. 2002). The first edition of the book was published in 1961.
2 Ibid., 662.
3 Ibid.
4 Ibid., 668.
5 Donald Grier Stephenson, Jr. "The Chief Justice as Leader: The Case of Morrison Remick Waite," 14 *Wm & Mary L. Rev.* 899, 900 (1973); See also Donald Grier Stephenson, Jr. "The Waite Court at the Bar of History," 81 *Denv. U.L. Rev.* 449 (2003).
6 Ibid., *The Chief Justice as Leader*, 900.
7 See Zaenal Abidin Aep and Lisa Suroso. *Setengah Abad Jimly Asshiddiqie, Konstitusi dan Semangat Kebangsaan* [Fifty Years of Jimly Asshiddiqie, Constitution and Spirit of Nationalism] (Jakarta: Perhimpunan Indonesia Tionghoa & Majelis Tinggi Agama Khonghucu Indonesia, 2006); See also Purwadi. *Pendekar Konstitusi Jimly Asshiddiqie* [Jimly Asshiddiqie, the Constitutional Warrior] (Yogyakarta: Hanan Pustaka, 2006).
8 See Zaenal Abidin Aep and Lisa Suroso. *Setengah Abad Jimly Asshiddiqie: Konstitusi dan Semangat Kebangsaan* [Fifty Years of Jimly Asshiddiqie: Constitution and the Spirit of Nationhood] (2006).
9 Presidential Decree No. 191 of 1998.
10 Presidential Decree No. 18 of 1999.
11 B. J. Habibie. *Decisive Moments: Indonesia's Long Road to Democracy.* (Jakarta: Ilthabi Rekatama, 2006), 428.
12 "Assembly Working Group Blasted Over Constitutional Amendments." The *Jakarta Post,* March 22, 2001.
13 "Government Names Seven Candidates for New Court." The *Jakarta Post,* August 13, 2003.
14 The Constitutional Court of Republic of Indonesia, *Annual Report of the Constitutional Court of the Republic of Indonesia 2003*, 2003.
15 Ibid.
16 For a detailed analysis of the major challenges that the Court had to face in its early days of operation, please see Stefanus Hendrianto. *From Humble Beginnings to A Functioning Court: Indonesian Constitutional Court, 2003–2008.* (Unpublished Doctoral Dissertation, University of Washington, School of Law, 2008).
17 See Sebastian Pompe. *The Indonesian Supreme Court: A Study of Institutional Collapse* (Ithaca, NY: Southeast Asia Program, Cornell University, 2005), 114–115.
18 "Mahkamah Konstitusi Dapat Dana Talangan 10,6 Miliar." [The Constitutional Court Received 10.6 Billion Contingency Fund], *Koran Tempo*, October 10, 2003.
19 Erman Rajagukguk, former Deputy Cabinet Secretary, in conversation with the author, August 10, 2006.
20 Harun Al Rasyid (Emeritus Professor of Law, University of Indonesia) in conversation with author, August 13, 2006.

21 Private conversation with Erman Rajagukguk.
22 Irmanputra Sidin, "Sembilan Pintu Kebenaran Konstitusi" [The Nine Constitutional Gates], *Kompas*, January 6, 2004.
23 Ibid.
24 Ibid.
25 See Sebastian Pompe. *The Indonesian Supreme Court*, 44.
26 "Negara dalam Negara" [Nation Within Nation], *Media Indonesia*, September 25, 2006.
27 Jimly Asshiddiqie. "Bermodal tiga lembar kertas" [With Three Pieces of Paper], *Republika*, January 11, 2004.
28 Jimly Asshiddiqie. "Setahun Mahkamah Konstitusi: Refleksi, Gagasan Dan Penyelenggaraan, Serta Setangkup Harapan" [The First Year of the Constitutional Court: Reflection, Idea, Action and Hope]. In *Menjaga Denyut Konstitusi: Refleksi Satu Tahun Mahkamah Konstitusi*, edited by Refly Harun, Zainal A. M. Husein, and Bisariyadi. (Jakarta: Konstitusi Press, 2004), 14.
29 Ibid., 15.
30 "Mahkamah Konstitusi Dapat Dana Talangan 10,6 Miliar." [The Constitutional Court Received 10,6 Billion Contingency Fund], *Koran Tempo*, October 10, 2003.
31 Jimly Asshiddiqie. *Setahun Mahkamah Konstitusi* [The First Anniversary of the Constitutional Court], 14.
32 "Komisi III Tolak Pembangunan Gedung Mewah MK." [The Commission III Rejects the Proposal for the Constitutional Court Luxurious Office Building], *Media Indonesia*, February 3, 2005.
33 Indonesian Constitutional Court. *Sejarah Pembangunan Gedung Mahkamah Konstitusi* [The History of the Constitutional Court Building], (Sekretariat Jenderal Mahkamah Konstitusi, August 2007)
34 Ibid., 28.

Although it appears that all of the Justices agreed to adopt the Greek style of architecture, there is no doubt that Asshiddiqie had a strong influence in choosing the design of the Court building. When I visited Asshiddiqie in his office in summer 2006, he was busy choosing designs for the Court Chamber.

35 Former President B. J. Habibie and Abdurrahman Wahid were invited but did not attend the opening ceremony.
36 Jimly Asshiddiqie. *Gagasan Kedaulatan Rakyat dalam Konstitusi dan Pelaksanaannya di Indonesia: Pergeseran Keseimbangan antara Individualisme dan Kolektivisme dalam Kebijakan Demokrasi Politik dan Demokrasi Ekonomi selama tiga masa demokrasi, 1945–1980-an* [The Concept of People's Sovereignty in the Indonesian Constitution: Collectivism and Individualism in the Political and Economic Policy, 1945–1980s] (Jakarta: Ichtiar Baru Van Hoeve, 1994).
37 Mohammad Hatta was credited as being the architect of Article 33. Hatta's idea was grounded in the socialist thinking of Europe in the 1920s; as a young man, he enjoyed a college education in the Netherlands during a period of history when socialist ideas of various kinds were spreading rapidly throughout the European intellectual community. Hatta, however, was not alone in endorsing an active role for state economic intervention and in being suspicious of the workings of the market. The Indonesian elite after the revolution was remarkably homogenous in their anti-capitalist economic outlook. See Benjamin Higgins. *Economic Development: Problems, Principles, and Policies* (New York: W.W. Norton, 1968); see also George Kahin. *Nationalism, and Revolution in Indonesia*, (Cornell University: Ithaca, New York, 1952).
38 Constitution of the Republic of Indonesia 1945, Article 33 (1, 2, 3). The English translation of Article 33 is my translation. For a comparison of the English translation of Article 33, please see the English translation of the Constitution of the

Republic of Indonesia by the Indonesia Constitutional Court, available at http://www.mahkamahkonstitusi.go.id/public/content/infoumum/regulation/pdf/uud45%20eng.pdf.

39 Constitution of the Republic of Indonesia 1945, Article 33 (4).

40 See Rizal Mallarangeng. *Liberalizing New Order Indonesia: Ideas, Epistemic Community, and Economic Policy Change, 1986–1992* (Unpublished dissertation, Ohio State University, 2000), 185–186. The dissertation was later published in Rizal Mallarangeng. *Mendobrak sentralisme ekonomi Indonesia, 1986–1992.* (Jakarta: Kepustakaan Populer Gramedia, 2002).

41 Thee Kian Wie. "The Soeharto Era and After: Stability, Development and Crisis, 1996–2000." In *The Emergence of A National Economy: An Economic History of Indonesia, 1800–2000*, edited by Howard Dick, Vincent J. H. Houben, J. Thomas Lindblad, and Thee Kian Wie. (New South Wales & Honolulu: Allen & Unwin and University of Hawai'i Press, 2002).

42 See Asshiddiqie. *Gagasan Kedaulatan Rakyat*, 221.

43 Ibid., 92.

44 Ibid., 102.

45 Ibid., 255.

46 Ibid., 272.

47 Ibid., 273.

48 Most of this essay and these articles were later compiled into a book titled *Format Kelembagaan Negara Dan Pergeseran Kekuasaan Dalam UUD 45* [The Format of State Institutions and the Shifting Power in the 1945 Constitution] (Yogyakarta: FH UII Press, 2004); and Jimly Asshiddiqie. *Hukum Tata Negara Dan Pilar—Pilar Demokrasi: Serpihan Pemikiran Hukum, Media dan HAM* [Constitutional Law and Democratic Pillars: Some Thoughts on Law, Media and Human Rights] (Jakarta: Konstitusi Press, 2005).

49 Jimly Asshiddiqie. *Pembangunan Hukum dan Penegakan Hukum di Indonesia* [Legal Development and Legal Enforcement in Indonesia], paper prepared for the 55th anniversary of Faculty of Law Gadjah Mada University, February 5, 2006.

50 Ibid., 9.

51 Ibid., 10.

52 Ibid.

53 Jimly Asshiddiqie. "Pidato Refleksi Akhir Tahun 2004: Agenda Konsolidasi dan Rekonstrusi Nasional Mengisi Paruh Kedua Era Transisi" [2004 End of Year Speech: Agenda for National Consolidation and Reconstruction to Fulfill Second Stage of Transition] (Jakarta, December 29, 2004), 4–5.

54 Ibid.

55 Private conversation with Jimly Asshiddiqie, July 31, 2006.

56 See Adnan Buyung Nasution. "Towards Constitutional Democracy in Indonesia," Inaugural Professorial Lecture, University of Melbourne, October 2O, 2010 (noting that during the democratic transition in Indonesia, human rights violations were common. The shooting of student activists, riots, illegal imprisonment, and the rapes and murders of ethnic Chinese were among some human rights tragedies that forced the Indonesians to think how to address this issue in the post-authoritarian period).

57 Private conversation with Jimly Asshiddiqie, July 31, 2006.

58 The Indonesian Constitutional Court Decision No. 011-017/PUU-I/2003, reviewing the Law No. 12 of 2003 on the Election of National and Regional Parliament (hereinafter *the Communist Party* case).

59 General Election Law No. 12 of 2003.

60 See Article 60 (g), the Law No. 12 of 2003.

61 For details of the impact of the anti-communist witch-hunts, see Ariel Heryanto. *State Terrorism and Political Identity in Indonesia: Fatally Belonging* (2006).
62 See the *Communist Party* case, 36–37.
63 Jimly Asshiddiqie. "Mahkamah Konstitusi: Bekas PKI Boleh Memilih dan Dipilih" [Constitutional Court: Former PKI May Cast a Vote and Elected], (*Tempointeraktif*, February 24, 2004).
64 For a detailed analysis of the government's reliance on this colonial legislation, please see Daniel S. Lev, "Colonial Law and the Genesis of the Indonesia State," in Daniel S. Lev, *Legal Evolution and Political Authority in Indonesia: Selected Essays* (The Hague: Kluwer Law International, 2000).
65 The Indonesian Constitutional Court decision, Case No. 013/PUU-IV/2006, reviewing the Indonesian Criminal Code (hereinafter the *Lèse Majesté* case).
66 Indonesian Criminal Code, Articles 134, 136, and 137.
67 The *Lèse Majesté* case, 61.
68 The Constitutional Court Decision No. 6/PUU-V/2007 (hereinafter the *Spreading Hatred* case).
69 Constitution of the Republic of Indonesia 1945, Art. 28E (3) and Art. 28F.
70 The *Spreading Hatred* case, para 3.18.6.
71 For a detailed analysis of the *Lèse Majesté* case and the *Spreading Hatred* case, please see Naomita Royan. "Increasing Press Freedom in Indonesia: The Abolition of the Lèse Majesté and 'Hate-Sowing' Provisions." 10(2) *Australian Journal of Asian Law* 290 (2008); see also Nono Anwar Makarim. "Press Freedom in Indonesia: A Case of Draconian Laws, Statutory Misinterpretation, but Still One of the Freest in Southeast Asia," 3 *J. Civ. L. Stud.* (2010).
72 The District Court Banda Aceh issued a criminal verdict on December 18, 2006 and sentenced Panji Utomo to three months' imprisonment. See the Banda Aceh District Court Decision No. 232/Pid.B/2006/PN-BNA, December 18, 2006. The Constitutional Court announced its decision on July 16, 2007.
73 Private conversation with Jimly Asshiddiqie, May 28, 2008.
74 Ibid.
75 For a detailed analysis of the IMF involvement in steering the Indonesian economic policy, please see Thomas Pepinsky. *Economic Crises and the Breakdown of Authoritarian Regimes: Indonesia and Malaysia in Comparative Perspective.* (Cambridge: Cambridge University Press, 2009).
76 See Richard Robison and Vedi R. Hadiz. *Reorganising Power in Indonesia: The Politics of Oligarchy in an Age of Markets* (London: RoutledgeCurzon, 2004); See "The Indonesian Letter of Intent to IMF," March 16, 1999, http://www.imf.org/external/NP/LOI/1999/031699.htm; "The Attachment to Indonesian Letter of Intent to IMF," January 20, 2000, http://www.imf.org/external/np/loi/2000/idn/01/.
77 Jimly Asshiddiqie. "Konstitusi Kita Bukan Konstitusi Liberal" [Our Constitution Is Not a Liberal Constitution], *Kontan*, September 22, 2003.
78 Law No. 22 of 2001 on Oil and Gas; Law No. 20 of 2002 on Electricity Law; Law No. 24 of 2004 on Government Securities; and Law No. 7 of 2004 on Water Resources Law.
79 Article 33 of the 1945 Constitution.
80 Constitutional Court Decision No. 001-021-022/PUU-I/2003 (hereinafter the *Electricity Law* case).
81 *Undang Undang No. 20 Tahun 2002 tentang Ketenagalistrikan* (Law no. 20 of 2002 on Electricity).
82 Ibid., 332.
83 Ibid., 333.
84 Ibid., 334.

85 Ibid., 346.
86 Ibid., 335.
87 Ibid., 345.
88 The *Electricity Law* case, 345. The Court used the term "*hajat hidup orang banyak,*" and I translated it loosely as "to the common good."
89 Ibid., 347.
90 Ibid., 347.
91 Ibid., 350.
92 The Constitutional Court Decision No. 002/PUU-I/2003 (hereinafter the *Oil and Gas Law I* case).
93 Ibid., 33.
94 Ibid., 224.
95 Ibid., 222.
96 Ibid., 230.
97 Ibid., 230.
98 Zen Zanibar, a senior lecturer at Faculty of Law, University of Sriwijaya and a former assistant to the Chief Justice in the Constitutional Court, also shared a similar view that Asshiddiqie's dissertation strongly influenced the Court decision in the Electricity case. See Zen Zanibar. "Perkembangan Ketatanegaraan Dalam Pandangan Jimly Asshiddiqie yang Tercecer" [The Forgotten Thought of Jimly Asshiddiqie]. In *Konstitusi dan Ketatanegaraan Indonesia Kontemporer*, edited by Rafiqul-Umam Achmad, 473.
99 Private conversation with Jimly Asshiddiqie, July 31, 2006.
100 Ibid.
101 Ibid.
102 Ibid.
103 The Presidential Regulation No. 55 of 2005.
104 Letter from the Chief Justice of the Indonesian Constitutional Court to the President of the Republic of Indonesia, October 6, 2005 (copy on file with the author).
105 The President of Republic of Indonesia to the Chief Justice of Constitutional Court, October 14, 2005 (copy on file with the author).
106 Ibid.
107 Private conversation with Jimly Asshiddiqie, May 28, 2008.
108 Private conversation with Jimly Asshiddiqie, May 28, 2008.
109 The Constitutional Court Decision, Case No. 072-073 /PUU-II/2004 (hereinafter, the *KPUD* case).
110 See Law No. 32 of 2004 on the Regional Governance.
111 Ibid., 12–15.
112 The Indonesian 1945 Constitution, Art. 22E (5).
113 The *KPUD* case, 15–16.
114 Ibid., 16.
115 Ibid., 111.
116 Ibid., 110.
117 Ibid., 116.
118 Jimly Asshiddiqie. "*Mereka Bacanya Sepotong—sepotong*" [They Read the Decision Partially], *Republika* daily newspaper, March 26, 2005.
119 Ibid.
120 Ibid.
121 Ibid.
122 See Jimly Asshiddiqie. *The 2004 End of Year Speech*, 8–9; Jimly Asshiddiqie, *Konstitusi & Konstitutionalisme Indonesia* [Constitution and Constitutionalism in Indonesia] (Jakarta: Sekretariat Jenderal Mahkamah Konstitusi, 2006).

123 Jimly Asshiddiqie. "*Fungsi Lembaga Negara Harus Ditinjau*" [The Function of State Institution Should Be Evaluated], *Kompas* daily newspaper, August 3, 2006.
124 Ibid.
125 The Constitutional Court Decision No. 005/PUU-IV/2006 (hereinafter the *Judicial Commission* case).
126 See the 1945 Constitution, Art. 24B (1).
127 Law No. 22 of 2004 on the Judicial Commission, Art. 21.
128 The conflict between the Supreme Court and Judicial Commission began after the Supreme Court disregarded the Judicial Commission's recommendation to give administrative sanctions to the judges of the West Java High Court, who issued a controversial ruling about the Depok mayoral election dispute. The conflict escalated when former president Soeharto's half-brother, Probosutedjo, claimed that the Supreme Court Chief Justice Bagir Manan received Rp 5 billion (U.S. $ 500,000) in a graft case involving reforestation funds. In response to the testimony of Probosutedjo, the Judicial Commission recommended that all of the Supreme Court Justices, including Chief Justice Bagir Manan, should be investigated. See "Supreme Court Delays Judicial Commission's Recommendations." The *Jakarta Post*, September 24, 2005; "Probosutedjo Admits to Bribing Judges." The *Jakarta Post*, October 12, 2005; "House Speaker Backs Performance Review of 49 Justices." The *Jakarta Post*, January 7, 2006.
129 "Commission to Grill 13 Justices." The *Jakarta Post*, February 20, 2006.
130 Apart from these three top officials, the Judicial Commission also summoned Titi Nurmala Siagian, Widayanto Sastrohardjo, Parman Soeparman, Artidjo Alkostar, Arbijoto, German Hediarto, Arbijoto, Tjung Abdul Mutalib, and Usman Karim.
131 See the *Judicial Commission* case, 8.Article 24B (1) of the 1945 Constitution provides that "there shall be an independent Judicial Commission which shall possess the authority to propose candidate for the Supreme Court justices and shall possess authority to maintain the honor, dignity, and behavior of judges."
132 Ibid.
133 Ibid., 11.
134 Ibid., 182.
135 Ibid., 187.
136 Ibid., 193.
137 Ibid., 201.
138 Ibid.
139 Jimly Asshiddiqie. *Sengketa Kewenangan Antarlembaga Negara* [State Institutional Dispute] (Jakarta: Konstitusi Press, 2005).
140 Ibid., 153–154
141 The former Deputy Minister of Justice Denny Indrayana even stated that the Chief Justice simply copied his treatise into the text of the Judicial Commission case. See Denny Indrayana, statement in public discussion "*Putusan Kontroversi MK tentang MA vs. KY dan Implikasinya terhadap Ikthiar Peradilan di Indonesia*" [The Controversy of the Constitutional Court Decision on the Conflict between the Supreme Court and Judicial Commission and Its Implication to the Indonesian Judiciary] Jakarta, August 31, 2006.
142 See Saldi Isra. "Hakim Konstitusi Juga Hakim" [The Constitutional Court Justice is also a Judge], *Kompas*, August 28, 2006; Irfan R. Hutagalung. "Putusan MK dan Kebingungan Pemahaman" [The Constitutional Court Decision and Misunderstanding], *Kompas*, August 28, 2006; Bivitri Susanti. "Benang Kusut Lembaga Peradilan" [The Entanglement of Judicial Institution], *Kompas*, August 29, 2006; M. Hadi Shubhan, "Problematika Yuridis Kewenangan KY" [Legal Problem of the Judicial Commission Authority], *Kompas*, August 29, 2006.

143 The *Judicial Commission* case, 201.
144 Asshiddiqie. *2004 End of Year Speech.*
145 Jimly Asshiddiqie. *Pokok—Pokok Hukum Tata Negara Indonesia Pasca Reformasi* [The Principle of Indonesian Constitutional Law in Post *Reformasi*] (Jakarta: Bhuana Ilmu Populer, 2007).
146 In the decade after the fall of the military government, at least eleven special courts were established by the legislature, such as the Commercial Court, the Human Rights Courts, the Anti-Corruption Court, the Fishery Court, the Labor Court, the Tax Court, the Juvenile Court, the Maritime Court, the Syariah Court for Aceh Province, the Customary Court for Papua Province, and the Traffic Court.
147 Asshiddiqie. *The Principle of Indonesian Constitutional Law*, 528.
148 Ibid., 529–530.
149 Government in Lieu of Law No. 2 of 2006 on the Postponement of the Creation of the Fisheries Court.
150 Asshiddiqie. *Pokok—Pokok Hukum Tata Negara*, 529–530.
151 The Constitutional Court Decision No. 012-016-019/PUU-IV/2006 (hereinafter the *Mulyana Kusumah* case).
152 See "House to Replace KPU Members Amid Graft Probe." The *Jakarta Post*, March 3, 2005.
153 See "8.5 years, Huge Fine Sought for Ex-KPU Chief." The *Jakarta Post*, November 17, 2005.
154 The *Mulyana Kusumah* case, 14–15.
155 Ibid.
156 Ibid., 282–283.
157 Ibid., 288–289.
158 Ibid.
159 Ibid., 295.
160 Ibid., 289.
161 Refly Harun. "Hakim Konstitusi Kelas Dua" [Second Class Justices], *Koran Tempo*, August 22, 2003.
162 Mukthie Fadjar's publication on constitutional law came out after his appointment as the Constitutional Court Justice. See Abdul Mukthie Fadjar. *Hukum Konstitusi & Mahkamah Konstitusi* [Constitutional Law and Constitutional Court] (Jakarta: Konstitusi Press; & Yogyakarta: Citra Media, 2006).
163 Palguna did not pursue his doctoral studies until he left the Court in 2008. He completed his doctoral studies at the University of Indonesia in 2011. In 2015, President Joko Widodo reappointed him as an associate justice of the Constitutional Court.
164 Marzuki's scholarly publication on constitutional law came out after his appointment as Constitutional Court Justice, see Laica Marzuki. *Berjalan Jalan di Ranah Hukum:* Pikiran-Pikiran Lepas Laica Marzuki [The Thought of Laica Marzuki] (Jakarta: Konstitusi Pers, 2005).
165 Asshiddiqie claimed that he had published more than 43 books throughout his academic career.Jimly Asshiddiqie, statement at the Opening Plenary Workshop on "the Constitutional Court & Democracy in Indonesia: Judging the First Decade." The University of New South Wales, Sydney, December 11, 2014.
166 Jimly Asshiddiqie. *Model—Model Pengujian Konstitusional di Berbagai Negara* [Constitutional Review in the Various Countries] (Jakarta: Konstitusi Press, 2005).
167 Private conversation with an associate justice of the Constitutional Court, July 28, 2006.
168 Private conversation with a senior associate justice of the Constitutional Court, May 28, 2008.
169 Private conversation with a senior associate justice, May 27, 2008.

4 (Un)heroic quasi-weak-form review

Prelude

Many people often compare the Greek heroic tales of the *Iliad* and *Odyssey* with the *Ramayana* and *Mahabharata* tales of the Hindu tradition.[1] Ramayana is the tale of how King Rama regained his wife Sita from the giant King Rahwana; Mahabharata tells of the great conflict and war between the Pandawa brothers and their cousins, the Kurawas. These heroic tales remain alive in modern day Indonesia, ranging from novels or comic books to the shadow play performances (*wayang*) given in connection with religious and life-cycle events such as births, weddings, circumcisions, and deaths, especially in Javanese society.[2]

Central to the epic *Mahabharata* are the heroic actions of the Pandawa brothers in the great *Bharata* war. But there is an important episode in the *Mahabharata* that displays a different kind of heroism shown by the Pandawa brothers: their 13 years of exile. In fact, the exile of the Pandawa brothers was the basis of the heroic plot of the epic. It all began when the Kurawa clan, headed by Duryudhana, was envious of the success of the Pandawa brothers at their kingdom Amartha.[3] The Kurawa clan challenged the Pandawa brothers to a dice game in the hope of winning the Pandawas' kingdom. Eventually, the Pandawas lost the game, and they were condemned to 12 years of exile in the forest and a thirteenth year to be spent incognito; if their cover was blown during the thirteenth year, another cycle of 13 years would ensue.

The forest exile culminating in the thirteenth year spent incognito can be viewed as a different sort of heroism. The Pandawas spent the thirteenth year assuming a variety of concealed identities in the court of Virata. Yudistira assumes the identity of game entertainer, Bima becomes a cook, Arjuna teaches dance and music as a eunuch, Nakula tends horses, and Sadewa herds cows. Their disguise as ordinary people is a complete reversal of their strength and heroism, as it makes them appear weak and powerless. In fact, they leave their weapons hanging on a tree outside of town. The fact that the Pandawas are able to accept their powerlessness gracefully is a sign of their heroic self-control. Through the exile, the Pandawas show themselves as models of the humble hero. Only humble heroes would be able to survive the exile and to live in humility. Nevertheless, when it becomes necessary for them to do battle in the defense of King Virata as the thirteenth year is ending, they resume their militaristic heroic identity.

The development of the Indonesian Constitutional Court is, in my view, similar to the episode of the Pandawa brothers in exile. In previous chapters, I explained how the heroic leadership of Chief Justice Asshiddiqie led the Court to issue many decisions that challenged governmental policies and pushed the government to abide by the Constitution. But like the Pandawa brothers in exile, Asshiddiqie knew how to minimize the Court's involvement in politically sensitive areas by tempering the remedial measures of the Court's decisions.

This chapter explores in more detail the less heroic or seemingly unheroic actions of the Constitutional Court. This chapter presents an interesting phenomenon that is unique to the Indonesian Constitutional Court. Under the leadership of Chief Justice Jimly Asshiddiqie, the Court began to adopt a quasi-weak form of judicial review, in which the Court allowed the law to remain valid as long as it was applied or implemented in the way the Court interpreted it. Like the Pandawa brothers who remain incognito in exile, the quasi-weak-form review makes the Court appear weak, but it is nonetheless a smart strategy in many ways, because the Court could issue ambitious constitutional interpretations without involving itself in a confrontation with the Executive and Legislative branches.

A weak judicial review approach

In analyzing the less heroic decisions of the Indonesian Constitutional Court, I would like to turn first to the notion of weak-form judicial review. The concept of weak-form review emerged in some of Mark Tushnet's articles on an alternative model of judicial review[4], and later this concept matured in Tushnet's *Weak Court's Strong Rights*.[5] The concept of weak judicial review has also been known by several other names, such as the ***dialogic judicial review model***[6] and the ***new Commonwealth model***.[7]

Weak judicial review stands for the idea that constitutional limitations can be enforced without bestowing a final and exclusive role to the judiciary. Under weak judicial review, the courts' interpretations merit great respect and carry a lot of weight, but their decisions can at times be overridden or rejected by legislatures. For instance, Tushnet characterizes the Constitutional Court of South Africa's socio-economic rights enforcement as a "weak-form" review because the Court allocates significant discretion to the legislature to enforce socio-economic rights based on the significant budgetary implications.[8] Thus, weak judicial review can be seen as a middle path between judicial supremacy and legislative power.

These theories on weak-form judicial review have focused almost entirely on the Commonwealth common law jurisdictions. One exception comes from Mark Tushnet and Rosalind Dixon, who have identified different models of "weak-form review" in civil law constitutional traditions as well.[9] Dixon and Tushnet posit that the closest model of weak-form review exists in Mongolia.[10] The Mongolian model has two components of review. First, a three-person panel of judges considers constitutional challenges to legislation. If the panel finds the law unconstitutional, the court then sends the decision to the nation's Parliament. In the second stage of review, the Parliament considers whether to accept or reject the court's interpretation.[11]

Tushnet and Dixon also identify the notion of quasi-weak-form review, under which the court may wholly defer to the legislature's interpretation of the constitution; or persist in its interpretation but acknowledge the legislature's power to disagree; or defer to the legislature's interpretation as displacing its own.[12] Tushnet and Dixon point out that the model of quasi-weak-form review exists in Japan. As evidence, Tushnet and Dixon cite many scholars who describe the Japanese Supreme Court as "conservative" because the Court rarely exercises its power of constitutional review to invalidate legislation.[13]

Apart from in Mongolia and Japan, the model of weak-form review also exists in South Korea. Although South Korea did not appear in Tushnet and Dixon's list, the South Korean Constitutional Court has put forth different types of constitutional remedies that fall under the category of quasi-weak-form review.[14] The first type of remedy involves declaring the law "unconformable to the Constitution," which means that the Court acknowledges a law as unconstitutional, but it remains valid while the National Assembly revises the law within a specified time period.[15] The second type of remedy is called "unconstitutional in certain contexts," which occurs whenever the Court prohibits a particular way of interpreting the law as unconstitutional, while upholding other interpretations of the same law as constitutional.[16] The third type of remedy is referred to as "constitutional in a certain context," which means that a law is constitutional if the government interprets it in a certain way.[17]

Indonesia as a civil-law country also shows that there is a quasi-weak-form review that could bolster constitutional review in new democracies. It is worth exploring the development of quasi-weak-form review in Indonesia because it will contribute to theory of weak-form review from the perspective of a civil-law constitutional tradition. The concept of quasi-weak-form review in Indonesia is unique because no formal mechanism exists that would allow political branches of the government to examine judicial rulings and to override the Court's decision by ordinary majority vote. In other words, the Court still has the exclusive power of constitutional review, but the judges often come out with a constitutional interpretation without involving themselves in complex political decision making.

Before proceeding further, let us consider Mark Tushnet's argument on weak remedies. Tushnet's analysis is helpful in better understanding the notion of quasi-weak-form review in Indonesia. Tushnet argues that there are two kinds of remedy: strong remedies and weak remedies.[18] The strong remedies are mandatory injunctions, in which the Court identifies certain goals for the government to achieve and sets specific deadlines for the accomplishment of those goals.[19] The weak remedies may come in certain forms—first and foremost is the declaratory remedy, in which the Court only has the authority to issue a declaratory judgment on the constitutionality of a statute.[20] The second type of weak remedy is whenever the Court requires government officials to develop plans that hold out some promise of eliminating the constitutional violation within a reasonably short period of time.[21]

This chapter argues that the experience of judicial review in Indonesia under the chairmanship of Asshiddiqie suggests that the Court frequently employed weak-form remedies insofar as the Court could provide a weak remedy but not resolve the injury that was suffered by the claimant—as, for example, when the Court declared that a terrorist must remain in prison despite the Court's decision to overturn the Anti-Terrorism Law that became the basis of his conviction,[22] which will be discussed in the following section of this chapter.

Prospective ruling

One of the driving forces behind the issuance of the weak remedies in the Indonesian Constitutional Court is a statutory limitation that constrains the Court—namely, that the effects of the Court's decision only begin on the day of the announcement of the decision.[23] In other words, the Court's rulings have a prospective effect.

The first case that involved the issue of weak remedy was the Constitutional Court's decision in the *Communist Party* case.[24] As explained in the previous chapter, the case involved the constitutionality of a provision in the General Election Law that barred former members of the Communist Party and its affiliate organizations from becoming legislators. The Court accepted the argument from the claimants and nullified the provision in the General Election Law that barred former Communists from becoming members of parliament. Nevertheless, in a press conference the day after the Constitutional Court issued the decision, Chief Justice Jimly Asshiddiqie announced that the decision would not have an immediate effect, as it would come into force for the 2009 General Elections.[25] Asshiddiqie explained that the decision had no immediate effect because the deadline for submitting legislative candidates for the 2004 election had passed by the time the Court issued its decision on February 24, 2004.[26]

The Court repeated this approach in the *Bali Bombing* case.[27] The *Bali Bombing* case involved the issue of the constitutionality of Law No. 16 of 2003, which allowed retroactive application of the Anti-Terrorism Law to the Bali bombing incident on October 12, 2002, when a suicide bomber detonated a high-explosive bomb inside a nightclub in the tourist district of Kuta, Bali. The claimant in the *Bali Bombing* case was Masykur Abdul Kadir, and he was on trial for his involvement in that suicide bombing.[28] In the criminal trial, Abdul Kadir was found guilty under Law No. 15 of 2003 on Anti-Terrorism for assisting the bomber, and he received 15 years' incarceration. Abdul Kadir filed a claim to the Constitutional Court and challenged the constitutionality of Law No. 16 of 2003, which authorized the police, prosecutors, and judges to apply the Anti-Terrorism Law No. 15 of 2003 to the *Bali Bombing* case, considering that the Law was not in force at the time the bomber prepared and detonated the bomb.[29]

On July 23, 2004, the Indonesian Constitutional Court—in a 5–4 decision—ruled that Law No. 16 of 2003, which allowed retroactive application of the

Anti-Terrorism Law, was unconstitutional. The Court majority declared the Law to be unconstitutional on several grounds. First, the Court held that the existing criminal code already covered an ordinary crime like the Bali bombing case.[30] Second, the Court held that the application of Law was contrary to the principle of separation of powers in the 1945 Constitution.[31] The Court explained that the legislators have no authority to apply statute as general and abstract norms to concrete cases, but rather it is the duty of the administration to apply abstract norms to concrete cases through administrative decisions.[32]

Surprisingly, in a press conference after announcing the decision, Chief Justice Jimly Asshiddiqie stated that the bombers must remain in jail because the effects of the Court's decision would only begin on the day of the announcement of the decision.[33] The chief justice explained further that the convict would not be able to enjoy the benefit of the favorable Constitutional Court decision.[34] In other words, the decision would only prevent future investigations, prosecutions and convictions under Law No. 16 of 2003, and the claimant, Masykur Abdul Kadir, could not enjoy the benefit of winning despite the Court's decision to issue a favorable decision for him.[35]

Having announced the effect of the Court's ruling through a press conference twice, the Court changed its approach in the *West Papuan* case,[36] in which the Court explicitly pronounced the effect of its decision in the body of its judgment.[37] Papua, the most easterly province of Indonesia, is home to a secessionist movement that has been involved in a struggle for independence for 40 years. As an attempt to weaken the independence movement, the Central Government divided the region into three provinces: Papua, West Papua, and Central Papua. The Central Government established the West Papua province in February 2003. After violent clashes on August 24–25, 2003, which left several people dead, however, the Central Government put plans on hold to further divide the province. John Ibo, the chair of the Papuan Provincial Parliament, filed a petition for judicial review to the Constitutional Court and claimed that the division of Papua was unconstitutional.

The Court decided to accept the claimant's request and ruled that Law No. 45 of 1999 on the division of Papua is unconstitutional. But the Court included an important statement at the end of its judgment, namely that the establishment of West Papuan province was lawful despite the unconstitutionality of the statute.[38] Chief Justice Asshiddiqie, again, had to explain the Court's decision through a press statement after the governors of the Papuan and West Papuan provinces begged for an explanation from the Court on how to interpret the decision. The chief justice explained that the West Papuan province already existed before the Court issued its decision, and therefore it would remain lawful. The establishment of the province of Central Papua, however, had not yet been realized, and therefore the Central Papuan province would not come into existence because the Law had since been declared unconstitutional.[39] Again, the Court issued a mind-bending logic decision, in which the claimant could not fully enjoy the benefit of winning despite the declaration of the unconstitutionality of the statute.

The Court further reaffirmed the use of weak remedies in the *Electricity Law* case, in which the Court invalidated the entire statute because it was proven to be inconsistent with Article 33.[40] At the end of its judgment, the Court stated:

> [A]ll agreement or contract and business permit in electricity industry that has been signed and issued based on Law no. 20 of 2002 on the Electricity shall remain valid until the expiration date of the contract or agreement and business permit.[41]

The Court explained that it should take such a measure "to prevent misunderstanding and doubt that may cause legal uncertainty in the electricity sector."[42]

The Court's holdings thus confirm that the Court could issue a weak remedy by pronouncing the consistency, or lack thereof, of a statute with the Constitution, and yet it would have no effect to rectify the injury suffered by the claimant. In the *Communist Party* case, the former Communist involved did not immediately enjoy the benefit of winning because the claimant would not be able to run as a legislative candidate in 2004; the decision would only apply to the 2009 General Election and beyond. In the *Bali Bombing* case, the claimant remained in jail despite the Court having ruled that the statute that had been the basis for his conviction was invalid. In the *West Papuan* case, the petitioner, John Ibo, filed for judicial review because, as the speaker of the Papuan Regional Parliament, he did not want to see the province divided into three different provinces. Nevertheless, Ibo did not enjoy the benefit of winning because the Court decision did not nullify the existence of West Papuan province, which he opposed. In the *Electricity Law* case, the nongovernmental organizations (NGOs) wanted to see the Court quash the privatization of the electricity industry, but the Court allowed all of the existing government contracts with the private sector to remain valid.

After the Court had issued its explicit holding in the *West Papuan* and the *Electricity Law* cases, it therefore become doctrine that the Court's decisions would not necessarily remedy the injuries suffered by the claimants. For instance, in the *Lèse Majesté case*, the applicants could not enjoy the benefit of winning although the Court had issued a favorable decision for them. As explained in previous chapter, Eggi Sudjana and Pandapotan Lubis were facing charges of insulting the president in criminal court proceedings. Both Sudjana and Lubis asked the Court to nullify the *lèse majesté* articles. The Constitutional Court accepted the complaint and nullified the *lèse majesté* articles. Despite the judgment of unconstitutionality, however, the District Court continued the criminal trial proceeding and sentenced the claimants to three months in jail. The District Court concluded that although the Constitutional Court had nullified the *lèse majesté* articles, the Constitutional Court decision only applies to future cases.

As mentioned earlier, one of the reasons that the Court took such an approach is because of a statutory limitation in which the Court's decisions only have a prospective effect. Another plausible explanation for the Court's taking such an approach is because this approach helps the Court to decide the cases without involving itself in complex political decision-making. For instance, in the

Bali Bombing case, by declaring that the statute was unconstitutional but that the claimant must remain in jail, the Court did not interfere with the government's effort to engage in a war on terror because the statute would still apply for all incidents from 2003 onward. In the *Communist Party* case, the Court did not want to interfere with the electoral process, as the deadline for submitting legislative candidates for the 2004 election had passed when the Court issued the decision on February 24, 2004. Similarly, in the *Electricity Law* case, the Court did not want to interfere with existing contracts that were part of the government's privatization program.

In the *West Papuan* case, Chief Justice Asshiddiqie explained further that the Court has limited jurisdiction in law-making processes, and therefore it should defer to the other branches of government. Chief Justice Asshiddiqie stated, "it is the government that has authority to decide further regulations on the establishment of Central Papuan province."[43] In other words, the Court respects its limits as a judicial branch, and, consequently, it worked to resolve cases without interfering with the authority of other branches of government.

In sum, the Court managed to mitigate the impact of its bold decisions through the issuance of weak remedies. The combination of statutory rules on prospective effect and the Court's minimalist approach led the Court to apply quasi-weak-form review, which enabled the institution to avoid confrontation with the Executive and Legislative branches while at the same time keeping its authority to issue constitutional interpretation. In addition to these factors, there is another aspect of the Court's structure that facilitates the application of quasi-weak-form review, that is, abstract statutory review. I will reserve the discussion of this issue for the final part of this chapter.

"Conditionally constitutional" decisions

The evolution of "conditionally constitutional" decisions

Apart from the issuance of weak remedy based on the prospective effect, the Court could also issue a weak remedy by refusing to declare a statute unconstitutional, and rather asking the government to interpret the statute in a certain way or prescribing specific directives to aid the government in interpreting the law. The Court called this approach a "conditionally constitutional" decision. The Court first utilized its "conditionally constitutional" remedy in the *Water Resources Law I* case.[44] The case involved the question of the constitutionality of the Water Resources Law, which accorded private corporations control over Indonesia's water resources.[45] The Court rejected the claimant's petition to declare the Water Resources Law unconstitutional, but in its dicta, the Court stated:

> The government must respect, protect and fulfill the right to clean water based on the guidelines provided by the opinion of the Constitutional Court. Therefore if the Law is interpreted differently to the Court's directive, then it can be reviewed further (conditionally constitutional).[46]

In other words, the Court viewed that the Law is constitutional as long as the government implements the Law according to the Court's interpretation, but if the government implements the law in different way, the claimant may challenge the statute for further review.[47]

Specifically, the Court provided guidelines on how the Executive branch should manage the water resources.[48] The Court stated that the government had obligations to fulfill citizens' access to clean water in several ways. First, they must issue licenses for water usage and provide daily supply and irrigation for community farming (*pertanian rakyat*). Second, regional-owned water companies should be positioned as the state's operational unit, not profit-oriented companies. Finally, the responsibility for providing clean water primarily belonged to central and regional governments. Private enterprises and cooperatives were only permitted to participate if the government was itself unable to provide fresh drinking water.[49]

Similarly, in the *Open Pit Mining* case,[50] the Court rejected the petition to nullify a government's decision to allow open-pit mining in forestry conservation areas, but expressed through its dicta that the Amendment of the Forestry Law is only conditionally constitutional. In 1999, the government enacted the Forestry Law, which banned open-pit mining in protected forests. The Mining and Energy Ministry, prompted by the concerns of mining investors, later pushed for the law to be revised. The government passed the Amendment of the Forestry Law, which provided that:

> Every license or contract for mining exploration in forestry areas that already existed before the enactment of Law no. 41 of 1999 on the Forestry, should be respected until the expiration date of the license or contract.[51]

Consequently, 13 giant mining companies were permitted to resume mining operations in protected forest areas. The claimants were environmental NGOs and individuals that challenged the Amendment of the Forestry Law. The applicants argued that open-pit mining in forestry conservation areas would have negative impacts on the environment, as well as on economic, social, and cultural life in the protected areas. Therefore, the claimants argued that the government had abandoned its constitutional duty to bring the greatest prosperity to the people of Indonesia under Article 33, instead of siding with foreign investors.

The Court held that it agreed with the claimants that mining exploration in a forestry conservation area would harm the environment, but it decided to reject the claimant's petition.[52] The Court wrote in dicta that:

> [T]he statute is not unconstitutional as long as the license and contract that already existed before the enactment of Law no. 41 of 1999 on Forestry comply with the Law.[53]

In other words, the Court prescribed that the existing license and mining contract must comply with the Forestry Law. Specifically, the Court provided a directive to the government that it must set up a program

> To monitor, to evaluate, to supervise and to modify the requirement for working contract (*kontrak karya*) and especially to anticipate the negative impact of mining activating that may harm the environment, plus an imposing obligation to rehabilitate or minimize the adverse impact on future generations ... including the commitment to repeal the license in mining industry whenever there is a breach of the licensing requirement.[54]

The Court therefore expressed through its dicta that the Law is constitutional under two conditions. First, the multinational company shall modify the contract according to the new statutory provision. Second, the government shall order the multinational mining company to minimize or restore the environmental damage caused by its exploration and, if necessary, the government shall repeal the working permit to those companies.[55] In sum, the Court refused to declare the challenged statute as unconstitutional, but it put forth certain directives for the government to implement the Forestry Law in a constitutional manner.

The Court continued to insert the "conditionally constitutional" remedy in the *Dawud Jatmiko* case.[56] Dawud Jatmiko filed for judicial review while he was facing criminal trial in the East Jakarta District Court. The Eradication of Corruption Law states:

> [A]nyone who illegally commits an act to enrich oneself or another person or a corporation that can create losses to the state's finances or state economy would face sentences of life imprisonment or minimum imprisonment of 4 (four) years and a maximum of 20 (twenty) years.[57]

Jatmiko argued that the term *can* in the provision regarding the creation of losses to the state had been interpreted widely by the prosecutor and thereby created legal uncertainty, which was a violation of the constitutional guarantee of legal certainty under Article 28D (1) of the Constitution.[58] The Court stated that the issue of the term *can* is a matter of implementation of regulations by the legal apparatus instead of being a constitutional issue. It was a matter of how the losses to the state's finances or state economy could be proved and calculated, and therefore the conclusion regarding such losses should be determined by someone who has expertise in the field.[59] The Court then expressed in its dicta that the statute is conditionally constitutional, as long as the prosecutor interprets the statute according to the Constitutional Court's directive, which includes involving experts to determine losses to the state.[60]

On April 14, 2008, the Court issued the decision in the *Film Censorship* case, in which the Court began to insert the declaration of "conditionally constitutional" in its holdings.[61] The claimants were an actress, movie directors, and producers who challenged the constitutionality of the Film Industry Law, especially the provisions that authorized the Censorship Board to censor films.[62] The claimants argued that the rules on censorship violated the freedom of expression as guaranteed by the Constitution. The Court held that the provisions on censorship were behind the "spirit of the times" (*semangat zamannya*), and that there was an urgency to pass a new law that was compatible with the spirit of democracy and respect for human rights.[63] Nevertheless, the Court considered that striking down the censorship provisions would create a vacuum of law and legal uncertainty, and, therefore, the Court held that the provisions shall remain in force, as long as the Censorship Board implements its authority by respecting democracy and human rights.[64] Thus, the Court held that censorship regulation and the existence of the Censorship Board were "conditionally constitutional."

Conditionally constitutional decisions in the electoral law cases

Before the Court's decision in the *Film Censorship* case, it first applied the conditionally constitutional ruling in judicial review of the electoral process.[65] On December 11, 2007, the Court issued a conditionally constitutional ruling in the *Political Crime I* case.[66] In this case, political activists challenged a provision in the Presidential Election Law that barred persons who had been previously convicted of an offense that imposes 5 years or more of incarceration from becoming a presidential candidate.[67] One of the claimants was Budiman Sudjatmiko, a former chairman of the People's Democratic Party, a leading opposition group during the military dictatorship. The New Order regime charged Sudjatmiko under the Anti-Subversive Act, and he was ordered to serve 13 years' incarceration. Sudjatmiko argued that the Law was unconstitutional because it did not make any distinction between politically motivated incarceration and general incarceration. The Court, however, held that the Law was constitutional as long as the prohibition does not include political crimes and minor offenses.[68] The Court defined a political crime as involving a political expression or political view that was contrary to the political view of the previous New Order Military regime.[69]

In the *Political Crime II* case,[70] the claimant challenged the Legislative Election Law, which provided that a candidate for a national legislator cannot be previously convicted of a crime with a penalty of 5 years' incarceration or more.[71] The Court re-affirmed its holding in the *Political Crime I* case that the Law was constitutional so long as the prohibition did not include political crimes and minor offenses. The Court, however, did not define the scope and meaning of minor offenses, as the claimant here had committed aggravated assault rather than a political crime.[72]

In the *DPD Residence* case,[73] some members of the Regional Representative Council (*Dewan Perwakilan Daerah*—DPD)[74] challenged the General Election Law, which did not require a candidate for the DPD to be domiciled in the province where he/she was seeking election.[75] The Court held that the Constitution required residency in a province for a DPD candidate, and therefore the requirement should be explicitly included in the General Election Law.[76] The Court further held, however, that the Law is conditionally constitutional, so long as it is interpreted to include the requirement that a DPD candidate must have a residence in the province where he/she seeks election.[77] In short, the Court recommended the General Election Commission to require a candidate for the DPD to be domiciled in the province where he/she was seeking election.

The Court issued a modification of its conditionally constitutional decisions in the *Independent Candidate* case.[78] The claimant was a legislator from Lombok Provincial Parliament who was unable to run in the West Nusa Tenggara governor election because the Regional Governance (*Pemerintahan Daerah—Pemda*) Law required that gubanatorial candidates needed to secure a nomination of political parties or an alliance of political parties that had either 15 percent of the seats in the regional parliament or 15 percent of the vote in the last local election.[79] The claimant was an independent candidate with no party backers, and therefore was legally barred from running for governor.

The claimant argued that the Regional Governance Law was inconsistent with the equal protection clause of the Constitution [Article 28D (1)] because it did not allow independent candidates to run in regional elections. In making the argument, the claimant referred to the provincial election in special territory Nanggroe Aceh Darussalam, which allowed independent candidates to run for local elections as stated in the 2006 Aceh Governance Law;[80] this arose as the consequence of a 2005 peace deal between the Indonesian government and the Aceh rebel movement.

The Court ruled for the claimant and held that the participation of independent candidates in regional elections should be allowed in other provinces outside Naggroe Aceh Darussalam province.[81] The Court's decision was meant to allow independent candidates to run in regional elections in the entire country; however, the Court realized that it had no authority to add new provisions in the statute that enabled independent candidates to run in regional elections. The Court ruled, "the declaration of unconstitutionality will not accomplish the goal of bringing an independent candidate to run in local elections."[82] Therefore, the Court deferred to the legislature to make a new provision that allows independent candidates to run in regional elections nationwide. The Court stated:

> The Court is not a lawmaking institution that can modify legislation by creating new laws. The Court could strike down the challenged provisions to make the statute consistent with the Constitution. But for a new regulation, it is up to lawmakers to formulate it.[83]

In sum, the Court refused to declare the Law unconstitutional, but it issued a directive for the legislature to prepare a new law to allow an independent candidate to run in regional elections.

After the Court announced its decision, there was a significant debate within the government on how to respond to the Court's decision. There was a debate as to whether the government should issue a government regulation in lieu of law, amend the law, or let the General Election Commission issue a regulation on independent candidates.[84] The debate arose because not only did the government not know what to do in response, but neither was it keen to implement the Court's decision. Politicians were willing to concede in Aceh for the sake of peace, but they did not want to concede in order to allow an independent candidate to run in regional elections nationwide. Traditional politicians from major political parties were opposed to independent candidates in the first place, because they saw independent candidates as a threat to the party establishment.

Having realized that his decision was being ignored by the government, Chief Justice Asshiddiqie went immediately to meet the president. They met in the airport before the president left the country for a foreign trip. The day after the meeting, Chief Justice Asshiddiqie held a press conference, at which he confirmed that the president and the DPR would soon issue a regulation that would regulate the participation of independent candidates.[85] Furthermore, Asshiddiqie tried to assure the public that the Court's ruling on independent candidates could be implemented in January 2008 (the Court announced its decision in July 2007).[86] Nevertheless, politicians kept delaying their action, and Chief Justice Asshiddiqie kept reminding the government that they should take action immediately.[87] It was not until April 2008 that the government and the House of Representatives (DPR) passed the Amendment to the Regional Election Law and set the rules for independent candidates.[88]

In sum, the Court solidified its doctrine on conditionally constitutional decisions through a series of judicial reviews of the electoral process. In those cases, the Court refused to invalidate the statutes, but it prescribed some directives for the government or the General Election Commission to interpret the law in a certain way.

"Progressive realization" in the right-to-education cases

As explained in Chapter 1, in a comparative context, courts in newer democracies sometimes apply the doctrine of "progressive realization" in the interpretation and enforcement of socio-economic rights. The idea has its origins in Article 2 of the International Covenant on Economic Social and Cultural Rights, which provides that states must progressively achieve the full realization of the rights in the Covenant.[89] The Indonesian Constitutional Court lent itself well to applying the doctrine of progressive realization in a series a series of right-to-education cases.

The crux of the matter of the right-to-education cases is the Fourth Amendment of the Constitution, which provides the education budget clause, "the state shall prioritize the budget for education to a minimum of 20 percent of the State Budget."[90] The Court then had to deal with a series of litigations that asked the Court to interpret the meaning of the education budget clause. In the *Education Budget II case*,[91] the claimant—the Union of Indonesian Elementary and Middle School Teachers (*Persatuan Guru Republik Indonesia*—PGRI)—challenged the constitutionality of the Law on the State Budget for Fiscal Year 2006, which allocated an education budget of 9.1 percent of the total budget.[92] The Court held that Article 31(4) is imperative and therefore that the government should fulfill the requirement without any further delay.[93] Nevertheless, the Court held that it would not declare the law unconstitutional because that would create chaos. Instead, the Court asked the Executive branch to transfer surplus from the State Budget to the education budget.[94] In other words, the Court refused to declare the Budget Law 2006 unconstitutional but instead issued a directive for the Executive to do something to fulfill its constitutional mandate.

Both the Executive and Legislature, however, ignored the Court's decision requiring them to transfer the surplus to the education budget. Consequently, the PGRI (the teachers' union) went back to the Court to challenge the Law on the State Budget for the Fiscal Year 2007.[95] The PGRI challenged the allocation of an education budget for that year that was only 11.8 percent of the total State Budget. The claimants argued again that this percentage did not comply with Article 31(4).[96] In the *Education Budget III* case,[97] the Court again ruled for the claimant. Nevertheless, the Court decided to defer to the legislature to fix the defect in the State Budget Law, with the Court holding:

> It was the lawmakers [who] should modify the State Budget to make it comply with the Constitution. The Court has no authority to push the lawmakers to change the State Budget, but the Court decision should stimulate the lawmakers to implement the Constitutional mandate.[98]

Therefore, the Court admitted it had no authority to force the legislature to do its job, but rather it could only call attention to what the Constitution required of the legislature. In this case, the Court agreed that the legislature was constitutionally bound to allocate 20 percent of the State Budget to education.

After the PGRI challenged the State Budget for Fiscal Year of 2007, two individual claimants also went to the Court to question the same law but on different grounds.[99] But the climax in this series of prominent education budget cases reached the Court in 2008. The case was significant because it related to the power struggle inside the Court at the end of the tenure of Chief Justice Asshiddiqie.[100] I will explain the issue of the power struggle in Chapter 6; the current chapter will solely focus on the Court's decision. On August 13, 2008, Chief Justice Asshiddiqie led the Court to issue the *Education Budget V* case.[101] The PGRI went back to the Court to challenge the Law on the State Budget for Fiscal Year 2008, which allocated an education budget of 15.6 percent. The Court noted that it had previously issued four decisions and that, apparently, the Executive and Legislature kept ignoring them.[102] The Court considered that it had given sufficient time for the lawmakers to fulfill their constitutional duty and that it was time for the Court to declare the State Budget unconstitutional.[103] The Court ruled that the president and the DPR were responsible for deliberate defiance of the Constitution and demanded that the Executive prepare the full allocation of the education budget in the 2009 cycle. The Court, however, still allowed the underfunded budget to stand until the 2009 budget cycle took effect, arguing that a delay was necessary "to avoid governmental disaster."[104] The Court further held that if the future State Budget Law failed to correspond to Article 31(4), it should be declared unconstitutional based on the Court's decision in the *Education Budget V* case.[105]

In the aftermath of the *Education Budget V* case, Chief Justice Asshiddiqie suspected that the Yudhoyono administration had orchestrated his removal due to the Court's declaring that the State Budget was unconstitutional.[106] The Court decided the *Education Budget V* case on August 13, 2008, and Asshiddiqie believes that the decision prompted the Yudhoyono administration to plot his removal at the election of a chief justice that took place on August 20, resulting in Mohammad Mahfud's election as second chief justice. I will address this issue in more detail in Chapter 6.

Regardless of any plot against Chief Justice Asshiddiqie, the Court's decisions in the education budget–related cases show that the declaration of unconstitutionality need not mean that laws became null and void, but rather that the Court can still allow laws to be valid for a limited period of time. Initially, the approach was successful in helping the Court avoid confrontation with the government. The Court did not declare the education budget unconstitutional, but it issued some directive for the government to fulfil its constitutional mandate. But as the executive and legislative branches ignored the Court's directives, the Court moved to declare the education budget unconstitutional. In its last attempt to mitigate the impact of its decision, the Court made a compromise to allow the underfunded budget to stand.

"Suspended declaration of invalidity"

In addition to the "progressive realization" technique, the Court also developed a different form of remedy that allows a statute to remain constitutional within a given period, during which the government must adopt a new plan to replace the law. As explained in Chapter 1, this form of remedy is known as a "suspended declaration of invalidity." For example, in the *Mulyana Kusumah* case,[107] the Court held that the Anti-Corruption Court must disband in 3 years unless the DPR enacted a new law to reform the Court. The case involved a constitutional challenge to the Anti-Corruption Commission Law,[108] which established the Anti-Corruption Court, one of a handful of new criminal justice system institutions formed during Indonesia's *Reformasi* period following the fall of the military dictatorship of General Soeharto. The case arose when the Anti-Corruption Court found two commissioners of the National Election Commission, Nazaruddin Sjamsudddin and Mulyana Kusumah, guilty, sentencing Sjamsuddin to a 7-year prison term and Kusumah to a 1.5-year sentence.

Kusumah and Sjamsuddin then filed a petition for judicial review in the Constitutional Court. They challenged the constitutionality of the Anti-Corruption Law on several grounds. One of the claimants' key arguments was that there is a dualism in the criminal justice system, in which both the Anti-Corruption Court and the General Court of Jurisdiction has the authority to try corruption cases. The claimants argued that the Anti-Corruption Court applied a different procedure than a general court in trying corruption cases—a violation of the constitutional guarantee of equality before the law (Article 28D § 1 of the Constitution). For instance, the Anti-Corruption Court does not recognize the procedure to terminate a case because of lack of evidence.[109] The claimant also filed a complaint about the absence of a pre-trial hearing in the Anti-Corruption Court procedure, in which the Law required a speedy trial within 90 days.[110]

The Court accepted the claimant's key argument and declared the provision that established the Anti-Corruption Court to be unconstitutional.[111] The Court then recommended lawmakers to pass a new Law on the Anti-Corruption Court, which would determine the Anti-Corruption Court as the only Court with the authority to try corruption cases. Nevertheless, the Court held that it should limit the effect of its decision by giving sufficient time for the lawmaker to create a new law consistent with the 1945 Constitution.[112] In the meantime, the Anti-Corruption Court would continue handling corruption cases. The Court further held that, based on its estimation, it would take 3 years for the lawmakers to enact a new law governing the Anti-Corruption Court. If the DPR was unable to meet this three-year deadline, then the authority to handle corruption cases would become the authority of General Courts of Jurisdiction.[113]

Unmasking quasi-weak-form review

The Indonesian model of quasi-weak-form review can be seen as closely related to the concept of the constitutional court in general. One of the distinct characteristics of a constitutional court model is the authority to perform an abstract review, and under abstract review, the subject matter is the question of whether a statute is compatible or incompatible with the constitution.[114] Furthermore, the purpose of the review is to safeguard the constitutional order, but not necessarily individual interests. Therefore, the remedy for a finding of unconstitutionality in an abstract case only affects the statute without affecting any particular legal rights. The constitutional court decisions in abstract review are typically binding upon all public authorities within the jurisdiction relevant to the subject matter decided by the Court, and/or any natural person or legal entities subject to the legal order of the respective domestic jurisdiction.[115]

In the further development of the constitutional court model, particularly in Western Europe after World War II, courts were assigned new authority to perform concrete review via constitutional complaint or referral mechanisms. One of the most important features of the constitutional court in European countries like Germany and Spain is the mechanism of a constitutional complaint, in which the court can review any act of a public authority as to its conformity with the protection of human rights under the constitution. In Germany, this mechanism was known as *verfassungsbeschwerden*, in which any person may enter a complaint of unconstitutionality if one of his or her fundamental substantive or procedural rights under the constitution has been violated by a public authority.[116] In Spain, this mechanism was known as the *recursos de amparo* (recourse for constitutional protection), in which individuals can bring a direct complaint to the constitutional court whenever his or her constitutional rights and liberties have been violated by public authorities.[117]

The constitutional court in a new democracy like South Korea also has adopted this mechanism. The Korean Constitutional Court provides two different kinds of constitutional complaints. First, the ordinary constitutional complaint is a common procedure by which any person who claims that his or her basic rights have been violated by an exercise or non-exercise of governmental power may file a constitutional complaint to the Constitutional Court.[118] Second, there is a constitutional complaint that is unique to the Korean system, in which an individual may directly file a complaint against a statute whenever his or her motion to the ordinary court for referring the constitutional question to the Constitutional Court was denied.[119]

Having explained briefly about the constitutional complaint mechanism in different jurisdictions, I would like to turn to the institutional design of the Indonesian Constitutional Court. The authority of the Indonesian Constitutional Court is limited to perform an abstract review, that is, to review the consistency of a statute with the Constitution. The Court has no authority of constitutional complaint or to hear a constitutional issue that arises from an ordinary court proceeding. Consequently, the Court's authority is limited to determining whether a statute is consistent with the Constitution. The Court cannot review issues that arise from a concrete case, either through the ordinary court proceeding or the conflict between the administration and the citizen. Therefore the Court only has the authority to hear questions regarding the constitutionality of statutes and not to resolve concrete cases that involve a dispute between citizens and government.

In the *Communist Party* case,[120] the Court dealt with the question of whether it is constitutional to prohibit a former Communist to run as a legislator. The Court did not review the decision of the General Election Commission to reject the candidacy of the aggrieved former Communist. Therefore, a favorable Court's decision did not remedy the claimant's injury. The court ruling therefore has no relation whatsoever to concrete cases in the General Election Commission; it just resolves the constitutional question on the constitutionality of the substance of General Election Law.

In the *Bali Bombing* case,[121] the Court was performing an abstract review of whether or not the application of the Anti-Terrorism Law to the Bali bombing case was consistent with the Constitution. The Court reviewed neither the constitutionality of the criminal trial of the claimant nor the Court decision that convicted Masykur Abdul Kadir, the claimant in the Bali bombing case. It was true that a retroactive law was applied to Masykur Abdul Kadir; however, he filed a separate claim for judicial review in the Constitutional Court that has no direct relation to his original case. Therefore, the Constitutional Court's decision would not reverse the decision of the district court, and more importantly, the Court itself has no authority to reverse the decision of the district court.

A similar pattern applies in the *West Papuan* case,[122] namely that the trigger of the case was the Presidential Instruction No. 1 of 2003 that led to the establishment of the new province. Similar to many other cases, because the Court had no authority to review the Presidential Instruction, the claimants had to challenge the statute that became the basis of the Presidential Instruction that is Law no. 45 of 1999. Therefore the Court only reviewed the constitutional question over the division of Papua province and the government's decision to create a new province based upon the Presidential Instruction. Therefore, the court ruling would not be able to reverse the government's decision because it has no bearing whatsoever on the government decision. In the end, however, the Constitutional Court's decision did complicate things further because the West Papuan province continued to exist while the statute that formed the basis of the province no longer had any legal effect.

Moreover, the Court itself explicitly stated that the Constitutional Court's proceeding does not involve the issue of concrete cases in the *Truth and Reconciliation Commission* case.[123] The claimants were six NGOs and two political activists who challenged the constitutionality of the Truth and Reconciliation Commission Law,[124] especially the provisions that ruled compensation for victims could only be given after perpetrators were granted amnesty[125] and the resolved cases could not be tried again in other courts.[126] The Court decided to nullify the entire Truth and Reconciliation Commission Law. This made the NGOs very upset because they only challenged the amnesty provisions in the Truth and Reconciliation Law, and, they invoked a prohibition for the Court to issue beyond what had been requested by claimant, known as *ultra petita* in the Indonesian civil law procedure.[127] The Court already anticipated the *ultra petita* argument, and, therefore, it held that

> Essentially, the procedural rule of judicial review that deals with the consistency of a statute with the Constitution binds general public (*erga omnes*), and therefore it is inappropriate to see the judicial review in the perspective of *ultra petita* in civil law procedure. That is a prohibition for the Court to issue beyond what had been requested by claimant ... Such notion (*ultra petita*) only exists in the context of private right.[128]

Here, the Court stated that it exercises the authority to review statutes that involve public interest and have greater implications than the individual benefit of the claimant. Therefore, the Court should not only focus on the claim that is asserted by the complainant.[129] In other words, the Court admitted that its model of judicial review is essentially an advisory system rather than an adversarial system. The Court reviews a case with no relation to the underlying concrete case, and consequently, the Court's decision does not aim to resolve the injury that suffered by the claimant.

The Court's structural limitation thus provides a fertile ground for the invention of the issuance of weak remedies. Considering that judicial review in Indonesia is primarily an abstract review, the Court's decisions should just be directed to the issue of compatibility of the challenged statute with the Constitution and the issuance of a declaratory remedy. A conditionally constitutional decision is a different form of declaratory remedy, in which the Court requires government officials to develop plans to eliminate the constitutional violation. In this way, the Court manages to issue constitutional interpretation and insert itself into some policy-making issues, but at the same time, the Court finds a way to minimize the impact of its decision in light of its structural limitations.

One of the telling examples of declaratory remedy is the *DPD Residence* case, where the claimants presented a constitutional question as to whether or not the Constitution requires a DPD candidate to have a residence in the province where he/she was seeking election. In this case, the Court did not deal with the validity of the application of the DPD candidate; rather, it dealt with the interpretation of the requirement of residency for a DPD candidate that was required by the Constitution. The Court then answered that the Constitution explicitly required a candidate to have a domicile in the province where he/she sought election, and, therefore, the General Election Commission must interpret the Electoral Law according to the Court's directive.

Apart from its structural limitations, the Court's survival strategy provided the driving force for its application of quasi-weak-form review. As explained in the previous chapter, through its intervention in some importance issues, the Court successfully created an image of a dynamic and robust judiciary. Not surprising, the politicians who designed the Court became upset to find out that their creation had turned against its creator. There are criticisms from the politicians that the Court abused its authority by issuing rulings beyond what had been requested by petitioners.[130]

While the Court was under pressure from politicians who wanted to curb its authority, it needed to find a way to balance the competing interests. In the earlier part of this chapter, I explained that the South Korean Constitutional Court adopted different types of decisions that fall under the category of the quasi-weak-form review. In the absence of the "political questions" doctrine found in the United States, the South Korean Constitutional Court came up with the idea of using different types of court decisions as the canon of constitutional avoidance in dealing with politically sensitive cases.[131] Indeed, the Indonesian Constitutional Court followed its Korean counterpart in creating a quasi-weak-form review. Specifically, and as covered above, the Indonesian Constitutional Court frequently applies the principle of prospective effect; the Court issued conditionally constitutional decisions, and in some cases, the Court held that the decision of constitutionality would only apply for a certain period of time.

Simon Butt argues that the Court's jurisprudential techniques, such as conditionally constitutional decisions, are pragmatism in disguise, and those techniques might even be considered hidden activism as the Court employed these techniques to make its decisions more politically palatable to the legislature.[132] In my opinion, the application of the different types of weak remedies, including conditionally constitutional decisions, exemplifies the strength of the Constitutional Court, because the Court finds a new way to balance the competing interests around them. By intervening in several important cases, the Court was quite successful in creating the image of a robust court. At the same time, the Court managed to avoid confrontation with the government or parliament by relying on weak-form remedies. With the application of weak remedies, the Court did not undo the decisions made by the elected politicians. Therefore, although the Court issued a favorable decision for the claimants, the decision did not automatically mean a total defeat for the lawmakers.

For instance, in the *Mulyana Kusumah* case, by declaring that the Anti-Corruption Court would remain constitutional for a period of 3 years, the Court avoided public criticism for issuing a pro-corruption decision.[133] But at the same time, the Court managed to avoid a bitter confrontation with the president and the DPR because the Court gave the president and the DPR a chance to prepare the new law.

Chief Justice Jimly Asshiddiqie was fully aware that the Court should move strategically in dealing with elected politicians, and therefore, he developed different types of weak remedies that might save the Court's reputation. The chief justice stated:

> A chaotic country like Indonesia needs an active court that can solve the problem, but there should be a limit ... if we frequently strike down statutes, they [the government and parliament] might launch a counterattack, and the Court has to avoid such situation.[134]

In short, Asshiddiqie was aware that he should lead the Court to issue many bold decisions, but at the same time, that he must find a way to avoid confrontation with the other branches of government. Asshiddiqie further explained that the application of the weak-remedy techniques is like an "art of turn around (*seni berkelit*)," in which the Court should "use its instinct and feeling to make a calculated decision when to hit and when to run."[135]

Despite its brilliant jurisprudential innovation, the Court had to face criticism from the public for the application of these techniques. For instance, the Constitutional Court decision in the *West Papuan* case received much criticism as a confusing decision.[136] It was not easy for the public to understand the logic behind the Court's decisions, especially regarding the way the Court's structural design impacts its rulings or the various political considerations behind its decisions. Moreover, many people criticized the Court for playing safe by invalidating the laws and at the same time avoiding confrontation with the government.[137] Nevertheless, regardless of the criticism of its jurisprudential techniques, the Court successfully balanced the competing interests around its existence as an institution.

Conclusion

Under the leadership of Jimly Asshiddiqie, the Indonesian Constitutional Court created different kinds of remedies that aim to minimize the effect of its decisions, such as the decisions that are conditionally constitutional, suspended invalidity, or progressive realization. Apart from institutional design reasoning, the Court took such an approach to avoid a political confrontation with elected politicians. In simple terms, by minimizing the impact of its decisions, the Court would avoid causing outrage among lawmakers, but at the same time, the Court managed to prove itself as an independent institution capable of issuing specific judicial remedies.

In sum, Asshiddiqie was quite successful in enhancing the Court's authority, but at the same time in defending the Court from any debilitating attack. Through the issuance of weak remedy, Chief Justice Asshiddiqie tried to find a balance between his desire to lead the Court into intervening in major policy decisions and avoiding confrontation with different branches of government. Thus, the Constitutional Court's unheroic weak remedy became its strength. The Court was relatively successful in preventing attacks from elected politicians with regard to the Court's decisions to invalidate some statutes. While in many instances, the government chose to ignore the Court's decision, Asshiddiqie kept the Court alive at least as an institution capable of addressing constitutional issues at an abstract level.

Notes

1 Laurie J. Sears. *Shadows of Empire: Colonial Discourse and Javanese Tales.* (Durham, NC: Duke University Press, 1996).
2 Ibid., 4–5.
3 Indonesia has a different version of the Mahabharata from the Indian version of Mahabharata in many parts of the story. In this book, I am using the Indonesian version of the story, including the name of the main characters.
4 Mark Tushnet. "New Forms of Judicial Review and the Persistence of Rights- and Democracy-Based Worries," 38 *Wake Forest L. Rev.* 813, 814 (2003); Mark Tushnet. "Alternative Forms of Judicial Review," 101 *Mich. L. Rev.* 2781 (2003). Tushnet coined the term "weak-form judicial review."
5 Mark Tushnet. *Weak Courts, Strong Rights: Judicial Review and Social Welfare Rights in Comparative Constitutional Law* (Princeton, NJ.: Princeton University Press, 2008); see also Mark Tushnet. "The Rise of Weak-Form Judicial Review." In *Comparative Constitutional Law*, edited by Tom Ginsburg and Rosalind Dixon. (Cheltenham, UK; Northampton, MA: Edward Elgar, 2011).
6 Po Jen Yap. *Constitutional Dialogue in Common Law Asia* (Oxford: Oxford University Press, 2015).
7 Stephen Gardbaum. *The New Commonwealth Model of Constitutionalism: Theory and Practice* (Cambridge: Cambridge University Press, 2013).
8 See Tushnet. *New Forms of Judicial Review*, 822; see also Tushnet. *Weak Courts, Strong Rights*, 242–244.
9 Mark Tushnet and Rosalind Dixon. "Weak-form Review and its Constitutional Relatives: An Asian Perspective." In *Comparative Constitutional Law in Asia*, edited by Rosalind Dixon and Tom Ginsburg. (Cheltenham, UK; Northampton, MA, USA: Edward Elgar, 2014).
10 Ibid., 105.
11 Ibid., 105.
12 Ibid., 107.
13 Ibid., 107.
14 Dongwook Cha. "The Role of the Korean Constitutional Court in the Democratization of South Korea" (PhD dissertation, University of Southern California, 2005), 67; see also the Constitutional Court of Korea, *The First Ten Years of the Korean Constitutional Court, 1988–1998* (Constitutional Court of Korea 2001) 86–93.
15 Cha. ibid., 68.
16 Ibid., 68. Between September 1988 and June 2009, the South Korean Constitutional Court declared 340 legal norms conditionally unconstitutional. See Aurel

Croissant. "Provisions, Practices and Performances of Constitutional Review in Democratizing East Asia," 23(5) *The Pacific Review* 549–578, 558 (2010).

17 Cha. ibid., 69.

18 Mark Tushnet. "Social Welfare Rights and the Forms of Judicial Review," 82 *Tex. L. Rev.* 1895 (2004).

19 Ibid., 1911.

20 Ibid., 1910.

21 Ibid., 1910.

22 See the Constitutional Court Decision No. 013/PUU-I/2003 (hereinafter the *Bali Bombing* case).

23 Law No. 23 of 2003 on the Constitutional Court, Art. 47.

24 See the Indonesian Constitutional Court Decision No. 011-017/PUU-I/2003 (hereinafter the *Communist Party* case).

25 Jimly Asshiddiqie. "Mahkamah Konstitusi: Bekas PKI Boleh Memilih dan Dipilih" [(Constitutional Court: Former PKI May Cast a Vote and Elected], *Tempointeraktif*, February 24, 2004.

26 Ibid.

27 See the Constitutional Court Decision No. 013/PUU-I/2003 (hereinafter the *Bali Bombing* case).

28 Simon Butt and David Hansell. "The Masykur Abdul Kadir Case: Indonesian Constitutional Court Decision No. 013/PUU-I/2003," 6(2) *Australian Journal of Asian Law* 177 (2004).

29 Six days after the explosion took place, the government passed the Emergency Law on Anti-Terrorism that created easier procedures for investigating, prosecuting, and convicting terrorists plus substantial penalties for terrorists and those who help terrorists. The Law was issued by the president under her emergency legislative powers and had to be ratified by the DPR at its following session. On the same day, the government also passed the Second Emergency Law, which merely states that the prosecutor could apply the First Emergency Law for the Bali bombings. Later, the DPR adopted the first Emergency Law as Law No. 15 of 2003 on Anti-Terrorism, and the second Emergency Law was passed as Law No. 16 of 2003.

30 The *Bali Bombing* case, 43. The Court, citing the Rome Statute of the International Criminal Court, 1998, held that the application of the retroactive principle in criminal law is only permitted in cases of gross violations of human rights, which include genocide, crimes against humanity, war crimes, and crimes of aggression.

31 Ibid., 44.

32 Ibid., 44.

33 See Jimly Asshiddiqie. *Hukum Acara Pengujian Undang—Undang* [Procedural Law of Statutory Review] (Jakarta: Sekretariat Jenderal dan Kepaniteraan Mahkamah Konstitusi, 2006).

34 Ibid., 317.

35 I cannot find any exact equivalents to this decision in other jurisdiction. The Constitutional Court of South Africa has a similar but different decision, in which South Africa's first housing-rights case provided no individual remedy because for practical reasons, the remedies for violations of social and economic rights cannot be "personal and present." Irene Grootboom, the lead litigant in South Africa's first housing-rights case, died homeless in her forties after she "won" South Africa's first housing case. See *Government of South Africa v Grootboom* (2001) 1 SA 46.

36 See the Indonesian Constitutional Court Decision, case No. 018/PUU-I/2003 (hereinafter the *West Papuan* case).

37 For a detailed analysis of Chief Justice Asshiddiqie's communication strategy, in which he used a press conference to announce the decision, please see Stefanus Hendrianto. "Judicial Power and Strategic Communication in Indonesia." In *Justices and Journalists: Global Perspective,* edited by Richard Davis. (Cambridge: Cambridge University Press, 2017).
38 Ibid., 135.
39 *Kompas.* "MK Sosialisasikan Putusan Papua" [the Constitutional Court explained the Papuan decision], December 13, 2004.
40 See the Constitutional Court Decision No. 001-021-022/PUU-I/2003 (hereinafter the *Electricity Law* case).
41 Ibid., 350.
42 Ibid.
43 *Kompas.* "MK Sosialisasikan Putusan Papua" [the Constitutional Court explained the Papuan decision], December 13, 2004.
44 The Constitutional Court Decision No. 058-059-060-063/PUU-II/2004 (hereinafter *Water Resources Law I* case).
45 Law No. 7 of 2004 on Water Resources (*Sumber Daya Air*).
46 The *Water Resources Law I* case, 495.
47 Ibid., 495.
48 Ibid., 492.
49 Ibid., 492.
50 The Constitutional Court Decision No. 003/PUU-III/2005 (hereinafter the *Open Pit Mining* case).
51 The Government Regulation in Lieu of Law No. 1 of 2004 on the Amendment of Law No. 41 of 1999 on Forestry, Art. 83A.
52 The *Open Pit Mining* case, 19.
53 Ibid., 19.
54 Ibid., 18.
55 Ibid., 19.
56 See the Constitutional Court Decision No. 003/PUU-IV/2006 (hereinafter the *Dawud Jatmiko* case).
57 Law No. 31 of 1999 on the Eradication of Corruption, Art. 2 (1).
58 Ibid., 7.
59 Ibid., 72.
60 Ibid., 72.
61 The Constitutional Court Decision No. 29/PUU-V/2007 (hereinafter the *Film Censorship* Case).
62 Law No. 8 of 1992 on Film Industry, Art. 33–34.
63 The *Film Censorship* case, 230.
64 Ibid., 231.
65 For a detailed analysis of the Court application of quasi-weak-form review in electoral cases, please see Stefanus Hendrianto. "A Curious Case of Quasi-Weak-Form Review: On Judicial Review of Electoral Process in Indonesia." In *Judicial Review of Elections in Asia*, edited Yap Po Jen. (London: Routledge, 2016).
66 The Constitutional Court Decision No. 14-17/PUU-V/2007 (hereinafter the *Political Crime I* case).
67 Law No. 23 of 2003 on the Presidential Election, Art 6 (T).
68 The *Political Crime I* case (n 37) 134.
69 Ibid., 132.
70 The Constitutional Court Decision No. 15/PUU-VI/2008 (hereinafter the *Political Crime II* case).
71 Law No. 10 of 2008 on Legislative Election, Art 50 (1.g).
72 "*Syarat Belum Pernah Dipidana Kembali Dipersoalkan.*" [The requirement of free from criminal charges was contested again] *Hukumonline.com.* http://www.huku-

monline.com/berita/baca/hol19316/syarat-belum-pernah-dipidana-kembali-dipersoalkan, accessed May 14, 2015.

73 The Constitutional Court Decision No. 10/PUU-VI/2008 (hereinafter the *DPD Residence* case).

74 The DPD was established by the Third Amendment to the Indonesian Constitution in 2001. The role of DPD was to represent a province as the Second Chamber of the People's Consultative Assembly (MPR). Nevertheless, the DPD was not given law-making powers, and it only has a limited power to submit bills to the DPR for approval.

75 Law No. 10 of 2008 on the Election of People's Representative Council, Regional Representative Council, Regional People's Representative Council, Art. 12 & Art. 67.

76 The Court made a reference to Article 22 C (1) of the 1945 Constitution, which provides that the members of the DPD shall be elected from every province through a general election.

77 The *DPD Residence* case, 215.

78 The Constitutional Court Decision No. 05/PUU-V/2007 (hereinafter the *Independent Candidate* case).

79 See Article 59 § 2 of the Law no.32 of 2004 on Regional Governance.

80 Law No.11 of 2006 on Aceh Governance, Art. 67 (1d).

81 Ibid., Para 3.15.15.

82 Ibid., Para 3.15.16.

83 Ibid., Para 3.15.16.

84 *Hukumonline*. "Pemerintah Bersikeras Tak Keluarkan Perpu Calon Independen" [the Government insisted not to issue Government Regulation in Lieu of Law], August 5, 2007.

85 *Jakarta Post*. "Independent Candidates Can Run in 2008," August 13, 2007.

86 Ibid.

87 See *Van Zorge Report*. "Press Briefing: Constitutional Court Chief Justice Jimly Asshiddiqie," February 12, 2008.

88 *Jakarta Post*. "Independents to Start Running in June," April 3, 2008.

89 See Article 2 of the International Covenant on Economic, Social and Cultural Rights.

90 Constitution of Republic of Indonesia 1945, Art. 31(4).

91 Constitutional Court Decision No. 026/PUU-III/2005 (the *Education Budget II* case).

92 Law No. 13 of 2005 on the State Budget for Fiscal Year (*Anggaran Pendapatan dan Belanja Negara*).

93 *The Education Budget Law II* case, 2005, 95.

94 Ibid., 86.

95 Law No. 18 of 2006 on the State Budget for Fiscal Year (*Anggaran Pendapatan dan Belanja Negara*).

96 Constitution of the Republic of Indonesia 1945, Art. 31(4).

97 Constitutional Court Decision No. 026/PUU-IV/2006 (the *Education Budget III* case).

98 Ibid., 94.

99 In the *Education Budget IV* case (Constitutional Court Decision No. 024/PUU-V/2007), a primary school teacher and a college professor claimed that they did not receive proper income as teachers in a public educational institution because the government failed to satisfy Article 31 (4). In this case, the Court instructed the Executive and Legislative branches to include the salaries of teachers in the education budget. The Court held, "'the inclusion of teachers' salary in the national education budget will help the Executive and Legislative fulfill the constitutional mandate to allocate a minimum 20 per cent of education budget."

100 On 20 August 2008, the Court held an election for chief justice, and a new associate justice, Mohammad Mahfud, defeated Chief Justice Asshiddiqie to become the second chief justice.
101 Constitutional Court Decision No. 13/PUU-VI/2008 (the *Education Budget V* case).
102 Ibid., 99.
103 Ibid., 100.
104 Ibid., 101.
105 Ibid., 101.
106 Private conversation with Jimly Asshiddiqie, December 22, 2014.
107 The *Mulyana Kusumah* case, Constitutional Court Decision No. 012-016-019/PUU-IV/2006.
108 Law No. 30 of 2002 on the Anti-Corruption Commission.
109 The *Mulyana Kusumah* case, 14–15.
110 Ibid.
111 The *Mulyana Kusumah* case, 283 (the case made reference to Article 53 of the Law No. 30 of 2002 on the Anti-Corruption Commission).
112 Ibid., 288.
113 Ibid., 289.
114 The Court's authority to conduct statutory review is based on the traditional concept of a constitutional court, which originated from the Austrian constitutional court. The original idea of Hans Kelsen is that a constitutional court is an institution that is directed at securing the observance of the rules of the constitution. It thus allowed select political entities that have a special interest in the constitutional validity or invalidity of legislation to demand a court judgment that identifies the compatibility of the law to the constitution. See Hans Kelsen. "Judicial Review of Legislation," 4(2) *Journal of Politics* 187 (May, 1942).
115 See Helmut Steinberger. "Decisions of the Constitutional Court and their Effects, in the Role of Constitutional Court in the Consolidation of the Rule of Law." In proceedings of *The Role of the Constitutional Court in the Consolidation of the Rule of Law* (Strasbourg: Council of Europe Press; Croton-On-Hudson, NY: Manhattan Pub., 1994), 82–85.
116 Article 93 § 1 (4a), The Basic Law of Germany. The public authority clauses permit constitutional complaints to be brought against any governmental action, including judicial decisions, administrative decrees, and legislative acts. See Donald P. Kommers. *The Constitutional Jurisprudence of the Federal Republic of Germany*, (Durham, N.C., Duke University Press: 1997), 14.
117 Article 191 § 1 (b) of the Spanish Constitution.
118 Article 68 § 1 of the Korean Constitutional Court Act.
119 Article 68 § 2 of the Korean Constitutional Court Act.
120 See the *Communist Party* case.
121 See the *Bali Bombing* case.
122 See the *West Papuan* case.
123 Constitutional Court Decision No. 006 PUU-IV/2006 (hereinafter the *Truth and Reconciliation Commission* case).
124 Law No. 27 of 2004 on the Truth and Reconciliation Commission.
125 Article 27 of the Truth and Reconciliation Commission Law 2004.
126 Article 44 of the Truth and Reconciliation Commission Law 2004.
127 See ELSAM. *Making Human Rights a Constitutional Right: A Critique of the Constitutional Court's Decision on the Judicial Review of the Truth and Reconciliation Commission Act and Its Implications for Settling Past Human Rights Abuses* (Briefing Paper Series, No. 1, January 2007), available at http://advokasi.elsam.or.id/assets/2015/09/20070100_Briefing-Paper_Making-human-rights-contitutional-right.pdf.

128 Ibid., 125.
129 Ibid., 126.
130 *Jakarta Post*. "Jimly Defends Right to Scrap Laws as Within Court's Powers," December 15, 2006.
131 Zoonil Yi, (professor of Constitutional Law and Legal Philosophy at Korea University), in discussion with the author, January 18, 2007.
132 Simon Butt. "Indonesia's Constitutional Court: Conservative Activist or Strategic Operator?" In *The Judicialization of Politics in Asia*, edited by Bjorn Dressel. (London: Routledge, 2012), 108.
133 See Denny Indrayana. "Mahkamah Konstitusi Antikorupsi" [The anti-corruption Constitutional Court], *Kompas*, December 21, 2006.
134 Private conversation with Jimly Asshiddiqie, July 31, 2006.
135 Ibid.
136 *Suara Pembaruan* Daily. "Putusan MK yang Membingungkan, [The Constitutional Court decision that was confusing], November 17, 2004; *Sinar Harapan*., "Kebingungan Usai Putusan" [The Confusion after the Constitutional Court issued the decision], November 22, 2004.
137 *Koran Tempo*. "Putusan MK Soal Irjabar Dinilai Ambivalen" [The Constitutional Court Decision on West Papuan issue was regarded as ambivalent], November 18, 2004.

5 A heroic social leadership

Prelude

David Danelski postulates that a chief justice who excels in social leadership will be able to relieve tensions, encourage solidarity and agreement, and attend to the emotional needs of his fellow judges.[1] Similarly, Diana Kapiszewski, Gordon Silverstein, and Robert Kagan describe the development of judicial power as a ship sailing on high seas, in which a chief justice as a judicial captain must contend with the worries, fears, aspirations, and conflicting views of their officers (fellow judges).[2] This conception of social leadership supports the observation by Walter Murphy that a man who wishes to exert influence over his fellows can do so most effectually if he is both intellectually disciplined and tactful in interpersonal relations.[3]

Having explained the intellectual leadership of Jimly Asshiddiqie and how he combined a maximalist and a minimalist approach, this chapter moves on to explore Asshiddiqie's social leadership style, through which he minimized conflict among the judges and increased their social cohesion. The primary legal focus of this chapter is on conflicting views on standing, specifically on how the chief justice influences the standing doctrine in the Court.

Standing can be seen as a reflection of how judges view their role. Essentially, the more cases that are heard by the courts, the more opportunity (and power) the courts have to engage with the other two branches of government. Therefore, standing determines the extent to which a judge could interfere with the functioning of and/or usurp the power of the other branches of government.[4] If judges want to have more power, one way to achieve that objective is through the expansion of standing rules.[5] On the flip side, judges could use standing as a tool to restrain the Court from usurping the power of the other branches of government.[6] In this chapter, I examine Chief Justice Asshiddiqie's influence on standing at the Indonesian Constitutional Court.

The scope and meaning of standing doctrine in the Indonesian Constitutional Court

Before delving into a detailed analysis of how Asshiddiqie built social cohesion and consensus on standing, we must first clarify the scope and meaning of the standing doctrine in the Indonesian Constitutional Court. *Standing*, or access to the court, in this book, refers to the question of whether either an individual or designated institution can bring a claim before the Indonesian Constitutional Court. What are the requirements that need to be fulfilled by either an individual or an institution to raise constitutional issues before the Court?[7]

The Indonesian Constitution is silent on standing, offering no rule regarding who may bring a claim to the Court. As explained in Chapter 2, the lawmakers intended to limit access to the Court. But in the end, the legislators reached a compromise by passing Law No. 24 of 2003 on the Constitutional Court, which states that:

> [C]laimants are parties who believe that their constitutional rights had been damaged (*dirugikan*) by the enactment of a statute; and they are individual citizens, customary communities (*masyarakat hukum adat*), public or private legal entities, or state institutions.[8]

Furthermore, the Law says that "the claimant must clearly describe his/her constitutional right that has been violated."[9] The pressing issue at the outset was how the Court would define the scope and meaning of standing in concrete cases. Would the Court apply strict standing rules as intended by politicians, or would it adopt a more generous approach to hearing the constitutional claims of aggrieved parties?

Actual versus potential harm

In 2003, the Court began to sketch its standing doctrine in the *Broadcasting Law* case, in which the Court explicitly stated that standing requires only a potential injury.[10] The claimants were six different television and radio associations that partially challenged the constitutionality of the Broadcasting Law No. 32 of 2002.[11] Specifically, the claimants challenged the authority of the Broadcasting Commission to issue administrative sanctions that include a range of sanctions from oral warnings to revocations of the license.[12]

The president signed the Broadcasting Law on December 28, 2002, but it took almost a year for the government to establish the Broadcasting Commission. At a time when the Broadcasting Commission was not yet in existence, the claimants came to the Court and argued that the Commission would administer its power in repressive ways. The issue was whether the claimants had the standing to raise a constitutional problem in such an abstract way. The Court majority ruled that the claimants had the standing because "constitutional injury (*kerugian konstitusional*) does not necessarily need to be real or actual … but potentially sufficient (*cukup bersifat potensial*)."[13]

The Court further solidified its approach to standing in the *Pemda Law III* case,[14] which came out in 2005, at the end of the Court's second calendar year. The claimant was a member of the Regional Representative Council (*Dewan Perwakilan Daerah*—DPD), the second chamber in the People's Consultative

Assembly (MPR), and he wanted to run for governor of Special Capital Territory Jakarta. The claimant could not run for governor as an independent candidate because the governing law required that the applicant must secure a nomination from a political party that had either a minimum of 15 percent of the seats in the Regional Parliament or a minimum of 15 percent of the votes in the local parliamentary election.[15]

The claimant argued that the *Pemda* Law did not comply with the equal protection clause in the Constitution and it had violated his constitutional right to run as an independent candidate for various reasons. First, the Law only allowed a political party to nominate the governor. Second, the requirement to nominate a candidate for the office of governor is much higher than the requirement for a presidential candidate.[16] The Law No. 23 of 2003 on Presidential Election requires that presidential candidate shall be nominated by a political party that has either 3 percent of the seats in the National Parliament or a minimum of 5 percent of the votes in the general election.[17] Finally, the claimant challenged the provision in the *Pemda* Law that required that the governor and vice governor shall be nominated on one ticket. The claimant argued that this provision did not comply with the regional election clause in the Constitution that mandated democratic elections.[18]

The claimant did not have any plan or intention to run as an independent candidate, nor had he been rejected by the Regional Election Commission as an independent candidate. The issue was whether the claimant had the standing to file a claim before the Constitutional Court. In this case, the Court came out with something similar to the five-prong standing test in the U.S. constitutional realm.

The Court ruled that the claimant must fulfill five requirements to establish constitutional injury (*kerugian konstitusional*). First, the claimant must have a constitutional right that is guaranteed by the Constitution. Second, the petitioner considers (*menganggap*) that the challenged statute has violated his or her constitutional rights. Third, the constitutional injury (*kerugian konstitusional*) should be concrete and actual or at least potential in character, which, according to reasonable logic, would be likely to occur. Fourth, there should be a causal relationship (*causal verband*) between the injury and the enactment of the challenged statute. Finally, there should be a possibility that with the issuance of a favorable decision, the constitutional injury would not occur or would not be repeated.[19]

While the Court sets the five-prong test, it never applies the test in a systematic way to judge whether the claimant has a standing. First, the Court held that the claimant could not prove in what way the provision that required the nomination of governor and vice governor on one ticket would bring immediate harm to him.[20] Second, the Court held that the different requirements between a presidential candidate and a gubernatorial candidate did not create any immediate harm to the claimant because it is the political party as candidate nominator that supposedly would suffer injury from those different sets of requirements.[21]

Nonetheless, the Court held that the claimant could assert simply a potential injury. Therefore, although the claimant never tried to run as a candidate for governor, there is a substantial likelihood that the claimant's candidacy would be turned down by the Electoral Commission because he would not be able to fulfil the requirement for the gubernatorial candidate. Therefore, the claimant was indeed found to have standing to file the case before the Court.

The Indonesian Constitutional Court's doctrine on standing therefore requires that to establish standing, there should be an immediate or likely harm to the applicant's constitutional rights. This requirement, however, is different from injury in fact standing found in an adversarial system like the United States. There, the Supreme Court adjudicates constitutional issues in what is known as *concrete review*, in which the parties request a resolution that immediately affects the determination of their rights in a concrete adversarial dispute.[22] The adjudication in an adversarial system may arise because the parties want to defend their rights against the enforcement of law or action by the state or private parties. Therefore, the standing rule in the adversarial system requires a claimant to claim the invasion of a legally protected right before the Court, and the Court decision is justified only to resolve the claim of injury. The Indonesian Constitutional Court's standing requirement, however, is more lenient than the standing rule in the adversarial system because it requires potential harm, instead of the requirement of injury in fact under the adversarial system.[23]

Generalized grievances standing

Apart from requiring a loose standing rule based upon potential injury, the Indonesian Constitutional Court also employed "generalized grievances standing," which enabled a claimant to assert an injury that all or a significant number of citizens shared together. In the context of U.S. constitutional theory, the U.S. Supreme Court has stated that there is a principle preventing standing when the asserted harm is a generalized grievance shared by all or a large class of citizens.[24] Thus, the prohibition against generalized grievances prevents individuals from suing if their only injury is as taxpayer[25] or citizen[26] concerned with having the government follow the Constitution.

Outside the U.S. constitutional realm, general grievances standing is not uncommon. In many jurisdictions, anyone, regardless of his or her own injury, may file a challenge to a law that affects the public at large.[27] There are a variety of terms to describe this mechanism, such as *actio popularis*, *jus tertii*, third-party standing, or public-interest standing.[28] In Israel, the Supreme Court has adopted the view that when the claim alleges a major violation of the rule of law (in its broad sense), every person in Israel has legal standing to sue.[29] The Indian Supreme Court has been well-known for developing procedural rules for third-party standing since the 1970s.[30] In Colombia, any citizen may file challenges to laws, constitutional amendments, and decrees issued by the government in exercise of delegated legislation powers or during states of exception.[31]

Similar to developing democracies worldwide, the Indonesian Constitutional Court in many instances does allow citizens to file a claim as a taxpayer or concerned citizen. In the 2003 *Government Securities Law* case,[32] the Court held for the first time that anyone could present a constitutional claim as a taxpayer. The claimants were 11 nongovernmental organizations (NGOs) who challenged the constitutionality of Law No. 24 of 2002 on the Government Securities Law.[33] The claimants argued that the Government Securities Law only benefited certain economic elites, and it was not compatible with the principle of economic democracy in the Constitution.[34] The claimants further argued that they had the standing to represent the public as nonprofit organizations because their primary mission is to defend and support human rights.[35]

The Court majority held that the claimants had the standing to bring the lawsuit because they are taxpayers. Based on the slogan "no taxation without participation, and no participation without tax," "their rights and interests intertwined with the government's loan, which naturally creates a burden for the citizen as taxpayers."[36]

The Court did not specify in what way NGOs have the capacity as a taxpayer or whether NGOs even pay taxes to the government. Nevertheless, the Court majority indicated that it would apply a broad interpretation of standing in at least one respect: A citizen may have standing to raise a constitutional issue as a taxpayer whenever a large class of citizens shares the injury.

The Court reaffirmed its taxpayer standing approach in the *Electricity Law* case.[37] In the *Electricity Law* case, three different groups of claimants challenged the constitutionality of the Electricity Law. The first group was made up of three human rights NGOs.[38] The second group was the Labor Union of Indonesian State Owned Electric Company (*Serikat Pekerja PLN*), and the third group was the Retired Union of State Electricity (*Ikatan Keluarga Pensiunan Listrik Negara*). The claimants argued that as nonprofit organizations, they had the standing to represent the public.[39]

The Court unanimously held "every citizen as the taxpayer has the constitutional right to question an economic policy that will implicate their welfare."[40] The Court held further that in addition to their status as taxpayers, the claimants also have standing as "electricity consumers or a group of people who have emotional ties (*hubungan emosional*) with the State Owned Electric Company (PLN)."[41] Essentially, the Court allowed the claimants to bring a case in their capacity as electricity consumers, in the case of the three human rights NGOs; or in their capacity as those who have emotional ties with the PLN, in the case of the Labor Union and the Retired Union.[42]

Through these cases, the Court therefore ruled that claimants are entitled to come before the Court as public defenders and assert an injury that a large number of people shared. By allowing taxpayers to raise constitutional issues, the Court opened its doors widely, in contrast to the approach sought by politicians who wanted a court with limited access and a resulting small amount of work to do.

"No standing rule" and advisory opinions

The Court did not stop with generalized grievances standing, going further by putting forth its unique standing rule that I would like to call the *no standing rule*. Under the no standing rule, the Court decided it could review a case despite a claimant's lack of standing. This kind of standing rule is different from an *actio popularis* because, under *actio popularis*, a claimant has the standing to raise constitutional issues in its capacity as defender of the public. Under the no standing rule, however, the claimant does not even have the ability to come before the Court as a public defender. But the Court nonetheless agrees to review the case, regardless of a claimant's capacity to otherwise raise constitutional issues.

A prominent example of the no standing rule is the *Susduk Law* case.[43] In 2003, some private-practice lawyers challenged Law No. 22 of 2003 on the Organization and Status of the Assembly, House, Regional Council and Local Parliament (*Susunan dan Kedudukan Anggota MPR, DPR, DPD dan DPRD—Susduk*). The crux of the matter was that the Susduk Law enabled the House (DPR) to compel anyone to appear before the DPR and give testimony as needed, and to have them detained for up to 15 days if they failed to comply with the summons.[44] The claimants argued that the Law did not comply with the Constitution because it had equipped the DPR with a law-enforcement function, which originally belonged to the other branches of government.[45]

The Court first held that the claimants had no standing because the enactment of the Law would not create either potential or actual injury to the complainants in any way, primarily because the DPR may only compel someone when it exercises its right of investigation (*hak angket*).[46] Moreover, none of the claimants had been compelled to testify by the DPR nor was called to testify before the DPR. Nevertheless, the Court held:

> [A]lthough the Court should dismiss the case on the ground of lack of standing, the Court must deliver an opinion on the merit of the case.[47]

Through its judgment, the Court signaled that it has the authority to issue advisory opinions whenever there is a constitutional issue at stake, regardless of the claimant's capacity to raise constitutional issues. The Court issued an advisory opinion that the act of compelling someone to testify before the DPR was constitutional because it was still within the corridors of legislative power.[48] The Court further stated that the punishment for someone who fails to comply with the DPR request would not be carried out by the DPR itself; instead, it would be conducted by law enforcement through a legal mechanism and due process.[49]

In sum, during its first few years of operation, the Indonesian Constitutional Court applied a generous approach to standing. The Court specifically developed a generalized grievances type of standing that enables the claimant to file for judicial review whenever there is a potential threat or injury to any citizen's constitutional rights. The Court expressly granted this standing to political activists and nongovernmental organizations (NGOs). In addition to this type of standing, the Court also developed what I call its *no standing rule*, under which the Court will issue advisory opinions regardless of the claimant's ability to establish standing.

The battle for standing

Having explained the Court's approach to standing, I will now turn to the internal dynamics within the Court with respect to standing issues. The battle over standing doctrine in the Indonesian Constitutional Court is evidenced by the conflicting visions of some justices regarding the role of the Court. In the midst of the conflict, Chief Justice Asshiddiqie played an important role as the mediator between two schools of thought in the Court.

Two schools of thought: Strict v. loose standing

In short, there were two different schools of thought on standing rules at the Court's inception. Under the intellectual leadership of Justice Achmad Natabaya, the first school of thought envisioned the Court as having a limited role and restricted access for citizens. Specifically, Justice Natabaya believed that the Constitutional Court has only a limited role in reviewing statutes. He argued that elected legislatures have the people's mandate to draft and pass laws, and, therefore, unelected judges must restrain themselves from invalidating a law.[50]

Furthermore, Justice Natabaya argued that it is wrong for the Court to review governmental policy. For instance, in the 2005 *National Education System* case,[51] the Court struck down a provision in the National Education Law (*Undang—Undang Sistem Pendidikan Nasional*),[52] which allows the government to fulfill the constitutionally required education budget (20 percent of the national budget) in an incremental way.[53] The claimants were individual activists, elementary and middle school teachers, and college teachers, who argued that the Law violated the education budget minimum of 20 percent required by the Constitution.[54]

The Court majority ruled for the plaintiffs and declared that the provision that allowed the government to fulfill the national education budget in an incremental way was unconstitutional.[55] Justice Natabaya issued a dissenting opinion and argued that the National Education System Law did not violate the Constitution because the government had a plan to increase the budgetary allocation for education every year until it reached the 20 percent requirement.[56] Natabaya believed that the Court's majority improperly invalidated the provision on the educational budget because this provision was a manifestation of governmental policy.[57] Natabaya further argued that the government made a policy decision to fulfill the constitutional mandate in an incremental way, and that the Court did not have the authority to invalidate a policy decision of the Executive branch.[58]

Based on his view of the limited role of the Court, Natabaya argued that the Court should apply a strict standing rule because only through restricted standing would the Court be able to avoid trespassing on the jurisdiction of the other governmental branches. Natabaya further believed that standing rules should require the claimant to assert a personalized and actual injury.[59] For instance, in the *National Education System* case, the Court held that, in their capacity as parents and teachers, the claimants had an interest in the fulfillment of the 20 percent requirement.[60] Thus, the Court ruled that the claimants had the standing to challenge the constitutionality of the National Education System Law. Three Justices—Natabaya, Roestandi, and Soedarsono—dissented that the complainants had no standing because they could not show any actual injury or even potential injury that would damage their constitutional rights.[61] Justice Natabaya argued that that the claimants could not even show what kind of injury or harm that they have suffered; for instance, the applicants could not prove that they had lost their salaries or their jobs because of the enactment of the National Education Law.[62]

According to Natabaya, there was a fundamental flaw in the standing mechanism in the Indonesian Constitutional Court because it allowed individual citizens to challenge a statute.[63] Natabaya believed that the ideal type of standing could be found in the mechanism of the France Constitutional Council, in which only a designated institution—president, prime minister, Upper House, Lower House, and Parliamentary minority—can challenge the constitutionality of a statute.[64]

Nevertheless, Natabaya acknowledged that in some legal systems, such as that of Germany, individual citizens may file constitutional complaints with certain requirements to establish standing, such as the complainant having to exhaust all the legal remedies available. Therefore, Natabaya proposed that if individual citizens would like to challenge a statute, they would then have to fulfill certain requirements to establish standing. Natabaya said that the U.S. five-prong standing test became a reference for him in believing that there should be a personalized and an actual injury.[65] As a scholar who studied in a U.S. law school,[66] Natabaya was familiar with U.S. standing doctrine and decided to follow the U.S. type of standing, which is reliant on proving injury. Moreover, Natabaya himself claimed that he was the only justice with real knowledge of the U.S. constitutional system.[67]

In addition to Justice Natabaya, Justice Ahmad Roestandi was also a proponent of the strict standing rule. Roestandi argued that standing is an essential element of Constitutional Court proceedings because not everyone should be able to come to the Court.[68] Roestandi, who proclaimed himself a "positivist," asserted that the Court should follow Law No. 24 of 2003 on the Constitutional Court, which requires the claimant to insert concrete harm or injury that was caused by the enactment of the statute.[69] Furthermore, Roestandi argued that constitutional injury should be factual injuries instead of potential injuries.

In contrast, the other school of thought believed that the Court should embrace open access to enable the Court to review important cases during Indonesia's transitional period. From the early days of the Court's operation, Justice Maruarar Siahaan consistently urged his brethren to apply a broad interpretation of standing, especially in the early period of Court service, and especially whenever there was a constitutional issue at stake.[70] Justice Siahaan repeatedly reminded his brethren:

> If the Court imposes a strict standing from its beginning, then no one would come to the Court, and, consequently, the Court would run out of business in a short period.[71]

In other words, Justice Siahaan believes that the Court should open its doors as wide as possible to the claimants so that that many people will bring cases before the Court.

In addition to Justice Siahaan, Justice Laica Marzuki also to some degree supported broad access to the Court. Justice Marzuki argued that potential injury is sufficient for the claimant to establish standing. For instance, in the *Communist Party* case,[72] Justice Marzuki argued that the claimants had the standing to challenge the prohibition against former Communists running to be legislators even though they never applied to run as legislative candidates.[73] Marzuki explained that the prohibition under the General Election Law clearly closed the door for the claimants to run for the legislature.[74]

Chief Justice Asshiddiqie himself sided with the proponents of this free-standing doctrine. Asshiddiqie argued that the Court should give priority to important issues that come before it.[75] In other words, he believed that the Court should not turn down a case solely based on administrative grounds. Asshiddiqie stated, "the Court should not let go an opportunity to review a major case simply because the claimant has no standing."[76] Thus, for Asshiddiqie, if an applicant presents an important case, the Court should not deny the case based on a lack of standing.

The standing battle and Article 50

Conflicting views on access to the Court had existed since the early days of the Court, when the Justices had to deal with the constitutionality of Article 50 of the 2003 Constitutional Court Law, which prohibited the Court from reviewing cases before 1999. Though Article 50 does not directly involve the standing issue, it was nonetheless closely related to the scope of judicial review authority of the Court, and therefore relevant to the evolution of the Indonesian Constitutional Court's standing doctrine.

When the Court decided its first case—the *Supreme Court Law I* case[77]—on December 23, 2003, it immediately had to deal with the issue of the prohibition of Article 50. The claimant was a district court judge who challenged the constitutionality of the Supreme Court Act, which set the requirements for becoming a Supreme Court Judge. The Law provided that the requirements for becoming a Supreme Court judge included that a career judge should have served 5 years as chief high court judge or have 10 years' service as high court judge; and for noncareer judges, 15 years' experience in legal practice.[78] The claimant argued that the provision clearly barred him from the possibility of becoming a Supreme Court judge and therefore the law violated his constitutional rights.

The issue was whether or not the Court had the authority to review the 1985 Supreme Court Law given that it was promulgated before Article 50's 1999 cut-off date. The Court's majority held that despite the statutory limitation set by Article 50, it had the authority to review the Supreme Court Law.[79] Nonetheless, the Court did not explicitly nullify Article 50. Instead, the Court decided "to set aside" (*mengenyampingkan*) Article 50 in this instance.[80] I will explain this case in more detail in the following section.

Three justices, Laica Marzuki, Achmad Roestandi, and Achmad Natabaya, wrote separate dissenting opinions in which they argued that the Court had no authority to review the case because of the limitation of Article 50.[81] The most articulate argument was the dissenting opinion of Roestandi, in which he argued that there is a strong constitutional basis for the enactment of Article 50. Roestandi referred to Article 24 C (6) of the Constitution, which provides that "the appointment and removal of constitutional justices, the judicial procedure, and other provisions concerning the Constitutional Court shall be regulated by law (statute)." Roestandi argued that the Constitution authorized lawmakers to regulate the constitutional court, which includes a limitation on the object of statutory review.[82]

The chance for the Court to again review Article 50 came soon thereafter, when a claimant directly challenged the constitutionality of Article 50 in the *Chamber of Commerce Law* case.[83] The claimants were members of the so-called Medium and Small-Scale Chambers of Commerce. The government refused the registration of Medium and Small-Scale Chambers based on the Chamber of Commerce Law of 1987, which states that there is only one Chamber of Commerce in the country. The claimant thought that the government's refusal infringed on their constitutional right, namely the freedom to organize.

The petitioners realized that there was a statutory limitation that prevented the Court from reviewing the Chamber of Commerce Law of 1987; therefore, the claimants asked the Court to review Article 50 to enable them to consider the 1987 Chamber of Commerce Law. The Court immediately took the chance to remove its biggest obstacle by nullifying Article 50 of the Constitutional Court Law of 2003. The Court, in a 6–3 decision, held that Article 50 was incompatible with the Constitution,[84] because "it curtailed the authority of the Constitutional Court as mandated by the Constitution."[85] In other words, the Court held that Article 50 contravened the Constitution because it reduced the authority of the Constitutional Court to review statutory regulation.

The three dissenters in the *Supreme Court Law I* case, Justices Marzuki, Roestandi, and Natabaya, issued dissenting opinions reaffirming their positions in the previous case: that the Constitution gives authority to Parliament and the president to create legislation on the appointment procedures for constitutional court justice and adjudication procedures.[86] In this case, the most articulate dissenting opinion was the one written by Justice Natabaya, in which he argued,

> [I]t was the province of the legislature to enact Law no. 24 of 2003 on the Constitutional Court, which includes a prohibition for the Court to review any statutes that were enacted before October 19, 1999 (Article 50).[87]

In other words, Natabaya believes that the legislative branch has the authority to set a statutory limitation on the Constitutional Court's power to conduct judicial review.

In the *Chamber of Commerce Law* case, the Court therefore removed one of the biggest obstacles preventing citizens from raising constitutional issues. By declaring Article 50 unconstitutional, the Court could now review any challenged statute. The Court decision signified that it had adopted an entirely different approach to the legislature's original intent on standing. The politicians who created the Constitutional Court initially wanted to create a court with limited access, but through the ruling in this case, the Court declared that it has the authority to review any statute regardless of the date it was passed.

The search for consensus on standing

As explained earlier, Asshiddiqie aligned himself with the proponents of loose standing. Nevertheless, as the Chief Justice, Asshiddiqie sees his role as the bridge builder. Therefore, he tried to find a middle ground between the competing camps in the early days of the Court's operation. Having realized that there was a division in the Court on the issue of standing, Asshiddiqie needed to find a strategy to bridge differences within the Court. Asshiddiqie then moved to build consensus among his fellow justices that, at least in its early years, the Court should impose more generous standing rules, and it could impose a stricter standing threshold in the future after the institution had earned trust and respect from the public.[88]

The proponents of strict standing doctrine relented and agreed to let the Court impose a lenient standing doctrine. Justice Roestandi explained that although he believed that the Court should not readily grant standing to the claimants, he had to respect the consensus among judges that in its early period, the Court would open its door widely, but that the Court would reconsider such policy later.[89] Another associate justice confirmed that the chief justice led the justices to reach a consensus that the Court had to build public trust in the first year of its operation by lowering the standing requirements, but the Court would reconsider such a standing policy in the future.[90] Such consensus is possible because as a country with a civil law tradition, Indonesia has no adherence to the principle of *stare decisis*, under which the Court will follow the previous Court's decision. Therefore, the Court may choose not to follow its previous decisions.

The Court's decision in the *Oil and Gas Law I* case provides clear evidence of how Asshiddiqie managed to achieve a consensus on standing. In the *Oil and Gas Law I* case,[91] the Court applied its generous standing approach when it held that public-interest NGOs have the standing to represent the public. The main claimants were four human rights–based NGOs,[92] who argued that they had the standing to represent the public as nonprofit organizations in challenging the privatization of the state-owned oil company, *Pertamina*.[93] On the issue of standing, the Court held that the claimants had the standing as public-interest advocacy groups.[94] It is worth noting that the Court ruling is very short and does not explain the details of the argument behind its holding, such as the meaning of public-interest advocacy. Nonetheless, the Court gave a clear-cut answer that the claimants had the capacity to act as defenders of the people. The Court decision thus signified that public-interest NGOs could come before the Court as advocates for the people.

The Court announced the *Oil and Gas I* case in its first calendar term, but the Court shifted its standing approach in its fifth calendar term. In the *Oil and Gas*

Law II case,[95] the Court refused to apply taxpayer standing doctrine. The petition for judicial review was filed by eight members of the DPR. They challenged the constitutionality of Article 11 (2) of the Oil and Gas Law, which states that the government should inform the DPR in writing of every cooperation contract on the production sharing of natural resources exploration and exploitation conducted with foreign contractors. The petitioners argued that the DPR has the right to give consent or to refuse the cooperation contracts instead of merely receiving a written notice, and therefore the provision violated their constitutional rights.

The Court refused to apply taxpayer standing and held that the claimants had no standing to file for judicial review.[96] Again, the Court did not provide a lengthy explanation on its reasoning, resulting in speculation that the Court declined to apply taxpayer standing because it is time to honor the consensus on standing.

The pressing question is how the chief justice managed to find a middle ground on the standing issue. I argue that his brilliant skill as a consensus builder was the key to his success in building bridges among justices. Most of the associate justices agreed that, as a chief justice, Asshiddiqie was excellent in leading deliberation meetings, and he usually managed to resolve conflicting opinions among his brethren. An associate justice expressed his admiration for the chief justice as follows:

> Mr. Chief Justice is very brilliant in leading deliberation meeting and most of the time he finds the way to unite all conflicting views among the Justices.[97]

An apt example of Asshiddiqie's brilliant skill in building bridges was in the *Supreme Court Law I* case, which involved the prohibition of Article 50.[98] During the deliberation meeting, the chief justice successfully persuaded his brethren that despite the prohibition of Article 50, the Court should review any statute that was promulgated before the 1999 Amendment.[99] In this case, the chief justice persuaded his brethren to choose a moderate approach, and therefore, instead of nullifying Article 50, the Court used the term "to keep aside" (*mengenyampingkan*) Article 50.[100]

In sum, Chief Justice Asshiddiqie managed to find a middle ground between two competing schools of thought on standing. While personally he preferred to side with the proponent of the loose standing approach, he did not ignore the voices of the opponents of loose standing. Moreover, Asshiddiqie also convinced the proponents of loose standing to take a more moderate approach in some cases.

The standing and "silent dissent"

As part of his strategy to build a consensus on standing, Asshiddiqie persuaded the proponents of strict standing to not express their dissent explicitly. As Simon Butt noted, the justices were conscious of not wanting to appear to disagree too strongly with each other, because too much open criticism within the Court might be seen to undermine the Court's authority.[101] One factor that explains why justices do not appear to disagree is an ostensible consensus among them over certain issues. For example, after three associate justices expressed their dissent in the two cases that related to the interpretation of Article 50, Asshiddiqie moved to persuade them to not express their dissent, and he went further by encouraging them to set aside their differences on the standing issue in the early years of the Court's operation.

In the *Government Securities Law* case,[102] in which the Court ruled on taxpayer standing, there were two Justices who filed dissenting opinions against the Court majority. Nevertheless, the dissenters did not write separate dissenting opinions. The Court summarized the dissent of two justices to be that the claimants had no standing because their injury was not specific enough, and furthermore, that they did not have standing as taxpayers because there was no sufficient link between tax payments that the claimants made and the issuance of the government securities.[103] The summary of the dissent signified that the minority preferred a personalized-injury type of standing, but the consensus among the justices was quite effective in containing the objections and keeping them under the radar.

In the *Broadcasting Law* case,[104] the dissenter also did not write a separate dissenting opinion. The Court only mentioned that there was a judge who argued that the claimant had no standing, but he did not mention the name of the judge.[105] A similar situation occurred in the *Oil & Gas Law* case,[106] under which the Court held that public-interest NGOs could have standing to represent the public. Here, the Court did not even summarize the dissenting opinions and only mentioned that two justices disagreed with the Court majority on the issue of standing.

In *Bram Manoppo* case,[107] the Court held that it would issue an advisory opinion for the sake of public interest even though the claimant had no standing. The claimant, Bram Manoppo, was a suspect in a major corruption case involving the purchase of a Russian helicopter for Aceh provincial government. Manoppo challenged a provision of the Anti-Corruption Commission Law, which authorized the Commission to take over all corruption cases that had not been settled by the police or prosecutors at the time the government established the Commission.[108] Manoppo argued that the provision was in conflict with the constitutional prohibition on retroactivity.[109]

The Court ruled that the claimant had no standing because the Court did not find any evidence that the police or prosecutors had ever investigated Manoppo, and it was only the Commission that had ever conducted investigations.[110] Nevertheless, the Court ruled that it should review the constitutionality of the challenged statute because of the public need for an answer on the scope of the Commission's operation.[111] Two judges disagreed with the majority approach because the claimant failed to establish standing. These two judges, however, did not write a dissenting opinion. Furthermore, the Court's judgment barely mentioned that there were two dissenters from the majority.[112]

It was not until the *Truth and Reconciliation Commission* case in December 2006 that the Court mentioned the names of the dissenters on standing for the first time.[113] The claimants were six NGOs and two political activists who challenged the constitutionality of the *Truth and Reconciliation Commission Law*.[114] The claimants challenged the provisions that provided compensation for victims only after perpetrators received amnesty,[115] and that the resolved cases could not be tried again in other courts.[116] In addressing the issue of standing, the Court first held that individual claimants were the victims of past abuse, and therefore they had the standing to challenge the statute.[117] For the NGO claimants, the Court majority held that they have the standing because they provide legal defense for the victims of past abuse in their capacity as public-advocacy NGOs.[118]

In its judgment, the Court explicitly mentioned that Justice Natabaya and Justice Roestandi were in the minority and that they questioned the claimants' status as the victims of gross human-rights violations. Nevertheless, the Court only summarized the opinion of Natabaya and Roestandi that the complainants had no standing because they were not victims of a gross violation of human rights.[119]

In sum, by persuading his brethren to not express their dissents publicly, Asshiddiqie was successful in building cohesion among the judges and leading the Court to follow the path that he had chosen, especially on the issue of standing. More importantly, Asshiddiqie also managed to lead the Court to take a slow approach in its initial years by showing a unity among the justices instead of taking an aggressive approach by displaying their disagreement publicly.

The role of "silent dissent" in fostering cohesion

As explained above, oftentimes the dissenter did not issue a separate dissenting opinion. This practice is not something unorthodox because the Courts in many different jurisdictions also apply a similar practice. For instance, while the German and Spanish Constitutional Courts do permit dissenting opinions, both have informal norms that discourage their frequent use and the public display of disagreement.[120] The Constitutional Courts in new democracies are also taking a similar approach. Take, for example, the decision of the Constitutional Court of Korea on May 14, 2004, which overrode the impeachment motion against President Roh Moo-Hyun. The decision was not unanimous, but, the Constitutional Court of Korea did not offer any dissenting opinion because the Court was concerned that the revelation of a dissenting opinion could have produced endless political confrontation.[121]

The Indonesian Constitutional Court's dissenting mechanism of merely summarizing dissenting views was compatible with Chief Justice Asshiddiqie's belief that dissenting opinions were a barrier to the culture of collegiality within the Court. During his tenure as chief justice, Asshiddiqie almost never issued a dissent. In a private conversation, Asshiddiqie admitted that he preferred to side with the majority and would choose not to disagree despite his initial position against the majority.[122] Asshiddiqie believed that if the chief justice frequently issued dissents, "the people will have some doubt about the Court's decision, and they might not respect the Court ruling."[123] According to Asshiddiqie, instead of giving clear guidance, dissenting opinions might create doubt because the public would see the Court as a divided institution.[124] In other words, Asshiddiqie believed that there was a negative aspect to dissenting opinions, and therefore he preferred not to express his dissent, instead siding with the Court majority.

A telling example of Asshiddiqie's deliberate choice to side with the majority is the *Death Penalty* case.[125] The death penalty is one of the remaining legacies of the New Order regime.[126] The Soeharto regime carried out and defended the death penalty both in the form of the mass killings in 1965–1966 (with estimates of up to 1 million people killed), as well as a part of the formal court system. In the 1980s, Soeharto also ordered extrajudicial killings of petty criminals, in which thousands were shot dead and left in the street.[127]

In the *Death Penalty* case, the claimants were two Indonesian women and three Australian men who had been caught smuggling heroin; all of them received a death sentence under the Narcotics Law.[128] They asked the Court to review whether the Narcotics Law, which allowed the imposition of the death penalty, contradicted the constitutional guarantee of the right to life.[129] With a split decision (6–3),[130] the Court upheld the Law and argued that a narcotics offense could jeopardize the right to life as guaranteed by the Constitution because drug crimes were like a murder in cold blood that deprived one of the right to life.[131]

Chief Justice Asshiddiqie sided with the majority, although he disagreed with the majority position. Asshiddiqie explained that initially, the result was five against four to retain the death penalty, but he could not convince one of the five to join four justices to nullify the death penalty.[132] Asshiddiqie explained:

> I had to make that decision … If I did that (filed a dissenting opinion) as chief justice, it could become a major problem for the legitimacy of the Court's ruling. That's why I decided not to write a dissenting opinion, even though, in substance, I was with the minority.[133]

In other words, Chief Justice Asshiddiqie believes that the legitimacy of the Court's ruling is far more important than his personal conviction on the death penalty.

The only case in which Asshiddiqie filed a dissenting opinion was the *Right to Recall* case.[134] In this case, the Court dealt with the authoritarian mechanism known as the *right to recall*. Under the New Order regime, political parties had the right to recall or replace any legislator who dared to speak up against the military government. After the fall of Soeharto, the DPR scrapped the right to recall based on the consideration that it was meant to silence opposition.[135] Nevertheless, due to various complaints from political parties, the right to recall was reinstated in the 2003 Law on the Composition of the Parliament.[136]

The claimant, Djoko Edhi Soetjipto Abdurahman, was a member of the DPR representing the National Mandate Party (*Partai Amanat Nasional*—PAN). The PAN National Executive recalled Abdurrahman from the DPR in late 2005 because he participated in a study tour to Egypt to study gambling laws, which sent a wrong signal concerning PAN's favor of gambling laws.[137] Abdurrahman asked the Court to nullify the right to recall provision. With a split decision (5–4), the Court majority rejected the petition and ruled that "just because parties have a recall mechanism, it does not mean that the recall mechanism is undemocratic."[138] The Court held further that the recall mechanism was necessary because "members of parliament, as the people's representatives, need to be kept accountable so that the people can control them through political parties."[139]

Chief Justice Asshiddiqie filed a dissenting opinion, in which Justice Siahaan joined.[140] In his dissent, Asshiddiqie wrote that the right of recall could undermine the functioning of parliament because the party's elite would likely recall any legislator who dared to break with party lines. Therefore, a parliamentarian would be more responsive to the interests of the party elite rather than speaking the truth.[141]

Apart from the *Right to Recall* case, Asshiddiqie always sided with the Court majority. One of the former law clerks explained that initially, Asshiddiqie had secured five votes to nullify the law, but one of the associate justices switched sides at the last minute, and, therefore, Asshiddiqie had no other choice than to be in the minority position.[142]

There are two plausible explanations for Asshiddiqie's approach on dissenting opinion. First, Asshiddiqie believed that there should be unity within the Court, and that too much dissenting opinion is a sign of division. In his calculation, by choosing to side with the majority, at least he would be able to show unity and minimize the public impression of a divided Court. Second, by always siding with the majority, Asshiddiqie tried to attend to the emotional needs of his associate justices by affirming their value as individuals and as Court members, especially when their views were asymmetrical to Asshiddiqie's own views. Through this strategy, Asshiddiqie sought to become the best-liked man in the Court and to play the role of a good social leader.

Conclusion

The social leadership of Chief Justice Jimly Asshiddiqie shows that he continued to apply a combination of maximalist and minimalist approaches on standing. In general, the Court applied loose standing rules that gave the Court a chance to review many important issues. The most important consideration in dealing with the standing issue was the significance of the constitutional issue at stake. In other words, when there was a constitutional issue at stake, then the Court should review the case regardless of whether the claimant had standing or not. Nevertheless, Asshiddiqie was attentive to fellow judges who preferred to apply strict standing rules. Even so, with the support of some associate justices, Asshiddiqie successfully built a consensus that the Court should apply lenient standing rules at least in the first few years of its operation, and that later the Court might reconsider this approach.

Moreover, Asshiddiqie led his brethren to take a slow approach in its initial years by showing a unity among the justices instead of taking an aggressive approach by displaying their disagreement through dissenting opinion.

Asshiddiqie tried to foster the culture of collegiality by minimizing dissent among the judges or at least persuading the dissenters not to express their dissent publicly. Asshiddiqie sees that dissenting opinion can be a sign of division with the Court. Therefore, Asshiddiqie always choose to side the majority opinion, even though he disagreed with the opinion. By siding with the majority, Asshiddiqie wants to show unity and minimize the public impression of a divided Court. Furthermore, Asshiddiqie also tries to affirm the aspirations of the associate justices, even if they disagree with the chief justice.

In sum, the critical success of the leadership of Chief Justice Jimly Asshiddiqie can be found in the combination of his intellectual superiority and his social leadership skills in uniting conflicting views on the bench. With the combination of these two factors, Asshiddiqie was able to unite the Court and persuade his fellow judges to move in the particular direction of his choosing. The question remains whether Asshiddiqie's leadership style would help or hurt him in continuing into a second term as chief justice, a topic discussed in the following chapter.

Notes

1 David J. Danelski. "The Influence of the Chief Justice in the Decisional Process." In *Courts, Judges, & Politics: An Introduction to the Judicial Process*, edited by Walter F. Murphy et al. (5th ed. 2002), 662–663.
2 Diana Kapiszewski, Gordon Silverstein, and Robert A. Kagan. "On Judicial Ships and Winds of Change." In *Consequential Courts: Judicial Roles in Global Perspective*, edited by Diana Kapiszewski, Gordon Silverstein and Robert A. Kagan. (New York: Cambridge University Press, 2013), 400–401.
3 Walter F. Murphy. "Marshaling the Court: Leadership, Bargaining, and the Judicial Process," 29 *U. Chi. L. Rev.* 640, 642 (1962).
4 Aharon Barak. *The Judge in a Democracy* (Princeton, NJ: Princeton University Press, 2006), 190; See also Aharon Barak. "A Judge on Judging: The Role of a Supreme Court in a Democracy," 116 *Harv. L. Rev.* 16 (November 2002).
5 Ibid., *The Judge in A Democracy*, 192.
6 Ibid.
7 There are several theories on the origin of the term *standing*. The first plausible explanation is that the term came from medieval Romano-canonic procedural writing, *excommunicatus non habet personam standi in iudicio*, under which someone lost his or her religious rights and was excluded from entry into the church, from the company of the faithful, and from pleading in secular and ecclesiastical courts. See F. Donal Logan, *Excommunication and the Secular Arm in Medieval England: A Study in Legal Procedure from the Thirteenth to the Sixteenth Century* (Toronto: Political Institute of Mediaeval Studies, 1968), 14. Joseph Vining, professor of Law, University of Michigan, suggested that the phrase does not seem to appear in classical Roman legal sources because the principle of excommunication came to apply for a time in secular English courts. Vining suggested that the term originated from nineteenth-century British parliamentary practice. The phrase is used in the practice of both the House of Parliament and the House of Lords with reference to the fact that there are standing orders that give certain classes of petitioners a *locus standi* or right to appear in opposition to any bill that may affect them. See Joseph Vining. *Legal Identity: The Coming of Age of Public Law* (New Haven, Yale University Press, 1978), 55.
8 Law No. 24 of 2003 on the Constitutional Court, Art. 51 (1).

9 Law No. 24 of 2003 on the Constitutional Court, Art. 51 (2).

10 The Constitutional Court Decision No. 005/PUU-I/2003 (hereinafter the *Broadcasting Law* case).

11 The claimants were the Television Journalists Association, The Union of National Commercial Radio Broadcasters, the Union of Indonesian Advertisers, the Indonesian Television Broadcasting Association, the Indonesian Union of Dubbing Specialists, and the Indonesian Television Community.

12 The *Broadcasting Law* case, 4.

13 Ibid., 76.

14 The Constitutional Court Decision No. 006/PUU-III/2005 (hereinafter the *Pemda Law III* case).

15 Law No. 32 of 2004 on the Regional Governance, Art. 59 (2).

16 See *Pemda Law III* case, 6–10.

17 See Article 101 of the Law No. 23 of 2003 on Presidential Election.

18 See Article 18 (4) of the Constitution.

19 See the *Pemda Law III case*, 16.

20 Ibid., 17–18.

21 Ibid.

22 For a detailed analysis of the distinction between standing in an adversarial system and in an advisory system, please see Richard S. Kay. "Standing to Raise Constitutional Issues: A Comparative Analysis." In *Standing to Raise Constitutional Issues: Comparative Perspectives*, edited by Richard S. Kay. (Bruxelles: Bruylant, 2005).

23 In this book, I will interchangeably use the term *generous rules* or *lenient rules* on standing. Simon Butt, in his study on the Indonesian Constitutional Court, used the terms *generous rules* on standing and *permissive approach* to standing. See Simon Butt. "Judicial Review in Indonesia: Between Civil Law and Accountability? A Study of Constitutional Court Decisions 2003–2005" (PhD dissertation, University of Melbourne, 2006), 52.

24 See Erwin Chemerinsky. *Constitutional Law: Principles and Policies* (New York: Aspen Law & Business, 2011), 91–98.

25 See *Frothingham v. Mellon*, 262 U.S. 447 (1923); *United States v. Richardson*, 418 U.S. 166 (1974); *Schlesinger v. Reservist Committee to Stop the War*, 418 U.S. 208 (1974); *Valley Forge Christian College v. Americans United for Separation of Church and State*, 454 U.S. 464 (1982); *DaimlerChrysler Corp. v. Cuno*, 547 U.S. 332 (2006); *Hein v. Freedom from Religion Foundation.*, Inc., 551 U.S. 587 (2007).

26 *Ex Parte Levitt*, 302 U.S. 633 (1937); *Lujan v. Defenders of Wildlife*, 504 U.S. 555 (1992). However, it should be noted that in subsequent cases the Court slightly changed its approach in addressing the generalized grievance doctrine; please see *Federal Election Commission v. Akins*, 524 U.S. 11 (1998); *Massachusetts v. EPA*, 549 U.S. 497 (2007).

27 For an excellent discussion on the application of *actio popularis* in developing democracies, please see Aparna Polavarapu. "Expanding Standing to Develop Democracy: Third-Party Public Interest Standing as a Tool for Emerging Democracies," 41 *Yale J. Int'l L.* 105 (2016).

28 One theory explains that *actio popularis* originated in ancient Roman law, in which a stranger could bring a case on behalf of an injured slave, where the slave had no "standing" in a Roman tribunal to bring the action him or herself; see Alfred P. Rubin. "Actio Popularis, Jus Cogens, and Offenses Erga Omnes?" 35 *New Eng. L. Rev.* 265, 268 (2001). Another theory, however, suggests that there was no general acceptance of *actio popularis* under Roman law; *actio popularis* was simply to indicate that it was one of a random group of actions that could be brought by anyone among the people (*quivus ex populo*); see Peter P. Mercer.

"The Citizen's Right to Sue in the Public Interest: The Roman *Actio Popularis* Revisited," 21 *U.W. Ont. L. Rev.* 89, 97–102 (1983).

29 Aharon Barak. "A Judge on Judging: The Role of a Supreme Court in a Democracy," 116 *Harv. L. Rev.* 16 (November 2002), 107–108.

30 In 1976, the Indian Supreme Court began to open its door to the relaxation of standing rules in *Maharaj Singh v. State of Utar Pradesh* (1976) 1 SCR 1072.

31 See the 1991 Colombian Constitution, Art. 241.The 1991 Constitution created two types of third-party standing: the abstract and concrete reviews of constitutionality. The first one is the public action of unconstitutionality by virtue of which any citizen can demand from the Court that a law or decree be declared unconstitutional, without him or her being a lawyer or having any particular interest in the issue. The second one is the *tutela* action, in which any person may directly request any judge to protect his or her fundamental rights when they are being violated by a state agent or an individual. The Court's rules on standing, even in concrete review cases, are relatively flexible.

32 The Constitutional Court Decision No. 003/PUU-I/2003 (hereinafter the *Government Securities Law* case).

33 See Law No. 24 of 2002 on Government Securities.

34 The 1945 Indonesian Constitution, Art. 33 (1 & 4).

35 The *Government Securities Law* case, 5–6.

36 Ibid., 49–50.

37 The Constitutional Court Decision No. 001-021-022/PUU-I/2003 (The *Electricity Law* case).

38 The Association of Indonesian Human Rights Lawyers (*Asosiasi Penasehat Hukum dan Hak Asasi Manusia Indonesia*—APHI); the Indonesian Legal Aid and Human Right Association (*Perhimpunan Bantuan Hukum dan Hak Asasi Manusia Indonesia*); and Foundation 234, an environmental-based NGO.

39 The *Electricity Law* case, 13–14.

40 Ibid., 327.

41 Ibid., 327.

42 Ibid., 327.

43 See the Constitutional Court Decision No. 014/PUU-I/2003 (hereinafter the *Susduk Law* case).

44 See Law No. 22 of 2003, Art. 30 (2–5). These provisions related to the DPR's right to an investigation (*hak angket*).

45 The 1945 Indonesian Constitution, Art. 27 (1).

46 The *Susduk Law* case, 31.

47 Ibid., 32.

48 Ibid., 34.

49 Ibid., 34.

50 Private conversation with Justice Natabaya, July 27, 2006.

51 Constitutional Court Decision No. 011/PUU-III/2005 (hereinafter the *National Education System* case).

52 Law No. 20 of 2003 on the National Education System (*Sistem Pendidikan Nasional*).

53 Ibid., the elucidation of Art. 49 (1).

54 Constitution of Republic of Indonesia 1945, Art. 31 (4).

55 The *National Education System* case, 102.

56 Ibid., 105.

57 Private conversation with Natabaya, July 27, 2006.

58 The *National Education System* case, 105.

59 Ibid.

60 Ibid.

61 The *National Education System Case*, 104–105.

62 Private conversation with Natabaya, July 27, 2006.
63 Ibid.
64 Ibid.
65 Ibid.
66 Natabaya earned his LLM degree from Indiana University School of Law, Bloomington.
67 Private conversation with Justice Natabaya, May 28, 2008.
68 Achmad Roestandi. *Mahkamah Konstitusi Dalam Tanya Jawab* [101 questions on the Constitutional Court] (Jakarta: Sekretariat Jenderal dan Kepaniteraan Mahkamah Konstitusi, 2006), 42.
69 Private conversation with Achmad Roestandi, August 8, 2006.
70 See the Constitutional Court Decision No. 006/PUU-I/2003, 796–797 (the *Anti-Corruption Commission Law I* case).
71 Private conversation with Justice Maruarar Siahaan, July 28, 2006.
72 The Indonesian Constitutional Court Decision No. 011-017/PUU-I/2003 (hereinafter the *Communist Party* case).
73 Laica Marzuki, Laica Marzuki, Berjalan Jalan Di Ranah Hukum. *Pikiran-Pikiran Lepas Laica Marzuki* [The Thought of Laica Marzuki] (Jakarta: Konstitusi Pers, 2005), 105.
74 Ibid.
75 Private conversation with Jimly Asshiddiqie, July 31, 2006.
76 Ibid.
77 The Constitutional Court Decision No. 004/PUU-I/2003 (the *Supreme Court Law I* case).
78 See Article 7 § 1 & 2 Law No. 14 of 1985 on the Supreme Court.
79 See the *Supreme Court Law I* case, 11–13.
80 Why did the Court not explicitly nullify Article 50? One plausible answer is because the claimant himself did not formally request the Court to invalidate Article 50. The claimant just challenged the constitutionality of the Supreme Court Law. Nevertheless, the Court had to deal with the issue of Article 50 because the challenged statute was enacted before the 1999 Constitutional Amendment.
81 See The *Supreme Court Law I* case, 18–31.
82 Ibid., 21.
83 The Constitutional Court Decision No. 066/PUU-II/2004 (hereinafter the *Chamber of Commerce Law* case).
84 Ibid., 55.
85 Ibid., 54–55.
86 The 1945 Indonesian Constitution, Art. 24C (6).
87 The *Chamber of Commerce Law* case, 65.
88 Ibid.
89 Private conversation with Justice Achmad Roestandi, August 8, 2006.
90 Private conversation with Justice Mukthie Fadjar, August 4, 2006.
91 The Constitutional Court Decision No. 002/PUU-I/2003 (the *Oil & Gas Law I* case).
92 Apart from the NGOs claimant, there were two other groups of NGOs: first, the Labor Union of the State Oil Company; and second, an individual academic who has concerns over oil and gas issues.
93 The *Oil and Gas Law I* case, 10.
94 Ibid., 200.
95 The *Oil and Gas Law II* case, the Constitutional Court Decision No. 20/PUU-V/2007.
96 Ibid., 98.
97 Private conversation with Justice Palguna, August 9, 2006.

98 The Constitutional Court Decision No. 004/PUU-I/2003 (hereinafter the *Supreme Court Law I* case).
99 Private conversation with Justice Palguna, August 9, 2006.
100 Ibid.
101 Simon Butt. *Judicial Review in Indonesia: Between Civil Law and Accountability*, 123.
102 The *Government Securities Law* case.
103 Ibid., 50.
104 The *Broadcasting Law* case.
105 Ibid.
106 The Constitutional Court Decision No. 002/PUU-I/2003 (the *Oil & Gas Law I* case).
107 The Indonesian Constitutional Court Decision No. 069/PUU-II/2004 (hereinafter the *Bram Manoppo* case).
108 See Law No. 30 of 2002 on the Anti-Corruption Commission, Art. 68.
109 See the 1945 Indonesian Constitution, Art. 28I (1).
110 See the *Bram Manoppo* case, 66.
111 Ibid., 67.
112 Ibid.
113 The Constitutional Court Decision No. 006/PUU-IV/2006 (the *Truth and Reconciliation Commission Law* case).
114 Law No. 27 of 2004 on the Truth and Reconciliation Commission.
115 Ibid., Art. 27.
116 Ibid., Art. 44.
117 The *Truth and Reconciliation Commission Law* case, 103.
118 Ibid., 103.
119 Ibid., 104. Article 18 § 1 (e) of the Truth and Reconciliation Commission Act states that the Commission shall clarify the status of perpetrators or victims of gross violations of human rights. When the claimants challenged the statute before the Court, however, the Commission had not yet been established.
120 See John Ferejohn and Pasquale Pasquino. "Constitutional Adjudication: Lessons from Europe," 82 *Tex. L. Rev.* 1671, 1692–1693 (2004). For a detailed analysis of dissenting opinion in the German Constitutional Court, please see Donald P. Kommers. *The Constitutional Jurisprudence of the Federal Republic of Germany* (2d ed. 1997), 26 (noting the reluctance of German constitutional justices to publish dissenting opinions).
121 See Jonghyun Park. "The Judicialization of Politics in Korea," 10 *Asian-Pacific L. & Pol'y J.* 62, 70–71 (2008); See also Chien-Chih Lin. "Pace of Constitutional Transition Matters: The Judicialization of Politics in Indonesia and Korea," 20 *UCLA J. Int'l L. & For. Aff.* 275, 307 (Fall, 2016).
122 Private conversation with Jimly Asshiddiqie, June 4, 2008.
123 Ibid.
124 Ibid.
125 The Constitutional Court Decision No. 2-3/PUU-V/2007 (hereinafter the *Death Penalty* case).For a detailed analysis of the *Death Penalty* case, please see Natalie Zeria.l, "Decision No. 2-3/PUU-V/2007 [2007] (Indonesian Constitutional Court)," 14 *Austl. Int'l LJ* 217 (2007).
126 For an excellent analysis on how the death penalty dates back to the New Order regime, please see Benedict Anderson. "Impunity and Reenactment: Reflections on the 1965 Massacre in Indonesia and its Legacy," 11(15) *The Asia-Pacific Journal* 1 (April 15, 2013).
127 For a detailed analysis of the extrajudicial killings that took place in the 1980s, please see David Bourchier. "Law, Crime, and State Authority in Indonesia." In *State and Civil Society in Indonesia*, edited by Arief Budiman. (Clayton, Victoria:

Centre for Southeast Asian Studies, Monash University, 1990); see also Geoffrey Robinson. "Rawan is as Rawan does." In *Violence and the State in Soeharto's Indonesia*, edited by Benedict R. O'Gorman Anderson (Ithaca, NY: Southeast Asia Program Publications, Southeast Asia Program, Cornell University, 2001).

128 Law No. 22 of 1997 on Narcotics.

129 The *Death Penalty* case, 6.

130 Justices Roestandi, Siahaan, and Marzuki filed dissenting opinions on the merit of the case. Also, Justice Harjono filed a dissenting opinion on the standing issue, but he sided with the majority on the merit of the case. On the standing issue, the Court majority ruled that the foreigners have no standing, but the Court proceeded to review the merit of the case because two other claimants had standing to bring the case.

131 The *Death Penalty* case, 359.

132 Tim Mann. "Missing History? Jimly Asshiddiqie on the Death Penalty in Indonesia." *Indonesia at Melbourne*. August 11, 2015b. Accessed February 10, 2016. http://indonesiaatmelbourne.unimelb.edu.au/missing-history-jimly-asshiddiqie-on-the-death-penalty-in-indonesia/.

133 Ibid.See also Jimly Asshiddiqie. *Islam, Democracy, and the Future of the Death Penalty*. Public Lecture presented by the Centre for Indonesian Law, Islam and Society, the Asian Law Centre and the Melbourne Law School, University of Melbourne, August 11, 2015a.

134 The Constitutional Court Decision No. 008/PUU-IV/2006 (hereinafter the *Right to Recall* case).

135 Patrick Ziegenhain. *The Indonesian Parliament and Democratization* (Singapore: Institute of Southeast Asian Studies, 2008), 125.

136 Law No. 22 of 2003 on the Composition and Position of the MPR, DPR, DPD and DPRD, Art. 85 (1).

137 "PAN Memecat Djoko Edhi." [PAN fired Djoko Edhi] Liputan6.com. December 22, 2005. Accessed February 09, 2016. http://news.liputan6.com/read/114597/pan-memecat-djoko-edhi.

138 The *Right to Recall* case, 55.

139 Ibid., 56.

140 Justice Mukthie Fadjar and Justice Laica Marzuki filed separate dissenting opinions.

141 The *Right to Recall* case, 71.

142 Private conversation with a former law clerk of the Constitutional Court, May 27, 2008.

Part III

The second-generation court

6 After the heroic court

The second-generation decline?

Prelude

The Javanese are numerically the largest and the most influential ethnic group in Indonesia, both culturally and politically. Most of the Javanese ruling class, including the presidents and many leading military generals, have been preoccupied with mystical Javanese religious views, which are represented in the shadow theatre tradition (*wayang*) of the heroic tales of *Mahabharata*.[1] Thus, in some way or another, the heroic tales of *Mahabharata* have spread into Indonesian political, religious, and cultural history.

The great Bharata war in the epic *Mahabharata* is a conflict that arose from a dynastic succession struggle between two groups of cousins, the Kurawas and the Pandawas. The battle produces complex conflicts of kinship, friendship, family loyalty, and duty over what is right and what is wrong. In the war, the chief adviser to the Pandawa brothers was Kresna. Nevertheless, Kresna's brother, Baladewa, took the side of the evil Kurawa clan. He did this out of loyalty to his wife, Herawati, and his father-in-law, King Salya. Salya felt duty bound to fight for the evil Kurawa because of his youngest daughter, Banowati, who had married the eldest of the Kurawas, Duryudhana. Nevertheless, deep in his heart, Baladewa harbored love for the Pandawa brothers. But would Baladewa take the Kurawas' side in the war? The legend says that Kresna instructed his younger brother to meditate at the place of thousand waterfalls, so he did not hear anything when the war broke out and, consequently, he missed the war.

The last three chapters remind us that the chairmanship of Jimly Asshiddiqie successfully transformed the first-generation Indonesian Constitutional Court into a functioning institution. The next three chapters explore what happened after the end of the era of the heroic Court under the chairmanship of Jimly Asshiddiqie. This chapter, in particular, will address the transition from the first-generation court under Chief Justice Asshiddiqie to the second-generation court under the presidency of Mohammad Mahfud.

The first part of this chapter explores the fall of Chief Justice Asshiddiqie and the rise of Chief Justice Mohammad Mahfud. The second part, which is the central portion of this chapter, examines the second-generation Court under the chairmanship of Mohammad Mahfud. This chapter will ask the following questions: Did Chief Justice Mahfud continue to employ the heroic leadership style of his predecessor? Was there anything unique about Mahfud's leadership style? To what extend did Mahfud understand himself to be the guardian of the legacy of the first-generation heroic Court? Or perhaps like Baladewa, he chose the wrong side of history even although, deep in his heart, he believed that the Court should play a heroic role.

Mohammad Mahfud came to office with a vision of judicial restraint. Nevertheless, Mahfud's leadership became something of a Frankenstein's monster possessed of the capacity to stand up to its creator. Mahfud led the transformation of the Court into a heroic social justice Court that struck down many anti-poor policies. In the name of substantive justice, the Court bypassed many procedural requirements and moved toward solving many political crises. Mahfud also led the Court to transform the quasi-weak form of review as a tool to issue strong remedies, without giving substantial deference to the legislature. In short, Mahfud chose to be a bold, aggressive judicial hero, which is very different from his predecessor's heroic leadership style.

The fall of Chief Justice Asshiddiqie

A skilled chief justice like Asshiddiqie might have been the proper figure to lead the Court in transition; nevertheless, he occupied a vulnerable position. Like the rest of the associate justices, Chief Justice Asshiddiqie had a limited term—the judge can only serve two 5-year terms—and therefore he had to please those who had the authority to reappoint him for a new term.[2] Moreover, the law states that the chief justice serves a 3-year term, though he can be reelected for a new term.[3] As chief justice, Asshiddiqie had to face reelection every 3 years and consequently was forced to please his associate justices in order to be reelected.

Initially, the nine justices of the Constitutional Court were due to reach the end of their first 5-year terms in August 2008. But three justices, Achmad Roestandi, Laica Marzuki, and Soedarsono, had to retire earlier because they would turn 67 years old, the mandatory retirement age.[4] Toward the end of the Court's calendar term in 2007, the vacancies in the Constitutional Court had become a major issue, as the media reported that President Susilo Bambang Yudhoyono had a plan to have his former confidant, Yusril Ihza Mahendra, chosen as chief justice of the Constitutional Court.[5]

Immediately Asshiddiqie went to the media and expressed his concern that the politicians might want to fight for the Constitutional Court seats because the political parties were unhappy with some of the Court's decisions.[6] Asshiddiqie made two appeals through the media. First, he urged that if the president or the House of Representatives (DPR) would like to nominate a member of the political party to be a Constitutional Court Justice, that candidate should relinquish his or her party membership.[7] Asshiddiqie made this statement about a potential nominee, Yusril Ihza Mahendra, who was the Chairman of the Star and Crescent Party. Second, Asshiddiqie called for his fellow academics to watch for and guard the Constitutional Court because he believed there was an attempt to subvert the "academic" culture of the Constitutional Court.[8]

As Justice Roestandi was approaching his mandatory retirement age in March 2008, the House Judiciary Committee prepared a fit and proper test for a candidate to replace Justice Roestandi. Moreover, the DPR also decided to proceed with a plan to find the replacement for two other justices who were to finish their first term in August 2008. Chief Justice Asshiddiqie stated that he would prefer not to run for a second term rather than to submit to the fit and proper test in the DPR. Asshiddiqie argued that there would be a conflict of interest if he chose to undergo the fit and proper test while he was still sitting as the chief justice. Asshiddiqie explained:

> Can you imagine that on Monday I have to hear an oral argument and on the following day, I have to undergo the fit and proper test in the DPR? On Wednesday, maybe I will announce a decision, and if the Court comes out with a decision to reject a petition, everybody then will think that the decision was simply to please the DPR.[9]

Surprisingly, the House Judiciary Committee decided to accommodate Asshiddiqie's concern and opened the door for him to skip the fit and proper test.[10] Initially, the House Judiciary Committee had closed the selection process for the Constitutional Court, but it then extended the nomination process to nominate Asshiddiqie as a Constitutional Court justice. The chair of the House Judiciary Committee, Trimedya Pandjaitan, explained that the DPR decided to accommodate Asshiddiqie's request because it was difficult for the DPR to find a qualified and capable candidate.[11]

Asshiddiqie immediately dropped his retirement plan and decided to stand for a second term.[12] In addition to Asshiddiqie, Justice Harjono also decided to join the selection process in the DPR. The DPR also approved Harjono's nomination to the Constitutional Court. Unlike other candidates who had to face the DPR interview session, Asshiddiqie and Harjono did not have to undergo a fit and proper test. They soon left the room upon signing a document that made their candidacy official.[13]

On March 14, 2008, the DPR appointed three candidates for the offices of Constitutional Court judge for the 2008–2013 period: Jimly Asshiddiqie, Mohammad Mahfud, and Akil Mochtar. Meanwhile, Justice Harjono failed to secure his second 5-year term because the DPR decided not to reappoint him for a second term.[14] In the meantime, the Supreme Court appointed Muhammad Arsyad and Muhammad Alim to replace Justice Laica Marzuki and Justice Soedarsono, who had reached the mandatory retirement age.[15]

As the Court was approaching the end of its calendar term in 2008, a few dramatic events symbolized the end of an era at the Court under the chairmanship of Jimly Asshiddiqie. On August 12, 2008, the Court issued a decision in the *Religious Court* case.[16] The Court rejected the claimant's petition, but it is worth noting the oral argument of the *Religious Court* cases, in which Chief

Justice Asshiddiqie was neither the center of attention nor was present.[17] It was a junior associate, Justice Muhammad Mahfud, who stole the attention during the oral argument.

The oral argument began with the claimant's argument that she wanted to conduct an *ijtihad* through her petition. *Ijtihad* is a term in Islamic Law that describes the process of making a legal decision by independent interpretation of the legal sources, the Qur'an and the Sunnah. The claimant challenged the constitutionality of the Amendment of the Religious Courts Law, which expanded the authority of the Religious Courts from adjudicating cases among Muslims ranging from family law, inheritance, and trust to dispute resolution on economic sharia and Islamic almsgiving (*zakat*).[18] The claimant argued that Islam required Muslims to adhere to Islamic Law in its entirety, including Islamic Criminal Law, and not to be limited to areas of Islamic Law under the Religious Court jurisdiction, from family law, inheritance, and trust to dispute resolution on economic sharia and Islamic almsgiving (*zakat*).

The claimant explained that two sources that inspired her petition were a news report in a local newspaper and a book titled *Penerapan Syariah Islam: Bercermin Pada Sistem Aplikasi Syariah Zaman Nabi* (The Implementation of Islamic Sharia: Learning from the Application of Sharia from the Era of the Prophet).[19] Mahfud began to grill the claimant by asking her why she took inspiration from a local news report and an obscure book instead of relying on the teaching of thousands of *ulama* (Islamic teachers).[20] Furthermore, Mahfud asked the claimant whether she could read Arabic books. Mahfud then recited from memory the definition of *Ijtihad* in Arabic and queried whether the applicant understood.[21] The claimant admitted that she did not know the Arabic quotation recited by Justice Mahfud.[22] Finally, Mahfud told the complainant she must check the primary sources in Arabic on the rule of *ijtihad* before making an attempt to conduct an *ijtihad* or otherwise she would be wasting her time with the petition.[23] The oral argument signified that Asshiddiqie was not the only intellectual quarterback in the Court, as was once the case. There was a new hero in town.

On August 13, 2008, the Court decided the *Education Budget V* case, which was discussed in Chapter 4. In sum, the Court held that the 2008 State Budget was in violation of the Constitution because it allocated less than the mandated budget (20 percent of the state budget).[24] The Court ruled that the president and the DPR were guilty of deliberate defiance of the Constitution and demanded the full allocation be met in the 2009 budget. But the Court still allowed for the current underfunded budget to stand until the 2009 budget cycle took effect, arguing that a delay was necessary "to avoid governmental disaster."[25] I will explain later why this decision was significant in marking the end of the Court under the chairmanship of Jimly Asshiddiqie.

Two days later, on August 15, 2008, the Court announced its decision in the *Wijaya & Lubis* case.[26] Both claimants, Risang Wijaya and Bersihar Lubis, were journalists who had been charged with the Criminal Code concerning defamation.[27] The claimants argued that their prosecution violated the constitutional guarantee of freedom of expression (Article 28E) and the right to communicate

(Article 28F). The Court unanimously decided against the claimant and ruled that the state has the authority to limit or regulate freedom of expression based on Article 28J (2).[28] Moreover, the Court held that the state must balance the freedom of expression so it would not harm other people's rights, which include a right to protect one's honor and reputation.[29]

This case marked a significant departure from the Court's previous jurisprudence in human rights–related cases. Interestingly, Asshiddiqie did not participate in the announcement of the Court's decision, and the decision was only signed by eight justices of the Constitutional Court. There was no record that Asshiddiqie recused himself from the case. The official explanation from the Court was that Asshiddiqie could not participate in the announcement of the decision because he had to attend the State of the Union address of President Yudhoyono.[30] Regardless of the reason for his absence, the decision signified the waning influence of Chief Justice Asshiddiqie.

On August 16, 2008, two new justices were sworn in. President Yudhoyono appointed two new justices, Maria Farida Indrati and Achmad Sodiki, and reappointed Justice Mukthie Fadjar for his second term. With the coming of these new justices, there were only three justices from the first-generation Court: Asshiddiqie, Siahaan, and Fadjar (Table 6.1).

When the Court opened its new term, Asshiddiqie was quite confident that he would continue to lead the Court. The law states that the Constitutional Court justices have the authority to elect the chief justice and deputy chief justice for a 3-year term.[31] Chief Justice Jimly Asshiddiqie became the chief justice in 2003, and later, in 2006, he was re-elected, so presumably, he would remain as chief justice until 2009.[32] Nevertheless, six new associate justices, who recently joined the bench, demanded the election of a new chief justice. Asshiddiqie relented, and on August 19, 2008, the Court decided to hold an election process to elect a new chief justice and a deputy chief justice. Surprisingly, a new associate justice, Mohammad Mahfud, beat Jimly Asshiddiqie by only one vote in the runoff after they each gained four votes in the first round.

Asshiddiqie suspected that the Yudhoyono administration orchestrated his removal due to the Court decision in the *Education Budget V* case.[33] The Court decided the *Education Budget V* case on August 13, 2008, and Asshiddiqie believed that the decision prompted the Yudhoyono administration to arrange for his removal during the election of the chief justice on August 20, 2008.[34] The president has no direct power to remove the chief justice because, according to the law, the chief justice was elected by associate justices in an internal election. But Asshiddiqie suspected that it was Vice President Jusuf Kalla who mobilized some associate justices to rally against him.[35]

If the plot of the Yudhoyono administration to remove Asshiddiqie can be proven to be true, it was just a proximate cause; there are different factors that became the ultimate cause of Asshiddiqie's ouster from the position of chief justice. The first factor was the Court's stability, which reflects the change in the Court's configuration. The appointment of six new associate justices in 2008 created instability within the Court. These new justices were the ones who

Table 6.1 Constitutional Court Justices 2008

Names	*Prior position*	*Nominator*	*Education*
Maria Farida Indrati	Professor of law	President	– LLB (UI, Indonesia) – Master of Law (UI, Indonesia) – PhD (UI, Indonesia)
A. Mukthie Fadjar	Professor of law	President	– LLB (UGM, Indonesia) – Master of Science (Unair, Indonesia)
Achmad Sodiki	Professor of law	President	– LLB (Unibraw, Indonesia) – PhD (Unair, Indonesia)
Jimly Asshiddiqie	Professor of law	DPR (House)	– LLB (UI, Indonesia) – Master of Law (UI, Indonesia) – PhD (UI, Indonesia
Mohammad Mahfud	Professor of law	DPR (House)	– LLB (UII, Indonesia) – MA (UGM, Indonesia) – PhD (UGM, Indonesia)
Akil Mochtar	Politician/MP	DPR (House)	– LLB (UPB, Indonesia)) – Master of Law (Unpad, Indonesia) – PhD (Unpad, Indonesia)
Maruarar Siahaan	Administrative court judge	Supreme Court	– LLB (UI, Indonesia)
Arsyad Sanusi	Administrative court judge	Supreme Court	– LLB (Unhas, Indonesia) – Master of Law (UII, Indonesia) – PhD (UI, Indonesia)
Muhammad Alim	High court judge	Supreme Court	– LLB (Unhas, Indonesia) – Master of Law (UII, Indonesia) – PhD (UII, Indonesia)

challenged Asshiddiqie's leadership and ousted him from the leadership position with the government's blessing.

The second factor is the term *limit*. Through Asshiddiqie's experience, it became apparent that the weakest point of the Court was the limited term of the associate justices and the chief justice. With such limited terms, the justices faced the reality that their term may not be renewed if they failed to please other elements of the government. Moreover, the chief justice also sits on the bench with some insecurity, since he might not be re-elected if he fails to please the government or the other associate justices. Mandatory term limits remain a weak point of the current structure of the Indonesian Constitutional Court. Although the government does not have direct control over the election of the chief justice, it can support associate justices likely to oust the chief justice from his leadership role. In sum, short mandatory term limits are a primary mechanism for the government to control the agenda and reach of the Indonesian Constitutional Court.

The last factor was Asshiddiqie's tactical mistake at the end of his tenure. Through the application of the quasi-weak form of review, Asshiddiqie was able to minimize the Court's involvement in complicated decision-making processes. Nevertheless, over time, Asshiddiqie did not make a prudential judgment by invalidating the State Budget in the *Educational Budget V* case. The Court had restrained itself in the previous four cases of the Educational Budget, but in the end, Asshiddiqie failed to make a prudential judgment and initiated unnecessary confrontation with the government.

Initially, Asshiddiqie remained as an associate justice; however, on October 8, 2008, he submitted his resignation from the Constitutional Court. During a press interview, he explained that he quit due to the "psychological" tension that had jeopardized his relations with the other eight justices and all court officials. Asshiddiqie said at a press conference, "I think this is the right time for me to leave, in the hope that it will help the chief justice, the other justices, and all the court officials conduct their duties with ease."[36] Chief Justice Mahfud, however, denied Asshiddiqie's claim about psychological tension within the Court.[37] For this reason, there was doubt about the real reason behind the resignation of Jimly Asshiddiqie, but one thing was clear: His decision to step down marked the end of an era and the beginning of the Court under the chairmanship of Mohammad Mahfud.[38]

Mohammad Mahfud and the court he made

Before reviewing the leadership of Chief Justice Mahfud, an overview of Mahfud's background is helpful to explain his leadership style after he took the helm as chief justice.

Political trajectories and intellectual vision

Mohammad Mahfud Mahmodin (commonly known as Mahfud MD) grew up in Madura, an Indonesian island off the northeastern coast of Java.[39] A majority of Madurese Muslims are proponents of *santri* tradition, a more orthodox version of Islam, which was influenced by Sunni Islam, the largest denomination of the religion. Mahfud grew up in a family with *santri* tradition, and his early education took place in an Islamic boarding school (*pesantren*).[40]

Mahfud pursued his undergraduate studies in law at the Indonesian Islamic University (*Universitas Islam Indonesia*) in Yogyakarta, where he was actively involved in the Indonesian Islamic Students Association (*Himpunan Mahasiswa Islam*).[41] Upon his graduation, Mahfud became a lecturer of law at his alma mater. Later, he obtained his doctoral degree in constitutional law from Gadjah Mada University, the oldest public university in the country. Mahfud rose to national prominence when the late President Abdurrahman Wahid appointed him minister of defense in 2000. There was some speculation that the appointment was solely based on Mahfud's affiliation with the *Nahdatul Ulama* (NU), the largest traditional Islamic organization in Indonesia, which was once led by President Wahid. For many Madurese like Mahfud, being a Muslim meant being a sympathizer of the NU, but this strong identification did not automatically mean that one became a member of the organization officially.[42]

After Mahfud had served for nearly a year as the minister of defense, President Wahid appointed him minister of justice. He did not hold that position for long, however, because the People's Consultative Assembly (*Majelis Permusyawaratan Rakyat*) impeached President Wahid in 2001. After Wahid's impeachment and removal from office, Mahfud became active in the National Awakening Party (*Partai Kebangkitan Bangsa*—PKB), which was founded by President Wahid. From 2004 to 2008, Mahfud represented PKB in the DPR and served as a member of the Judiciary Committee. By the time Mahfud assumed the role of chief justice, he was the only politician in Indonesia who had served in all three branches of government. With his background and experience, Mahfud was a credible contender against a high-profile chief justice like Jimly Asshiddiqie. Mahfud's social and political connections also advanced his ability to compete with someone like Jimly Asshiddiqie.

While he was serving as a member of the House Judiciary Committee, Mahfud expressed his disagreement with Asshiddiqie's approach to judicial review. He accused Asshiddiqie of steering the Court in the wrong direction, and he urged the Court to exercise judicial restraint to get back on track. He proposed a formula of "10 taboos" that could serve as a template for the Court's self-restraint.[43] His first taboo was that the Court should not create any new rule or regulation in its decisions. Second, the Court should not review any governmental policy. Third, the Court should make its decisions solely based on the Constitution. As the fourth taboo, he stated that the Court should not impinge upon the jurisdiction of the legislature. The fifth was that the Court should not make reference to any constitutional theories or case precedents from foreign countries. As the sixth taboo, he posited that the Court should recuse itself when it had a self-interest in certain cases, such as the cases addressing Article 50 that involved the Court's jurisdictional limitation. Giving interviews in the news media or offering public comments formed the seventh taboo. The eighth taboo was that the Court should not build close relationships with any groups or help them to bring cases before the Court. Mahfud envisioned the ninth taboo as a general prohibition on the justices engaging in any activism outside of the Court. Finally, he was convinced that the justices should not criticize the Constitution.[44] With this vision of extreme judicial restraint, Mahfud appeared to be the ideal candidate to dismantle Jimly Asshiddiqie's work as the Court's first leader.

During the confirmation hearing in front of the House Judiciary Committee on March 12, 2008, Mahfud reaffirmed his "10 taboos."[45] Some members of the House Judiciary Committee were quite impressed with Mahfud's vision on judicial restraint.[46] Surprisingly, they did not bring up Mahfud's previous legal writing for further scrutiny and confirmed him with the highest vote.

If the House Judiciary Committee wanted to know Mahfud's legal vision, they were supposed to trace Mahfud's intellectual works before the formulation of the "10 taboos." While pursuing his doctoral studies at Gadjah Mada University, Mahfud was deeply influenced by a local "radical" theoretician, Satjipto Rahardjo, a proponent of the so-called progressive legal approach (*hukum progresif*). The idea of the progressive legal approach draws on the premise that law can only be actualized with human intervention, and it held that judges should be free from the reign of absolute rules.[47] Therefore, if changes occur in society and legal texts are unable to cope with the new development, judges then must not be enslaved by legal texts that are no longer relevant.[48]

Mahfud wrote his doctoral dissertation on the role of the political configuration in the creation of law regarding elections, regional government, and land reform in Indonesia.[49] In his dissertation, Mahfud was strongly influenced by the idea of responsive law, which derived from the slender book by Philippe Nonet and Philip Selznick, *Law and Society in Transition*.[50] Nonet and Selznick posit three modes of legal order: repressive law, autonomous law, and responsive law.[51] Each is distinguished from the other by purpose, method, and source of legitimacy. Responsive law focuses on the substantive goals of the community and views law as an instrument for achieving them.[52] Responsive law pursues accountability not solely regarding compliance with rigid rules but also through fidelity to the substantive aims of the law.[53] The bottom line is that responsive law reflects a concern with substance. The concept of responsive law was the primary theoretical framework for Mahfud's doctoral dissertation, and it would continue to influence his legal thinking throughout his career.

If the House Judiciary Committee had traced Mahfud's writing, they would have been more cautious in appointing him to the Constitutional Court. Knowing Mahfud's intellectual conviction concerning progressive and responsive law, the House Judiciary Committee would have thought twice about whether they had found the right man to make the Court more subservient to the other branches of government.

Mixed record on individual rights cases

Mahfud was sworn in as the second chief justice of the Constitutional Court on August 21, 2008. As Mahfud came to the bench with a vision of strong judicial restraint, the issue was whether he would be able to fulfill what he had promised. A brief overview of some of the Court's decisions is helpful to evaluate his leadership style and how faithful he was to his vows of judicial restraint.

Some of the Mahfud Court decisions in the area of civil and political rights signified a substantial departure from the Court's earlier approach. The Court under the chairmanship of Jimly Asshiddiqie believed that it was the duty of the Court to correct governmental infringement upon constitutional rights and therefore that the court should protect such rights. On the contrary, the Court under the chairmanship of Mahfud seemed to defer to the government in the areas of civil and political rights.

The Court decisions in the *Pornography Law* case[54] and the *Blasphemy Law I* case[55] were examples of the Court's strong tendency to defer to the government in the areas of civil and political rights.[56] In both cases, the Court relied on Article 28J (2), which provide general limitations to the bill of rights.[57] In the *Pornographic Law* case, the Court rejected the claimant's petition and held that although the Constitution guarantees some fundamental rights, including freedom of expression, there is a general limitation of those rights as stipulated in the Constitution by Article 28J (2).[58] Similarly, the Court took a similar approach in the *Blasphemy Law I* case and held that the Blasphemy Law was the manifestation of Article 28J (2); therefore, the state has the authority to limit liberty as long as it is based on the recognition of other people's rights and freedoms.[59] This restriction pertains to morality, religion, and public order in a democratic society.[60]

The Court reaffirmed the application of Article 28J (2) in the *Blogger I* cases.[61] The claimant challenged the Information and Electronic Transaction Law, which prohibits the making available of electronic information and documents that contain insults or defile one's good name.[62] The Court decided against the claimant and argued that the Information and Electronic Law is not contrary to the Constitution because there is always a limit to press freedom.[63] The Court held that the state has the authority to restrict or regulate press freedom based on Article 28J (2).[64]

Despite its less favorable treatment of individual rights-related cases, in some instances, the Court tried to protect the constitutional rights of citizens. In the *Book Banning* case,[65] the Court invalidated the authority of the Attorney General Office to ban books and printed materials.[66] The Court, however, did not make any explicit ruling on freedom of speech. Instead, the Court seemed to consider the books as "property." The Court ruled that the authority of the Attorney General to ban and seize books and printed materials without any judicial proceedings was to be considered an extrajudicial execution that violated the right to own property.[67] The Court made reference to the Constitution, which stipulates that "every person shall have the right to own personal property, and such property may not be unjustly held possession of by any party."[68] Despite the issuance of a favorable decision to the claimants, the *Book Banning* case had no significant impacts on free-speech rights in Indonesia. The Court approached neither the right to speech nor the freedom of expression as fundamental individual rights.

In sum, the Court under the leadership of Mohammad Mahfud took a different approach on human rights-related cases. The Court's jurisprudence on individual rights-related cases was not defined by its meaning but rather by its limitation. The most interesting part of the Court's jurisprudence under the chairmanship of Mahfud was the recognition of a general limitation of individual rights under Article 28J (2).

A heroic social justice court

The Court during the presidency of Mahfud also had to deal with the interpretation of Article 33. The remaining question was whether Mahfud would exercise heroic judgment and second guess governmental economic policy as his predecessor did. On the surface, the Mahfud Court seemed to take a heroic approach like the Asshiddiqie Court in reviewing Article 33–related cases. Nevertheless, there are some significant differences between the heroism of the Asshiddiqie Court and the Mahfud Court in Article 33 cases. Asshiddiqie had the vision to reconstruct the Indonesian economy in a transitional period, and therefore, he tried to implement his vision through the Court's decisions. In other words, Asshiddiqie's heroic mission was to rescue the Indonesian economy from the waves of a free market and globalization. Mahfud had no economic vision like Asshiddiqie, and there was no sign that he had the ambition to lead the Court to reconstruct the Indonesian economy.

The Court under the chairmanship of Mohammad Mahfud took a different approach in dealing with Article 33 cases, in which the Court put emphasis on the phrase "the greatest benefit of the people" (*sebesar—besarnya kemakmuran rakyat*). This approach led Mahfud to display a different kind of heroism in being the savior of poor people: fishermen, farmers, local miners, and so on. As Mahfud stated, his Court was not anti-free market or anti-foreign investment, but rather it was a "pro-social justice court."[69] In sum, Mahfud directed his crusade to provide benefits for lowly people instead of second-guessing the government's macroeconomic policy, as his predecessor had done.

The Court began to solidify its Article 33 jurisprudence in the *Coastal and Remote Islands Law* case.[70] In this case, some fishermen located in coastal areas, along with some NGOs, challenged various provisions of the 2007 Law on the Management of Coastal Areas and Remote Islands. The crux of the matter was whether some provisions in the Law, which authorized the government to grant Coast Water Concessions Right (*Hak Pengusahaan Perairan Pesisir*—HP3) (Article 16) to private business entities (Article 18), including foreigners (Article 23 § 7), were contrary to the Constitution.

The Court ruled that the key point to determine state control is the phrase "the greatest benefit of the people" (*sebesar—besarnya kemakmuran rakyat*) in Article 33 (3).[71] The Court held that the Coast Water Concessions Right (HP3) could not achieve the greatest benefit of the people because it would deprive the traditional or indigenous community of their rights to natural resources, upon which they relied for their subsistence needs and livelihoods.[72]

The Court used a similar approach in the *Tin Mining* case.[73] In this case, two miners from Bangka islands–the biggest tin producing area in the country—challenged the 2009 Mining Law.[74] The claimants argued that some provisions in the Law contradicted Article 33 as it only protected high-capital companies and did not offer the same legal protection to smaller businesses or individual miners.[75] The Court ruled that the minimum mining area requirement of 5000 hectares could threaten small and medium-scale mining operations as they usually operate in a much smaller mining area. The Court held that to achieve the greatest benefit of the people, the government should give priority to small and medium-scale industry to manage mineral and coal mining.

The Court did not deal with the challenge against any governmentally significant economic policies until it had to review the government privatization policies in the *Oil and Gas Law III* case.[76] The claimants were 12 Islamic-based organizations and 30 individuals, chiefly led by *Muhammadiyah*, one of the largest Islamic organizations in the country. The complainants challenged some of the key statutory provisions in the Oil and Gas Law, which mandated the government to establish a Regulatory Agency (*Badan Pelaksana Minyak and Gas—BP Migas*) to supervise the oil and gas upstream sector and to take over the regulatory and administrative functions of *Pertamina* (State Owned Oil Company).[77]

First, the Court decided to apply generalized grievances standing and held that *Muhammadiyah* and others had the standing to bring the case because their constitutional rights might potentially be injured by the application of the law.[78] In its ruling, the Court did not explicitly state that *Muhammadiyah*, as a religious-based NGO, may enter the stage of constitutional litigation as a public defender. Nonetheless, by granting standing to *Muhammadiyah*, the Court under the leadership of Mahfud continued to apply a loose standing doctrine like the previous Court.[79]

On the merit of the case, the Court began its judgment by referring to the *Coastal and Remote Islands Law* case, in which the Court held that that the key point in determining state control is the phrase "the greatest prosperity of the people" (*sebesar—besarnya kemakmuran rakyat*). The Court then moved to consider that *BP Migas* only maintains a monitoring and supervisory function, and consequently, the services of *BP Migas* did not violate constitutional "state control" within the meaning of Article 33.[80] The Court further considered that when *BP Migas* entered into a contract with private enterprises, the private companies would potentially control the benefits of oil and gas, therefore minimizing the benefits that the people were supposed to enjoy. Thus, the Court decided that the establishment of *BP Migas* contradicted the constitutional mandate of state control for the greatest benefit of the people.

By transforming the Court into a social justice court, Mahfud broke his taboo, as the Court had to review some governmental policies. Moreover, the Court continued to employ generalized grievance standing to open the door to reviewing administrative policies.

The transformation of quasi-weak-form review

After Mahfud had taken over the helm as chief justice, there were some significant shifts in the issuance of the quasi-weak-form decisions. First, the Court issued far more conditional decisions than the previous Court.[81] Second, the Court began to issue "conditionally unconstitutional decisions," which means that the challenged statute is invalid unless implemented according to the Court's interpretation. Furthermore, the Court also became more explicit in stating the condition in the Court's holding.

The Court under the chairmanship of Mahfud began to cement its "conditionally unconstitutional" approach in the *Tobacco Excise Tax* case.[82] The claimant—the Provincial Government of West Nusa Tenggara—challenged a provision in the Excise Tax Law that required the allocation of 2 percent of central government excise tax on tobacco to "tobacco-producing regions."[83] The claimant argued that the application of the law is contrary to the principle of economic democracy under Article 33.[84]

The Court accepted the claimant's argument, but it refused to invalidate the provision on tobacco-producing regions because the invalidation of the provision would cancel the allocation of the excise tax on tobacco to different provinces.[85] The Court held that the challenged provision was "unconstitutional as long as tobacco producer regions were not included as those are entitled to receive the tobacco excise."[86] To make sure that the government would include producer regions as the recipient of the tobacco excise, the Court ordered the government to allocate tobacco excise in the state budget. The Court announced the decision on April 13, 2009 and it ordered the government to apply the decision in the 2010 State Budget.

Furthermore, the Court presented a crucial statement on the shift from conditionally constitutional decisions to conditionally unconstitutional ones. The Court stated:

> Experience has shown that some of the conditionally constitutional decisions have not been followed, and, therefore the Court's holdings were not effective. For the sake of upholding the Constitution, the Court rules that the challenged provision (tobacco excise tax) conditionally violates the Constitution. The ruling means that the provision is unconstitutional if the conditions the Court stipulates are not met, namely the claimant as a tobacco producer province is entitled to receive the government's allocation of the excise tax on tobacco. Therefore, the challenged provision has no binding force if the requirements stipulated by the Court are not fulfilled.[87]

The Court continued its "unconstitutional conditionally" approach in the *SJSN IV* case,[88] which dealt with the workers' participation provision in the law on the National Social Security System (*Sistem Jaminan Sosial Nasional* or SJSN).[89] The SJSN Law provides that employers must register their employees as participants in a social security program, by which they would be entitled to receive the benefits bestowed by the program.[90] Some labor unions went to the Court and argued that the Law curtailed their rights to social security, as the fulfillment of social security rights would be dependent upon the employers' good faith in registering their employees in the program.[91]

The Court held that the worker participation provision was "conditionally unconstitutional," which means the challenged provision would be declared unconstitutional if it was interpreted as a way to eliminate workers' rights to be registered in the social security program when their employers failed to register them.[92] The Court held that the provisions should be interpreted as follows: "employers must register their employees as participants in a social security program and workers have the right to register for a social security program if their employers fail to register their employees with the Social Security Administrative Body."[93]

As mentioned earlier, the Court under the leadership of Mahfud became more explicit in stating the condition in the Court's holding. In the *ID Card* case,[94] the Court created a new rule about voting registration in its conditionally constitutional decision. In this case, the Court dealt with the constitutionality of a provision in the Presidential Election Law, which required that to cast a vote, a voter must be registered in the Final Electoral Roll (*Daftar Pemilih Tetap*—DPT).[95] The Court held that the Law is conditionally constitutional, so long as it does not deprive those citizens not registered in the Final Electoral Roll of their voting rights.[96] The Court ruled that the Law must be interpreted as follows: "all citizens who were not registered in final electoral roll (*Daftar Pemilih Tetap*—DPT) could show their IDs to cast a vote and for those who are living overseas can use their passports to cast a vote."[97] The Court ruled further that "voters using an ID card must also show their family card (*Kartu Keluarga*) and may only cast their ballot in their residential neighborhood."[98]

The Court continued to prescribe specific conditions in the *Leftover Votes* case.[99] In this case, the Court had to deal with the issue of how to determine "leftover" votes (*sisa suara*) in national legislative elections to allocate "leftover" seats (*sisa kursi*) in the parliament. Law no. 10 of 2008 on the Legislative Election prescribed that there must be a "second round" of seat allocations to fill the leftover seats, under which political parties' votes must meet at least 50 percent of the Voting Division Number (*Bilangan Pembagi Pemilih*—BPP) to obtain a seat.[100] The Court held the provisions to be conditionally constitutional as long as they were interpreted to mean that any parties that fulfill 50 percent or more of the BPP would receive a seat in the second round of counting.[101] If any seats remained, those seats would be allocated in the third round of seat allocation. Finally, the Court held that the Law is "conditionally constitutional" as long as votes used to obtain a seat in the first round would be exhausted and could not be used again in the second round.[102]

In the *Attorney General* case,[103] the Court ruled that the Public Prosecutor Law created legal uncertainty because it did not provide any clarity concerning when the attorney general shall begin and end his term in office.[104] Nevertheless, the Court held that the Law is "conditionally constitutional," as it should be interpreted that the attorney general should serve a 5-year term as a member of the president's cabinet and the president can remove the attorney general at any time.[105]

The Court ruled that the Law is conditionally constitutional, but it did not explicitly rule that the appointment of the then attorney general, Hendarman Supandji, was unconstitutional.[106] Having realized that there was an ambiguity in the Court's decision, the president's legal adviser argued that Supandji was still a legitimate attorney general. Initially, Mahfud said that he did not care whether or not the president would comply with the Court's decision.[107] But later, Mahfud decided to intervene by urging the president to dismiss Attorney General Hendarman Supandji immediately.[108] Mahfud explained that he must intervene in his capacity as the chief justice, otherwise there would be an endless conflict of interpretation on the status of Hendarman Supandji as the attorney general.[109]

Some scholars argue that the Court under the leadership of Mahfud usurped the legislative power by using the conditionally constitutional technique as a tool to correct legislation and prescribe an amendment to a challenged statute.[110] While this argument has its validity, I argue that there is a different way to see the transformation of the conditionally constitutional technique. While Asshiddiqie relied on this technique as a tool to issue weak remedies to minimize the impact of the Court's ruling, Mahfud used this technique to issue strong remedies. Under the leadership of Mahfud, the Court would enforce robust remedies fully, without giving substantial deference to legislative judgments, especially when the justices concluded there was a legal vacuum that needed to be filled.

Towards responsive/progressive law approach

By the time the Court began its new court term in August 2010 (two years after Mahfud took office), it was already evident that Mahfud had broken his enumerated taboos multiple times. Mahfud explained, "If I follow those restrictions, then there will be no justice at all. We don't live in a perfect world, with the assumption that everyone is a good person."[111] According to Mahfud, he broke his taboos to uphold "substantive justice."[112] Some scholars argued that Mahfud did not elaborate what "subjective justice" meant.[113] But, apparently, Mahfud was referring to the idea of responsive law, which put emphasis on fidelity to the substantive aims of the law instead of compliance to rigid rules.

The Court began to make reference to the idea of substantive justice in the *East Java* case,[114] in which the Court ruled that it must not let procedural limitations hamper and neglect substantive justice. In this case, the Court dealt with the Regional Administration Law, which prescribed that the object of a regional election dispute could only concern the final result of the regional election.[115] The Court, however, went the extra mile to review any infringement upon local election processes, including both administrative and criminal offences.[116] Nevertheless, the Court did not make any connection between the idea of substantive justice and the concept of responsive law.

The Court made an explicit reference to the notion of responsive law in the presidential election dispute between President Yudhoyono and his opponents, Jusuf Kalla and Megawati Soekarnoputri.[117] Chief Justice Mahfud wrote a long opinion on the meaning of substantive justice in conjunction with the responsive law. In sum, Mahfud wrote, "in dealing with general election dispute, the Court must aim to uphold substantive justice."[118] Mahfud explained further, "with emphasis on substantive justice, although an action is legally justified, if it's substantially in breach of justice, then it could be declared wrong."[119] Mahfud further clarified that by upholding substantive justice, it did not mean that the Court would always disregard the statutory text. Mahfud wrote:

> As long as the statutory text brings a sense of justice, the Court will rely on it in the decision making process. But if the statutory text won't render justice,

> the Court could ignore it and then make its own decision. That's the essence of responsive law or progressive law.[120]

The Court rejected the petition of the presidential candidates, Jusuf Kalla and Megawati Soekarnoputri, in the 2009 Presidential Election dispute and voted in favor of President Yudhoyono. But the Court concluded that in dealing with a general election dispute, the Court would not stop to examine the electoral result, but it would go the extra mile to evaluate the electoral process.[121]

Interestingly, Mahfud began to equate the notion of responsive law and progressive law. It appeared that Mahfud needed to convince his fellow judges of the idea of responsive law, which was derived from Nonet and Selznick. One way for Mahfud to win them over to the notion of responsive law was by convincing his fellow judges that such an idea is parallel with the concept of progressive law (*hukum progressif*), which was fostered by a local scholar, Satjipto Rahardjo. Indeed, Satjipto Rahardjo was a big cheerleader for the Court under the leadership of Mahfud. Rahardjo especially gave high praise to the Court's decision in the *ID Card* case as the best example of how the Court had employed the progressive approach.[122]

An apt example of Mahfud's "progressive" approach is the Court's decision in the *Hamzah & Riyanto* case.[123] The claimants—Chandra Hamzah and Bibit Riyanto—were the commissioners of the Anti-Corruption Commission. The Commission managed to wiretap a high-ranking police official on the suspicion that the official was taking bribes. The Indonesian National Police then moved to incriminate Hamzah and Riyanto, alleging that they abused their power.[124] As Hamazh and Riyanto's trial loomed, there was significant public pressure on President Yudhoyono to save the Anti-Corruption Commission. Chief Justice Mahfud advised President Yudhoyono of a Government Regulation in Lieu of Law (*Peraturan Pemerintah Pengganti Undang—Undang* or PERPU) that gave himself the power to appoint the Anti-Corruption Commissioner if three or more commissioner positions became vacant.[125] Mahfud argued that he had advised President Yudhoyono to pass the PERPU in order to save the Anti-Corruption Commission, and he had no hidden agenda whatsoever.[126]

In the meantime, Hamzah and Riyanto went to the Constitutional Court and asked the Court to issue an interim injunction to prevent their dismissal before the Court could hear their case. Considering that the Court's authority was limited to determining the constitutionality of a statute and issuing appropriate declaratory remedies as claimed, in theory, the Court had no power to issue an injunctive remedy to prevent the criminal investigation of Hamzah and Riyanto. Surprisingly, the Court decided that it could issue an injunction. But on the question of to whom the injunction would be directed, the Court admitted that it lacked jurisdiction to order police and prosecutors to postpone the criminal investigations against Hamzah and Riyanto.[127] Nevertheless, the Court ordered the president to refrain from suspending Hamzah and Riyanto until a final verdict was issued.[128]

Having realized that the Court lacked the authority to stop the criminal proceeding, Chief Justice Mahfud criticized the police in the media and urged the police to bring the commissioners' alleged abuses of power to the State Administrative Court instead of the Criminal Court.[129] Furthermore, he stated that if he were the president, he would remove the chief of the National Police.[130] After the press conference, Chief Justice Mahfud met with President Susilo Bambang Yudhoyono privately and tried to convince the president to drop the case because the police had no basis for incriminating the commissioners of the Anti-Corruption Commission.[131]

Collegiality

As the Court moved to embrace the notion of responsive/progressive law, it appeared that Mahfud's intellectual vision had influenced the Court's jurisprudence. Nevertheless, Mahfud was aware that he did not have total control over his fellow judges, and he learned a valuable lesson from his predecessor on the necessity of building a culture of trust and collegiality. For instance, Mahfud was quite successful in creating consensus among his fellow justices that the Court should play the heroic role as the savior of the lowly people. In the *Oil and Gas Law III* case, Mahfud assigned Associate Justice Hamdan Zoelva to prepare the draft of the judgment that focused on the scope and meaning of the phrase "the greatest benefits of the people." By assigning the draft to Hamdan Zoelva, Mahfud showed that his fellow justices were behind him in his crusading heroism to uphold social justice for the greatest benefit of the people.

Like his predecessor, Mahfud was also conscious of the need for the justices to avoid opposing each other and to give the impression that the justices were usually in agreement and that there was consensus among them on the main issues. An apt example is the Court's decision in the *PERPU* case.[132] The crux of the matter was whether the Court had the authority to review the constitutionality of the Government Regulation in Lieu of Law (*Peraturan Pemerintah Pengganti Undang—Undang*—PERPU). With a split decision (8–1), the Court majority held that it had the authority to review PERPU because PERPU has legal effects like a statute.[133] Mahfud disagreed with the Court's majority opinion, but he decided to issue a concurring opinion instead of a dissenting opinion. Mahfud argued that essentially his concurring opinion was a dissenting opinion, but he did not believe it appropriate for him as chief justice to issue a dissent.[134] Mahfud explained that there were several reasons for him to side with the majority. First, Mahfud believed that his fellow associate justices were genuine in their argument and that they had no personal interest.[135] Second, Mahfud saw that his adversaries always had a reasonable argument and therefore, Mahfud chose to side with the majority so that the case could be resolved quickly.[136]

Similarly, Mahfud tried to avoid issuing a dissenting opinion in the *International School* case.[137] The Court ruled that the provision of the international standard state school (*Satuan Pendidikan yang Bertaraf Internasional*) was unconstitutional because international schools could charge higher fees than other public schools, thereby precluding enrollment by students from disadvantaged families.[138] Mahfud admitted that personally, he loved the idea of the international school, but he could not convince his brethren to agree with his position.[139] The Court unanimously declared the Law unconstitutional, but Mahfud did not issue a dissenting opinion. In Mahfud's view, there was no reason for him to issue a dissenting opinion after he lost a debate with the majority.[140]

Mahfud saw the Court as a symphony orchestra that performs musical compositions. According to Mahfud, like the "symphony," which means "sound together," the justices must always come together on important issues.[141] Mahfud explained further that all the justices always support the majority opinion despite their dissent, and even some dissenting justices helped to craft the majority opinion to show the weight of the Court's majority opinion.[142]

Chief Justice Mahfud at twilight

Despite his strength, Mahfud occupied a vulnerable position, in which he had a limited term. Mahfud had to sit on the bench with uncertainty as to whether he would be re-elected as the chief justice and whether he would be renewed for a second term. Before addressing this issue, there were at least two dramatic events that marked Mahfud's leadership.

The corruption scandal

One of the biggest challenges for Mahfud was to maintain the image of a transparent Court. Unfortunately, Mahfud failed to preserve this image, as the Court he led was tainted by several alleged corruption scandals. These scandals brought serious challenges to Mahfud's legitimacy as the chief justice of the Constitutional Court. One of these high-profile scandals involved Associate Justice Mohammad Arsyad and centered on allegations that he manipulated the Court's decision in a regional election dispute. In 2009, the Court examined a dispute over the Head of Regency Election in South Bengkulu. A candidate for the position, Nirwan Mahmud, bribed both Arsyad's daughter and Arsyad's brother-in-law to convince Justice Arsyad to sway the Court's decision in Mahmud's favor. Justice Arsyad admitted that his daughter indeed met the candidate; however, he denied that his daughter had introduced the candidate to him.[143] Arsyad maintained that he did not commit any crime; nevertheless, he tendered his resignation and left the Court in disgrace.[144]

A few months after Arsyad left office, a new scandal surfaced. While he was in office, Arsyad was allegedly involved in the forgery of a letter that gave a seat in the DPR to a losing candidate.[145] The disgraced Justice Arsyad launched a counterattack and accused Mahfud of being an incompetent chief justice because he neglected the Court's administration and focused too much on building his popularity outside of Court activities.[146] Arsyad maintained that he was innocent, and Mahfud wanted to find a scapegoat for the maladministration in the Court. The truth behind Arsyad's statement remains unknown; nevertheless, Arsyad's scandals and his counterattack tainted the Court's reputation and the leadership of Chief Justice Mahfud.

The 2011 amendments

While the Court was still recovering from the shock of Arsyad's scandals, it had to deal with another pressure as the DPR enacted the Amendment of the Constitutional Court Law.[147] The amendment process itself went largely unnoticed, and thus it created an impression that the DPR wanted to avoid public discourse on the bill.[148] The Amendment established the Honorary Council of Judges of the Constitutional Court, which aimed to supervise the performance of the Constitutional Court justices. The council members included some members of the DPR.[149] The Amendment also prescribed that the Court's judgment should not exceed what a claimant requested.[150] The then minister of law and human rights, Patrialis Akbar, explained that the Court would be forbidden from deciding a matter it had not been asked to make a decision upon, such as the nullification of a whole statute.[151] Moreover, the amendment also prohibited the Court from issuing declarations of "conditionally constitutional" or "conditionally unconstitutional."[152]

The Amendment also reduced the tenure of chief justice to 2.5 years, implying that the DPR wanted to have more control over the Court.[153] The decision to reduce the term of chief justice signified that this position was quite important. By reducing the term of chief justice, the DPR wanted to minimize the position's influence on Indonesian constitutional politics.

Chief Justice Mahfud, however, responded positively to the Law and stated that the Court would accept it without reservation.[154] Moreover, Mahfud overruled any possibility that the Court would review the Law. He promised to stick with his old taboos: that the Court should recuse itself when it had self-interest in certain cases that involved the Court's authority.[155] One plausible explanation of Mahfud's "compliance" with the new law was that he was seeking for re-election as the chief justice. In August 2011, Mahfud had to run for re-election as the chief justice, so he once again implemented judicial restraint to avoid any possible interference from the Executive and Legislative branches in the election process.

On August 18, 2011, Mahfud was re-elected as chief justice until 2014.[156] Not long after his re-election, Mahfud returned to his heroic role and led the Court to strike down the Amendment of the Constitutional Court Law. In the *2011 Amendment Law I* case,[157] the Court invalidated Article 45A, which prohibited the Court from issuing a judgment that exceeds beyond what a claimant requested, commonly known as *ultra petita*. The Court considered that *ultra petita* was derived from a civil procedure that related to an individual interest.[158] The Court held that the prohibition of *ultra petita* arose from "a misunderstanding of the judicial review function ....The Constitution requires judges to guard the Constitution for the sake of public interest, which is bigger than individual interests."[159]

In the *2011 Amendment Law II* case, the Court invalidated Article 27A, which allowed the Honorary Council to supervise the performance of the Constitutional Court justices.[160] The Court held that the establishment of the Honorary Council that involved the DPR, government, and Supreme Court threatened the Court's independence.[161] Moreover, the Court also invalidated Article 50A, which prohibited the Court from using another statute as the basis for its legal considerations.[162] As Simon Butt noted, the Court's decision was ambiguous because it denied that the Court had ever used another statute as a basis for its considerations.[163]

Nevertheless, the Court held that the provision reduced the Court's authority in exercising its judicial powers to uphold the law.[164]Although invalidating Article 50A was unnecessary, the Court wanted to show that it was a defiant judiciary. As Chief Justice Mahfud stated, "We were being mistreated by the Legislatures, and, therefore, we decided to invalidate the Law."[165]

There are at least two major narratives about the factors that triggered the adoption of the 2011 Amendment. First, Mahfud's responsive law approach brought discomfort to the DPR and the president.[166] Some cases that were decided by the Court under the framework of responsive law had upset the DPR, which eventually led them to initiate the 2011 Amendment. The other trigger for the 2011 legislative amendments was a series of corruption scandals that provided justification for the Court's opponents to create a mechanism to supervise the judges.[167]

It is beyond the scope of this book to analyze the real motives of the politicians in adopting the 2011 Amendments, but I will address a difficult question arising from the 2011 Amendment, that is, the question of principal–agent relationships, in which judges are agents or servants of the political branches that appoint them.[168] This question was based on the assumption that Mahfud chose not to represent the interest of the principals or masters who appointed him, and therefore, the DPR, as the principal, decided to launch an attack.

I argue that the principal–agent model does not map so neatly onto the experience of the Constitutional Court, especially concerning the 2011 Amendment. First, it was not clear to what extent the DPR envisioned Mahfud as their judicial agent in the first place. Looking back at Mahfud's appointment process, clearly, the DPR had no clear strategy about the judicial appointment as they did not even bother to check Mahfud's legal writings. Moreover, the DPR did not seem to have any strategic plan to place Mahfud as the new chief justice. If the DPR wanted to elevate Mahfud, they could refuse to re-appoint Asshiddiqie for his second term, but the DPR decided to enable Asshiddiqie to apply for his second term.[169] Moreover, the DPR provided special treatment for Asshiddiqie by letting him skip the confirmation hearing and by re-appointing him for his second term.[170]

Neither does the principal–agent theory fit in the Indonesian judicial context, especially if we try to explain the chairmanship of Mohammad Mahfud on the basis of the attitudinal model. The attitudinal model holds that judges decide cases according to their ideological attitudes and values. Two leading proponents of this model describe this approach as "Rehnquist votes the way he does because he is extremely conservative; Marshall voted the way he did because he is extremely liberal."[171] This model does not work in the Indonesian context because Mahfud could not be put in a particular ideological category. As Donald Horowitz put it, although in many instances Mahfud defended a progressive point of view and a flexible constitutional interpretation, the Court decisions in the *Pornography Law* case[172] and the *Blasphemy Law I* case[173] were far from progressive and flexible interpretations.[174] Furthermore, many of the Court's decisions regarding individual rights were often inconsistent with Chief Justice Mahfud's rhetoric.[175] Thus, it was not clear to what extent ideology played a role in the decision-making process and to what extent Mahfud upset the DPR.

Last days of Chief Justice Mahfud

Having survived the 2011 Amendments, Mahfud continued to the lead the Court, and he was supposed to serve as the chief justice until 2014.[176] Surprisingly, in November 2012, Mahfud told the DPR that he intended to leave his job in April 2013. Considering that the DPR appointed Mahfud, he had to inform the DPR earlier so that they would have sufficient time to appoint his predecessor. There were rumors that Mahfud was a potential candidate for president in the 2014 election.[177] Therefore, his decision to resign, some believe, was part of his larger plan to run for president.

While Mahfud did not shy away from showing his ambition to run as a presidential contender,[178] some additional factors prompted his early departure from the Court. Mahfud could make a strategic calculation that he might not be reappointed for his second term. Mahfud was initially sworn in as an associate justice on April 1, 2008, which meant that his first term would end on April 1, 2013. Thus, Mahfud needed to win a nomination from either the president or the DPR for his second term. But there was a high likelihood that neither the president nor the DPR would appoint him for his second term.

On April 1, 2013, Chief Justice Mahfud officially resigned from the Court and reaffirmed his aspiration to run in the presidential race. "If the opportunity is there, I am ready to be nominated as a presidential candidate," said Mahfud on his last day at Court.[179] Mahfud's presidential ambitions indicate that he utilized the role of heroic chief justice as political capital to run for presidency.[180]

Conclusion: A different type of heroism

The leadership of Chief Justice Mahfud, for the most part, was the embodiment of the bold, aggressive, heroic leader. In many different cases, Mahfud led the Court to employ the progressive law approach and issue strong remedies. In the name of substantive justice, the Court bypassed many procedural requirements and moved toward solving many political crises. An apt example is the *ID Card* case, in which the Court did not summon the government and parliament at all.[181] Chief Justice Mahfud explained that the Constitutional Court justices had a conference on the morning of Monday, July 6, 2009, and they unanimously agreed to decide the case on the same day.[182] In other words, the Court decided the case based on the written argument prepared by the petitioner.

In the *Mohammad Sholeh* case,[183] Mahfud showed that he could be a street fighter. In this case, the Court ordered the General Election Commission to assign seats to any candidate who won the most number of votes in a district.[184] The General Election Commission, however, refused to comply with the Court's decision. Chief Justice Mahfud issued a press statement and warned the Election Commission that there would be political and criminal consequences for all commissioners who refused to comply with the Court's decision.[185] He argued that the situation forced him to speak out; otherwise, the General Election Commission would have never followed the Court's decision.[186]

Interestingly, Mahfud refused to lead the Court to invalidate some provisions related to individual rights. It was not clear why Mahfud declined to employ his progressive law approach in individual rights-related cases and chose to defer to the government instead. But it is interesting to note that Mahfud did not seem to highly appreciate some of the NGOs that filed the cases. In the aftermath of the *Blasphemy Law I* case, Chief Justice Mahfud responded by accusing the NGOs who filed the complaint of merely seeking attention, and he questioned their credibility as human-rights advocates.[187]

To some degree, Mahfud displayed arrogance and pride in relation to different governmental branches. In Mahfud's view, he could criticize the house speaker publicly when the DPR committed wrongdoing.[188] Similarly, Mahfud stated that he could be very candid to the president if he had a different opinion than the president.[189] Mahfud made an analogy in which the governance structure is a soccer team in which the president is the captain of the team, the DPR is the defender, and the Court is the forward. Mahfud argues that, as a team, they share a similar goal of winning the game, and so each member has right to yell at and criticize some of his teammates when they mess up during the match.[190] But Mahfud forgot to acknowledge that his analogy represents a pervasive problem on a lot of athletic teams, where the better athletes somehow feel that they have a right to get angry at and criticize their less skilled teammates. As Mahfud frequently criticized the president and the DPR, he implied that he was more knowledgeable than other leaders of different governmental branches.

Some scholars argue that there was a trend of decline in the Court under the chairmanship of Mahfud, especially regarding the quality of reasoning.[191] The decline in the quality of reasoning, coupled with the Court's intrusion into legislative territory through its "conditionally constitutional approach," triggered the 2011 Amendments. It is beyond the scope of this book to measure the quality of reasoning under the chairmanship of Mahfud. I, however, argue that the main issue is the type of heroism that was displayed by Chief Justice Mahfud. The combination of aggressiveness and the enforcement of strong remedies, without substantial deference to legislative judgments, were the factors that provoked some retaliation from the other branches of government against the Court.

In sum, what made the difference between the first-generation and the second-generation Courts is the heroic leadership style of the two chief justices. Asshiddiqie relied more on a combination of maximalist and minimalist approaches, in which he employed a quasi-weak form of review as a tool to minimize the impact of the Court's decision. Mahfud, however, transformed the quasi-weak form of review into a means to issue strong remedies without giving substantial deference to the legislature. Moreover, Mahfud also displayed some aggressiveness and arrogance toward the Executive branch and Legislature. While Asshiddiqie was not immune from pride and arrogance, at least he did not show it publicly as Mahfud did.

Given Mahfud's aggressive leadership style, there was a looming question as to whether his successors would be able to maintain the legacy of the second-generation court. In the next two chapters, I will explore how his successors would be lesser heroic figures and how leadership style will affect the future of the Court.

Notes

1 Laurie J. Sears. *Shadows of Empire: Colonial Discourse and Javanese Tales* (Durham, NC: Duke University Press, 1996), 218–221. Sears explains how the first president, President Soekarno, who led the nation for independence, often identified himself with *Mahabharata* heroes such as Bima, who is known for his courage; and Gathutkaca, who is known for his patriotism. See also Helen Pausacker. "Presidents as Punakawan: Portrayal of National Leaders as Clown-Servants in Central Javanese Wayang," 35(2) *Journal of Southeast Asian Studies* 231–233, 218 (2004). Pausacker explains that the second president, President Soeharto, liked to identify himself with Semar, the divine and wise figure in the *Mahabharata*. The status of Semar is a servant, but he is the incarnation of God. Thus, Semar's character is the combination of grassroots and God.

2 Law No. 24 of 2003 on the Constitutional Court, Art. 22.

3 Ibid., Art. 4 (3).

4 Ibid., Art. 23 (1c).

5 *Jakarta Post*. "Politicians Should Keep Out of Court, Says Jimly," December 27, 2007.

6 *Hukumonline*. Jimly Asshiddiqie. "Pergantian Hakim Konstitusi Jangan Sampai Mengubah Kultur MK [Don't Let the Appointment of New Justices Change the Constitutional Culture], December 14, 2007. http://www.hukumonline.com/berita/baca/hol18177/pergantian-hakim-konstitusi-jangan-sampai-mengubah-kultur-mk.

7 Ibid.

8 Ibid. The chief justice made reference to the Anti-Corruption Commission and the General Election Commission because both institutions have been undermined by the appointment of new commissioners who can be considered weak appointees. See *Jakarta Post*. "Anti-Graft Candidates Show No New Ideas," September 4, 2007; see also *Jakarta Post*. "House Taps Seven for Poll Body: Questions Raised about Experience," October 5, 2007.

9 *Hukumonline*. "Beralasan Menjaga Etika, Jimly Emoh Melamar ke DPR, [In Order to Maintain Ethical value, Jimly Declines to Apply to the House], February 18, 2008.

10 *Jakarta Post*. "Lawmakers Support Jimly For New Term," February 26, 2008.

11 *Hukumonline*. "Demi Jimly, Independensi DPR Dipertaruhkan" [The House Sacrifices its Independence for Jimly], February 25, 2008. http://www.hukumonline.com/berita/baca/hol18626/demi-jimly-independensi-dpr-dipertaruhkan.

12 *Jakarta Post*. "Jimly Drops Retirement Plan, to Stand for Second Term at MK," March 8, 2008.

13 *Jakarta Post*. "House Begins Testing Constitutional Court Candidates," March 12, 2008.

14 *Jakarta Post*. "Two Politicians Elected as Constitutional Court Judges," March 15, 2008.

15 Muhammad Arsyard was sworn in on May 29, 2008, and Muhammad Alim was sworn in on June 26, 2008.
16 The Constitutional Court Decision No. 19/PUU-VI/2008 (hereinafter the *Religious Court* case).For a detailed analysis of the *Religious Court* case, please see Simon Butt. "Islam, the State and the Constitutional Court in Indonesia," 19 *Pac. Rim L. & Pol'y J.* 279 (2010).
17 Minutes of the Oral Argument on the Case No. 19/PUU-VI/2008, July 31, 2008.
18 Law No. 3 of 2006 on the Amendment of Law No. 7 of 1989 on Religious Court, Art. 49.
19 Khatimah, Husnul, and Zubaedi. *Penerapan Syari'ah Islam: Bercermin pada Sistem Aplikasi Syari'ah Zaman Nabi.* (Yogyakarta: Pustaka Pelajar, 2007).
20 The Minutes of the Oral Argument on the Case No. 19/PUU-VI/2008, July 31, 2008, para . 25, 27.
21 Ibid., para. 29, 33.
22 Ibid., para. 36.
23 Ibid., para. 37.
24 The Constitutional Court Decision No. 13/PUU-VI/2008, reviewing Law No. 16 of 2008 on the Amendment of Law No. 45 of 2007 on the 2008 State Budget (hereinafter *Education Budget V* case).
25 Ibid., 101.
26 The Constitutional Court Decision No. 14/PUU-VI/2008 (hereinafter the *Wijaya & Lubis* case).
27 Risang Wijaya, general manager of the *Radar Jogja* newspaper, was criminally charged for defamation. Wijaya was sentenced to six months imprisonment for the *Radar Jogja* report that the general manager of its rival newspaper, *Kedaulatan Rakyat*, had sexually harassed a female employee. Bersihar Lubis was a veteran journalist who had been convicted for writing a column in the *Koran Tempo* newspaper, in which he called the Attorney General's Office a "fool" for banning school history books. Lubis was charged under the Criminal Code, which imposes a maximum of 18 months imprisonment for publicly insulting, orally or in writing, a public institution or authority.
28 The *Wijaya & Lubis* case, para. 3.24.
29 Ibid.
30 "Pasal Penghinaan Tidak Langgar UUD." [Defamation Articles Don't Violate the Constitution], August 6, 2008, KOMPAS.com. Accessed July 12, 2016. http://nasional.kompas.com/read/2008/08/16/00140453/pasal.penghinaan.tidak.langgar.uud.
31 The Constitutional Court Law No. 24 of 2003 on the Constitutional Court, Art 4 (3).
32 *Jakarta Post.* "Jimly Asshiddiqie: The Face of Controversial Constitutional Court," January 3, 2008.
33 Private conversations with Jimly Asshiddiqie, December 22, 2014.
34 Ibid.
35 Ibid. Few facts may support Asshiddiqie's suspicion that Vice President Jusuf Kalla orchestrated his removal. First, Mahfud admitted that Vice President Jusuf Kalla asked him to run against Asshiddiqie. See Rita Triana Budiarti. *On the Record: Mahfud M.D. di balik putusan Mahkamah Konstitusi* [Mahfud behind the Constitutional Court Decisions] (Jakarta: Murai Kencana, Konstitusi Press, 2010), 54. Second, Justice Mukthie Fadjar acknowledged that the then minister of justice, Andi Mattallata, briefed the president's appointees to vote against Asshiddiqie. Justice Fadjar further explained that a close confidant of Vice President Jusuf Kalla—the then Ambassador to Russia, Hamid Awaludin—called him on the night before the election and tried to persuade him to vote for Mahfud.

See A. Mukthie Fadjar. *2037 Hari Mengawal Konstitusi* [2037 days to guard the Constitution] (Malang, Indonesia: In-Trans Publishing, 2010), 16–19.

36 *Jakarta Post*. "Jimly Quits MK for Personal Reasons," October 8, 2008.

37 Rita Triana Budiarti. *On the Record: Mahfud M.D.: Di Balik Putusan Mahkamah Konstitusi (Mahfud: Behind the Constitutional Court Decisions)* (Jakarta: Konstitusi Press, 2010), 36–37. The book was later republished under a different title, *Kontroversi Mahfud MD Jilid 1* (Jakarta: Konstitusi Press, 2012).

38 After his resignation from the Court, Asshiddiqie initially took a break from politics. He came back to the national political stage in 2010 when President Yudhoyono appointed him as a member of the Presidential Advisory Board. Having spent six months as one of the president's advisors, Asshiddiqie tendered his resignation because he wanted to make a bid to be selected for the top post as Anti-Corruption Commission leader. Despite the massive public support for Asshiddiqie as a potential chief of the Anti-Corruption Commission, he did not even make it through to the final selection test before the House Judiciary Committee. In 2012, Asshiddiqie was appointed chairman of the Honorary Council of General Electoral Officers (*Dewan Kehormatan Penyelenggara Pemilu*). In 2015, Asshiddiqie made his second attempt to make a bid to be selected as the Anti-Corruption Commission Chief. Again, Asshiddiqie did not make it through to the final list. Moreover, many people became more cynical with his political overture and began to see him as a political opportunist. Apparently, Asshiddiqie's resignation from the Court and his constant failure to secure a position in the Anti-Corruption Commission marked his waning political influence.

39 Mahfud rarely uses his complete name, Muhammad Mahfud Mahmodin, and he commonly uses Mahfud MD. But in this book, I will use Muhammad Mahfud instead. Mahfud explains that the name of Mahmodin is his father's name and his primary-school teacher added the name to his original name to distinguish him from many other students who were also named Mahfud. See Aguk Irawan. *Biografi Mahfud: Cahayamu Tak Bisa Kutawar* [Mahfud's Biography: I Cannot Deny Your Light] (Yogyakarta: Ar-Ruzz Media, 2014), 87–88.

40 Ibid., 34.

41 Ibid., 220.

42 Yanwar Pribadi. *Religious Networks in Madura: Pesantren, Nahdatul Ulama, and Kiai as the Core of Santri Culture,* 51(1) *J. Islamic Stud, Al-Jami'ah* 14 (2013). http://journal.aljamiah.org/index.php/AJ/article/viewFile/147/pdf.

43 Mohammad Mahfud. *Konstitusi dan Hukum Dalam Kontroversi Isu* [Constitution and Law in Controversial Issues] (Jakarta: Rajawali Pers, 2009), 281–284.

44 Ibid., 281–284.

45 Rita Triana Budiarti. *Biografi Mahfud MD: Terus Mengalir* (Jakarta: Konstitusi Press, 2013), 419.

46 *Hukumonline*. "Sepuluh Rambu Hakim Konstitusi Ala Profesor Mahfud," March 13, 2008. Accessed July 21, 2016. http://www.hukumonline.com/berita/baca/hol18749/sepuluh-rambu-hakim-konstitusi-ala-profesor-mahfud.

47 Satjipto Rahardjo. *Membedah Hukum Progresif* (Jakarta: Penerbit Buku Kompas, 2006), 56.

48 Satjipto Rahardjo. "Hukum Progresif, Hukum Yang Membebaskan," 1(1) *Jurnal HukumProgresif* 5–6 (2005).

49 Mohammad Mahfud MD. *Perkembangan Politik Hukum: Studi Tentang Pengaruh Konfigurasi Politik Terhadap Produk Hukum di Indonesia* (unpublished doctoral dissertation, Gadjah Mada University, 1993). A modified version of this dissertation was later published in Mohammad Mahfud MD. *Politik Hukum di Indonesia* [Legal Politics in Indonesia] (Jakarta: LP3ES, 1998).

50 Philippe Nonet and Philip Selznick. *Law and Society in Transition: Toward Responsive Law* (New York: Octagon Books, 1978).While writing his dissertation,

Mahfud did some library research in the United States at Columbia University and Northern Illinois University; presumably he found this book during his library research in the United States.

51 Ibid., 16.

52 For the origin of the responsive law, which derived from American legal realism, please see Robert A. Kagan. "On Responsive Law." In *Legality and Community: On the Intellectual Legacy of Philip Selznick*, edited by Robert A. Kagan, Martin Krygier, and Kenneth I. Winston. (Lanham, MD: Rowman & Littlefield, 2002).

53 Nonet and Selznick. *Law and Society in Transition*, 108–109.

54 The Constitutional Court of the Republic of Indonesia, 10-17-23/PUU-VII/2009 (hereinafter the *Pornography Law* case). For background information on the litigation, see Donald Horowitz. *Constitutional Change and Democracy in Indonesia* (Cambridge: Cambridge University Press, 2013), 252–253.

55 The Constitutional Court of the Republic of Indonesia, No. 140/PUU-VII/2009 (hereinafter *Blasphemy Law I* case). For a detailed analysis of the Court's decision in the *Blasphemy Law I* case, see Melissa A. Crouch. "Law and Religion in Indonesia: The Constitutional Court and the Blasphemy Law," 7(1) *Asian J. COMP. L.* 46 (2012); Melissa Crouch. *Law, and Religion in Indonesia: Conflict and the Courts in West Java* (London: Routledge, 2014). See also Stewart Fenwick. *Blasphemy, Islam and the State: Pluralism and Liberalism in Indonesia* (New York: Routledge, 2017).

56 Horowitz. *Constitutional Change and Democracy in Indonesia*, 253–254.

57 Article 28J (2) of the 1945 Constitution provides, "In exercising his/her rights and freedoms, every person shall have the duty to accept the restrictions established by law for the sole purposes of guaranteeing the recognition and respect of the rights and freedoms of others and of satisfying just demands based upon considerations of morality, religious values, security and public order in a democratic society."

58 The *Pornography Law* case, 381.

59 The *Blasphemy Law I* case, 293.

60 Ibid., 293.

61 The Constitutional Court Decision No. 50/PUU-VI/2008 (hereinafter the *Bloggers I* case).

62 Law No. 11 of 2008 on the Information and Electronic Transaction Law, Art. 27 (3).

63 The *Bloggers I* case, 108.

64 Ibid. In the *Bloggers II* case, several bloggers went back to the Court and challenged the Information and Electronic Transaction Law. But the Court dismissed the case on legal technical grounds, in which the Court cannot hear a challenge on the same statutory provisions that was challenged in a previous case. See the Constitutional Court Decision No. 2/PUU-VII/2009 (hereinafter the *Bloggers II* case).

65 The Constitutional Court Decision No. 6-13-20/PUU-VIII/2010, (hereinafter the *Book Banning* case).

66 The case originated from the 1963 Law on Securing Printed Materials, which allowed the Attorney General's Office (AGO) to confiscate and ban the distribution of books whose content could disrupt the public order. In 2009, the AGO banned five books, which included the book *Pretext for Mass Murder: The September 30th Movement and Soeharto's Coup d'état in Indonesia* by John Roosa of the University of British Colombia. See the *Jakarta Globe*. "Court Hears Author's Legal Case Against Book Bans", March 9, 2010, http://www.thejakartaglobe.com/archive/court-hears-authors-legal-case-against-book-bans/.

67 The *Book Banning* case, 241.

68 The Constitution of the Republic of Indonesia 1945, Art. 28H (4).

69 Rita Triana Budiarti. *Kontroversi Mahfud: Di Balik Putusan Mahkamah Konstitusi Jilid 2* [Mahfud's Controversies: Behind the Constitutional Court Decisions, Volume 2] (Jakarta: Konstitusi Press, 2013), 240–241.
70 The Constitutional Court Decision No. 3/PUU-VIII/2010 (hereinafter the *Coastal and Remote Islands Law* case).
71 Ibid., para. 3.15.4.
72 Ibid., para. 3.15.4.
73 The Constitutional Court Decision No. 25/PUU-VIII/2010 (hereinafter the *Tin Mining* case).
74 Law No. 4 of 2009 on Mineral and Coal Mining.
75 Law No. 4 of 2009 on Mineral and Coal Mining, Art. 52 (1), provides that every holder of the Mining Business Permit for exploration of metal mineral shall be granted a minimum area of 5000 hectares and a maximum of 100,000 hectares.
76 The Constitutional Court Decision No. 36/PUU-X/2012 (hereinafter the *Oil and Gas III* case).
77 The Oil and Gas Law, Art. 1 (23) & Art. 4 (3).
78 The *Oil and Gas III* case, 179–180.
79 Ibid., 214. There is a dissenting opinion in which Justice Harjono argued that the plaintiffs have no standing to bring the case. Justice Harjono did not write a lengthy dissent, and he only criticized the Court majority for their lack of consideration concerning the standing issue. He believed that the Court did not provide sufficient legal reasoning in reaching a conclusion that the plaintiffs have the standing to argue before the Court. For a detailed analysis of the *Oil and Gas Law III* case, please see Simon Butt and Fritz E. Siregar. "State Control over Natural Resources in Indonesia: Implications of the Oil and Natural Gas Law Case of 2012," 31(2) *Journal of Energy & Natural Resources of Law* 107 (2013).
80 The *Oil and Gas Law III* case, para. 3.13.3.
81 The rate of conditionally constitutional decisions increased from 15 decisions under Asshiddiqie to 54 decisions under Mahfud. See Simon Butt. *The Constitutional Court and Democracy in Indonesia* (Leiden, the Netherlands: Brill, Nijhoff, 2015), 64; see also Fritz Edward Siregar. *Indonesian Constitutional Politics 2003–2013* (unpublished SJD Thesis, the University of New South Wales, 2016), 207.
82 The Constitutional Court Decision No. 54/PUU-VI/2008 (hereinafter the *Tobacco Excise Tax* case).
83 Article 66A (1) Law No. 39/2007.
84 The crux of the matter was that the government interpreted the "tobacco-producing regions" as a region where there was a cigarette factory. The claimant complained that West Nusa Tenggara did not receive a portion of tobacco tax excise because it had no cigarette factories, despite the fact that it is one of the biggest tobacco growers in the country.
85 The *Tobacco Excise Tax* case, para. 3.23.
86 Ibid., para. 5.
87 Ibid., para. 3.22.
88 The Constitutional Court Decision No. 70/PUU-IX/2011 (hereinafter the *SJSN IV* case). Apart from this case, the Mahfud Court also dealt with a series of cases that involved social security matters. See the Constitutional Court Decision No. 50/PUU-VIII/2010 (the *SJSN II* case), The Constitutional Court Decision No. 51/PUU-IX/2011 (the *SJSN III* case), the Constitutional Court Decision No. 70/PUU-IX/2011 (the *SJSN IV* case) and the Constitutional Court Decision No. 82/PUU-X/2012 (the *SJSN V* case). For a detailed analysis of these cases, please see Stefanus Hendrianto. "The Divergence of a Wandering Court: Socio-Economic Rights in the Indonesian Constitutional Court," 16(2) *The Australian Journal of Asian Law* article 5 (2016).

89 *Undang Undang No. 40 Tahun 2004 tentang Sistem Jaminan Sosial Nasional* (Law No. 40 of 2004 on the National Social Security System—hereinafter the *SJSN* law).
90 The *SJSN* law, Art. 13 (1).
91 The *SJSN IV* case, 7.
92 Ibid., 44.
93 Ibid.
94 The Constitutional Court Decision No. 102/PUU-VII/2009 (hereinafter the *ID Card* case).
95 Law No. 42 of 2008 on the Presidential Election, Art. 28 and 111 (1).
96 The *ID Card* case, 19.
97 Ibid., 19–20.
98 Ibid., 17.
99 The Constitutional Court Decision No. 110-111-112-113/PUU-VII/2009 (hereinafter *the Left Over Votes* case).
100 Law No. 10 of 2008 on the Legislative Election, Art. 205 (4).
101 The *Leftover Votes* case, 103.
102 Ibid., 104.
103 The Constitutional Court of the Republic of Indonesia, No. 49/PUU-VIII/2010, (hereinafter the *Attorney General* case). The case originated from the political conflict between the Yudhoyono administration and his former confidant, Yusril Ihza Mahendra. In May 2007, President Yudhoyono dismissed Mahendra from his position as state secretary due to his alleged involvement in several high-profile graft cases. On June 24, 2010, the Attorney General's Office named and charged Mahendra under the Anti-Corruption Law for his approval of the Ministry of Justice's online corporate registration system (*Sistem Administrasi Badan Hukum*—Sisminbakum). Mahendra fought back by filing a petition to the Constitutional Court, in which he challenged the appointment of the then attorney general, Hendarman Supandji. Mahendra argued that Supandji was an illegitimate attorney general because he had never been formally re-appointed as the attorney general after he finished his first term in office.
104 Ibid., para. 3.31.
105 Ibid., para. 3.32.
106 *Jakarta Globe.*, "Surprise Ruling Sees Attorney General Lose Job," Accessed February10,2016.http://jakartaglobe.beritasatu.com/archive/surprise-ruling-sees-attorney-general-lose-job/.
107 *Tribunnews.com.* "Mahfud: Memangnya Saya Pikirin Mau Dilaksanakan Atau Tidak" [Mahfud: Do You Think I Care Whether or Not the Decision Was Implemented], September 23, 2010. Accessed July 28, 2016. http://www.tribunnews.com/nasional/2010/09/23/mahfud-memangnya-saya-pikirin-mau-dilaksanakan-atau-tidak.
108 *Hukumonline.* "Mahfud MD: Hendarman Supandji Harus Berhenti" [Mahfud MD: Hendarman Supandji Must Leave], September 22, 2010. http://www.hukumonline.com/berita/baca/lt4c9a327ade2d2/hendarman-supandji-harus-berhenti.
109 Rita Budiarti. *Biografi Mahfud MD: Terus Mengalir* [Biography of Mahfud MD: Keep Flowing] (Jakarta: Konstitusi Press, 2013), 430.
110 Simon Butt. *The Constitutional Court and Democracy in Indonesia*, 123–126.
111 Rita Budiarti. *Biografi Mahfud MD: Terus Mengalir*, 424.
112 Ibid.
113 See Simon Butt. *The Constitutional Court and Democracy in Indonesia*, 63.
114 See the Constitutional Court Decision No. 41/PHPU.D-VI/2008, on the Dispute of Regional Election East Java Province.

115 Law No. 12 (2008), Concerning Amendment of Law No. 32 of 2004 on Regional Administration, Art. 236C.
116 For a detailed analysis of the expansion of the Constitutional Court authority in regional election disputes, see Iwan Satriawan et al. *Studi Efektifitas Penyelesaian Sengketa Hasil Pemilukada oleh Mahkamah Konstitusi* [Study on the Effectiveness of the Settlement of Local Election Dispute by the Constitutional Court] (2012).
117 The Constitutional Court Decision No. 108-109/PHPU.B-VII/2009, Presidential Election Dispute, *Jusuf Kalla v. Susilo Bambang Yudhoyono* and *Megawati Soekarnoputri v. Susilo Bambang Yudhoyono.*
118 Ibid., 324–325.
119 Ibid., 325.
120 Ibid., 325.
121 Ibid., 325.
122 Satjipto Rahardjo. "Tribut Untuk Mahkamah Konstitusi." In *Penegakan Hukum Progresif*, edited by Satjipto Rahardjo. (Jakarta: Penerbit Buku Kompas, 2010). The original version of this essay was published in *Kompas Daily* newspaper on July 14, 2009.
123 The Constitutional Court Decision No.133/PUU-VII/2009 (hereinafter the *Hamzah & Riyanto* case).
124 For a detailed analysis of the background of the conflict between the Anti-Corruption Commission and the National Police, see Simon Butt. *Corruption and Law in Indonesia* (London: Routledge, 2012).
125 See Government Regulation in Lieu of Law No. 4 (2009), Art. 33A (1). Before the enactment of this PERPU, the Law required the positions to be filled using a rigorous fit and proper test in the parliament. Under the PERPU, the president had the authority to appoint temporary commissioners to fill the vacant positions with commissioners who had the same rights, powers, and obligations as did commissioners serving full terms.
126 Budiarti. *On the Record: Mahfud Behind the Constitutional Court Decisions*, 105–107.
127 The Constitutional Court Decision No. 133/PUU-VII/2009, on the injunctive decision, 31.
128 Ibid., 32.
129 *Jakarta Post.* "The President Set to Issue Regulation on KPK Today," Sept. 23, 2009.
130 *Kalau Saya President Sudah Saya Pecat Kapolri.* [If I were President I Would Remove the National Chief of Police], *Tempointeraktif*, Sept. 28, 2009, http://www.tempointeraktif.com/hg/hukum/2009/09/28/brk,20090928-199729,id.html.
131 Rita Triana Budiarti. *On the Record: Mahfud: Behind the Constitutional Court Decisions* (2010), 160.
132 The Constitutional Court Decision No. 138/PUU-VII/2009 (hereinafter the *PERPU* case).
133 Ibid., 21.
134 Rita Triana Budiarti. *Mahfud's Controversies: Behind the Constitutional Court Decisions*, Volume 2, 28–30.
135 Ibid., 31.
136 Ibid., 31.
137 The Constitutional Court Decision No. 5/PUU-X/2012 (hereinafter the *International School* case).
138 Ibid., 194–195.
139 Budiarti. *Mahfud's Controversies: Behind the Constitutional Court Decisions*, Volume 2, 245.

140 Ibid., 256.
141 Budiarti. *On the Record*, 217.
142 Ibid., 218.
143 *Jakarta Post*. "MK to Examine Judge Arsyad's Daughter Next Week," December 11, 2010. http://www.thejakartapost.com/news/2010/12/11/mk-examine-judge-arsyad%E2%80%99s-daughter-next-week.html.
144 *Antara News Agency*. "Supreme Court to Find Substitute for Arsyad Sanusi," February 11, 2011.
145 *Antara News Agency*. "Arsyad Questioned over Alleged Court Document Forgery," July 1, 2011. The scandal arose from the General Election dispute in 2009 between a politician from the People's Conscience Party (Hanura), Dewi Yasin Limpo, and a politician from the Greater Indonesian movement (Gerindra), Mestariani Habie. The Constitutional Court officially ruled that the seat should be given to Habie, yet Justice Arsyad collaborated with the Court's clerk to forge a letter to award a DPR seat to the losing candidate, Dewi Yasin Limpo.
146 *TribuneNews*. "Arsyad: Mahfud tidak becus memimpin MK" [Arsyad: Mahfud Is Incompetent to Lead the Court], June 28, 2011. http://www.tribunnews.com/nasional/2011/06/28/arsyad-mahfud-md-tak-mengerti-administrasi-peradilan.
147 Law No. 8 of 2011 on the Amendment of the Law No. 24 of 2003 on the Constitutional Court.
148 *PolMark Indonesia*. "Revisi UU MK Cermin Ketakutan DPR" [Amendment of the Constitutional Court Law Indicates the Fear of the Legislators], June 22, 2011. http://www.polmarkindonesia.com/index.php?option=com_content&task=view&id=2338.
149 Law No. 8 of 2011 on the Amendment of Law no. 24 of 2003 on the Constitutional Court, Art. 27A (2).
150 Ibid., Art. 45A.
151 Dina Indrasafitri. "Minister Lauds New Constitutional Court Bill." *The Jakarta Post*, June 4, 2011.
152 Art. 57 (2a).
153 Law No. 8 of 2011, Art. 4 (2).
154 *REPUBLIKA*. "Soal Revisi UU MK, Mahfud MD Bilang Terserah" [With Regard to the Amendment of the Constitutional Court Law, Mahfud Says Whatever] (Jakarta), June 21, 2011. http://www.republika.co.id/berita/nasional/hukum/11/06/21/ln4kil-soal-revisi-uu-mk-mahfud-md-bilang-terserah.
155 *KOMPAS*. "Mahfud: MK Hormati Revisi UU MK" [Mahfud: The Court Respects the Amendment of the Constitutional Court Law] (Jakarta), June 22, 2011. http://nasional.kompas.com/read/2011/06/22/00571396/Mahfud.MK.Hormati.Revisi.UU.MK.
156 *Antara News Agency*. "Mahfud Retakes Oath as Constitutional Court Chairman," Aug. 22, 2011. http://www.antaranews.com/en/news/75006/mahfud-md-retakes-oath-as-constitutional-court-chairman.
157 The Constitutional Court Decision No. 48/PUU-IX/2011 (hereinafter the *2011 Amendment Law I* case).
158 Ibid., 93.
159 Ibid., 93.
160 The Constitutional Court Decision No. 49/PUU-IX/2011 (hereinafter the *2011 Amendment Law II* case), 80.
161 Ibid., 72.
162 Ibid., 80.
163 Simon Butt. *The Constitutional Court and Democracy in Indonesia*, 137.
164 The *2011 Amendment II* case, 74.
165 Budiarti. *Terus Mengalir*, 429.

166 See Fritz Siregar. *Indonesian Constitutional Politics 2003–2013*, 168–176.

167 See Simon Butt. *The Constitutional Court and Democracy in Indonesia*, 43–44, 121.

168 See Chien-Chih Lin. *The Judicialization of Politics in New Democracies* (unpublished doctoral dissertation, University of Chicago, 2015). In his dissertation, Lin compares the judicialization of politics in Indonesia, Korea, Taiwan, Bolivia, Brazil, and Mexico. Lin relies on principal–agent theory and argues that the judicialization of politics occurs because both politicians—particularly those in power—and citizens increasingly see courts as their agents.

169 *Jakarta Post*. "Lawmakers Support Jimly For New Term," February 26, 2008.

170 *Jakarta Post*. "House begins Testing Constitutional Court Candidates," March 12, 2008.

171 Jeffrey Segal and Harold J. Spaeth. *The Supreme Court and the Attitudinal Model Revisited* (Cambridge: Cambridge University Press, 2002), 86.

172 The Constitutional Court of the Republic of Indonesia, No. 10-17-23/PUU-VII/2009 (hereinafter the *Pornography Law* Case). For background information on the litigation, see Donald Horowitz, *Constitutional Change and Democracy in Indonesia*, 252–253.

173 The Constitutional Court of the Republic of Indonesia, No. 140/PUU-VII/2009 (hereinafter the *Blasphemy Law I* Case).

174 Horowitz., *Constitutional Change and Democracy in Indonesia*, 253–254.

175 Ibid., 254.

176 *Antara News Agency*. "Mahfud Retakes Oath as Constitutional Court Chairman," Aug. 22, 2011. http://www.antaranews.com/en/news/75006/mahfud-md-retakes-oath-as-constitutional-court-chairman.

177 *Antara News Agency*. "Mahfud Says He has No Posture for Presidency," Aug. 22, 2011. http://www.antaranews.com/en/news/75010/mahfud-says-he-has-no-posture-for-presidency.

178 *Jakarta Post*. "Mahfud Says He's Ready for Presidential Race," April 2, 2013.

179 Ibid.

180 Mahfud's party, the National Awakening Party (PKB), had indeed considered him as a potential candidate for the 2014 presidential election. Unfortunately, the PKB only garnered 9.04 percent of the popular vote (i.e. 8.39 percent of seats), which is far below the presidential threshold. Having realized that it would not be able to nominate Mahfud for president, the PKB buried Mahfud's presidential ambition and decided to join the coalition that nominated the governor of Jakarta, Joko Widodo, as president. Mahfud could not hide his disappointment and decided to support Widodo's rival, a retired three-star general, Prabowo Subianto. In a dramatic turn, he accepted an offer to become the head of Subianto's election campaign. In the presidential election that took place on July 9, 2014, Joko Widodo, commonly known as Jokowi, defeated his archrival Prabowo Subianto. Widodo received 53.1 percent of the votes (71 million), and his opponent won 46.85 percent (62.5 million). Mahfud admitted that he had failed to deliver a victory for Prabowo Subianto. Subianto, however, refused to concede and claimed that fraud had denied him victory, and he immediately challenged the election result in the Constitutional Court. Soon after the General Election Commission announced the official results of the 2014 presidential election, former Chief Justice Mahfud resigned from his position as chairman of Subianto's presidential campaign team.

181 The Constitutional Court Decision No. 102/PUU-VII/2009 (hereinafter the *ID Card* case).

182 Mahfud Md. "Putusan Itu Hanya Butuh Sepuluh Menit" [It Took Only Ten Minutes to Reach the Decision], *Tempo Magazine*, July 13, 2009.

183 The Constitutional Court Decision No. 22-24/PUU-VI/2008 (hereinafter the *Mohammad Sholeh* case).
184 Ibid, 107.
185 Budiarti. *On the Record: Mahfud: Behind the Constitutional Court Decisions*, 92.
186 Rahmat Sahid. "Kalau KPU Ngotot Akan Terjadi Bencana Besar" [There Will Be a Disaster if the Election Commission Refuses to Comply], *Seputar Indonesia,* Feb. 21, 2009.
187 *KOMPAS.* "Itu Genit yang Kebablasan" [When Flirting Becomes Too Much], April 22, 2010. http://nasional.kompas.com/read/2010/04/22/22444396/mahfud.md.itu.genit.yang.kebablasan.
188 Budiarti. *Terus Mengalir*, 435.
189 Ibid., 436.
190 Ibid., 437.
191 Theunis Roux and Fritz Siregar. "Trajectories of Curial Power: The Rise, Fall and Partial Rehabilitation of the Indonesian Constitutional Court," 16(2) *Australian Journal of Asian Law* article 2 (2016).

7 Miscarriage of chief justices

The anti-heroes

Prelude

In Indonesia, for people who are conversant with the epic *Mahabharata*, there is a notion of the anti-hero in the character of Karna. Karna is an illegitimate son of Kunti, the mother of the Pandawa brothers. Afraid of being an unwed mother and having a bastard, Kunti placed the baby in a basket and set him afloat on a river. A charioteer found the boy and raised him as his son. The boy later grew up to become a great warrior. But he was always resentful because he did not know whose child he was. He could not come to terms with being labeled "low-born." The bitterness made him into a nasty and ugly character in the *Mahabharata*. He wanted to be somebody he was not. Because of this obsession, Karna became a close friend of the eldest of the Kurawa clan, Duryudana, who later crowned him king. Karna's friendship with Duryodhana turned his life story into a disaster, as he collaborated with Duryodhana in his evil plots to destroy the Pandawas. Finally, Karna sided with the evil Kurawa against his half-brothers in the war and died tragically in the end.

This chapter explores the quasi-second-generation Indonesian Constitutional Court, which draws from the leadership of Akil Mochtar and Hamdan Zoelva. After the departure of Chief Justice Mahfud, Chief Justice Akil Mochtar took over the role of chief justice for six months and was followed by Chief Justice Hamdan Zoelva after a little over a year. I will consider this period as a quasi-second-generation period, because many judges from the second-generation court were still sitting on the bench. Moreover, the brief of leadership of Mochtar and Zoelva, which only lasted for 20 months, signified that there was no discrete discontinuity with the second-generation Court. The issue that I will address is whether the new chief justices were capable of maintaining the heroic leadership of their predecessors. What was the impact of the leadership of the new justices on the Court's performance? How did the leadership of the new chief justices compare to that of the previous chief justices?

The chairmanship of Akil Mochtar (2013)

Akil Mochtar had the shortest tenure as chief justice in Indonesian legal history. Mochtar held his presidency for 182 days (from April 4, 2013, to October 2, 2013).

Despite his brief tenure as a chief justice, it is worth examining his leadership; by considering his leadership, this chapter will show how the Court was transformed further from a first-generation heroic court into a less heroic one.

Political trajectories and appointment

As mentioned in the previous chapter, in March 2008, the House Judiciary Committee prepared a fit and proper test for candidates to replace the three justices who were about to finish their first 5-year term. As a result, the DPR appointed two new justices, Mohammad Mahfud and Akil Mochtar, and re-appointed Jimly Asshiddiqie.

Mochtar had no towering academic credentials like Asshiddiqie and Mahfud; he graduated from a lower-tier undergraduate law program at Panca Bhakti University, located in a provincial town, Pontianak, West Kalimantan.[1] When the DPR appointed him associate justice of the Constitutional Court in 2008, Mochtar was still pursuing his doctoral studies at Padjajaran University Faculty of Law. About a year after his appointment, Mochtar defended his doctoral thesis on shifting the burden of proof in corruption cases according to Indonesian law.[2] Nonetheless, there was much skepticism about Mochtar's academic achievements. Regardless of his doctoral degree, Mochtar is not a professional academic like Asshiddiqie and Mahfud.

Mochtar began his legal career as a lawyer in small town, Singkawang. He earned fame by defending three farmers in the case of Lingah, Pacah, and Sumir.[3] These farmers were convicted by a Supreme Court of murder in 1987. Five years later, a wholly unknown figure, Asun, emerged and confessed in a separate criminal trial that he was the murderer. Based on this new evidence, Mochtar and his teammate filed a special review procedure (*peninjauan kembali*) in the Supreme Court. The Supreme Court, however, rejected the review on the grounds that Asun's testimony was inadmissible, as he was never investigated, charged, or indicted.

Having earned his fame as a defender of poor and innocent people, Mochtar jumped into politics by joining Golkar, the former ruling party under the military dictatorship. He began to serve as a member of the DPR after the fall of the military government in 1998. In his second term as the member of the DPR, he served as the deputy chairman of the House Judiciary Committee.[4]

In 2007, Akil Mochtar ran for West Kalimantan governor and lost. But his failure in that election became a turning point for his political aspirations. In his bid for governor, Mochtar went against his party candidate, the then governor, Usman Djafar. Thus, Golkar party officials saw Mochtar as a traitor who split Golkar's vote, which resulted in the party's loss.[5] Having realized that he would never be nominated for legislative candidacy again by Golkar, Mochtar lobbied politicians for consideration to be appointed as a Constitutional Court justice.

On March 14, 2008, the House Judiciary Committee confirmed the appointment of Akil Mochtar as an associate justice of the Constitutional Court with 32 out of 49 votes. Mochtar was sworn in as an associate justice on August 16, 2008.

In his first 5 years as an associate justice, Mochtar did not display impressive achievements. In 2010, he was linked to a bribery scandal that related to a case involving an election dispute in the Simalungun district. Refly Harun, the lawyer of the head of Simalungun District, accused Mochtar of receiving money from his client in exchange for a promise of a favorable decision in return.[6] The then Chief Justice Mahfud established an independent ethics council to investigate the allegation. The Ethics Council, however, did not find any incriminating evidence and cleared Mochtar of all charges.

On March 5, 2013, the DPR re-appointed Mochtar for his second term as an associate justice. Following the resignation of Chief Justice Mahfud, the Court elected Akil Mochtar as the new chief justice for the period 2013–2015.[7] Akil Mocthar's election as the chief justice is rather puzzling for many people, especially considering his poor record. The election of Akil Mochtar could be explained by two components. The first element is that Mochtar's predecessors, Asshiddiqie and Mahfud, were extraordinary figures. The second element is that most judges are mediocre, and the Indonesian Constitutional Court had been staffed by mediocre judges in its first 10 years. As explained in Chapter 3, Asshiddiqie was a towering figure partly because his associate justices were mediocre judges. Similarly, Mahfud also led many mediocre judges during his tenure as chief justice. Akil Mochtar was a more ordinary chief justice. He was a mediocre judge during his first 5-year tenure, and later he was elected by his fellow mediocre justices to be the leader of the pack.

The parade of mediocre doctors

When Akil Mochtar took the helm as chief justice in May 2013, the Court's composition had changed significantly. There was only one judge from the first-generation Court sitting on the bench, Justice Harjono. As mentioned earlier, initially the House Judiciary Committee did not re-appoint Harjono for his second term. Nevertheless, Jimly Asshiddiqie resigned in November of 2008, and the House Judiciary Committee had to rush to find a replacement for Asshiddiqie. The DPR decided to call Harjono out of retirement and re-appoint him as associate justice of the Constitutional Court. Apart from Justice Harjono, two other judges from the first-generation Court initially served for a second term, Justice Siahaan and Justice Fadjar; nevertheless, both of them reached their mandatory retirement age in December 2009.

The composition of the Court had also changed because of the 2011 Amendment of the Constitutional Court Law. It is important to note that in 2011, the DPR passed a new law that amended the requirements for a Constitutional Court justice.[8] One of the requirements was that a candidate must have a doctorate and master's degree and an undergraduate degree in law.[9] In September 2012, however, the Court struck down the master's degree requirement.[10] The Court held that a candidate must have a doctorate, but not necessarily a master's degree. The Court explained that there are many law graduates from overseas who hold doctorates without holding master's degrees.[11] It was not clear what the Court meant by its holding; one plausible explanation is the lack of understanding of academic degrees in the American law school system. Presumably, the Court thought that a JD degree was equivalent to a PhD or SJD degree, and therefore the Court assumed that a person who holds a JD degree does not necessarily have an LLM degree. Based on a false understanding that a JD degree is an equivalent to a doctoral degree in law, the Court tried to make a JD degree sufficient to meet the requirement.

It is interesting to note that the requirement of the doctoral degree to be a constitutional court justice represents an unresolved issue in intellectual life in Indonesia. One of the legacies of the New Order military regime was the co-optation of intellectuals into a component of the ruling regime. For many years, the majority of Indonesian scholars served the interest of the military government instead of taking an interest in their intellectual pursuits.[12] Moreover, for Indonesian intellectuals, the aim of their career was an administrative position, because these posts were more prestigious than being scholars.[13] Such a phenomenon is quite contrary to life in Western academia, where academics prefer to remain scholars instead of taking up administrative positions. Under these circumstances, a doctoral degree meant a ticket to a higher administrative position inside academia or public office. In other words, the primary motivation for a person to pursue a doctoral degree was to obtain prestige and advance their career instead of manifesting intellectual pursuit.

When the legislatures wrote the law that required a constitutional court justice to have a doctoral degree, they turned the Court into a new venue for an unhealthy intellectual culture in which administrative or public positions are more prestigious than academic achievement. By the time the Court celebrated its tenth anniversary on August 13, 2013, five new associate justices had come to the Court with their doctoral degrees. Most of them pursued their legal education in medium-tier law schools, and they did not show any robust scholarship in their academic research. The majority of these new justices were either politicians or career judges, but they managed to obtain doctoral degrees to advance their careers.

The Supreme Court appointed two career judges with doctoral degrees in the second-generation Court. First, the Supreme Court appointed Fadlil Sumadi to succeed Justice Maruarar Siahaan, who reached mandatory retirement age in December 2009. Sumadi initially graduated from the Syariah Department of Semarang State Islamic Institute and later obtained a degree in civil law from Muhammadiyah University Faculty of Law in Yogyakarta. Sumadi spent most of his legal career as a judge in the Religious Court. While he was serving as the deputy chief of Yogyakarta High Religious Court, Sumadi began his doctoral studies at Diponegoro University and wrote a dissertation on the role of the Indonesian Supreme Court in the management of the lower courts.[14] Looking at his background, Sumadi was not a lifelong constitutional scholar or lawyer. Sumadi served as chief clerk of the Constitutional Court (2003–2008), but the position only equipped him with an understanding of the legal technicalities and internal mechanisms of the Court instead of sufficient knowledge of constitutional matters.

In 2011, the Supreme Court moved to fill the Court's vacancy due to the resignation of Justice Arsyad Sanusi in 2010. As explained in the previous chapter, Arsyad resigned in disgrace due to corruption allegations: that he manipulated the Court's decision in a regional election dispute. The Supreme Court appointed Anwar Usman, a career judge from Jakarta High Court. Usman graduated from a low-tier law school at the Jakarta Islamic University. Later, he obtained a master's degree in law at the Institute of Business Law and Legal Management (IBLAM), Jakarta. IBLAM is also listed in the low-tier of institutions of higher legal education. Usman claimed that he obtained his doctoral degree from the prestigious Gadjah Mada University. The official web page of the University explained that Anwar Usman wrote his dissertation on judicial independence in Indonesia, but the University never specified that Usman obtained his doctoral degree in law.[15] The official web page of the Constitutional Court mentioned that Usman obtained his doctoral degree in public policy.[16]

Usman's appointment raised a burning question on the requirements of a constitutional court justice. The 2011 Amendment requires that a constitutional court justice must have a doctoral degree with an undergraduate degree in law. But it was not clear whether one must obtain a doctoral degree in law to be qualified as a constitutional court justice. The Supreme Court interpreted the requirement as a doctoral degree in any field, and therefore, they appointed Usman, who had a doctoral degree in public policy. This interpretation prompted a further question on the merits of a doctoral requirement. The logic behind the inclusion of a doctoral requirement was to improve the quality of judges in the constitutional adjudication process. Nevertheless, this logic does not correlate with the reality that anyone with a doctoral degree in any field could potentially become a constitutional court justice.

President Yudhoyono appointed two politicians, who also came to the bench with doctoral degrees. First, President Yudhoyono appointed Hamdan Zoelva to succeed Justice Mukthie Fadjar, who reached the mandatory retirement age in January 2010. I will explain the background of Hamdan Zoelva later in this chapter. In a nutshell, Zoelva was a politician from the Star and Crescent Party. He obtained his doctoral degree in law from Padjajaran University. Nevertheless, apart from his doctoral works, there was no evidence that Zoelva ever published any serious scholarly works.

The second presidential appointee was Patrialis Akbar. Akbar obtained his bachelor degree in legal studies from the medium-tier Muhammadiyah University Jakarta Faculty of Law. Akbar began his legal career at the legal clinic of Muhammadiyah University. Muhammadiyah is one of the largest Islamic organizations in the country. During the 32-year reign of the Soeharto military dictatorship, the regime marginalized Muhammadiyah and other Islamic political forces.[17] After the fall of the Soeharto regime, Muhammadiyah began to re-appear on the political stage with close links to the National Mandate Party (*Partai Amanat Nasional*—PAN). The then chairman of Muhammadiyah, Amien Rais, established the National Mandate Party, and he subsequently became its first chairman. Through his connection with Muhammadiyah, Patrialis Akbar joined the National Mandate Party and represented PAN for two terms in the DPR.

In 2009, President Yudhoyono appointed Akbar as the minister of justice in his administration. President Yudhoyono, however, dismissed Akbar at the end of 2011 due to his poor performance.[18] After his dismissal, Akbar resumed his doctoral studies at Padjajaran University, which he had begun to pursue when he was a member of parliament. Akbar wrote his dissertation on presidential veto in Indonesian and successfully defended his dissertation on December 3, 2012.[19] In August 2013, President Yudhoyono appointed Akbar to succeed Justice Achmad Sodiki, who had finished his term. There was some speculation that, following Akbar's dismissal as the minister of justice, President Yudhoyono had promised him a position that could heal Akbar's resentment. In other words, Akbar's appointment was merely a consolation prize to compensate for his dismissal.[20]

The drama of the appointment of Patrialis Akbar continued when two non-governmental organizations (NGOs) challenged the validity of his appointment at the Jakarta Administrative Court, arguing that the nomination of a constitutional court justice must be transparent and participatory, yet President Yudhoyono had appointed Akbar without public hearing. The Jakarta Administrative Court ruled that the appointment process of Patrialis Akbar did not fulfill the requirements of being transparent and participatory. On appeal, however, the High Administrative Court ruled that the NGOs who brought the case lacked the standing to challenge the presidential decision. On February 25, 2015, the Supreme Court affirmed the High Administrative Court's decision that the NGOs lacked standing because the presidential decision did not cause any immediate harm to the claimants' interests.

The last doctoral degree holder to come to the Court in 2013 was Arief Hidayat. Hidayat was an exception because he was the only professional academic among the five new appointees. Hidayat began his career as a lecturer in law at Diponegoro University. In 2006, Hidayat obtained a doctoral degree in constitutional law with a dissertation on the development of freedom of assembly in Indonesia from the beginning of independence to the post-authoritarian period.[21] Having obtained his doctoral degree, Hidayat was subsequently promoted to the position of full-time professor and dean of the Faculty of Law at Diponegoro University. Despite his position as the Dean of the Diponegoro Faculty of Law, however, Hidayat had not published many academic works when he came to the Court, unlike the first chief justice, Jimly Asshiddiqie (Table 7.1).

The parade of doctoral degree holders did not guarantee an improvement in the quality of the judges who sat in the Constitutional Court. All of them graduated from Indonesian academic institutions. The fact of the matter is that most Indonesian educational institutions lack a full capacity for doctoral training, and they have not developed a national capacity in research due to the lack of a nationwide academic network.[22] Moreover, the number of international linkages developed by Indonesian academic institutions has remained at a minimum. Under these circumstances, domestically trained doctoral students may not have had a rigorous training, let alone experience in cross-country research projects.

Most of the newly appointed judges lacked significant achievements before their appointments. Neither Fadlil Sumadi nor Anwar Usman showed remarkable ability during their long careers as lower court judges. Patrialis Akbar gave a poor performance as a minister of justice, and President Yudhoyono dismissed him from the position.

Table 7.1 Constitutional Court Justices 2013

Names	*Prior position*	*Nominator*	*Education*
Maria Farida Indrati	Professor of law	President	– LLB (UI, Indonesia) – Master of Law (UI, Indonesia) – PhD (UI, Indonesia)
Hamdan Zoelva	Politician/MP	President	– LLB (Unhas, Indonesia) – Master of Law (Unpad, Indonesia) – PhD (Unpad, Indonesia)
Patrialis Akbar	Politician/ minister of justice	President	– LLB (UMJ, Indonesia) – Master of Law (UGM, Indonesia) – PhD (Unpad, Indonesia)
Arief Hidayat	Professor of law	DPR (House)	– LLB (Undip, Indonesia) – Master of Law (Unair) – PhD (Undip, Indonesia)
Harjono	Professor of law	DPR (House)	– LLB (Unair, Indonesia) – Master of Comparative Law (Southern Methodist University, Dallas, USA) – PhD (Unair, Indonesia)
Akil Mochtar	Politician/MP	DPR (House)	– LLB (UPB, Indonesia) – Master of Law (Unpad, Indonesia) – PhD (Unpad, Indonesia)
Fadlil Sumadi	Administrative clerk/judge	Supreme Court	– LLB (UMY, Indonesia) – Master of Law (UII, Indonesia) – PhD (Undip, Indonesia)
Anwar Usman	Administrative court judge	Supreme Court	– LLB (UIJ, Indonesia) – Master of Law (IBLAM, Indonesia) – PhD (UGM, Indonesia)
Muhammad Alim	High court judge	Supreme Court	– LLB (Unhas, Indonesia) – Master of Law (UII, Indonesia) – PhD (UII, Indonesia)

I will explain in more detail about the track record of Hamdan Zoelva and Arief Hidayat, but in a nutshell, they also gave mediocre performances in their careers. In sum, the Court was filled with mediocre judges. These judges were the ones who elected Akil Mochtar as the third chief justice of the Constitutional Court.

Socio-economic rights

Although the tenure of Akil Mochtar was very short, he nevertheless led the Court to issue several important decisions in some policy areas. First, the Court continued to deal with socio-economic issues. In the *Indigenous Forest I* case,[23] the Court dealt with the constitutionality of the Forestry Law. The case was unique because it has been written by "two hands," as Chief Justice Mahfud handed it over to Akil Mochtar.

Mahfud finished the deliberation meeting on the case on March 26, 2013. Nevertheless, Mahfud left the Court on April 1, 2013, and he handed over the case to Akil Mochtar, who announced the decision on May 16, 2013. The claimants were NGOs, chiefly led by the Indigenous Peoples Alliance of the Archipelago (*Aliansi Masyarakat Adat Nusantara*—AMAN), who claimed that they represented indigenous people across the archipelago.[24] The cruxes of the matter were some provisions in the Forestry Law, which defined indigenous forest (*hutan adat*) as State Forest (*hutan negara*) located within an indigenous community area. The claimants argued that these provisions allowed the State to grant rights over indigenous forest to private legal entities without obtaining consent from the indigenous community and without providing any compensation to the indigenous community. The claimants posited that the Law excluded the indigenous community from accessing the forestry resources that they had managed for many generations.

In the *Indigenous Forest I* case, the Court reaffirmed its jurisprudence, which defined that state control over natural resources "should be used to allocate natural resources justly for the greatest benefit of the people."[25] The Court made reference to the *Coastal and Remote Islands Law* case,[26] which required the state to observe existing rights, both individual and collective, held by customary law communities and other rights of the indigenous community. Based on its holding in the *Coastal and Remote Islands Law* case, the Court considered that the decision to classify indigenous forest (*hutan adat*) as part of the State Forest (*hutan negara*) was meant to undervalue the indigenous people's rights. The Court decided that classification of indigenous forests (*hutan adat*) as State Forests (*hutan negara*) was contrary the Constitution.[27]

The Court stated further that indigenous forests (*hutan adat*) must be classified as part of the "forests subject to rights" (*hutan hak*) category instead of as State Forest (*hutan negara*).[28] Nevertheless, the Court held that the Law was "conditionally unconstitutional"—that it would be unlawful and unbinding unless the Law was to be interpreted in such a way that indigenous forests (*hutan adat*) were not classified under State Forests (*hutan negara*). Although the signature of Akil Mochtar was at the bottom of the Court's decision, the decision reflected the ideological lines of Mohammad Mahfud with his preferential option for the poor.

Akil Mochtar issued a decision on socio-economic rights for the first time on July 18, 2013, in the *Plant Cultivation System Law* case.[29] The claimants were NGOs and individuals, chiefly led by the Indonesian Human Rights Committee for Social Justice (IHCS). The applicant argued that the Plant Cultivation System Law,[30] adopted in 1992 by the New Order military regime, was meant to constrain peasants' rights and creativity regarding the need for seed.[31] The claimants argued that the Law was contrary to the Constitution, especially Article 33 (2 & 3) because it allowed the government to issue various policies to determine the type, amount, and timing of seed production and circulation without any participation or input from local farmers. Furthermore, the Law also regulated criminal sanctions. If farmers or seed-breeders refused to comply with the government's policies, they would be penalized with imprisonment of up to 5 years and a maximum fine of 2.5 billion rupiahs.[32]

The Court ruled that the government had the authority to set policies to determine the type, amount, and timing of seed production and circulation.[33] The Court ruled further that although the farmers have the liberty to produce and use some of the crop seed to breed, sell, and trade, it did not mean that they had the unlimited freedom to do so. The Court stated that the government has the authority to restrict citizens' rights for the sake of the public interest based on the general limitation of the Bill of Rights clause (Article 28J [2]) in the Constitution.[34]

Despite its conservative ruling, the Court ruled that the government should protect the status of poor farmers instead of requiring them to obtain a permit for collecting and producing local seeds.[35] The Court held that the provision, which required a license for collecting and producing local seeds, was conditionally unconstitutional as long as it excluded an individual poor farmer. The Court further held that the provision, which stipulates that the government has the authority to control and release seed production, was conditionally unconstitutional as long as it excluded the products of poor local farmers. These conditionally unconstitutional rulings meant that poor local farmers were neither prohibited by nor did they need permission from the government any longer to collect local seeds, produce seed, and distribute seed.

Religion-related cases

During his brief tenure, Akil Mochtar also led the Court to issue two important decisions relating to the status of religion in public life. The first case was the *Blasphemy Law II* case.[36] The claimants are members of Shiite Muslim minority.[37] The first claimant, Tajul Muluk has been convicted by the Sampang District Court for blasphemy because he propagated Shiite teachings.[38] Three other claimants—Hasan Alaydrus, Ahmad Hidayat, and Umar Shabab—had never been convicted of blasphemy, but they asserted that as Shiite preachers, they would be likely to be convicted in the future. In addition to these Shiite members, the last claimant was an individual who had been found guilty by the District Court of Ciamis for blasphemy over his Facebook comments about Islam.[39]

First, the Court compared the nature of the *Blasphemy I* case and the *Blasphemy II* case. The comparison is necessary because, before 2011, the Court could not review a case about a legal provision that had already been challenged in a previous case.[40] Nevertheless, the 2011 Amendment to the Constitutional Court Law allowed the Court to review a constitutional challenge to the same legal provision as long as the claimant brought a new argument.[41] The Court considered that the claimants in the *Blasphemy I* case sought to nullify the Blasphemy Law entirely.[42]

Nevertheless, the claimants in the *Blasphemy II* case sought to declare the key provision in the Blasphemy Law conditionally unconstitutional as long as criminal charges were applied without any warning and in order to stop the blasphemous act.[43] In other words, the claimant sought to include the prior warning and order to stop blasphemous acts before the prosecutor could file criminal charges.

Considering that the *Blasphemy II* case brought a different argument, the Court then proceeded to review the merits of the case. First, the Court made reference to the *Blasphemy Law I* case, in which the Court ruled that although the Blasphemy Law was imperfect, it was necessary to keep the Law for the purpose of constraining any blasphemous acts and avoiding societal conflicts.[44] Based on its previous ruling, the Court ruled that the claimants' petition had no legal basis and was irrelevant.[45] The Court ruled further that the applicants' concern involved the application of the Blasphemy Law, which falls under the ambit of the general court of jurisdiction. The Court held that the *Blasphemy Law II* case was about the application of law instead of constitutional issues.[46] Therefore, the Court rejected the claimant's petition entirely.

There are several significant twists in this case. First, the case had been written by "two hands," as Chief Justice Mahfud handed it over to Akil Mochtar. Mahfud led the Court to finish the deliberation meeting on April 9, 2013, but it was Akil Mochtar who signed and announced the decision on September 19, 2013. Second, Justice Patrialis Akbar was the minister of justice who represented the government in the *Blasphemy Law I* case, but after his appointment as an associate justice, he did not recuse himself in the *Blasphemy Law II* case.[47] The last twists are the inconsistency of argument: The Court relied on the general limitation of the Bill of Rights clause (Article 28J [2]) to reject the claimant's petition in the *Blasphemy I* case, but the Court did not make any reference to Article 28J (2) at all in the *Blasphemy Law II* case.

The second religion-related case under the tenure of Akil Mochtar was the *Sharia Banking* case.[48] In 2006, the Indonesian Legislature approved an amendment to the Religious Court Law, which expanded the authority of the Religious Courts from adjudicating cases among Muslims on family law, inheritance, and trust to dispute resolution on economic Sharia and Islamic almsgiving (*zakat*).[49] The elucidation of the statute clarified the meaning of economic Sharia as commercial activities carried out according to the principles of Sharia.[50] The opponents of the Law argued that the judges who staffed the Islamic Courts lacked the expertise to adjudicate complex financial questions.[51] The debate over the jurisdiction to resolve Islamic commercial disputes resurfaced during the discussion of the Sharia Banking Bill in 2008. In the end, the Sharia Banking Law provided that the Islamic Court has the authority to settle any dispute that arises from Sharia banking. Nevertheless, the Law allows the parties involved to pick a forum to resolve their dispute, which includes mediation, Sharia arbitration, or any arbitration hearing or civil court.[52]

The claimant was a debtor to *Mualamat* Bank, and he was in default as he could not pay back his loan. The loan agreement did not specify the forum of the settlement of the dispute; nevertheless, the bank decided to file a claim in the civil court. The claimant argued that the Sharia Banking Law created legal uncertainty as it did not provide clarity as to the jurisdiction in which to settle the dispute. In a short opinion—less than three pages—the Court accepted the claimant's argument and ruled that the Law has created a conflict of jurisdiction between the Islamic Court and the Civil Court in settling the Sharia Banking dispute.[53] The Court emphasized that although it had no authority to review an actual case, that is, the dispute between the claimants and the bank, it was evident that the applicant had been deprived of his rights to seek legal certainty in Sharia banking litigation.[54] Therefore, the Court declared the legal provision, which allowed a choice of forum, as being contrary to the Constitution, which guarantees the right of certainty (*kepastian hukum*) before a just law.[55]

Again, the case has been written by the "two hands" of chief justices. Mahfud led the conclusion of the deliberation meeting on March 28, 2013, and Akil Mochtar signed and announced the decision on August 29, 2013. The Court's reasoning was quite narrow as it did not explain at length in what way the choice of the forum might violate the Constitution. Although the Court stated it had no authority to review a concrete case, the Court nevertheless reached its decision based on a concrete dispute. While the claimant asserted his constitutional harm before the Court, his case was merely a loan dispute instead of a constitutional dispute. Furthermore, it is clear that the loan dispute should be settled by the Islamic Court, considering that both parties never reached any agreement to resolve the conflict outside the Islamic Court.

Freedom of expression case

During his short tenure, Akil Mochtar led the Court to issue an important decision in the area of freedom of expression, the *Twitter* case.[56] In this case, a controversial lawyer, Farhat Abbas, went to the Court and sought a judicial review of the 2008 Electronic Information and Transaction Law (ITE), which bans hate speech made and distributed through electronic documents.[57] The police named Abbas as a suspect in libel charges against the then deputy governor, Basuki Tjahaja Purnama, commonly known as Ahok. Ahok was a controversial figure who was notorious for his straightforward and blunt speaking. He was a Christian of Chinese descent, which made him a rare breed of politician, considering religion is often important in a predominantly Muslim country like Indonesia. Moreover, Indonesia has a long history of discrimination against its Chinese minority.

The libel case originated from Ahok's statement at city hall about the use of plate numbers for high state officials. As the deputy governor, Ahok was supposed to use Plate B2 Capital. Nevertheless, Ahok complained that Plate B2 Capital was owned by someone else.[58] Ahok never specified who allegedly owned the Plate B2 Capital, even though the police claimed the number was available. Farhat Abbas posted on his Twitter, "Ahok is protesting here and there that a police officer sold the Plate B2 Capital to someone. That is Ahok, making an issue over a mere plate number. Whatever his plate number, he remains a Chinese."[59]

One of Ahok's supporters considered Abbas's Twitter post an insult and reported Abbas to the police.[60] The police then charged Abbas under the Electronic Transaction and Information Law, which provides a maximum sentence of 6 years in jail or 1 billion rupiahs in fines for someone who spreads hate speech involving ethnic affiliations, religion, race, or societal groups (*suku, agama, ras dan antar-golongan*—SARA). Abbas asked the Constitutional Court to nullify the provision in the Law because it was contrary to the constitutional guarantee of freedom of expression.[61]

The Court considered that there was a general limitation to the Bill of Rights in the Constitution under Article 28J (2). Although the Constitution guaranteed the freedom of expression, the Court ruled that such freedom is not absolute and can be restricted based upon considerations of morality, religion, and public order in society.[62] The Court ruled that any hate speech involving ethnic affiliations, religion, race, or a societal group was a threat to public order in society. Therefore, the Court rejected the claimant's petition entirely.

The Court's decision signified continuity with the approach of the previous Court under the chairmanship of Mahfud in the area of freedom of expression. Akil Mochtar continued to apply his predecessor's approach to the application of Article 28J (2) in the field of freedom of speech. In other words, the Court did not define the meaning of freedom of speech based on its content but rather on its limitation.

In short, there is no clear pattern to the Court's decisions under the presidency of Akil Mochtar. Mochtar mostly inherited cases from the Mahfud Court, and so some of the Court decisions were marked by Mahfud's leadership approach. While Mochtar led the Court to issue a few decisions during his brief tenure, these decisions were quite conservative as the Court consistently invoked the general limitations of the Bill of Rights clause (Article 28J [2]).

The tragic fall of Akil Mochtar

As mentioned earlier, Mochtar had escaped from corruption allegations once during his first term in the Court. But three years after the first allegation, Mochtar could not escape corruption charges when the Anti-Corruption Commission arrived with a warrant for his arrest and confiscated approximately USD 260,000 from his residence. The money was allegedly given so Mochtar would rule the Gunung Mas regional election dispute in the incumbent's favor.[63]

Why did the Court have to deal with the Regional Election dispute? The authority to review regional election disputes is one of the most unsettling issues in the Indonesian constitutional history. The Constitution is vague on the issue; nevertheless, the 2004 Regional Government Law assigned the Supreme Court to handle the regional election dispute, which included elections for governor and head of regency (*Bupati*).[64] Nevertheless, one of the most visible problems facing the Supreme Court was the extensive backlog that plagued the Court for several decades.[65] The jurisdiction over regional elections disputes did not help the Supreme Court in overcoming this backlog.

While he was still in office, Chief Justice Asshiddiqie made a proposal that the Constitutional Court should take over the regional election disputes to ease the burden on the Supreme Court.[66] On April 28, 2008, the DPR passed a new law that authorized the Constitutional Court to handle the Regional Election dispute.[67] The Constitutional Court then took over the jurisdiction for regional election disputes from the Supreme Court on October 29, 2008.[68]

Since 2008, however, the Court had received an average of 130 cases of regional election disputes per year. The Court's docket was overloaded, especially with the regional election disputes. Also, Law No. 32 of 2004 on Regional Governance mandates that the Court settle election disputes within 14 days. The unintended consequence of this provision was that the Court would delay its rulings in judicial review cases, considering that there was no time constraint for the Court to render a judgment on statutory review.

Akil Mochtar came to the bench right before the Court took over the jurisdiction to handle regional election disputes. From the day the Court took over the regional election disputes on October 29, 2008, to his arrest on October 2, 2013, Mochtar sat on multiple panels of regional election disputes. Budiman Tanuredjo, the chief editor of *Kompas*, the leading daily newspaper in Indonesia, wrote a detailed report on the involvement of Akil Mochtar in multiple bribery offenses in regional election disputes.[69] Under the tenure of Chief Justice Mahfud, Mocthar sat on the same panel of judges as Justice Hamdan Zoelva and Justice Mohammad Alim, the panel tasked with examining some of the regional election dispute cases.[70] Tanuredjo reported that in many instances, Akil Mocthar received a bribe for the Court to rule in favor of particular candidates.[71] After he had become the chief justice, Mochtar shuffled the panel of judges that examine the regional election disputes. Mocthar assigned himself to sit on a panel of magistrates with Justice Maria Farida and Justice Anwar Usman.[72] Tanuredjo reported that Mochtar received many bribes to issue favorable rulings to individual candidates.[73] The question is how Mochtar could steer the Court's decision without the knowledge of his brethren who sat on the same panel. There were two plausible explanations for Mochtar's bribery practice. First, Mochtar steered the Court's decision in collaboration with his fellow justices who sat on the same panel. Second, he received bribes alone, but he was able to use his insider position to advocate strongly for certain positions while the other judges were oblivious.[74]

As explained in Chapter 2, the Constitutional Court Law prescribes that the president has the authority to remove a justice upon the request of the chief justice.[75] Before being removed, justices shall be given the opportunity to defend themselves before the Constitutional Court Honorary Council (*Majelis Kehormatan Mahkamah Konstitusi*).[76] On October 5, 2013, President Yudhoyono announced that he had decided to remove Akil Mochtar temporarily from the position of chief justice.[77] The president dismissed the chief justice based only on the request of the Chief Justice Constitutional Court.[78] After the president had removed Mochtar from his position, the Court established the Honorary Council to investigate Mochtar. On November 1, 2013, the Council came out with a verdict to grant dishonorable discharge to Mochtar.

As I explained in Chapter 2, Mochtar's removal took place in the absence of an impeachment mechanism for a sitting chief justice. The Honorary Council removed Mochtar from his position in a speedy trial. Moreover, the Council decided to remove Mochtar before his criminal trial began. It was not until June 30, 2014, that the Jakarta Anti-Corruption Court found Mochtar guilty of corruption and money laundering during his tenure as associate justice and chief justice, between 2010 and 2013. The Jakarta Anti-Corruption Court then sentenced him to life imprisonment.[79]

The arrest of Akil Mochtar not only tarnished the Court's reputation but also eroded the Court's legitimacy. Shortly after Mochtar's arrest, an angry crowd ransacked the courtroom where a trial was being held.[80] At that time, eight justices were reading out a verdict concerning a dispute over the governor's election in Maluku province. The supporters of the losing candidate stormed the courtroom, and the justices immediately exited the courtroom after one of the angry supporters hurled a microphone at them. The attack signified the lack of trust on the part of the general public.

The tragic episode of Akil Mocthar meant a significant shift from the first-generation heroic court to a much less heroic court. The chief justice holds a crucial position in the Indonesian constitutional constellation. Akil Mochtar had shown himself to be a villain instead of a hero. In his capacity as the chief justice, Akil Mochtar was the personification of the Court, and thus, the public could easily equate his crimes with the Court. Under the chairmanship of Jimly Asshiddiqie, the Court had the reputation of a transparent and functioning institution. Mochtar's arrest, however, turned the Court into another corrupt legal institution in the country, similar to the Supreme Court or the Attorney General's office.

The chairmanship of Hamdan Zoelva (2013–2015)

Political trajectories

After the arrest of Akil Mochtar, Deputy Chief Justice Hamdan Zoelva took over the leadership of the Constitutional Court and subsequently was elected as the fourth chief justice of the Constitutional Court on November 1, 2013. Zoelva was born and grew up in Bima, a city on the eastern coast of the island of Sumbawa in central Indonesia's province, West Nusa Tenggara (*Nusa Tenggara Barat*). Like his predecessors, Zoelva had a strong Islamic background;[81] Zoelva grew up in *santri* tradition, a more orthodox version of Islam, which was influenced by Sunni Islam, the largest denomination of the religion. His father was a leader of an Islamic Boarding School (*pesantren*) in Bima, and Zoelva's early education took place entirely in the Islamic boarding school.

Upon the completion of his Islamic boarding school training, Zoelva initially decided to pursue both civil law education and Sharia law education. For his civil law training, Zoelva enrolled in a medium tier law school, the Faculty of Law, Hassanuddin University in Makassar, South Sulawesi. At the same time,

Zoelva also enrolled in the Sharia Faculty, National Islamic Institute Alauddin in Makassar. Nevertheless, after some years of study, Zoelva chose to focus more on his study of civil law and abandoned his Sharia law training.

Zoelva began his legal career as a private practitioner in the capital city, Jakarta. Having spent a decade in legal practice, he decided to enter politics and joined the Crescent Star Party (*Partai Bulan Bintang*). The Crescent Star Party claims to be the continuation of the Council of Indonesian Muslim Associations (*Partai Majelis Syuro Muslimin Indonesia* or commonly known as *Masyumi*), a major Islamic political party in Indonesia in the 1950s.[82] When the party was re-established in 1999 after the fall of Soeharto regime, the original plan was to use the *Masyumi* name again, but after consideration, they settled on the Crescent Star Party.[83]

Zoelva held many strategic positions in the Crescent Star Party.[84] He was the secretary of the Crescent Star caucus in the DPR from 1999 to 2004. During the constitutional reform process in 1999–2002, Zoelva was the sole representative of the Star and Crescent Party in the Ad Hoc Committee of the People's Consultative Assembly (*Majelis Permusyawaratan Rakyat*—MPR). During the debate on a constitutional amendment in the MPR, Zoelva was the first person to raise the idea of the establishment of a constitutional court.[85] After the adoption of the Constitutional Court of the Third Amendment of 2001, Zoelva sat on the Special Committee that drafted the bill of the Constitutional Court in 2003. As the deputy chairman of the House Judiciary Committee, Zoelva participated in selecting the first-generation justices of the Constitutional Court. In sum, Zoelva played an instrumental role in the birth of the Constitutional Court.

When Zoelva was entering politics for the first time in 1999, he filed his candidacy for a seat in the DPR in his home province, West Nusa Tenggara. Nevertheless, having represented his home province for five years, Zoelva ventured to contest a seat in the DPR in the second district of Special Capital Territory, Jakarta. In the 2004 legislative election, however, Zoelva was beaten badly for the seat in the second district of Jakarta and only received 8.342 votes (0.25 percent of the total vote).[86] After his exit from politics, Zoelva went back to legal practice, and at the same time, he began to pursue a graduate degree at the Faculty of Law, Padjajaran University.

Despite the failure of his 2004 congressional bid, Zoelva continued to nurture his political ambitions in the 2009 legislative election. Zoelva decided to switch back to his home province and contested his old seat. But Zoelva was defeated soundly and decisively in his attempt at a political comeback. In the 2009 Legislative Election, Zoelva obtained 49,043 votes (2.56 percent of the total vote).[87] For Zoelva, the failure of his political comeback turned to be a blessing in disguise. The first blessing came when President Yudhoyono appointed Zoelva as an associate justice of the Constitutional Court on January 7, 2010.[88] At around the same time, Zoelva was finishing his doctoral dissertation on legal aspects of presidential impeachment in Indonesia.[89] A few months after his appointment as an associate justice, Zoelva obtained a doctoral degree in law from Padjajaran University.[90]

In August 2013, the Constitutional Court justices elected Zoelva as the deputy chief justice to succeed Justice Achmad Sodiki, who was retiring. Three months later, Zoelva became the fourth chief justice, replacing Akil Mochtar, who resigned in disgrace.

Political background and conflict of interest

When Zoelva took up the office of chief justice on November 6, 2013, he inherited a court in crisis. One of the major tests of Zoelva's efficacy in restoring public confidence in the Court lay in his ability to deal with criticism over his political background. As mentioned earlier, Zoelva was a career politician, and he resigned from the Crescent Star Party only after President Susilo Bambang Yudhoyono nominated him as an associate justice of the Constitutional Court in 2010. Zoelva's appointment as the chief justice had drawn criticism from political activists, who believed that his background as a politician would only serve to weaken the public's waning trust in the Court.[91] In this section, I will review two cases that presented challenges for Zoelva's impartiality as the chief justice.

The Presidential Threshold *case*

In the *Presidential Threshold* case,[92] Zoelva faced a significant test of his leadership. Many critics expressed concern that Chief Justice Zoelva might try to steer the Court's decision in favor of his political ally. This concern was based on the fact that the founder of the Crescent Star Party, Yusril Ihza Mahendra, was a high-profile lawyer and former minister of justice who was involved in the *Presidential Threshold* case.

The Presidential Election Law requires that a presidential candidate shall be nominated by a political party or a coalition of political parties who hold at least 20 percent of the seats in the DPR or obtain at least 25 percent of the popular votes in the legislative election.[93] Nevertheless, on December 8, 2013, Mahendra announced his candidacy for the presidency despite his party having no seats in the DPR and little prospect of fulfilling either the seat or popular vote threshold in the 2014 legislative election.[94]

Realizing that he had a slim chance of fulfilling his political ambitions, Mahendra launched a legal challenge in the Constitutional Court to enable him to run for president on his party's ticket, the Crescent Star Party. In the petition, Mahendra postulated that the Constitution did not specify any threshold for the presidential election. Mahendra referred to the Constitutional provision that states, "each ticket of presidential candidates shall be proposed before the holding of general elections by political parties or coalitions of political parties which are participants in the general elections."[95] Mahendra asserted that there were 12 political parties in the 2014 election, and therefore, he urged the Court to declare that all these parties have the right to nominate their candidates for president.[96]

On March 20, 2014, the Court issued a decision that addressed Mahendra's complaint. The Court considered that Mahendra had requested the Court to issue an advisory opinion in regard to the meaning of Article 6(2) of the Constitution. The Court made a distinction between a declaratory judgment and an advisory opinion: The former aimed to resolve real controversies, and the latter did not.[97] The Court held that it had no authority to issue an advisory opinion, and thus that it could not grant Mahendra's petition.[98]

The Court's decision to turn down Mahendra's request boosted hope in Chief Justice Zoelva's ability to defend judicial independence in Indonesia. Nevertheless, the public would keep questioning Zoelva's impartiality if he did not recuse himself from any cases that involved his former party. The fact of the matter was that Zoelva never considered recusing himself from any case that involved the Star and Crescent Party.

The 2014 presidential election dispute case

Soon, Zoelva's impartiality would be questioned again with the presidential election dispute that involved the Crescent Star Party. On July 22, 2014, the General Election Commission declared Jokowi and his running mate, Jusuf Kalla, as the presidential election winners, with Joko Widodo and Jusuf Kalla gaining 70,997,833 votes and Prabowo Subianto and Hatta Rajasa winning 62,576,444 votes. The defeated candidate, Prabowo Subianto, however, refused to concede, claiming that fraud had denied him victory, and he immediately challenged the election result in the Constitutional Court.[99]

Many critics were skeptical that the Court would be impartial in reviewing the case.[100] The concerns were again based on the fact that Zoelva was a member of the Star and Crescent Party that supported the losing candidate, Prabowo Subianto. In addition to Zoelva, Justice Patrialis Akbar was a member of the National Mandate Party (PAN) and the chairman of PAN; Hatta Rajasa was the running mate of Prabowo Subianto. Therefore, there was a concern that Chief Justice Zoelva, with some help from Justice Patrialis Akbar, might steer the Court's decision in favor of Prabowo Subianto.

Prabowo Subianto argued that his opponents employed different *modus operandi* to commit electoral fraud, such as a miscounting of the results by the KPU, partisan local government bureaucracy, and fraud surrounding the higher number of unregistered voters who were still able to vote using IDs.[101] Having spent more than three weeks reviewing the case, the Court rejected all of Subianto's complaints and ruled that there was no evidence of systematic and massive electoral fraud in favor of Widodo.[102]

Many people praised the Court's decision to reject Subianto's challenge. Moreover, for Zoelva personally, the decision elevated his credibility. After the Court had announced the decision, Zoelva responded to the critics: "Whatever I said, people would not believe me. I had repeatedly stated that the Court would be independent, but no one believed us."[103] Indeed, Chief Justice Zoelva turned the skepticism into delight by proving his impartiality. But, even as his political background continued to haunt him, Zoelva never considered that it was necessary to recuse himself as the way to address the criticism of his impartiality.

Judicial review of the electoral process

One of the major politically sensitive issues that the Court had to deal with was the judicial review of the electoral process. The first-generation Court did not deal much with the judicial review of the electoral process because at that time, Indonesia had just begun its democratic experiment. The 2004 General Election took place within a few months after the Court opened. In the era of the second-generation Court, more complex electoral process issues had begun to arise. By the time Zoelva had taken the helm as chief justice, Indonesia had enjoyed democracy for a decade, and the Court had to deal with many cases related to judicial review of the electoral process.

The first significant electoral process claim that the Court had to decide was the *General Election Schedule* case.[104] A political activist, Effendi Ghazali, challenged the Presidential Election Law No. 42 of 2008, which prescribed two separate election schedules for legislative and presidential elections. Why were there two different election schedules? According to Law No. 42 of 2008 on the presidential election, a presidential candidate shall be nominated by a political party or a coalition of political parties that hold at least 20 percent of the seats in the DPR or obtain at least 25 percent of the popular vote in the legislative election. Apparently, the legislators designed the Law to allow only a few big parties to nominate a presidential candidate. Under these arrangements, political parties cannot nominate a candidate until they find out the official result of the legislative election. The Presidential Election Law, therefore, states that the parliamentary and presidential elections must be held at least three months apart.[105]

In its decision, the Court decided to strike down the provision that decreed that the legislative and presidential elections be scheduled three months apart. First, the Court ruled that the presidential election must be organized in accordance with constitutional structures of government, which is based on the presidential system.[106] The Court opined that the current system, which set the presidential elections to depend upon the result of the legislative election, would give political parties too much leverage over a president elect and consequently, would undermine the presidential system.[107]

Second, the Court held that the drafters of the Constitution never intended to hold two separate elections, but rather a simultaneous general election, which includes the presidential and legislative elections.[108] Finally, the Court argued that the current election mechanisms are expensive and for the most part, the elections are paid for by taxpayers. The Court ruled that the simultaneous election would save taxpayers money on election costs.[109]

The Court finally held that the legislative election and the presidential election should be held simultaneously. Nevertheless, the Court held that the decision could not be applied right away because it would likely disrupt the 2014 General Election preparations.[110] The Court cited its previous decision in the *Mulyana Kusumah* case,[111] in which the Court held that the Anti-Corruption Court must disband in three years and the DPR was to prepare a new law to reform the

Anti-Corruption Court within three years.[112] Finally, the Court ruled that the decision would only be applied in the upcoming 2019 general election.

The case was written by "two hands" of chief justices. Mahfud finished the deliberation meeting on March 26, 2013, but it was Hamdan Zoelva who signed and announced the decision on January 23, 2014. The Court's decision signified the continuation of the "suspended declaration" remedy. Moreover, the Court's decision did not aim to redress the claimant's injury on the violation of his voting rights. The Court only issued a declaratory judgment, which declared that the presidential election and legislative election should be held simultaneously in the future.

After the Court had decided the *General Election Schedule* case, many different groups challenged Law No. 42 of 2008 on the Presidential Election on various grounds. In the first instance, the *Armed Forces Voting Right* case,[113] two political activists challenged a provision in the Presidential Election Law that provided, "in the Presidential Election of 2009, a member of the Indonesian Armed Forces and National Police shall not use its voting rights."[114] The claimants argued that such a prohibition should also be applied to the 2014 General Election because there was still the necessity for the Armed Forces and National Police to maintain their neutrality during the General Election. The Court accepted the claimants' argument and declared that the provision was conditionally unconstitutional, so long as it would not be interpreted to include the 2014 General Election.

Here the Court continued to employ a quasi-weak-form review; instead of declaring the Law unconstitutional, it stated that the Law was conditionally unconstitutional because it only applied to the 2009 General Election. Nevertheless, if Law No. 42 of 2008 on the presidential election were interpreted to include the 2014 General Election, then it would deem it constitutional.

In the *Presidential Candidate* case,[115] some political activists challenged a provision on how to determine a president elect. The Presidential Election Law stipulated that a president elect is a presidential candidate who obtains more than 50 percent of the total votes in the presidential election with at least 20 percent of votes in each province spread throughout more than half of the provinces in Indonesia.[116] The claimants argued that the provision was ambiguous because it did not specify whether the formula was to be applied when there were multiple presidential candidates or two candidates. The Court concurred with the claimants and declared that the Law was conditionally unconstitutional, so long as it was not to be applied when there were two presidential candidates.[117]

Again, the Court framed its decision in the context of the quasi-weak-form review. The Court considered that the Law should not be applied if there are only two presidential candidates.[118] In other words, if there are only two presidential candidates in the presidential election, the candidate with the most votes would be declared the winner.

The Court under the leadership of Hamdan Zoelva continued to apply the quasi-weak-form review technique. The pressing issue was whether Zoelva intended to minimize the impact of the Court's decision as a strategy to deal with the Executive, or it was a sign of weakness in that Chief Justice Zoelva did not believe that the Court had the strength to overrule the Executive and Legislature decisions. This question cannot be answered based on the Court's decisions on the judicial review of the electoral process alone, and so I will come back to this issue after having considered some of the Court's decisions in different policy areas.

Socio-economic rights

One of the most delicate issues throughout the Court's history has been the judicial review of governmental policies that involve socio-economic rights. The Court under the chairmanship of Hamdan Zoelva could not avoid dealing with some cases that involved socio-economic rights issues. In the *Private Hospital* case,[119] the Court had to deal with the issue of a private healthcare provider. In this case, Muhammadiyah, one of the largest Islamic organizations in the country, challenged article 7(4) of the Hospital Law, which provided that private hospitals can only be set up by private legal entities that operate solely in the hospital industry (*bidang perumahsakitan*).[120] The claimant also challenged Article 21, which provided that all private hospitals must be run by profit-oriented legal entities in the form of limited companies.[121]

Muhammadiyah is an Islamic nonprofit organization that runs 78 hospitals that already have permits and the legal status to operate. This Law threatened to jeopardize these hospitals because a private corporation did not own them.[122] Muhammadiyah invoked the argument that the Hospital Law violated the socio-economic rights provision in the Constitution, especially the right to health care under Article 28H (1).[123] It also argued that the Law violated the right to receive similar opportunities and benefits to achieve equality, fairness, and property rights.[124]

The Court ruled that the Law would cripple the claimant's ability to provide health-care services, and this situation would potentially deprive many people of health-care services.[125] The Court held the Law to be "conditionally unconstitutional" as long as it did not provide an exception for hospitals run by nonprofit corporations (*badan hukum yang bersifat nirlaba*).[126] In other words, the Court declared the Law to be "unconstitutional" unless it provided some exception as prescribed by the Court.

The *Private Hospital* case was also written by "two hands" of chief justices. Akil Mochtar led the conclusion of the deliberation meeting on August 12, 2003, but then the Court took more than six months to announce its decision. By the time it did so on May 22, 2014, it was already under the chairmanship of Hamdan Zoelva.

Hamdan Zoelva had the opportunity to lead his first deliberation meeting on the socio-economic rights issue in the *Farmers' Protection and Empowerment* case.[127] The claimants were NGOs chiefly led by the Indonesian Human Rights Committee for Social Justice (IHCS). After their success in the *Plant Cultivation System Law* case,[128] they came back to the Court to challenge the constitutionality of Law No. 19 of 2013 on Farmers' Protection and Empowerment. The crux of the matter was that the Law provides that the government is obliged to guarantee "the expansion of farmers' land area" (*luasan tanah pertanian*) by providing facilities to obtain free land that is intended or designated as an agricultural area.[129] The Law then mandated the government to give an area of 2 hectares to farmers who did not own land and had worked on the land for 5 years in a row.[130] Nevertheless, the Law refused to use the term "land reform." The Law provided that the land shall be given to the farmers in several ways: as the lease of land by the state (*hak sewa*), a license to develop (*izin pengusahaan*), a license to cultivate (*izin pengelolaan*), or a license to utilize (*izin pemanfaatan*).[131] The claimants argued that the lease of land and licensing system were contrary to the constitutional mandate to guarantee the greatest benefit of the people (Article 33 section 2).[132]

Apart from the socio-economic rights claims, the claimant also brought the issue of freedom of association. The Law provided that the government is obliged to facilitate and encourage the establishment of farmers' organizations (*kelembagaan petani*) and farmer's economic organizations (*kelembagaan ekonomi petani*). Nevertheless, the Law set a limit to the farmers' association into four categories: a farmers' club (*kelompok tani*), an association of farmers' clubs (*assosiasi kelompok tani*), an association of agricultural commodities (*assosiasi komoditas pertanian*), and the board of national agricultural commodities (*Dewan Komoditas Pertanian Nasional*).[133] The claimants argued that the arrangement of farmers' organizations as stated in the Law was the legacy of the military regime, in which the government had the sole authority to determine the form of the farmers' organizations.[134] The claimant posited that the Law is contrary to the constitutional guarantee of freedom of association and freedom of assembly.[135]

The Court considered that the lease of land by the state is a feudal practice and a legacy of colonialism, and therefore, it must stop.[136] The Court held that the lease of land (*hak sewa*) should be declared unconstitutional as it was contrary to Article 33, which mandates the state to control land and natural resources for the greatest benefit of the people.[137] Nevertheless, the Court held that the state has the authority to issue different kinds of licenses for the farmers to use the land, as long as such a licensing system would bring the greatest benefit for the people.[138] The Court's reasoning was very narrow and it did not elaborate in what way the lease of land would hamper the greatest benefit of the people. Furthermore, the Court did not clarify whether the decision meant that farmers could control the land as private property or if the farmers' control over the land would be limited to a license to cultivate, develop, and utilize it.

Concerning the issue of freedom of association, the Court ruled that the state has the authority to establish farmers' associations with the purpose of empowering farmers, but it did not mean that farmers were forbidden to create other organizations.[139] The Court held further that there should not be any coercion imposed on farmers to join government-sponsored institutions as they were free to establish and to join nongovernmental farmers' associations.[140] The Court then declared the Law was conditionally unconstitutional as long as it did not recognize the existence of nongovernmental farmers associations. In other words, the Law would be deemed constitutional only if it allowed farmers to join and to establish nongovernmental farmers associations.

Freedom of association cases

Considering that the Court only partially dealt with the subject of freedom of assembly in the *Farmers' Protection and Empowerment* case, it is important to examine a case that solely dealt with freedom of association because it will show the Court's pattern in dealing with the issue. In the *Ormas* case,[141] the Court reviewed the constitutionality of the Mass Organization Law (*Undang—Undang tentang Organisasi Kemasyarakatan*—Ormas), which set a variety of vague obligations and prohibitions on NGO activities and requirements for the establishment of NGOs.[142]

The claimant was again Muhammadiyah, the Islamic organization that was at the forefront of constitutional litigation in Indonesia. Muhammadiyah long considered itself to be engaged in a struggle for social justice in Indonesia, and since its involvement in the *Oil and Gas III* case, Muhammadiyah termed judicial review a "constitutional jihad" and part of their "great legal struggle."[143] The claimant argued that the Law should be declared entirely unconstitutional because it was contrary to the constitutional guarantee of freedom of assembly. In short, the applicant argued that the Law had gone too far to regulate the purpose, scope, function, symbol, coat of arms, and article association of NGOs.[144] The claimant objected to the prohibition against receiving donations from anonymous donors and the obligation to publish an annual report to the public. Moreover, the plaintiff also objected to some rules, such as the requirement that NGOs be nationwide in scope.[145]

The Court concurred with the claimant that the Law provided too many details in regulating the existence of NGOs. Nevertheless, the Court argued that it could not declare a law unconstitutional simply because it represented meticulous legislation. More importantly, the Court ruled that the Constitution authorized the government to regulate freedom of assembly and association based upon the considerations of morality, religion, and public order in a democratic society (Article 28J, [2]). Therefore, the Court rejected the claimant's petition to nullify the Law entirely.

Despite the rejection, the Court decided to declare the nationwide scope requirement as unconstitutional because it curtailed the freedom of association. The Court opined that Article 28J (2) did not justify the nationwide scope requirement, as local NGOs would not bring any harm to morality, religion, and public order in a democratic society.[146] Apart from nullifying the nationwide scope requirement, the Court also held that the provision on the objectives of NGOs should be declared conditionally unconstitutional. The Law set the goals of NGOs so as to provide public services; to preserve religious values; to maintain the values, morals, ethics, and cultures in society, and so on.[147] The Court held that such objectives must be interpreted as an option for NGOs to embrace instead of an obligation to be followed strictly.

The decision did not signify any significant departure from the conservative approach of the Mahfud Court. Zoelva followed the Court's pattern to invoke the general limitation of the Bill of Rights clause (Article 28 J [2]) in justifying the government's authority to limit the Bill of Rights. Moreover, the Court only applied the conditionally unconstitutional technique to the nationwide scope provision instead of to key provisions of the Law. Apparently, the Court used the conditionally unconstitutional decision to sugar-coat its decision to reject the claimant's petition.

In sum, the Court under the chairmanship of Hamdan Zoelva continued to apply the quasi-weak-form review techniques of the previous courts. Nevertheless, there is no clear pattern to the application of such techniques. As mentioned in the previous chapters, Chief Justice Asshiddiqie relied more on a combination of maximalist and minimalist approaches, in which he employed quasi-weak-form review as a tool to minimize the impact of the bold Court's decisions. Chief Justice Mahfud, however, transformed quasi-weak-form review as a means to issue strong remedies without giving substantial deference to the legislature. The Court under the chairmanship of Hamdan Zoelva did not issue many bold decisions on the merits of the cases, but rather jumped directly to the declaration of "conditionally unconstitutional." Despite the issuance of many conditionally unconstitutional decisions, the Court did not provide strong remedies and only issued short directives on how to interpret the Law.

The end of the regional election dispute

When Zoelva took over the helm as chief justice, he was acutely aware that many scandals, which originated from regional election disputes, had tarnished the Court's reputation. The regional election dispute did not only become a source of corruption but also created extra work for the Court. Since the incorporation of regional election disputes into the Court's jurisdiction in 2008, the Court received an average of 130 cases of regional election dispute per year, in addition to an average of 80 judicial review cases per year. The Court's docket was overloaded with regional election disputes. Furthermore, Law No. 32 of 2004 on Regional Governance mandated the Court to settle election disputes within 14 days. This provision led the Court to delay its rulings in judicial review cases since there was no time constraint for the Court to render a judgment in statutory review.

After the arrest of Chief Justice Mochtar, many constitutional stakeholders began to urge the president and the DPR to reevaluate the Court's authority to handle these disputes. Nonetheless, neither the president nor the DPR took any steps to address the issue. The Court thus took the issue into its own hands in its decision in the *Regional Election Dispute* case.[148]

The case originated in a claim made by a group of NGOs, chiefly led by the Law and Constitutional Assessment Forum (*Forum Kajian Hukum dan Konstitutsi*). The claimants posited that the Constitution only equipped the Court with the authority to handle national election disputes, not regional election disputes.[149] Based on this presupposition, the claimant concluded that the Court's authority to handle regional election disputes was unconstitutional.

The claimants also put forward a claim that the Court had shifted its energy and resources toward handling regional election disputes instead of statutory review.

According to the claimants, the Court's new priority caused immediate harm to them because it lessened their ability to bring meaningful statutory review cases.[150] The nature of the claim was very abstract, with the petitioners asking the Court to re-evaluate its authority to handle regional election disputes.

The Court's majority sustained the claimant's petition and held that the drafters of the Constitution never intended to include the election of the governor and the head of district (*Bupati*) within the textual phrase "general election."[151] The Court ruled that the drafters intended only to include the presidential election and the legislative election, including the members of the national parliament and the regional parliament.[152] The Court held that many regional election disputes were not within the scope of its authority.[153] Thus, the Court decided to remove regional election disputes from its docket entirely.

The closing chapter of Hamdan Zoelva

President Susilo Bambang Yudhoyono appointed Zoelva as an associate justice on January 7, 2010, which meant he would finish his first 5-year term on January 7, 2015.[154] As Chief Justice Zoelva approached the end of his first 5-year term, the new Jokowi administration hinted that he would not be re-appointed for his second term.[155] On November 11, 2014, President Jokowi established a selection committee to find a successor for Hamdan Zoelva. Chief Justice Zoelva implied that he was prepared to be reappointed if Jokowi wanted him to keep the position. When the selection committee opened a public competition for Zoelva's position, Zoelva put aside his ego and applied for his job.

Chief Justice Zoelva soon realized that the Jokowi administration would not give him an easy pass when the selection committee called him for an interview. Zoelva sent a letter stating his objection to attend the interview with the selection committee. He said he had already fulfilled the requirement to serve on the bench when he was interviewed to become an associate justice in 2010.[156] The selection committee maintained that Chief Justice Zoelva would not receive any special treatment and he could not take any shortcuts. The committee finally decided to drop the bid of Chief Justice Hamdan Zoelva.[157]

On January 14, 2015, a little over a year after he took the helm as chief justice, Zoelva bid farewell to the Constitutional Court justices and their staff. Before he left the office, Chief Justice Zoelva urged the lawmakers to reform the term limit for Constitutional Court justices and chief justice.[158] He argued that a longer-term limit was necessary to preserve judicial independence. Indeed, there is some truth in Zoelva's proposal, because life tenure or a long fixed tenure would allow judges to be more independent in exercising their authority. Moreover, the humiliating exit of Chief Justice Zoelva re-affirmed the weak spot of the institutional design of the Indonesian Constitutional Court. First, the potential pool of candidates for the Constitutional Court is not large. Indonesian legal academia and society have not been able to generate a significant number of constitutional scholars and lawyers who are capable of sitting as constitutional court justices. Consequently, it is hard to find good potential candidates to fill the Constitutional Court in a

5-year cycle. Second, a quick turnover of judges has given many opportunities for the legislators, the president, and the Supreme Court to appoint their favorite judges and dismiss sitting judges who do not serve their interests.

In sum, during his short tenure as the fourth chief justice of the Constitutional Court, Zoelva was not able to play a heroic role like his predecessors. First, the leadership of Hamdan Zoelva was marred by his background as a politician, and he failed to recuse himself from many important cases presented before the Court. Second, the Court's advocacy of quasi-weak-form review may be a sign of weakness; Chief Justice Zoelva did not believe the court had the strength to issue bold decisions, and therefore, played it safe through the issuance of conditionally unconstitutional decisions minus bold rulings. Finally, the Court's decision that upheld Jokowi's electoral victory could also be interpreted as a sign of weakness, because the Court was merely affirming a popular electoral result.

Conclusion

The founding chief justice, Jimly Asshiddiqie, and his immediate successor, Mohamad Mahfud, were both extraordinary figures. Their successors, however, were ordinary chief justices. Both Mocthar and Zoelva were mediocre politicians before they were appointed to be constitutional court justices. Despite their doctoral degrees, neither were serious academics like Asshiddiqie and Mahfud. Neither Mochtar nor Zoelva could not maintain the role of judicial heroism to solve social and political problems in the country, as they were plainly less innovative and bold in their rulings. Mochtar defined himself as a villain. His arrest immediately led public perception to put the Court on the same level as other corrupt legal institutions in the country. Zoelva appeared to pursue a path of retreat, underscoring the Court's weakness in relation to other branches of government. But the fact of the matter is that the Court under Zoelva did not retreat under pressure or chose a safe position and toe the political line; it was rather that Zoelva was not a heroic chief justice like his predecessors. As President Jokowi decided not to re-appoint him for the second term, Zoelva was forced to exit the Court as the victim of the new Jokowi administration.

Notes

1 See the official biography of Akil Mochtar at the Indonesian Constitutional Court website, http://www.mahkamahkonstitusi.go.id/index.php?page=web.ProfilHakim&id=8.
2 Akil Mochtar. *Pembalikan Beban Pembuktian Tindak Pidana Korupsi* [On Shifting the Burden of Proof in Corruption Cases] (Jakarta: Sekretariat Jenderal dan Kepaniteraan, Mahkamah Konstitusi, 2009).
3 For a detailed analysis of the Lingah-Pacah case, please see Budiman Tanuredjo. *Lingah-Pacah: Berjuang Menggapai Keadilan* [Lingah-Pacah: The Struggle for Justice] (Jakarta: Lembaga Studi dan Advokat Masyarakat, 1995).
4 See the Constitutional Court of the Republic of Indonesia, *Upholding the Constitutional Democratic State*, the 2011 Annual Report of the Constitutional Court, xxi.

5 Prodita Sabarini. "Akil Mochtar: Turning the Tide." The *Jakarta Post*, May 2, 2013. http://www.thejakartapost.com/news/2013/05/02/akil-mochtar-turning-tide.html.
6 *Jakarta Post*. "Honor Council for Justice Akil: MK chief," (December 12, 2010), http://www.thejakartapost.com/news/2010/12/22/honor-council-justice-akil-mk-chief.html.
7 *Jakarta Post*. "Akil Mochtar Chosen as New MK Chief Justice," April 3, 2013.
8 Law No. 8 of 2011 on the Amendment of the 2003 Constitutional Court Law.
9 Ibid., Art. 15 (2).
10 The Constitutional Court Decision No. 68/PUU-IX/2011 (the *Constitutional Court Justice Requirement* case).
11 Ibid., para. 3.23.
12 For an excellent analysis of the role of intellectuals as the support of the military regime, please see Daniel Dhakidae. *Cendekiawan dan Kekuasaan dalam Negara Orde Baru* [Intellectuals and Authority under the New Order State] (Jakarta: Gramedia Pustaka Utama, 2003).
13 For a detailed analysis of the shift from academic to administrative authority in Indonesian academia, please see Heru Nugroho. "The Political Economy of Higher Education: The University as an Arena for the Struggle for Power." In *Social Science and Power in Indonesia*, edited by Vedi R. Hadiz, and Daniel Dhakidae. (Jakarta: Equinox Publishing, 2005).
14 Ahmad Fadlil Sumadi. *Pengawasan dan pembinaan pengadilan: Fungsi Manajemen Mahkamah Agung terhadap Pengadilan di Bawahnya setelah Perubahan UUD 1945* [Supervision and Development of the Judiciary: The Supreme Court Management on Lower Court After the Amendments of the 1945 Constitution] (Malang: Setara Press, 2013).
15 The Postgraduate Program of Gadjah Mada University only published a blurb of Anwar Usman's dissertation without specifying that he earned his doctorate at the Law School. See http://www.pasca.ugm.ac.id/v3.0/promotion/id/82. The website says that Anwar successfully defended his dissertation, titled *Bentuk-bentuk Intervensi Terhadap Independensi Kekuasaan Kehakiman: Relevansinya bagi Penegakan Hukum dan Keadilan di Indonesia* [The Forms of Intervention on the Independence of Judiciary: Its Relevance for the Law Enforcement and Justice in Indonesia].
16 See the official biography of Anwar Usman at the website of the Indonesian Constitutional Court, available at http://www.mahkamahkonstitusi.go.id/index.php?page=web.Berita&id=13021&menu=2#.V9mrA5grK00.
17 Jacqueline Hicks. "The Missing Link: Explaining the Political Mobilization of Islam in Indonesia," 42(1) *Journal of Contemporary Asia* 46 (2012).
18 Andi Hajramurni. "Ministers Get Poor Grades, Reshuffle Suggested." The *Jakarta Post*, January 22, 2010. Accessed September 13, 2016. http://www.thejakartapost.com/news/2010/01/22/ministers-get-poor-grades-reshuffle-suggested.html.
19 Patrialis Akbar. *Hubungan Lembaga Kepresidenan dengan Dewan Perwakilan Rakyat dan Veto Presiden* [The Relationship between the President and the People's Representative Council, and Presidential Veto] (Yogyakarta: Total Media, 2013).
20 *Jakarta Post*. "Patrialis Akbar Appointed as New Constitutional Court Judge," July 30, 2013. Accessed September 13, 2016. http://www.thejakartapost.com/news/2013/07/30/patrialis-akbar-appointed-new-constitutional-court-judge.html.
21 Arief Hidayat. *Kebebasan Berserikat di Indonesia: Suatu Analisis Pengaruh Perubahan Sistem Politik Terhadap Penafsiran Hukum* [Freedom of Assembly in Indonesia: An Analysis of the Influence of the Changing of Political System into Legal Interpretation] (Semarang: Badan Penerbit Universitas Diponegoro, 2006).

22 Simon Marginson and Erlenawati Sawir, "University Leaders' Strategies in the Global Environment: A Comparative Study of Universitas Indonesia and the Australian National University," 52(2) *Higher Education* 343–373 (2006).
23 The Constitutional Court Decision No. 35/PUU-X/2012, reviewing Law No. 41 of 1999 on Forestry (hereinafter *the Indigenous Forest I* case).
24 See *Aliansi Masyarakat Adat Nusantara* [Indigenous Peoples Alliance of the Archipelago], Organization Profile, http://www.aman.or.id/profile-kami/.
25 *The Indigenous Forest I* case, para. 3. 12.4.
26 The Constitutional Court Decision No. 3/PUU-VIII/2010 (hereinafter the *Coastal and Remote Islands Law* case).
27 Ibid., para. 3.13.1.
28 Ibid., 179.
29 The Constitutional Court Decision No. 99/PUU-X/2012 (hereinafter the *Plant Cultivation System Law* case).
30 Law No. 12 of 1992 on the Plant Cultivation System.
31 The *Plant Cultivation System Law case*, 19–20.
32 Law No. 12 of 1992, Art. 60 (1.i).
33 The *Plant Cultivation System Law* case, para. 3.18.
34 Ibid., para. 3.19.
35 Ibid., para. 3.20.
36 The Constitutional Court Decision No. 84/PUU-X/2012 (hereinafter the *Blasphemy II* case). For a detailed analysis of the *Blasphemy II* case, please see Melissa Crouch. "Constitutionalism, Islam and the Practice of Religious Deference: The Case of the Indonesian Constitutional Court," 16(2) *Australian Journal of Asian Law* 1–15 (2016).
37 The population of Shia Muslims in Indonesia is approximately one million, while Indonesia has the largest number of Sunni Muslims, an estimated 205 million people. For an excellent analysis of the history of Shiite Muslims in Indonesia in comparison with Shiite Muslims in Southeast Asia, please see Chiara Formichi and R. Michael Feener. *Shi'ism in Southeast Asia: 'Alid piety and sectarian constructions.* (Oxford; New York, NY: Oxford University Press, 2015).
38 See the Decision of the Sampang District Court No. 69/Pid.B/2012/PN.Spg.
39 See the District Court Decision of Ciamis No. 278 / Pid.Sus /2012 / PN.CMS (November 6, 2012). The claimant filed an appeal, but the Supreme Court rejected his appeal; see Supreme Court Decision No. 777 K/Pid.Sus/2013 (April 23, 2013).
40 Law No. 24 of 2003 on the Constitutional Court, Art. 60.
41 Law No. 8 of 2011 on the Amendment of the Constitutional Court Law, Art. 60 (2).
42 The *Blasphemy Law II* case, Para 3.11.1.
43 Ibid., para. 3.11.1.
44 Ibid., para. 3.12.
45 Ibid., para. 3.13.
46 Ibid., para. 3.15–3.16.
47 Patrialis Akbar came to the Court in August 2013, long after the Court finished its deliberation meeting on April 9, 2013. Nevertheless, Akbar joined the majority opinion, and his name was listed in the Court's decision.
48 The Constitutional Court Decision No. 93/PUU-X/2012 (hereinafter the *Sharia Banking* case).
49 Law No. 3 of 2006 on the Amendment of Law No. 7 of 1989 on Religious Court, Art. 49.
50 Ibid., the elucidation of Article 49 (i).
51 Mark E. Cammack and R. Michael Feener. "The Islamic Legal System in Indonesia," 21 *Pac. Rim L. & Pol'y J.* 13 (2012).

52 See Law No. 3 of 2006, the elucidation of Article 55 (2).
53 The *Sharia Banking* case, para. 3.21.
54 Ibid., para. 3.22.
55 The 1945 Indonesian Constitution, Art. 28D (1).
56 The Constitutional Court Decision No. 52/PUU-XI/2013 (hereinafter the *Twitter* case).
57 Law No. 11 of 2008 on the Electronic Information and Transaction, Art. 28 (2).
58 Bayu Marhaenjati and Ezra Sihite. "Police Deny Selling Plate Numbers." The *Jakarta Globe,* January 15, 2013. Accessed July 6, 2017. http://jakartaglobe.id/archive/police-deny-selling-plate-numbers/.
59 "Lawyer Named a Suspect Over Allegedly Racist Tweet Aimed at Basuki." The *Jakarta Globe,* May 24, 2013. Accessed July 6, 2017. http://jakartaglobe.id/news/lawyer-named-a-suspect-over-allegedly-racist-tweet-aimed-at-basuki/.
60 *Jakarta Post.* "Facing Libel Charges, Lawyer turns to MK to defend Himself," June 4, 2013. http://www.thejakartapost.com/news/2013/06/04/facing-libel-charges-lawyer-turns-mk-defend-himself.html.
61 The 1945 Indonesian Constitution, Article 28 E (2).
62 The *Twitter* case, para. 3.12.
63 *Jakarta Post.* "MK Chief Justice, Golkar Lawmaker Arrested for Bribery Charges." October 3, 2013. http://www.thejakartapost.com/news/2013/10/03/mk-chief-justice-golkar-lawmaker-arrested-bribery-charges.html.
64 Law No. 32 (2004), Concerning Regional Administration, Article 106(4). Law of the Republic of Indon.
65 Sebastian Pompe. "Supreme Court Causes Backlogs, Not the Law," *Jakarta Post,* December 23, 2003.
66 *Hukumonline.* "Penyatuan Rezim Pilkada dengan Pemilu Tergantung DPR dan Pemerintah" [Unification of Local and National Elections Depends on the House and Government], August 15, 2006. http://www.hukumonline.com/berita/baca/hol15318/penyatuan-rezim-pilkada-dengan-pemilutergantung.
67 See Law No. 12 of 2008 on the Amendment of the Regional Governance Law, Art. 236C.
68 *Hukumonline.* "MA Resmi Limpahkan Sengketa Hasil Pilkada ke MK" [MA Formally Handed over the Regional Election Dispute to MK], October 29, 2008. http://www.hukumonline.com/berita/baca/hol20397/ma-resmi-limpahkan-sengketa-hasil-pilkada-ke-mk.
69 Budiman Tanuredjo. *Akal Akal Akil* [The Tricks of Akil] (Jakarta: Penerbit Buku Kompas, 2014).
70 Ibid., 109–115.
71 Ibid., 110–111.
72 Ibid., 78–104.
73 Ibid., 83–105.
74 Ibid., 120.

In the Central Tapanuli Regional Election case, Mochtar received the bribe even when he was not a sitting judge who examined the case. The Court ruled in favor of the candidate who bribed Mochtar. As a non-sitting judge, Mochtar would not be able to steer the Court decision unless he built collaboration with the sitting judges.

75 See Constitutional Court Law No. 24 of 2003, Art. 23 (4).
76 Ibid., Art. 23 (3).
77 SINDONEWS.COM. "SBY Berhentikan Sementara Akil Mochtar" [President SBY Removed Akil Mochtar Temporarily]. http://nasional.sindonews.com/read/791201/13/sby-berhentikan-sementara-akil-mochtar-1380966478.
78 See Constitutional Court Law No. 24 of 2003, Art. 23 (2a) & 23 (4).
79 Tanuredjo. *The Tricks of Akil,* 138–139.

80 Bayu Marhaenjati. "Farce in Constitutional Court as Maluku Ruling Turns to Riot." *Jakarta Globe*, November 14, 2013. http://thejakartaglobe.beritasatu.com/news/farce-in-constitutional-court-as-maluku-ruling-turns-to-riot/.
81 See Nadisryah Hosen. "The Constitutional Court and 'Islamic' Judges in Indonesia," 16(2) *Australian Journal of Asian Law* article 4, 2016).
82 See Bernhard Platzdasch. *Islamism in Indonesia: Politics in the Emerging Democracy* (Pasir Panjang, Singapore: Institute of Southeast Asian Studies, 2009), chapter 1.
83 For details of the debate on the adoption of the name of Bulan Bintang, see Ibid. 63–68.
84 Ibid., 353.
85 See Minutes of 2nd meeting, BP MPR, October 6, 1999.
86 Pemilu DPR 2004-Indonesia. (The 2004 Indonesian Legislative Election), available at http://www.pemilu.asia/?lang=ind&c=54&opt=3&s=11&y=2004&id=32524.
87 Pemilu DPR 2009-Indonesia (The 2009 Indonesian Legislative Election), available at http://www.pemilu.asia/?lang=ind&c=54&opt=3&s=11&y=2009&id=116413.
88 Erwida Maulia. "Two New Constitutional Court Justices Sworn In." *Jakarta Post*, January 7, 2010.
89 Hamdan Zoelva. *Pemakzulan Presiden di Indonesia* (Jakarta: Sinar Grafika, 2011).
90 *Hukumonline*. "Presiden Jangan Takut Dimakzulkan." August 2, 2010. http://www.hukumonline.com/berita/baca/lt4c566d3549050/presiden-jangan-takut-dimakzulkan.
91 Rizky Amelia. "Hamdan Zoelva's Selection Stirs Debate." *Jakarta Globe*, November 4, 2013. http://www.thejakartaglobe.com/news/hamdan-zoelvas-selection-stirs-debate/.
92 The Indonesian Constitutional Court Decision No. 108/PUU-XI/2013, reviewing the Law No. 24 of 2008 on the Election of President and Vice President (hereinafter the *Presidential Threshold* case).
93 Law No. 24 of 2008 on the Election of President and Vice President, Article 9.
94 *Jakarta Globe*. "Yusril and Crescent Star Party Throw Hat in 2014 Presidential Race." December 9, 2013. http://thejakartaglobe.beritasatu.com/news/yusril-and-crescent-star-party-throw-hat-in-2014-presidential-race/.
95 The Constitution of the Republic of Indonesia, Art. 6 (2).
96 See the *Presidential Threshold* case, 12.
97 Ibid., 21.
98 Ibid.
99 "Prabowo Files Challenge to Election Result at Constitutional Court." *Jakarta Globe*, July 25, 2014. http://jakartaglobe.beritasatu.com/news/prabowo-challenges-election-result-constitutional-court/.
100 *Jakarta Post*. "Game Over, Prabowo!" August 22, 2014. http://www.thejakartapost.com/news/2014/08/22/game-over-prabowo.html.
101 *Jakarta Globe*. "As Court Deliberates, Doubts on Prabowo's Claims of Vote Fraud," August 6, 2014. Accessed July 6, 2017. http://jakartaglobe.id/news/court-deliberates-doubts-prabowos-claims-vote-fraud/.
102 The Constitutional Court Decision No. 1/PHPU-Pres-XII/2014 reviewing the Presidential Dispute between Prabowo Subianto and Joko Widodo.
103 Dian Triyuli Handoko. "Hamdan Zoelva: This Was Our Toughest Case." *Tempo.com*, August 27, 2014. http://en.tempo.co/read/news/2014/08/27/241602631/Hamdan-Zoelva-This-was-our-toughest-case.
104 The Constitutional Court Decision No. 14/PUU-XI/2013 (hereinafter the *General Election Schedule* case).
105 Law No. 42 of 2008 on the Presidential Election, Art. 112.
106 The *General Election Schedule* case, para. 3.17.

107 The *General Election Schedule* case (No. 103) 80–81.
108 Ibid., 82.The Court made reference to the minutes of discussion of the Commission of "A" in the General Assembly Meeting on November 5, 2001. The Court concluded that the drafters envisioned a simultaneous general election to elect president/vice president, national legislatures, members of regional representative councils, provincial legislatures, and regency-level legislatures.
109 Ibid., 84.
110 Ibid., para. 3.20.
111 The *Mulyana Kusumah* case, the Constitutional Court Decision No. 012-016-019/PUU-IV/2006.
112 The *General Election Schedule* case, 86.
113 The Constitutional Court Decision No. 22/PUU-XII/2014 (the *Armed Forces Voting Right* case).
114 Law no. 42 of 2008 on the Presidential Election, Art. 206.
115 The Constitutional Court Decision No. 50/PUU-XII/2014 (hereinafter the *Presidential Candidate* Case).
116 Law No. 42 of 2008 on the Election of President and Vice President, Art. 159 (1).
117 The *Presidential Candidate* Case (No. 112) 40.
118 Ibid., 39.
119 The Constitutional Court Decision No. 38/PUU-XI/2013 (the *Private Hospital* case).
120 Law No. 44 of 2009 on Hospitals (*Rumah Sakit*), Art. 7 (4).
121 Ibid., Art. 21.
122 *Jakarta Post.* "Muhammadiyah Turns to MK to Annul Hospital Law," April 19, 2013. Accessed July 6, 2017. http://www.thejakartapost.com/news/2013/04/19/muhammadiyah-turns-mk-annul-hospital-law.html.
123 The *Private Hospital* case, 11–12.
124 Ibid., 11–12.
125 Ibid., 82.
126 Ibid., 84.
127 The Constitutional Court Decision No. 87/PUU-XI/2012 (hereinafter the *Farmers' Protection and Empowerment* case).
128 The Constitutional Court Decision No. 99/PUU-X/2012 (hereinafter the *Plant Cultivation System* Law).
129 Law no. 19 of 2013 on Farmers' Protection and Empowerment, Article 58 (1 &2).
130 Ibid., Art. 58 (3).
131 Ibid., Art. 59.
132 The *Farmers' Protection and Empowerment* case, 25–27.
133 Law No. 19 of 2013 on Farmers' Protection and Empowerment, Article 70.
134 The *Farmers' Protection and Empowerment* case, 32.
135 The 1945 Indonesian Constitution, Article 28E (3).
136 The *Farmers' Protection and Empowerment* case, para. 3.19.
137 Ibid.
138 Ibid.
139 Ibid., para. 3.20.
140 Ibid.
141 The Constitutional Court Decision No. 82/PUU-XI/2013 (hereinafter the *Ormas* case).
142 Law no. 17 of 2013 on Mass Organization.
143 *Jakarta Post.* "Muhammadiyah Proceeds with Judicial Review," May 19, 2012. Accessed July 6, 2017. http://www.thejakartapost.com/news/2012/05/19/muhammadiyah-proceeds-with-judicial-review.html.
144 The *Ormas* case, 15.

145 Ibid., 16.
146 Ibid., 124–125.
147 Law No. 17 of 2013 on Mass Organization, Article 5.
148 The Indonesian Constitutional Court Decision No. 97/PUU-XI/2013, reviewing the Law No. 12 of 2008 on the Amendment of Law No. 32 of 2004 on Regional Governance (hereinafter the *Regional Election* case).
149 Ibid., 3.
150 Ibid., 21–22.
151 Ibid., 60.
152 Ibid., 59.
153 Ibid., 60.
154 Chief Justice Zoelva was elected as chief justice on November 1, 2013, and he was supposed to stay in office until 2016. The problem arose because the term of chief justice does not run concurrently with the term of Constitutional Court justices.
155 There was some speculation that President Jokowi did not re-appoint Chief Justice Zoelva because the Court did not rule in favor of Jokowi's political party, the Indonesian Democratic Party of Struggle (PDI-P) in some cases before the Court. For instance, the PDI-P challenged the Law on the election of the Speaker of the House (commonly known as MD3 Law). The Court held that the PDI-P has no standing to challenge the Law. See the Constitutional Court Decision No. 73/PUU-XII/2014 (hereinafter the *MD3 Law* case). Also, Zoelva's political affiliation was with the Star and Crescent Party, which opposed Jokowi in the last presidential election.
156 Ezra Sihite and Carlos Paath. "Constitutional Court in Fresh Crisis as Hamdan Zoelva Skips Selection Interview," *Jakarta Globe* (December 23, 2014). http://jakartaglobe.beritasatu.com/news/constitutional-court-fresh-crisis-hamdan-zoelva-skips-selection-interview/.
157 Ina Parlina. "Team Disqualifies Hamdan from MK Race." *Jakarta Post* (December 24, 2014). http://www.thejakartapost.com/news/2014/12/24/team-disqualifies-hamdan-mk-race.html.
158 *Hamdan Zoelva, interview with Metro TV News*, https://www.youtube.com/watch?v=Tl9LdEw83ls.

8 A good hero is hard to find

Toward a less heroic court?

Prelude

Apart from the apocalyptic war, the core story of Mahabharata is about three generations of families. The first generation is the five Pandawa brothers, who successfully developed the barren and hostile lands and built a great and lavish kingdom and thus came to be known as Amartha. After the Pandawas had won the apocalyptic war against their cousins, the Kurawas, they were supposed to retire and hand over the kingdom to the second generation. But all of the potential crown princes died heroically on the battlefield.

The legend says that the Pandawa brothers ruled the kingdom for 36 long years until their grandchildren achieved sufficient age to reign. In the 37th year of the Pandawas' rule, they all decided that the time had come for them to renounce the kingdom, and they all left for the path of liberation toward heaven. By that time, Parikesit (grandson of Arjuna, the third Pandawa Prince) was crowned king. But Parikesit was a reckless leader, so chaos and discontent slowly started creeping into his reign and eventually led to his tragic death. In short, the story of three generations of Pandawas can be summarized as follows: The first generation worked hard to build the kingdom, and the second generation sacrificed their lives heroically defending the kingdom. The third generation, however, lost that heroic drive and become soft.

Certainly, the last chapter reminds us of the second-generation lapse. This chapter continues my exploration of what happened after the heroes left the scene. The focus of this chapter is the chairmanship of Arief Hidayat; at this stage, the Indonesian Constitutional Court fully entered into the third-generation period. Concerning the third-generation period, this chapter will address some questions: whether Chief Justice Arief Hidayat was endowed with a forceful personality like the first two chief justices, whether the Court was still capable of standing up to governmental branches, and whether Chief Justice Hidayat shared insights into the intricate links between personal status and institutional power.

The rise of Chief Justice Arief Hidayat

In November 2012, Chief Justice Mohammad Mahfud told the House of Representatives (DPR) that he intended to leave his job in April 2013. As the departure of Mahfud was imminent, the DPR began to conduct a selection process to find his replacement. On March 4, 2013, the House Judiciary Committee began to interview the first candidate, Arief Hidayat, a law professor at Diponegoro University.

Hidayat had not been in the public spotlight before his nomination, so there was not much information available about his background.[1] He obtained his bachelor degree in legal studies from Diponegoro University in Semarang, Central Java. Upon his graduation, Hidayat became a lecturer at his alma mater. After obtaining a Master of Law degree at Airlangga University, Hidayat went back to Diponegoro University to pursue his doctoral studies. In 2006, Hidayat obtained a doctoral degree in constitutional law under the guidance of Professor Satjipto Rahardjo, the father of the progressive legal movement in Indonesia. He wrote his doctoral dissertation on the development of freedom of assembly in Indonesia from the beginning of independence to the post-authoritarian period.[2] Having obtained his doctoral degree, Hidayat was subsequently promoted to the position of full-time professor and dean of the Diponegoro University Faculty of Law.

In 2011, some constitutional law professors, chiefly led by Saldi Isra of Andalas University, challenged the 2011 Amendment on the Constitutional Court Law.[3] Arief Hidayat was one of the constitutional law professors who filed the petition. These law professors invoked third-party standing and challenged some provisions, including the prohibition for the Court to issue a judgment that exceeds what a claimant requested, commonly known as *ultra petita*. Furthermore, they also challenged the requirement that a constitutional justice must have government service experience and the provision that requires the establishment of an Honorary Council to supervise the performance of the Constitutional Court Justices. Apart from invoking the third-party standing, the claimants explained that they were concerned citizens who had been campaigning for new constitutionalism and constitutional order, and therefore, they had standing to challenge the Law.

During the confirmation hearing, some legislators expressed their criticism of the leadership style of the outgoing chief justice, Mohammad Mahfud. One of the objects of criticism concerned *ultra petita*. Based on his position against the prohibition of *ultra petita* in the *2011 Amendment II* case, presumably, the DPR would grill Hidayat on the issue of *ultra petita*. Surprisingly, the central concern of the legislatures was Hidayat's position on atheism and same-sex marriage instead of *ultra petita*.

When a member of the Judiciary Committee pressed Hidayat on the issue of same-sex marriage and atheism, he firmly expressed his conviction by denouncing both. Hidayat stated, "We shall not construe the constitutional guarantee of religious freedom to allow citizens not to adhere to any religion. Consequently, Indonesian citizens shall not become an atheist."[4] About same-sex marriage, Hidayat argued that, theologically, marriage is between a man and a woman, and same-sex marriage was prohibited by every religion.[5] Hidayat further argued that there was no constitutional right to have same-sex marriage under the Indonesian Constitution because there was a general limitation in the bill of rights based on the consideration of religion and public order.[6]

The reasons the House Judiciary Committee focused on the issues of atheism and same-sex marriage are not entirely clear. One plausible reason is that the two subjects had become a hot topic in Indonesia before Hidayat's hearing. Just one year before the hearing, the Indonesian public had been shocked by the case of a Civil Service candidate who denied the existence of God on his Facebook page.[7] The Muaro Sijunjung District Court later sentenced the man to 2.5 years in prison for being a self-proclaimed atheist. Similarly, same-sex marriage had become an important debate in the country before the confirmation. In 2012, the Minister of Religious Affairs, Suryadharma Ali, warned the public about the attempt of the gay and lesbian community to legalize same-sex marriage by challenging the Marriage Law.[8]

After the hearing, Hidayat was confirmed by the House Judiciary Committee with 42 out of 48 votes.[9] The chair of the Judiciary Committee, Gede Pasek Suardika, explained that the DPR voted in favor of Hidayat because of his knowledge and character. "He is very courageous on the issue of same-sex marriage and Human Rights. Such courage is necessary for his role in the Constitutional Court," said Suardika.[10] Nevertheless, the chair of the Judiciary Committee warned Hidayat not to be a "political analyst" like his predecessor.[11]

It was not entirely clear why the House Judiciary Committee picked Hidayat as their judicial agent. On the surface, it appeared that some members of the Judiciary Committee voted in favor of Hidayat as their ideological proxy. The issue was whether Hidayat was the right candidate to be an ideological proxy of politicians in the DPR. Based on his record, obviously, Hidayat was not the best candidate to defend the DPR's interest in the issues of *ultra petita* and conditionally constitutional decisions. Moreover, looking at his academic background, Hidayat was not a good fit to replace Mahfud either. Hidayat studied under the auspices of Satjipto Rahardjo, the father of the progressive legal movement, who was Mahfud's role model. Or perhaps politicians saw an urgent need for the DPR to find an ideological proxy to combat same-sex marriage and atheism.

Another plausible explanation for the appointment of Hidayat was because the House Judiciary Committee did not have many choices, as they had to appoint someone to fulfill its constitutional mandate. During the confirmation hearing, a member of the House Judiciary Committee requested to postpone the hearing because he didn't see any candidates adequate for the position.[12] But the chairman of the Judiciary Committee refused to delay the hearing and proceeded with the confirmation process. Presumably, Arief Hidayat was the best candidate that the DPR could find, and he was their best option.

Arief Hidayat was sworn in as an associate justice in front of President Yudhoyono at the presidential palace on April 1, 2013. After he was sworn in, Hidayat made two important statements. First, he humbly asked help from fellow justices to guide him. Second, Hidayat assured the public that he would not be a corrupt judge, as he had inherited a huge amount of money from his parents.[13]

After the humiliating departure of Chief Justice Hamdan Zoelva, the Indonesian Constitutional Court justices unanimously elected Arief Hidayat as Zoelva's successor. After his election, Hidayat said he would ensure that the Court would continuously try to improve the quality of its rulings, as well as ensuring that all state officials and citizens would obey those rulings. Hidayat stated, "[Hopefully] we can work together to build the country in achieving the country's goals because the judicial, legislative and executive branches share a similar goal of a just and prosperous people."[14] On January 14, 2015, Hidayat was sworn in as the fifth chief justice of the Indonesian Constitutional Court.

The composition of the third-generation court

By the time Hidayat was sworn in as the fifth chief justice, there had been some significant changes to the composition of the Constitutional Court. Justice Maria Farida Indrati was the only remaining judge from the second-generation court. Justices Patrialis Akbar and Anwar Usman came to the bench during the transition between the leadership of Mahfud and that of Akil Mochtar. In the term of 2014–2015, five new justices came to the bench.

Before we proceed further, let us briefly review the background of these five new justices. Following the arrest of Akil Mochtar and the retirement of Justice Harjono, the DPR appointed two new associate justices: Aswanto (one name only) and Wahidudin Adams. Aswanto was the dean of the Hasanuddin University Faculty of Law, Makassar. He held a doctoral degree in Criminal Law from Airlangga University, in addition to his master's degree in National Security from Gadjah Mada University. Wahidudin Adams was a career bureaucrat in the Ministry of Justice. Before his appointment as an associate justice, Adams was the general director of Statutory Regulation (*Direktur Jendral Perundang—Undangan*) of the Ministry of Justice. Interestingly, Adams's primary legal training was in Islamic Law, and he held a doctoral degree in Islamic Law. Adams did not hold a civil law degree until 2005.

At the beginning of 2015, the Supreme Court had the opportunity to appoint two new justices: Suhartoyo (one name only) and Manahan Sitompul. Suhartoyo was the chief justice of South Jakarta District Court, and he held a doctoral degree from a medium-tier school, Jayabaya University. Suhartoyo's appointment was quite problematic because the Judicial Commission protested the appointment of Suhartoyo given an investigation into his involvement in suspected ethics violations.[15] Suhartoyo sat on a panel of judges in the South Jakarta District Court that had cleared bribery suspect Sudjiono Timan of all charges in a case involving funds dispersed by Bank Indonesia Liquidity Assistance (BLBI) during the 1997–1998 financial crisis. Nevertheless, the Supreme Court stood by its decision to appoint Suhartoyo as a new justice in the Constitutional Court (MK). In addition to Suhartoyo, the Supreme Court appointed Manahan Sitompul, who was also a career judge. Sitompul held a doctoral degree from North Sumatera University, and he wrote his doctoral dissertation on bankruptcy procedure in the Indonesian Commercial Court.[16]

The appointment of these new justices continued the parade of mediocre doctors in law. All of them held a doctoral degree from a local university, and none of them had shown any robust academic scholarship throughout their career. Their appointment continued to beg the question on the merit of the doctoral requirement. As explained in the previous chapter, the logic behind the inclusion of a doctoral requirement was to improve the quality of judges in the constitutional adjudication process. Nevertheless, this logic does not correlate with the reality that someone with a doctoral degree in any field—criminal law (Aswanto), Islamic law (Adams), and bankruptcy law (Sitompul)—could become a constitutional court justice.

It is interesting to note the appointment of I Dewa Gede Palguna by President Jokowi in January 2015. Initially, Palguna was part of the first-generation Court

Table 8.1 Constitutional Court Justices 2015

Names	*Prior position*	*Nominator*	*Education*
Maria Farida Indrati	Professor of law	President	– LLB (UI, Indonesia) – Master of Law (UI, Indonesia) – PhD (UI, Indonesia)
I Dewa Gede Palguna	Professor of law	President	– LLB (Udayana, Indonesia) – Master of Law (Unpad, Indonesia) – PhD (UI, Indonesia)
Patrialis Akbar	Politician/ minister of justice	President	– LLB (UMJ, Indonesia) – Master of Law (UGM, Indonesia) – PhD (Unpad, Indonesia)
Arief Hidayat	Professor of law	DPR (House)	– LLB (Undip, Indonesia) – Master of Law (Unair) – PhD (Unpad, Indonesia)
Wahidudin Adams	Bureaucrat of the Ministry of Justice	DPR (House)	– LLB, (IAIN Syarif Hidayatullah, Indonesia) – Master of Law (UIN Syarif Hidayatullah, Indonesia) – PhD (UIN Syarif Hidayatullah, Indonesia)
Aswanto	Professor of law	DPR (House)	– LLB (Unhas, Indonesia) – Master of Science (UGM, Indonesia) – Ph.D. (Unair, Indonesia)
Suhartoyo	Head of the South Jakarta District Court	Supreme Court	– LLB (UII, Indonesia) – Master of Law (Untar, Indonesia – Ph.D. (Jayabaya University, Indonesia)
Anwar Usman	Administrative court judge	Supreme Court	– LLB (UIJ, Indonesia) – Master of Law (IBLAM, Indonesia) – Ph.D. (UGM, Indonesia)
Manahan Sitompul	High court judge	Supreme Court	– LLB (USU, Indonesia) – Master of Law (USU, Indonesia) – Ph.D. (USU, Indonesia)

under the chairmanship of Jimly Asshiddiqie. He retired in 2008 because he wanted to complete his doctoral studies. In 2011, Palguna finished his doctoral dissertation on the idea of constitutional complaint.[17] In 2015, President Jokowi appointed him to be the Constitutional Court justice for the second time. Palguna was a professor at a medium-tier school, Udayana University Faculty of Law, Bali. He published some books during his first tenure as an associate justice, but those books were either a collection of his speeches[18] or a compilation of his short articles.[19] Also, he also wrote a memoir of his first 5 years as an associate justice[20] (Table 8.1).

In sum, the arrival of new justices in the Court did not change the overall picture of the Court. The Court was still filled with many mediocre judges who held doctoral degrees in law, but who showed little rigorous academic scholarship. These mediocre justices then elected Arief Hidayat as the leader of their pack. The question was whether Arief Hidayat would prove himself to be an extraordinary chief justice like his earlier predecessors or would simply be an ordinary one.

Toward a less heroic court?

In the previous chapter, I explained that under the short tenure of Akil Mochtar and Hamdan Zoelva, although the Court continued to apply some techniques from the first-generation Court, it became less innovative and bold in its rulings. In this section, I will explore the Court's decisions under the chairmanship of Arief Hidayat and assess whether Arief Hidayat was able to lead the Court to innovation and boldness.

Socio-economic rights

Some scholars argue that a Court should reduce its policy-making role when the democratic system begins to function better. The problem is that, despite the success of democratic consolidation, the Court still has to deal with complex policy-making issues that come before its doors. In this section, I will explore the Court's decision in the area of socio-economic rights, which involved complex socio-economic issues.

The Water Resources Law II *case*

In the *Water Resources Law II* case,[21] the Court had to deal with the privatization of the water industry. At the center of the dispute was the issuance of a government regulation about the Water Supply System, which allowed private corporations to manage water resources.[22] The regulation was based on Article 40 (2) of the Water Resources Law, which provides that water supply systems shall be managed by the central government and regional government. The claimant was again Muhammadiyah, the Islamic organization that had been at the forefront of constitutional litigation in Indonesia. As mentioned in the previous chapter, Muhammadiyah long considered itself in the path of a "constitutional jihad." Muhammadiyah argued that the law violated their socio-economic rights under

Article 28H (1) and, more importantly, deprived the state of control over water as mandated by Article 33 (2 and 3).[23] The claimant framed its petition in the context of the Court's previous decision in the *Water Resources Law I* case.

As explained in Chapter 4, in the *Water Resources Law I* case, the Court provided guidelines on how the Executive branch should manage the water resources.[24] The Court ruled that the government had obligations to fulfill citizens' access to clean water in several ways: First, by issuing licenses for water usage and providing daily supply and irrigation for community farming (*pertanian rakyat*). Second, regionally owned water companies should be positioned as the state's operational unit, not as profit-oriented companies. Finally, it was primarily the responsibility of the central and regional governments to provide clean water. Private enterprises and cooperatives were only permitted to participate if the government was unable to provide clean water.[25]

In the *Water Resources II* case, the claimant posited that the Executive did not follow the guidelines prescribed by the Court. The claimant pointed to the issuance of the Government Regulation on the Water Supply System, which provided that State Owned Enterprises (*Badan Usaha Milik Negara*—BUMN) shall manage the water supply system. Moreover, the Regional Owned Enterprises (*Badan Usaha Milik Daerah*—BUMD), cooperatives, private corporations, or local communities (*kelompok masyarakat*) also have the authority to manage the water supply system.[26] The claimant argued that the Executive had cheated in creating a privatization in disguise, allowing private corporations to get involved in the water industry.[27]

The Court concurred with the claimant and held that the Executive had not fulfilled the Court's prescriptions in the *Water Resources Law I* when it introduced a series of government regulations.[28] Since the Court's decision in the *Water Resources Law I* case, the Yudhoyono administration had issued six different governmental regulations aimed at implementing the Water Resources Law.[29] Although the claimant disputed only one of those six regulations, the Court considered all the regulations in its judgment. The Court ruled that none of them followed the guidelines prescribed by the Court in the *Water Resources Law I* case.[30] It, therefore, declared the Water Resources Law unconstitutional in its entirety.[31]

In this case, the Court was mostly judging the application of the Water Resources Law by the Executive instead of reviewing the scope and meaning of water rights protected under the Constitution. The Court's decision seemed quite radical considering that it had no jurisdiction to review the application of the Law by the Executive, only the statutes. The decision was quite bold and gave a sign that the Court might return to its heroic mode. Nevertheless, the decision did not fully represent the leadership of Arief Hidayat because it was written by "two hands." The Court finished its deliberation meeting on September 17, 2014 under the chairmanship of Hamdan Zoelva, but it was Chief Justice Arief Hidayat who announced the decision on February 18, 2015. Despite the Court's bold decision, we need to gather more evidence before concluding that the Court was on its way to reclaiming its heyday. Thus, it is necessary to review more socio-economic rights cases under the chairmanship of Arief Hidayat.

The Forestry and P3H Law *case*

In the *Forestry and P3H Law* case,[32] the Court, however, took a more conservative stance than in the *Water Resources Law II* case. In this case, a group of farmers and environmental NGOs challenged the constitutionality of the Forestry Law. The claimants challenged several key provisions in the Forestry Law,[33] which provided that no one shall exploit and/or use and/or occupy forest area illegally. No one shall encroach forest area, harvest or collect forest produce in a forest illegally, and herd cattle in forest areas not specially designated for that purpose. Finally, there was a prohibition against anyone bringing in any devices commonly used to fell, cut, or split trees in a forest area without the consent of competent authorities. The Forestry Law further states that anyone whomsoever caught intentionally violating the prohibition shall be subject to imprisonment ranging from a minimum 5 years to a maximum of 15 years and a penalty of a maximum of five billion rupiahs.[34] The claimant argued that those provisions threatened some indigenous communities that live in the forest area and rely on forest produce for their livelihood.[35]

In conjunction with their challenge to the Forestry Law, the claimants also challenged some key provisions in the Law on the Prevention and Eradication of Forest Destruction (*Pencegahan dan Pemberantasan Perusakan Hutan*—P3H).[36] The claimants challenged several key provisions in the P3H Law. For the sake of the limits of this chapter, I will focus on two key provisions among many. First, the claimant argued that the definition of forest destruction created legal uncertainty, especially the phrase, "the permit in forest land (*kawasan hutan*) declared, designated or being processed by the government."[37] The claimants argued that some members of indigenous communities had to face criminal charges for destroying forests that had been designated as forest land.

The claimant further challenged a different provision, which provided, "the people living in and around forest land and cutting trees outside conservation forest land and protected forest for their own interest and not for commercial purposes shall secure a permit from the authorized official according to the law and regulation." The claimants argued that the provision threatened the existence of indigenous communities as they had to obtain a permit to use forest produce. Furthermore, many indigenous communities that relied heavily on forest produce would face criminal charges for destroying forests under the P3H Law.

The claimants, however, did not frame their argument in the context of Article 33, but rather they relied on Article 28H (1), which provides that every person shall have the right to live in physical and spiritual prosperity, to have a home, and to enjoy a good and healthy environment. Interestingly, it was the government who framed their argument based on Article 33. The government's legal team argued that the Forestry and P3H Law were necessary to fulfill the constitutional mandate of Article 33 for the government to control natural resources for the greatest benefit of the people.

The Court ruled that Article 33 mandated the state to control forest resources by regulating and managing forest resources, which included the issuance of permits to use forest resources.[38] The Court then rejected the claimants' argument entirely on the constitutionality of the P3H Law. The Court ruled that the claimant's arguments were not clear enough and did not have a sufficiently strong legal basis for the court to approve them.

Concerning the constitutionality of the Forest Law, the Court declared some of the challenged provisions were conditionally unconstitutional as long as it was interpreted to exclude indigenous communities that lived for generations in the forest land and sustained their lives by using forest resources for commercial purposes. In other words, the Court held that some key provisions in the Forest Law provided an exception for indigenous communities that had lived for generations in the forest land and sustained their lives by cutting trees and collecting forest produce for noncommercial purposes. The Court issued a similar ruling about the prohibition against herding cattle in forest areas—that the provision should be interpreted to give an exception for indigenous communities, as long as the herding was part of daily necessity for indigenous people who lived from generation to generation inside forest areas.

The Chevron Pacific *case*[39]

The claimant in this case was Bachtiar Abdul Fatah, a former general manager of Chevron Pacific Indonesia. The case arose from the so-called bioremediation project for land contaminated by hazardous and poisonous waste ("B3-classified waste") program that began in 2006 at Chevron's drilling facilities on the island of Sumatra. Chevron Pacific Indonesia hired two local contractors to do the work, which entailed removing or neutralizing contaminants in soil or water. Prosecutors said that the companies were not qualified and did not have the proper permits, and that the clean-up was unnecessary because the area was not sufficiently contaminated.[40] The prosecutors then charged five of the Chevron employees on the grounds that they had violated corruption laws by causing the state to lose $9.9 million. The loss was tied to a reimbursement that the state was due to pay for the clean-up as part of its contract with Chevron.

The claimant filed a claim with the Constitutional Court and challenged the constitutionality of Law No. 32 of 2009 on the Protection and Management of the Environment, which became the basis of his convictions. The claimant primarily challenged the provision that provided "the management of B3-classified wastes must obtain a permit from the minister, governor or regent/mayor by their respective authority."[41] The claimant argued that the challenged provision was contradictory to a different provision in the Law that states that parties who produce B3-classified waste are under an obligation to manage that waste,[42] and if such waste management is not conducted, there is a threat of criminal sanctions.[43] The claimant argued that he was prosecuted because he was deemed to have conducted waste management operations on B3-classified waste without a permit, even though the company he was working for had applied for the renewal of its previous permit; the permit had yet to be issued by the authority, however.

The claimant argued that the Law on the Protection and Management of the Environment was contrary to the Constitution, which guarantees that every person shall have the right to live in physical and spiritual prosperity, to have a home, and to enjoy a good and healthy environment.[44] The claimant opined that the current regulatory system allowed environmental destruction, as B3-classified waste cannot be contained while the producer of B3-classified waste was applying for a permit.[45]

Interestingly, the Court framed its argument based on the Preamble of the 1945 Constitution, which mandated the state to improve public welfare.[46] The Court argued that the promulgation of the Law No. 32 of 2009 on the Protection and Management of the Environment was to fulfill the constitutional mandate to improve public welfare. Under the framework of improving public welfare, the Court ruled that B3-classified waste is a dangerous waste that, if improperly released into the environment, could have disastrous effects on the environment, health, and human life.[47] Therefore, the provisions, which state that industries that produce B3-classified waste must manage such waste and must also obtain permits from the relevant authorities, were correct and constitutional.[48]

The Court then moved to address the procedural aspect of the issuance of the permit. The Court ruled that producers of B3-classified waste who had previously held a permit but whose permit expired had not yet formally obtained the permit when they were in the process of applying for a renewal of such permit.[49] Nevertheless, in substance, that party should be considered as already having the permit, especially when the delay in the issuance of the permit was not based on the fault or negligence of the party applying for the permit.[50] The Court then declared the challenged provision conditionally unconstitutional as long as it did not give any exception for any parties who are managing B3-classified waste and are still waiting for a permit renewal.[51] In other words, the producers of B3-classified waste whose application for a permit renewal was still in process must be deemed to have the permit already.

In short, the Court's decision was quite narrow. Although the Court cited the Preamble of the Constitution, it did not define the scope of socio-economic rights in the Constitution under Article 28H (1) or Article 33. The Court did not define the meaning of the right to enjoy a healthy and good environment in the context of the management of B3-classified waste. The Court simply decided the case on the procedural ground of the issuance of the permit.

The Electricity Law III *case*[52]

As explained in Chapter 3, one of the landmark decisions of the first-generation Court was the *Electricity Law I* case,[53] in which the Court declared the 2002 Electricity Law unconstitutional. The founding chief justice, Jimly Asshiddiqie, once stated that the *Electricity* case was one of the most crucial decisions under his leadership.[54] Although the Court struck down the Law entirely, however, the government disobeyed the decision through the issuance of a governmental regulation that prescribed the formula of privatization under the old Law. In 2009, the government enacted a new electricity law that resurrected the privatization of policy.[55] Under the 2009 Electricity Law, the State Electricity Company (*Perusahaan Listrik Negara*—PLN) no longer had a monopoly in supplying electricity to end-users, and it opened up the market for independent power producers (IPPs) to be involved in supplying electricity.

In the *Electricity Law III* case, a leader of the State Electricity Company Workers Union (*Serikat Pekerja Perusahaan Listrik Negara*—SPPLN) challenged the 2009 Electricity Law in the Constitutional Court. The claimant's central concern was the provision that provides that public power-supply businesses shall include different types of business such as power generation, power transmission, power distribution, and power sale.[56] The Law further states, "electricity supply business for public interest may be conducted in an integrated manner."[57] The claimant argued that the provision meant to split the electricity industry into different business units under the management of different business entities (an unbundling system).[58] The claimant argued that the 2009 Electricity Law was contrary to Article 33 (2) of the Constitution, which mandated state control over an important sector of the industry. The claimant posited that the law would deprive the state of control over important sectors of the industry, as the PLN would no longer be the caretaker of the electricity industry in Indonesia.[59]

The claimant also challenged the provision that provides, "electricity supply business for public interest shall be conducted by state-owned enterprises, regional-owned enterprises, private enterprises, cooperatives and non-profit organization that engaged in the business of electricity supply."[60] The claimant argued that the provision was obviously contrary to Article 33 (2) because it was only state-owned enterprises and regional-owned enterprises that could control important sectors of industry like electricity.[61] The claimant asserted that private enterprises, cooperatives, and nonprofit organizations have no constitutional mandate to provide electricity to the public.

First, the Court concurred with the claimant that the 2009 Electricity Law could potentially deprive the state of control over an important sector of the industry.[62] Therefore, to avoid any doubt and to achieve a consensus on the meaning of state control, the Court declared the provision conditionally unconstitutional if construed to allow electricity supply to the public sector to be managed on an unbundled basis.[63]

The Court then moved to address the issue of the involvement of private business entities in the electricity industry. The Court cited the *Electricity Law I* case, in which the Court held that "domestic or foreign private enterprises may only be involved whenever they are asked to be involved through cooperation, loan agreement, and share purchase agreement with the state-owned enterprises."[64] Based on the 2004 decision, the Court concluded that there was no prohibition against private enterprises being involved in the electricity industry as long as the government maintained supervision over those private enterprises. Considering the involvement of private enterprises in the electricity industry, the Court opined that there was no compelling reason to prohibit cooperatives and nonprofit enterprises in the electricity industry.[65] Nevertheless, the Court argued that the 2009 Electricity Law did not explicitly rule that the involvement of private enterprises, cooperatives, and nonprofit organizations was within the framework of state control over the electricity industry.[66] Therefore, the Court declared the provision conditionally unconstitutional if construed so that the principle of "state-controlled" is not required in the involvement of private enterprises, cooperatives, and nonprofit entities in the electricity industry.

The Court decision on the judicial review of the 2009 Electricity Law signified significant differences between the current court and the first-generation court. Obviously, Chief Justice Arief Hidayat did not show intellectual leadership like Chief Justice Asshiddiqie in dealing with the issue of the privatization of the electricity industry. The Court's decision was much less rigorous compared to the 2004 decision. For instance, the Court did not go into as much detail regarding the notion of "controlled by the state" under Article 33 as the 2004 decision did. Furthermore, the decision signified a lack of boldness in the Court under the chairmanship of Arief Hidayat: The Court refused to declare the law unconstitutional, and it chose to issue a conditionally unconstitutional decision without any strong remedies. This decision is one of the most crucial decisions under the chairmanship of Arief Hidayat, as it signified the trajectory toward a less heroic court.

Judicial review of electoral process

Some scholars believe that Indonesia's democratic consolidation had been accomplished by the time of the second-generation court, and that therefore the Court needed to step back and allow the democratic system to function.[67] But the fact of the matter is that democratic consolidation could be a longer process than one could imagine. In more than a decade since the Court's inception, the Court still dealt with the judicial review of the electoral process, especially about the election of governor, *bupati* (regent), and mayor, commonly known as "regional election head" (*Pemilihan Kepala Daerah*—Pilkada).

The political dynasty *case*[68]

One of the central concerns of the election of governor, *bupati*, and mayor is the issue of political dynasty. By 2013, there were at least 23 political dynasties at the provincial and district level (*Kabupaten*) throughout Indonesia that occupied various political offices such as governor, mayor, *bupati* or head of the Regional Parliament.[69] Law No. 8 of 2015 on Regional Elections tried to address the political dynasty issue by prohibiting candidates who have family ties with the incumbent. The Law stated that a candidate in a regional election must not have a conflict of interest with the incumbent (regional head).[70] The elucidation of the statute stated that "conflict of interest" meant that a candidate must not have any blood or marital ties to the incumbent governor, district head or mayor, or the respective deputy positions unless the incumbent had passed the nonconsecutive terms limit (*jeda satu Kali Jabatan*).

The claimant, Adnan Purichta Ichsan, was a member of influential political dynasties in South Sulawesi. He was the son of the incumbent Gowa district head, Ichsan Yasin Limpo, and a nephew of the incumbent governor, Syahrul Yasin Limpo. His grandfather was also a former Gowa district head. Moreover, the Limpo family had brothers, sisters, sons, and in-laws in key posts in regional legislatures and the DPR. Adnan Ichsan was considering running in the regional election in December 2015 to replace his father as Gowa district chief. The claimant argued that the Law impinged on his constitutional rights, especially the right to be free from discriminative treatment.

The Court accepted the claimant's argument and ruled that the provision on political dynasties violated the constitutional rights of citizens to obtain equal opportunities in government.[71] Moreover, the Court ruled that the elucidation of the statute was not only discriminative but also created a new rule by adding a nonconsecutive terms clause.[72] The Court ruled that a nonconsecutive terms clause did not exist in the body of the statute, and that therefore it could not be a basis for further regulation on the regional election.

The *Political Dynasty* case signified that the Court under the chairmanship of Arief Hidayat had retreated from the progressive positions of the first-generation court. As explained in Chapter 3, the founding chief justice, Jimly Asshiddiqie, envisioned that the Court would be involved in repairing the harm done by the military regime by correcting past authoritarian practices. The Court under the chairmanship of Arief Hidayat did not share such a vision, as it chose to reverse the Court's stance on the practices of patronage, cronyism, and nepotism, which were among the pillars of the New Order regime.[73] Patronage, cronyism, and nepotism under the military regime had long been used to concentrate control over political power and economic resources.[74] By revoking the prohibition on political dynasty, the Court restored the opportunities for a small number of families to control power and economic resources.

Religion-related cases

One aspect of the Indonesian constitutional history is the long contestation between the secular and Islamist forces. The struggle for marriage reform in Indonesia in the last 40 years is the manifestation of the struggle between Islamic and secular nationalist views.[75] In 1974, the New Order military regime attempted to curb arbitrary divorce and polygamy rules on marriage under Islamic Law by restricting a Muslim husband's power to unilaterally repudiate his wife or by requiring judicial approval for a Muslim man who wanted to take a second wife.[76] Opposition to the law was vociferous, as a large segment of the Muslim community perceived the bill as contradictory to the Islamic doctrine on marriage.[77] In the end, the government reached several compromises with the Islam leaders, such as keeping the legal restrictions on polygamy and divorce procedures, especially for civil servants, in exchange for keeping the authority of the Islamic Courts over marriage among Muslims.[78]

The Marriageable Age *case*

In the *Marriageable Age* case,[79] the Court dealt with the issue of the minimum marriage age. Forty years ago, the military regime tried to reduce child marriage by imposing a minimum marriage age of 18 for girls and 21 for boys. After facing voracious opposition from the Islamic forces, the government reached a compromise to change the marriageable age from 21 to 19 for men and from 18 to 16 for women. For the secular forces, the marriageable age rule does not provide sufficient protection for women and children. In recent years, a few women's rights NGOs challenged the constitutionality of the provision, which provides a minimum marriageable age of 16 years for women.[80] They argued that the provision discriminated against girls due to the different minimum age of marriage for boys. They sought an increase in the minimum marriageable age for women to 18 years, arguing that the current marriage age was inconsistent with the statutory regulation on child protection, which defines a child as being a person below the age of 18 years.[81]

In an 8–1 decision, the Court decided to reject the claimants' petition entirely. The Court began its judgment by citing its previous decision that dealt with the Marriage Law, the *Polygamy* case.[82] In the *Polygamy* case, the claimant objected to the provisions in the Marriage Law that prevented him from engaging in polygamy. The claimant then argued that the Marriage Law deprived him of his freedom to worship as guaranteed by the Constitution (Article 29 § 2), as he believed that polygamy was a type of worship under Islamic doctrine. In the *Polygamy* case, the Court considered that polygamy was not the invention or creation of Islamic teaching as it had existed long before the Prophet Muhammad received the revelation. The Court believed that the Islamic teaching on polygamy aimed to protect the dignity of women and to ensure that men would not practice polygamy arbitrarily.[83]

The Court then moved to discuss the purpose and nature of marriage according to Islamic teaching, which is to achieve a peaceful heart (*sakinah*), as a man and a woman in a marital relationship will have peace.[84] According to the Court, a couple could achieve *sakinah* if they could maintain a loving relationship without hoping for anything in return, and only desire to make sacrifices to bring happiness to each other (*mawaddah*).[85] The Court concluded that Islamic law tries to achieve *mawaddah* by requiring that a man seek permission from his wife before entering into another marriage.

Based on the *Polygamy* case, the Court concluded in the *Marriageable Age* case that marriage has intrinsic sacred religious value and each religion has its own rules on marriage.[86] For instance, Islamic Law does not set any age limit for marriage; the only requirement from Islamic Law's perspective is that the couple has reached maturity (*akil baligh*) and is capable of distinguishing between good and evil. The Court ruled that it would not intervene into the religious domain on the requirement of marriage, especially on the age limit.[87] Moreover, the Court ruled that even if the claimant's assertion was correct, the Court ruled that it is not in the domain of the judiciary to increase the age limit of marriage, but rather it is the domain of the legislature.[88]

The Interfaith Marriage *case*[89]

In the *Interfaith Marriage* case, the Court continued to deal with the contestation between Islamic and secular forces over marriage reform. When the government introduced the bill of Marriage Law in 1973, it stated:

> Marriage is legitimate if it has been performed in front of the civil registrar; registered by the civil registrar who witnesses the marriage; and performed according to the Law and /or rules of marriage that adhered by parties concerned, as long as it does not contrary to the Law.[90]

For the Islamic forces, this provision meant marriage would be governed simply by civil law, and religion would be excluded entirely from governing marriage. Moreover, this provision opened a door for interreligious marriage; any interreligious marriage would be legitimate as long as it was performed and registered by a civil registrar. Indeed, the bill allowed interreligious marriages, as it stated, "any differences of nationality, ethnicity, citizenship, place of origin, religion/belief system, shall not become an obstacle to marriage."[91]

In dealing with opposition from the Islamic forces, the government agreed to modify the provision to state that a "marriage is legitimate if it has been performed according to the laws of the respective religions and beliefs of the parties concerned."[92] The Law further states that "every marriage must be registered according to the regulations of the existing regulation."[93]

This compromised provision in some way closed the door to interreligious marriage because, for a marriage to be lawful, a recognized religion must conduct it. In interreligious marriages, at least one of the parties might adhere to a religion that does not allow a person to marry someone of a different faith. Furthermore, for Muslim marriage, it must be registered with the local Office of Religious Affairs, which would refuse to register the interfaith marriage.[94]

In the *Interfaith Marriage* case, three lawyers and a law student challenged the provision on the legality of marriage and argued that the provision prevented couples of different religions from registering their marriage. The claimants came to the Court as concerned citizens, and they posited that there was a high probability that they might engage in interreligious marriage.[95] The claimants argued that there are many couples with different faith backgrounds who could not register their marriages. Consequently, these couples would try to bend the Law in many different ways, such as marrying in a foreign country, subjecting themselves to the religious rule of one party, or changing religion temporarily before the marriage. The claimants challenged the provision on the basis that it was inconsistent with several constitutional provisions, primarily the right to form a family and to procreate based upon lawful marriage.[96] Furthermore, the claimants argued that the Marriage Law violated the constitutional guarantee of religious freedom because the Law allowed the state to interfere into the religious realm in determining the legitimacy of marriage.[97]

The Court unanimously rejected the claimants' petition and ruled that, although the Constitution guaranteed a right to marry and to procreate, there was a general limitation of the Bill of Rights clause (Article 28J [2]) that allows the state to limit such rights based upon consideration of religious values.[98] The Court did not address the issue of freedom of religion, and obviously, it repeated the pattern of the second-generation Court in rejecting a politically sensitive case by relying on the general limitation of the Bill of Rights under Article 28J (2).

Bowing down to the president?

As explained in Chapter 3, one of the top priorities of founding Chief Justice Asshiddiqie was to fight for judicial status—the fight for recognition that the chief justice has an equal position to the president. Asshiddiqie was aware that for many years, the chief justice of the Supreme Court had been considered a second-class officer in the governmental hierarchical line. Therefore, he tried hard to place himself on equal footing with the president; for instance, he took an oath by himself, while President Yudhoyono stood behind him.

Unlike Asshiddiqie, Arief Hidayat, however, portrayed himself as subordinate to the president. The most telling example is the series litigation of the Tax Amnesty case. The tax amnesty policy, the pet project of President Jokowi, aimed to improve tax compliance in Indonesia. The Indonesian government estimates that some approximately $303 billion dollars of "Indonesian money" is secretly stashed abroad in tax havens such as Singapore, Panama, London, Hong Kong, and the British Virgin Islands. By offering tax incentives and immunity from prosecution, the Indonesian government, therefore, tried to make it attractive for tax evaders to declare their offshore funds to Indonesia's tax authorities and—if desired—repatriate these funds into Indonesia.[99]

In July 2016, some activists, under the banner of the One Justice Foundation (*Yayasan Satu Keadilan*) and Indonesian People's Struggle Union (*Serikat Perjuangan Rakyat Indonesia*), filed for judicial review by the Constitutional Court. They claimied that the tax amnesty program turned money laundering into a legal practice, protected criminals, taught Indonesian citizens not to pay taxes, and constituted an unfair program from a social point of view. Apart from these two groups, the Indonesian Prosperity Workers Union (*Serikat Buruh Sejahtera Indonesia*—SBSI) and some individuals also filed two separate claims against Law No. 11 of 2016 on the Tax Amnesty. One of the largest Islamic NGOs and leader in constitutional litigation in Indonesia, Muhammadiyah, also planned to challenge the constitutionality of the tax amnesty policy in the Constitutional Court.

The Jokowi administration decided to defend the tax amnesty program. First, the Jokowi administration moved to lobby Muhammadiyah to drop the challenge to the Law. Considering that Muhammadiyah had scored much success in the Constitutional Court, presumably the Jokowi administration realized that they needed to convince Muhammadiyah to drop their challenge. On September 14, 2016, the finance minister, Sri Mulyani Indrawati, accompanied by the chief of presidential staff, Teten Masduki, and the director general of taxation, Ken Dwijugiasteadi, visited Muhammadiyah's headquarters. During the 3-hour meeting, the finance minister explained to Muhammadiyah's leaders the objectives and benefits of the tax amnesty program.[100] Surprisingly, Muhammadiyah canceled its plan to file for judicial review against the Tax Amnesty Law after a visit from the finance minister. One of the leaders of Muhammadiyah explained that the plan to file for judicial review in the Constitutional Court had not yet become Muhammadiyah's official stance, but it was the personal view of some people in the organization.[101] It was not clear what led to Muhammadiyah's decision to cancel its legal challenge against the Tax Amnesty Law. But apparently, the Jokowi administration's lobby affected Muhammadiyah's view of the tax amnesty policy.

Apart from lobbying Muhammadiyah, the Jokowi administrative moved to "pressure" the Court. After the hearing process for the judicial review of the Tax Amnesty Law had begun, President Jokowi summoned Chief Justice Arief Hidayat to the presidential palace. Chief Justice Arief Hidayat denied that the meeting was to discuss the tax amnesty case, but rather to discuss the meeting of the Asian Constitutional Court Conference in Bali.[102] Hidayat stated further, "In the case of Tax Amnesty, there is no Presidential intervention to the Court. But we are building collaboration to advance the national interest."[103] Hidayat also denied that the director general of taxation, Ken Dwijugiasteadi, was present at the meeting, despite the fact that Dwijugiastedi arrived at the presidential palace 10 minutes after Hidayat's arrival.[104] It was not clear what Hidayat meant by "building collaboration," with the Executive, but obviously, the chief justice did not make a wise decision by attending a meeting with the president while there were cases pending in the Court.

As mentioned earlier, there are four different cases that involved the constitutionality of the Tax Amnesty Law. For unknown reasons, the Court did not consolidate those cases, but instead, issued four separate decisions. For the sake of the limits of this chapter, I will only review two cases below.

The Tax Amnesty Law I *case*[105]

In the first case, the Indonesian People's Struggle Union (*Serikat Perjuangan Rakyat Indonesia*) argued that the Tax Amnesty Law was discriminatory because tax evaders were being rewarded for their tax crimes, while honest tax payers who fulfilled their tax obligations did not receive any appreciation from the government.[106] The claimant posited that the Tax Amnesty Law had changed the compulsory nature of the taxation system and it would encourage (faithful) Indonesian citizens not to pay taxes.[107] The claimant further argued that the tax amnesty program could undermine the criminal justice system in Indonesia as the Law prevents the Tax Authority, the Attorney General Office, and the Anti-Corruption Commission from using all the data from the tax amnesty program as evidence for criminal investigations.[108]

The Court unanimously rejected the petition. First, the Court argued that the compulsory nature of the taxation system was not arbitrary but must be carried out within the context of human-rights protection. The Court then made reference to the constitutional guarantee of property rights,[109] which meant that the government cannot arbitrarily impose taxes upon the citizens. Second, the Court argued that all the data submitted to the tax amnesty program shall be protected, or otherwise nobody would be interested in participating in the tax amnesty program. Therefore, that data shall not be used as evidence in a criminal investigation.[110] Third, the Court ruled that the Law never aimed to prevent law enforcement from conducting criminal investigations of tax evaders, as long as they rely on evidence that was obtained outside the tax amnesty program. The Court stated that the tax amnesty law only provides immunity for tax-related crimes, but it never provides immunity for other crimes committed by tax evaders.[111]

The Tax Amnesty Law II *case*[112]

In the second case, the One Justice Foundation (*Yayasan Satu Keadilan*) made similar but different arguments to the first claimant. First, the claimant made reference to Article 23A of the Constitution, which provides, "all taxes and other levies for the needs of the State of a compulsory nature shall be regulated by law." The claimant argued that the government's taxing authority is compulsory in nature, and therefore the government has no constitutional mandate to issue a tax amnesty law, which by nature is an absolution instead of a compulsory act.[113] Second, the claimant argued that the tax amnesty program would protect criminals by turning many financial crimes into legal practice. The claimant made reference to a specific provision in the Tax Amnesty Law, which provides that "all data and information from the tax amnesty program shall not be used as evidence for criminal investigation or criminal charges against taxpayers."[114] The claimant further pointed to the elucidation of the Law, which states, "The scope of the criminal investigation in this provision shall include tax crimes and other types of crime."[115]

The Court unanimously dismissed the case by arguing that the claimant made a similar argument to the claimant in the *Tax Amnesty I* case. The Court ruled that it would not address the issues in the current case, as the Court's ruling in the *Tax Amnesty I* case should be applied to this case also.[116] Nevertheless, in its dicta, the Court addressed the issue of the scope of the criminal investigation of taxpayers. The Court wrote that the challenged provision should be declared "conditionally constitutional," as long as it did not provide immunity to any other crimes outside the realm of tax crimes.[117] In other words, the Law would be deemed constitutional if it provided immunity for tax-related crimes only, but not to other crimes committed by the tax evaders. The Court wrote further in its dicta that if in the future, the law enforcement could not investigate other crimes committed by the taxpayers, then the Law could be reviewed further.[118]

The claimants in these cases did not seem to provide compelling arguments on taxing power and whether the government has a constitutional mandate to issue a tax amnesty program. Similarly, in the *Tax Amnesty III*[119] and the *Tax Amnesty IV*[120] cases, different claimants also repeated the argument of the claimant in the first case that the Tax Amnesty Law has changed the compulsory nature of the taxing authority, and the Court moved immediately to dismiss the cases. Despite the weak arguments presented by the claimants, the Court also showed weakness in its judgment. In the *Tax Amnesty II*, the Court only issued the conditionally constitutional decision in its dicta instead of its holding. Presumably, the Court did not want to issue a conditionally constitutional decision in its holding because this would toe the political line.

I presented in Chapter 1 the idea of the judicial soldier, who understands or portrays himself as subordinate to the elected branches of government; who essentially does what elected politicians have him do. In the Tax Amnesty cases, Arief Hidayat portrayed himself as a judicial soldier by his failure to resist the pressure from President Jokowi, who wanted the Court to uphold the Tax Amnesty Law. The fact of the matter is that Chief Justice Hidayat did not refuse President Jokowi's summons to see him in the presidential palace while the Court was examining the judicial review cases against the Tax Amnesty Law.

Ethics scandal and corruption crisis continue

Chief Justice Hidayat's ethics scandal

Arief Hidayat's immediate predecessors were either in prison or disgraced. Considering the fates of his predecessors, one presumed that Hidayat would be more prudent in his actions and judgment. But it appears that Hidayat did not learn from his predecessors. Barely one year into his tenure as chief justice, Hidayat shocked the public with indications of an ethics violation.[121]

Hidayat allegedly wrote a letter to Widyono Pramono, the then assistant attorney general for special crimes, concerning Hidayat's recommendation for Pramono's appointment as professor at the University of Diponegoro Law School, where Hidayat was previously dean. In return, Hidayat requested special treatment for his "family member," Zainur Rochman, an assistant district attorney at Trenggalek Regency, East Java.[122]

Following this disclosure, the Constitutional Court's Ethics Council moved to investigate the allegations of an ethics violation. Hidayat admitted before the Ethics Council that he did write the letter, but he never intended to seek any special treatment for his "relative."[123] Hidayat argued that he simply wrote that he was "entrusting you (Pramono) to take him (Rochman) under your wing and to treat him like your son."[124] According to Hidayat, what he meant by those words was a simple request for Pramono to be a mentor for Rochman regarding improving his skill and knowledge as a young prosecutor, rather than any request for illicit special treatment.[125]

The Ethics Council ruled that the chief justice acted with a lack of prudence in issuing the letter of recommendation because it could create negative perceptions.[126] Nevertheless, it did not find any gross violations of ethics and largely accepted Chief Justice Hidayat's version of the events.[127] On March 2016, the Ethics Council recommended that Chief Justice Hidayat be given a private warning (*sanksi teguran*).[128]

Regardless of the result of the investigation of the Ethics Council, the scandal over the letter of recommendation was just the tip of the iceberg in terms of ethical problems in the Indonesian Constitutional Court. The Court moved to establish the permanent Ethics Council following the arrest of Chief Justice Akil Mochtar in 2013 on serious corruption charges (for which he is currently serving a life sentence). The Council was composed of a former justice of the Constitutional Court, a law professor, and a community figure.[129] It had the authority to investigate complaints of judicial misconduct and judicial incapacity, and it could recommend whether to suspend a justice temporarily and/or to establish an Honorary Council, which has the authority to remove that justice permanently.[130] It was, however, doubtful whether the Council had proved effective in disciplining justices on the Court.

Apart from the scandal over the letter of recommendation, one of the fundamental ethical problems in the Indonesian Constitutional Court is the absence of any recusal mechanism. As mentioned in the previous chapter, Chief Justice Hamdan Zoelva never recused himself in cases that involved his former political party, the Crescent Star Party. Nevertheless, Zoelva was not alone on this issue. The second chief justice (2008–2013), Muhammad Mahfud, never recused himself in the series of cases that involved constitutional challenges to the Legislative Election Law. Before taking up his position as chief justice, Mahfud was a member of the House Judiciary Committee and was involved in drafting the Legislative Election Law. Mahfud argued that it was unnecessary for him to recuse himself from the cases because he played two different roles as a legislator and a judge.[131]

Under the chairmanship of Arief Hidayat, three Constitutional Court Justices refused to recuse themselves in a case that involved a constitutional challenge by the Association of Indonesian Judges (*Ikatan Hakim Indonesia*—IKAHI), despite the fact they had been members of IKAHI.[132] One of the parties involved in the case filed a complaint with the Ethics Council. After examining the complaint, the Ethics Council ruled that there was no conflict of interest in the case because IKAHI was an association for career judges, and those justices had ceased to be members of IKAHI when they were appointed to the Constitutional Court.[133]

Justice Patrialis Akbar corruption case

As explained in Chapter 7, the appointment of Justice Patrialis Akbar in 2003 was quite problematic because of his poor record as the minister of justice. Apparently, Akbar's appointment was merely a consolation prize after his dismissal from the position of minister of justice. During his four years' tenure as an associate justice, Akbar did not give a stellar performance. On January 25, 2017, in another major blow to the reputation of the Constitutional Court, the Anti-Corruption Commission arrested Patrialis Akbar for allegedly receiving bribes of U.S. $20,000 (RP 266 million) from a prominent beef-importing businessman. The businessman, Basuki Hariman, admitted giving U.S. $20,000 to an aide of Justice Patrialis Akbar, and the aide assured Hariman that Patrialis Akbar would help to sway the judicial review of the *Animal Health and Husbandry Law II* case[134] in favor of beef importers.[135]

In 2009, the DPR passed the Animal Health and Husbandry Law, which allowed the import of beef and cattle from disease-free zones, regardless of the disease status in the country as a whole. On October 14, 2009, NGOs and individual farmers challenged key provisions of the Animal Health and Husbandry Law, such as Article 59 (2), which provides that live animals imported to Indonesia come from a country or a zone within a country that already fulfills the health standard.[136] The claimants argued that the law was not effective in preventing animal diseases entering Indonesia because it abolished a maximum security principle that aimed at preventing the importation of live animals from countries contaminated with animal diseases.[137] The claimants believed that the Law could harm consumers, local farmers, and eventually the Indonesian economy because of the possible spread of foot and mouth disease from unsafe countries.[138] On August 25, 2010, the Court under the chairmanship of Mohammad Mahfud issued a decision on the *Animal Health and Husbandry Law I* case[139] and declared that the phrase "a zone within a country" in Article 59 (2) was unconstitutional. The Court considered that the import of live animals from a country or a zone within a country is the manifestation of imprudent and dangerous policy because the disease may spread into the zone from unsafe parts of the country.[140]

In 2014, the government enacted a new law that reinstated the provision that allows animals imported into Indonesia to come from a country or a zone within a country that already fulfills the health standard. On October 29, 2015, some claimants from the *Animal Health and Husbandry Law I* case came back to the Court and challenged the new law that reinstates the zone-based system of animal import. The Court finished the examination process on May 12, 2006, but for unknown reasons, it took a long time for the Court to finish its deliberation meeting. After long delay, the Court completed deliberations on January 18, 2017, and initially, the Court clerks scheduled the ruling issuance for Wednesday, February 7, 2017. But the Anti-Corruption Commission arrested Akbar on January 25, 2017.

On February 7, 2017, the Court announced its decision on *the Animal Health and Husbandry Law II* case. The Court considered that after the issuance of the 2010 decision, the Parliament revised the zone system requirement. Thus, the Court opined that there was a difference between the object norms that had been reviewed in the first case and the second instance. The Court decided that Law No. 41 of 2014 was "conditionally unconstitutional"—that the implementation of the zone system was allowed when there was urgent domestic demand for which the government needed to import from other countries.[141]

The Court reached the decision unanimously, and Justice Patrialis Akbar cast his vote in the final deliberation meeting. It was not clear how much influence Akbar had to sway the Court's decision. The fact of the matter is that nine justices made the ruling and Akbar only had one vote. Regardless of what happened behind the scenes, the arrest of Patrialis Akbar tainted the legitimacy of the Court's decision in this case.

We now return to the arrest of Patrialis Akbar. Chief Justice Arief Hidayat did not seem to know how to respond to the crisis. In a press statement, Hidayat said, "I am begging God's mercy for my failure to keep Court's reputation."[142] Following Hidayat's bewildered response, some constitutional stakeholders began to ask for his resignation.[143] Hidayat refused to resign because he said that he had nothing to do with Akbar's corruption cases, and moreover, all the constitutional court justices still trusted him as chief justice.[144]

As explained in Chapter 2, the Court assigns the role of disciplining judges to the Ethics Council, and in the meantime, the ad hoc Honorary Council plays the role of "impeaching" judges. In the aftermath of the arrest of Patrialis Akbar, the chair of the Ethics Council, Mukthie Fadjar, admitted that the Council had received many reports from the public about Akbar's alleged ethical violations, but he claimed there was no solid evidence to support the reports.[145] The inability of the Ethics Council to discipline Akbar then raised some doubt as to the Council's effectiveness in disciplining judges on the Court. On January 27, 2017, the Ethics Council of the Constitutional Court reached the conclusion that Akbar's alleged involvement in a graft scandal was a "grave offense." The Court then decided to release Akbar temporarily from his duty as an associate justice of the Constitutional Court.[146] The Ethics Council also recommended that the Court establish an Honorary Council to investigate Akbar's case.

On January 30, 2017, however, Patrialis Akbar tendered his resignation as an associate justice. In response to Akbar's resignation, Chief Justice Arief Hidayat stated that the Court would proceed with the establishment of an Honorary Council and that the Council would decide on the removal of Patrialis Akbar from the Court.[147] The Court completed the formation of the Honorary Council on January 31, 2017.[148]

It was not clear why the Court needed to proceed with the "impeachment trial" after Akbar had tendered his resignation. As in the Akil Mochtar case, the Honorary Council usually conducted a speedy trial in the absence of criminal charges against the judge. On February 6, 2017, the Honorary Council recommended a temporary dismissal (*pemberhentian sementara*) of Justice Patrialis Akbar.[149] In the meantime, the Honorary Council stated that it would continue its investigation and gather more evidence to reach a conclusive decision.[150] Having heard nine witnesses in a closed-door hearing, the Honorary Council announced its final decision on February 16, 2017, and issued a verdict to grant dishonorable discharge for Akbar on the grounds that he committed a "grave offense" (*pelanggaran berat*) against the Code of Ethics and Conduct of Constitutional Court justices.[151] The criminal trial of Patrialis Akbar, however, did not start until June 13, 2017, and on September 4, 2017, Jakarta District Corruption Court sentenced Akbar to eight years in prison.[152]

The ethical scandals and the arrest of Patrialis Akbar tainted the reputation of the Constitutional Court. Nuno Garoupa and Tom Ginsburg postulate the theory of judicial reputation, which plays two important roles in judicial politics.[153] First, judicial reputation conveys information to the general public about the quality of the judiciary.[154] Second, reputation fosters both self-esteem and esteem in the eyes of the public for the judges as a team and as individuals.[155]

The Court under the presidency of Arief Hidayat did not see the importance of both the individual reputation and the collective reputation of the Court. Hidayat did not care about his individual reputation when he got involved in an ethics scandal. Moreover, he did not know how to respond to the arrest of Patrialis Akbar, which tainted the Court's collective reputation.

After the arrest of Patrialis Akbar, on April 11, 2017, President Jokowi appointed academic-cum-activist Saldi Isra as the new associate justice of the Constitutional Court.[156] With his long track record as an anti-corruption activist, Saldi Isra could be a bold, aggressive judge, and there were great expectations that he would be able to repair the Court's reputation.[157] Whether he could do so remained to be seen.

On July 14, 2017, the Constitutional Court Justices reached a unanimous consensus to re-elect Hidayat for his second term as the chief justice, and, therefore, there was no need to hold an open voting as had happened in previous elections.[158] Some Indonesian NGOs had voiced objections to Hidayat's re-election, considering that Hidayat failed to lead the Constitutional Court adequately during his 2.5-year tenure, during which time he was accused of breaching the court's ethical codes in 2015 and failing to deal with the corruption scandals involving Patrialis Akbar.[159] Hidayat's re-election, however, did not come as an unjustified surprise. As I have argued in this book, the Indonesian Constitutional Court has been occupied by many mediocre judges, and these mediocre judges chose to re-elect mediocre judges as their leaders. Arief Hidayat was re-elected as the Constitutional Court chief justice for the term 2017–2020. Nevertheless, Hidayat's 5-year term as a justice will end in April 2018, and there is a possibility that the DPR will not renew his term. Under this scenario, there would then be another chief justice election in 2018.

Conclusion

When Chief Justice Mahfud retired in 2013, politicians in the DPR were tired of Mahfud's leadership style, in which he led the Court to issue many bold decisions. When the DPR appointed Arief Hidayat as Mahfud's successor, it appeared that they made a mistake in appointing someone who shared a similar view to Mahfud. Nevertheless, looking at the performance of the third-generation Court, apparently, the DPR appointed the right person to transform the Court into a less heroic institution.

During his short tenure, Chief Justice Hidayat did not show strong intellectual leadership like the founding chief justice, Jimly Asshiddiqie. Although he was under the tutelage of Satjipto Rahardjo, the father of the Indonesian progressive legal movement, Hidayat did not show progressive legal ideas while leading the Court. Under the chairmanship of Arief Hidayat, the Court retreated from the advanced position of the first-generation court. In most cases, the Court chose to retreat, avoiding backlash or political pressure. In other words, Arief Hidayat portrayed himself as a judicial soldier who refused to challenge the elected branches of government. The defining feature of Hidayat's judicial soldiering became apparent when the Executive put pressure on the Court in the Tax Amnesty case, in which the Court chose to retreat further instead of fighting back.

The Court continued to apply the quasi-weak-form review technique; nevertheless, the application of this technique underscores the Court's weakness toward other branches of government. Instead of relying on the quasi-weak-form review to temper the Court's bold decisions, the Court simply refused to issue bold decisions to challenge the Executive and Legislative branches. In other words, Arief Hidayat transformed the quasi-weak-form review as a way of judicial soldiering, in which he would defer to the will of his superiors.

Apart from judicial soldiering, the defining feature of Arief Hidayat's tenure as chief justice was a lack of attention to judicial reputation. Hidayat did not see that a judiciary with a good reputation is likely to garner more public support and be more insulated from political actors who might want to undermine the Court's authority. Hidayat did not care about his individual reputation when he became involved in a major ethical scandal. Moreover, Hidayat did not have any strategies to guard the collective reputation of the Court, as was evident when he failed to show strong leadership when Patrialis Akbar was arrested over bribery allegations.

In sum, the Court under the chairmanship of Arief Hidayat became less robust and less innovative than the earlier generation heroic court. Arief Hidayat was a mediocre chief justice, who was out of his depth in politics and preferred a compromised solution rather than defending the Constitutional Court's interest in other branches of government.

Notes

1 For the biography of Arief Hidayat, I rely on his official biography at the Indonesian Constitutional Court website, available at http://www.mahkamahkonstitusi.go.id/index.php?page=web.ProfilHakim&id=669.

2 Arief Hidayat. *Kebebasan Berserikat di Indonesia: Suatu Analisis Pengaruh Perubahan Sistem Politik Terhadap Penafsiran Hukum* [Freedom of Assembly in Indonesia: An Analysis on the Influence of the Changing of Political System into Legal Interpretation] (Semarang: Badan Penerbit Universitas Diponegoro, 2006).

3 The Constitutional Court Decision No. 49/PUU-IX/2011 (hereinafter the *2011 Amendment II* case).

4 *Tribunnews.com*. "Calon Hakim Konstitusi Tolak Pernikahan Sesama Jenis." [A Candidate for Constitutional Court Justice Rejects Same-sex Marriage]. (March 4, 2013). Accessed July 18, 2016. http://www.tribunnews.com/nasional/2013/03/04/calon-hakim-konstitusi-tolak-pernikahan-sesama-jenis.

5 Ibid.

6 *DetikNews*. "Calon Hakim MK Arief Hidayat Tolak Ide Legalisasi Pernikahan Sejenis." [The Constitutional Court Justice Nominee, Arief Hidayat, Rejects the Notion of the Legalization of Same-sex Marriage] (March 4, 2013). Accessed January 10, 2018. https://news.detik.com/berita/2184835/calon-hakim-mk-arief-hidayat-tolak-ide-legalisasi-pernikahan-sejenis.

7 Meghan Neal. "Man Jailed in Indonesia for Atheist Facebook Posts." *NY Daily News*, (June 15, 2012). Accessed July 19, 2016. http://www.nydailynews.com/news/world/man-jailed-indonesia-atheist-facebook-posts-article-1.1096779.

8 *Republika Online*. "Ada Upaya Melegalkan Perkawinan Sejenis" [There is an Attempt to Legalize Same-Sex Marriage] (April 10, 2012). Accessed July 19, 2016.

http://www.republika.co.id/berita/nasional/hukum/12/04/10/m29g7d-ada-upaya-melegalkan-perkawinan-sejenis.

9 "Arief Hidayat Elected to Replace Outgoing Constitutional Court Judge Mahfud MD." *Jakarta Globe*. Accessed July 19, 2016. http://jakartaglobe.beritasatu.com/news/arief-hidayat-elected-to-replace-outgoing-constitutional-court-judge-mahfud-md/.

10 *Republika Online*. "Arief Hidayat Terpilih Sebagai Pengganti Mahfud MD Di MK" [Arief Hidayat Was Chosen to Succeed Mahfud in the Constitutional Court] (March 4, 2013). Accessed July 19, 2016. http://nasional.republika.co.id/berita/nasional/umum/13/03/04/mj55ce-arief-hidayat-terpilih-sebagai-pengganti-mahfud-md-di-mk.

11 *Kompas.com*. "Gantikan Mahfud MD, Arief Diminta Tak Jadi Pengamat Politik" [Succeeding Mahfud, Hidayat was Asked Not to Play Politics] (March 4, 2013). Accessed July 18, 2016. http://nasional.kompas.com/read/2013/03/04/21313056/Gantikan.Mahfud.MD..Arief.Diminta.Tak.Jadi.Pengamat.Politik.

12 *Kompas.com*. "Ahmad Yani: Tak Satu Pun Calon Hakim MK Yang Negarawan" [Ahmad Yani: No One among The Candidates for Constitutional Court Justices are Statesmen]. (March 4, 2013). Accessed July 19, 2016. http://nasional.kompas.com/read/2013/03/04/20265794/ahmad.yani.tak.satu.pun.calon.hakim.mk.yang.negarawan?utm_source=RD&utm_medium=box&utm_campaign=Kaitrd.

13 *Antara News*. "Hakim Konstitusi Arief Hidayat akui punya banyak warisan." [Constitutional Justice Arief Hidayat claimed that He Inherited a Huge Amount of Fortune (April 1, 2013). Accessed January 10, 2018. https://www.antaranews.com/berita/366443/hakim-konstitusi-arief-hidayat-akui-punya-banyak-warisan.

14 *Jakarta Post*. "New MK Chief Justice Promises Integrity, Fair Rulings," January 13, 2015. http://www.thejakartapost.com/news/2015/01/13/new-mk-chief-justice-promises-integrity-fair-rulings.html.

15 *Jakarta Post*. "Supreme Court Defends Suhartoyo for MK," (December 8, 2014). http://www.thejakartapost.com/news/2014/12/08/supreme-court-defends-suhartoyo-mk.html.

16 See Manahan Sitompul. "Penyelesaian Sengketa Utang-Piutang Perusahaan Dengan Perdamaian Di Dalam atau Di Luar Proses Kepailitan: Studi Mengenai Lembaga Penundaaan Kewajiban Pembayaran Utang" [The Corporate Debt Settlement Inside or Outside Bankruptcy Procedure: Studies on the Postponement of Debt Payment], unpublished doctoral dissertation, North Sumatera University, 2009.

17 I Dewa Gede Palguna, *Pengaduan Konstitusional: Upaya Hukum Terhadap Pelanggaran Hak-hak Konstitusional Warga Negara* [Constitutional Complaint: Legal Remedy for the Violation of the Citizens' Constitutional Rights], (Jakarta: Penerbit Sinar Grafika, 2013).

18 I Dewa Gede Palguna, *Nasionalisme, identitas, dan kegelisahan: Kumpulan orasi I Dewa Gede Palguna, hakim konstitusi periode 2003–2008* [On Nationalism in Indonesia: Speeches of the Indonesian Constitutional Judge for the period 2003–2008] (Jakarta: Sekretariat Jenderal dan Kepaniteraan, Mahkamah Konstitusi, 2008).

19 I Dewa Gede Palguna. *Mahkamah Konstitusi, judicial review, dan welfare state: kumpulan pemikiran*. [Thoughts on Role and Task of Indonesian Constitutional Court, Judicial Review, and Welfare State Concept in Indonesia and Several Countries] (Jakarta: Sekretariat Jenderal dan Kepaniteraan, Mahkamah Konstitusi, Republik Indonesia, 2008). See also I Dewa Gede Palguna, *Saya sungguh mencemaskan Bali: Sebuah kumpulan tulisan* [Essays on Social Conditions, Arts, Spiritualism, Adat Law, and Local Government in Bali] (Jakarta: Sekretariat Jenderal dan Kepaniteraan, Mahkamah Konstitusi, 2008).

20 I Dewa Gede Palguna, *Jalan panjang hingga ke Medan Merdeka Barat: Perjalanan & pemikiran hukum I Dewa Gede Palguna (Hakim Konstitusi periode 2003–2008)* [On Role and Task of Indonesian Constitutional Court: Festschrift in Honor of I Dewa Gede Palguna, Former Indonesian Constitutional Judge] (Jakarta: Sekretariat Jenderal dan Kepaniteraan, Mahkamah Konstitusi, 2008).
21 Constitutional Court Decision No. 85/PUU-XI/2013 (the *Water Resources Law II* case).
22 Government Regulation No. 16 of 2005 on the Water Supply System (*Sistem Penyediaan Air Minum*).
23 *Water Resources Law II* case, 2013, 9.
24 *Water Resources Law I* case, 2004, 492.
25 Ibid., 492.
26 *Water Resources Law II* case, 2013, 20.
27 Ibid., 20.
28 Ibid., 144.
29 Government Regulation No. 16 of 2005 on Drinking Water Supply System (*Pengembangan Sistem Penyediaan Air Minum*); Government Regulation No. 20 of 2006 on Irrigation (*Irigasi*); Government Regulation No. 42 of 2008 on Water Supply Management (*Pengelolaan Sumber Daya Air*); Government Regulation No. 43 of 2008 on Groundwater (*Air Tanah*); Government Regulation No. 38 of 2011 on Rivers (*Sungai*); and Government Regulation No. 73 of 2013 on Swampland (*Rawa*).
30 *Water Resources Law II* case, 2013, 144.
31 Ibid., 145.
32 The Constitutional Court Decision No. 95/PUU-XII/2014 (hereinafter the *Forestry and P3H Law* case)
33 Law No. 41 of 1990 on Forestry. Article 50 (3) a,b,e,i,k.
34 Ibid., Article 78.
35 The *Forestry and P3H Law* case, 90.
36 Law No. 18 of 2003 on the Prevention and Eradication of Forest Destruction.
37 Ibid., Art. 1 (3) stipulates that forest destruction is a process, method or act of destroying forests through illegal logging, illegal use of forest land, or use of permit, contradicting the purpose and aim of the permit in forest land (*kawasan hutan*) declared, designated or being processed by the government.
38 The *Forestry and P3H Law* case, para 3.11.
39 The Constitutional Court issued Decision No. 18/PUU-XII/2014 (hereinafter the *Chevron Pacific* case).
40 Joe Cochrane. "Chevron Criticizes Ruling by Indonesia's Supreme Court on Corruption." The *New York Times*, (October 24, 2014). Accessed July 11, 2017. https://www.nytimes.com/2014/10/25/business/chevron-criticizes-ruling-by-indonesias-supreme-court-on-corruption.html.
41 Law No. 32 of 2009 on the Protection and Management of the Environment, Article 59 (4).
42 Ibid., Art. 59 (1).
43 Ibid., Art. 59 (3).
44 The 1945 Indonesian Constitution, Article 28H (1).
45 The *Chevron Pacific* case, para 3.10.
46 Ibid., para 3.16.
47 Ibid., para 3.16.
48 Ibid., para 3.18.
49 Ibid., para 3.18.
50 Ibid., para 3.18.
51 Ibid., 126–127.

52 The Constitutional Court Decision No. 111/PUU-XIII/2015 (hereinafter the *Electricity Workers Union* case).
53 The Constitutional Court Decision No. 001-021-022/PUU-I/2003 (hereinafter the *Electricity* case).
54 See Jimly Asshiddiqie. Address at the Opening Plenary Workshop on "Constitutional Court and Democracy in Indonesia: Judging the First Decade," University of New South Wales, December 11, 2014.
55 Law No. 30 of 2009 on Electricity Industry.
56 Ibid., Art. 10 (1).
57 Ibid., Art. 10 (2).
58 The *Electricity Law III* case, 26.
59 Ibid., 32.
60 Ibid., Art. 4 (1–2).
61 The *Electricity Law III* case, 35–36.
62 The Court also made reference to the Constitutional Court Decision No. 149/PUU-VII/2009, in which the government's lawyers argued that the 2009 Electricity Law does not adopt the unbundling system. In this case, the Court ruled that there is no explicit provision that signifies the adoption of the unbundling system in the 2009 Electricity Law. The Court then compared the 2009 Electricity Law with the 2002 Electricity Law, which explicitly adopted the unbundling system. Furthermore, the Court argued that it gave the benefit of the doubt to the government, which has reaffirmed that the 2009 Electricity Law did not adopt the unbundling system.
63 The *Electricity Law III* case, 107 (para 3.12).
64 The *Electricity Law I* case, 348.
65 The *Electricity Law III* case, 111.
66 Ibid., 111–112.
67 Theunis Roux and Fritz Siregar. "Trajectories of Curial Power: The Rise, Fall and Partial Rehabilitation of the Indonesian Constitutional Court," 16(2) *Australian Journal of Asian Law* article 2 (2016).
68 The Constitutional Court Decision No. 33/PUU-XIII/2015 (hereinafter, the *Political Dynasty* case).
69 See Yoes Chandra Kenawas. *The Rise of Political Dynasties in Decentralized Indonesia*, unpublished master's thesis, Rajaratnam School of International Studies, 2013.
70 Law No. 8 of 2015 on the Amendment of Regional Election Law, Art. 7R.
71 The *Political Dynasty case*, para 3.16.3.
72 Ibid., para 3.16.5.
73 For a detailed analysis of corruption as one of the pillars of the New Order regime, please see George J. Aditjondro. *Dari Soeharto ke Habibie: Guru kencing berdiri, murid kencing berlari; Kedua puncak korupsi, kolusi, dan nepotisme rezim Orde Baru.* [From Soeharto to Habibie: Monkey See, Monkey Do: The Twin Peaks of the Corruption, Collusion, and Nepotism of the New Order Regime] (Jakarta: Masyarakat Indonesia Untuk Kemanusiaan, 1998).
74 For a detailed analysis of patronage, cronyism, and nepotism under the military regime, please see Richard Robison. *Indonesia: The Rise of Capital* (North Sydney, NSW, Australia: Allen & Unwin, 1986); and Harold A. Crouch. *The Army and Politics in Indonesia* (Ithaca: Cornell University Press, 1988).
75 For a detailed analysis of marriage law reform as a political contestation, please see Kathryn Robison. *Gender, Islam and Democracy in Indonesia* (London: Routledge, 2015), 60–67.
76 Mark Cammack, Lawrence Young, and Tim B. Heaton. "Legislating Social Change in an Islamic Society: Indonesia's Marriage Law," 44 *American Journal of Comparative Law* 1 (1996).

77 Bachtiar Effendy. *Islam and the State in Indonesia* (Singapore: Institute of Southeast Asian Studies, 2003). Parliament reached a compromise with the orthodox demands, wherein all provisions contrary to Islamic doctrine were removed.
78 Mark Cammack. "Indonesia's 1989 Religious Judicature Act: Islamization of Indonesia or Indonesianization of Islam?" 63(April, 1997) Indonesia 143–168 (1997).
79 The Constitutional Court Decision No. 30-74/PUU-XII/2014 (the *Marriageable Age* case).
80 Law No. 1 of 1974 on Marriage, Art. 7 (1).
81 Law No. 23 of 2002 on Juvenile Protection.
82 The Constitutional Court Decision No. 12/PUU-V/2007 (the *Polygamy* case).
83 Ibid., para 3.15.1.
84 Ibid., para 3.15.2.
85 Ibid.
86 The *Marriageable Age* case, para 3.13.1.
87 Ibid., para 3.13.2.
88 Ibid., para 3.13.2.
89 The Constitutional Court Decision No. 68/PUU-XII/2014 (hereinafter *the Interfaith Marriage* Case).
90 See the 1973 Bill on Marriage Law, Art. 2 (1).
91 See the 1973 Bill on Marriage Law, Art. 11 (2).
92 Law No. 1 of 1974 on Marriage, Art 2 (1).
93 Ibid., Art. 2 (2).
94 In terms of official recognition of inter-religious marriages, in 1983, a Presidential Decision instructed the Civil Registry to refuse to formalize marriages involving Muslims, and in 1984, the Ministry of Religion issued guidance to marriage registry officials at the Office of Religious Affairs, stating that they could only register marriages between Muslims.
95 The *Interfaith Marriage* case, 9.
96 The 1945 Indonesian Constitution, Art. 28B (1).
97 The *Interfaith Marriage* case, 16.
98 Ibid., para 3.12.3.
99 The tax amnesty program ran between July 2016 and 31 March 2017. A total of 965,983 people joined the program. But the program failed to attract new taxpayers into the system; only 44,232 out of the total number of amnesty participants had never before paid taxes. This number means tax evasion remains rampant in Indonesia. See I Made Sentana. "Indonesia President Faces Setback as Tax Amnesty Falls Short," the *Wall Street Journal*, (March 29, 2017). Accessed October 24, 2017. https://www.wsj.com/articles/indonesia-tax-amnesty-likely-to-fall-short-in-setback-for-president-joko-widodo-1490791170.
100 *Kontan English Edition/* "Finance Minister Lobbied Muhammadiyah for Amnesty," (September 15, 2016). http://english.kontan.co.id/news/finance-minister-lobbied-muhammadiyah-for-amnesty.
101 *Jakarta Post.* "Muhammadiyah Changes Mind on Tax Amnesty After Sri Mulyani Visit," (September 15, 2016). http://www.thejakartapost.com/news/2016/09/15/muhammadiyah-changes-mind-on-tax-amnesty-after-sri-mulyani-visit.html.
102 *Suara.com.* "Temui Jokowi, Hakim MK Klaim Tak Bahas Gugatan Tax Amnesty," [Meeting with President Jokowi, the Chief Justice Denied to Discuss the Tax Amnesty case] (September 1, 2016). Accessed July 11, 2017. http://www.suara.com/news/2016/09/01/150944/temui-jokowi-hakim-mk-klaim-tak-bahas-gugatan-tax-amnesty.

103 *CNN Indonesia*. "MK: Jokowi Tidak Intervensi Perkara Uji Materi UU Tax Amnesty," [MK: Jokowi did not Intervene in the Judicial Review of the Tax Amnesty Law] (September 1, 2016). http://www.cnnindonesia.com/nasional/20160901161857-12-155440/mk-jokowi-tidak-intervensi-perkara-uji-materi-uu-tax-amnesty/.
104 Hendra Kusuma. "Dipanggil Jokowi, Ketua MK Jamin Tak Ada Intervensi Uji Materi Tax Amnesty" [Being Summoned by President Jokowi, Chief Justice Ensures That There Is No Intervention on the Judicial Review of the Tax Amnesty Law). *Economy.okezone.com*. (September 1, 2016). Accessed July 12, 2017. http://economy.okezone.com/read/2016/09/01/20/1478641/dipanggil-jokowi-ketua-mk-jamin-tak-ada-intervensi-uji-materi-tax-amnesty.
105 The Constitutional Court Decision No. 57/PUU-XIV/2016 (hereinafter the *Tax Amnesty Law* I case).
106 Ibid., 3.
107 Ibid., 4.
108 Ibid., 5. Here the claimant made a reference to Article 20 of the Tax Amnesty Law.
109 Article 28 G (1) of the 1945 Constitution provides that every person shall have the right to protection of his/herself, family, honor, dignity, and property, and shall have the right to feel secure against and receive protection from the threat of fear to do or not do something that is a human right.
110 The *Tax Amnesty Law I* case, 405–406.
111 Ibid., 406.
112 The Constitutional Court Decision No. 58/PUU-XIV/2016 (the *Tax Amnesty Law II* case).
113 Ibid., 19.
114 Law No. 11 of 2016 on Tax Amnesty Program, Art. 20.
115 Ibid., elucidation of Art. 20.
116 Ibid., 353.
117 Ibid., 354–355.
118 Ibid., 356.
119 The Constitutional Court Decision No. 59/PUU-XIV/2016 (the *Tax Amnesty Law IV* case).
120 The Constitutional Court Decision No. 63/PUU-XIV/2016 (the *Tax Amnesty V* case).
121 *Jakarta Globe*. "Constitutional Court Chief under Fire for Memo to AGO," (January 21, 2016). http://jakartaglobe.beritasatu.com/news/constitutional-court-chief-fire-memo-ago/.
122 *Indonesia Law Reform Weekly Digest*. "Ethics Violation Allegedly Committed by Constitutional Court Chief Justice,"(February 15, 2016). http://www.pshk.or.id/id/publikasi/lrwd-edition-01-january-2016-2/. Hidayat and Rochman did not have any familial relationship, but Indonesia has an extended family system and, in one way or another, people can claim that they have a familial relationship.
123 Ethics Council Decision No. 13/Info-III/BAP/DE/2016, March 15, 2016, 5.
124 Ibid., 2. The original wording in the letter says, "Mohon titip dan dibina, dan dijadikan anak Bapak."
125 Ibid., 5.
126 Ibid., 23.
127 Ibid., 25.
128 Ibid., 25.
129 Constitutional Court Regulation No. 2 of 2014, Art. 15 (1).
130 Constitutional Court Regulation No. 1 of 2014, Art. 4.

131 See Rita Triana Budiarti. *Kontroversi Mahfud MD: Di Balik Putusan Mahkamah Konstitusi* [Controversy of Mahfud MD: Behind the Constitutional Court Decisions] (Jakarta: Konstitusi Press, 2013), 239.
132 The Constitutional Court Decision No. 43/PUU-XIII/2015 (hereinafter the *IKAHI* case).
133 The Ethics Council Decision No. 11/LAP-II/BAP/DE/2015, 25.
134 The Constitutional Court Decision No. 129/PUU-XIII/2015 (hereinafter *the Animal Health and Husbandry Law II* case).
135 See *Jakarta Post.* "Beef Importer Basuki Reportedly Confesses to Bribing Constitutional Court Aide," (January 27, 2017). http://www.thejakartapost.com/news/2017/01/27/beef-importer-basuki-reportedly-confesses-to-bribing-constitutional-court-aide.html; See also *Jakarta Post.* "KPK Names MK Justice Patrialis Akbar Suspect in Bribery Case," (February 27, 2017). http://www.thejakartapost.com/news/2017/01/27/kpk-names-mk-justice-patrialis-akbar-suspect-in-bribery-case.html.
136 Law No. 18 of 2009 on Animal Health and Husbandry (*Peternakan dan Kesehatan Hewan*), Art. 59 (2).
137 Ibid., 9–10.
138 Ibid., 11–13.
139 Constitutional Court Decision No. 137/PUU-VII/2009 (the *Animal Health and Husbandry I* case).
140 Ibid., 133.
141 The *Animal and Health Husbandry Law II* case, para 3.13.
142 *Tribunnews.com.* "Ketua MK: Mohon Ampun Tidak Bisa Jaga MK" [The Chief Justice: Please Forgive Me for My Failure to Guard the Court] (January 26, 2017). http://www.tribunnews.com/nasional/2017/01/26/ketua-mk-mohon-ampun-tidak-bisa-jaga-mk.
143 *Tribun Timur.* "Ketua MK Arief Hidayat Diminta Mundur" [Chief Justice Arief Hidayat was Asked to Resign] (January 27, 2017). Accessed July 11, 2017. http://makassar.tribunnews.com/2017/01/27/ketua-mk-arief-hidayat-diminta-mundur.
144 *Tribunnews.com.* "Arief Hidayat Tidak Akan Mundur Dari Jabatan Ketua MK." (Arief Hidayat Won't Resign From the Position of Chief Justice) (January 27, 2017). Accessed July 11, 2017. http://www.tribunnews.com/nasional/2017/01/27/arief-hidayat-tidak-akan-mundur-dari-jabatan-ketua-mk.
145 *Pikiran Rakyat.* "Dewan Etik Sebut Patrialis Akbar Sering Diperingatkan" (Ethics Council Has Repeatedly Warned Patrialis Akbar) (January 26, 2017). http://www.pikiran-rakyat.com/nasional/2017/01/26/dewan-etik-sebut-patrialis-akbar-sering-diperingatkan-391837.
146 Yustinus Paat and Eko Prasetyo. "Patrialis Akbar Dismissed from Constitutional Court," the *Jakarta Globe* (January 28, 2017). http://www.jakartaglobe.beritasatu.com/news/patrialis-akbar-dismissed-constitutional-court/.
147 *Hukumonline.com.* "Patrialis Akbar Mundur dari MK" [Patrialis Akbar Resigned from the Court] (January 30, 2017). Accessed July 11, 2017. http://www.hukumonline.com/berita/baca/lt588f36fe30ede/patrialis-akbar-mundur-dari-mk.
148 *Jakarta Post.* "Judicial Commission Appoints Vice Chairwoman to Join MK Honorary Council," (February 1, 2017). http://www.thejakartapost.com/news/2017/02/01/judicial-commission-appoints-vice-chairwoman-to-join-mk-honorary-council.html. The membership of the Council comprised Associate Justice Anwar Usman; a former Constitutional Court justice, Achmad Sodiki; the former chief justice of the Supreme Court, Bagir Manan; a former deputy chief of the State Intelligence Agency, As'ad Said Ali; and the deputy chairwoman of the Judicial Commission, Sukma Violetta.
149 The Honorary Council Decision No. 1/MKMK-SPP/II/2017.

150 Ina Parlina. "Panel to Rule on Patrialis' Alleged Ethics Breach Next Week," the *Jakarta Post* (February 3, 2017). Accessed May 15, 2017. http://www.thejakartapost.com/news/2017/02/03/panel-to-rule-on-patrialis-alleged-ethics-breach-next-week.html.
151 The Honorary Council Decision No. 1/MKMK-SPL/II/2017.
152 *Jakarta Post*. "Former MK Justice Sentenced to 8 Years in Prison," (September 4, 2017). Accessed September 29, 2017. http://www.thejakartapost.com/news/2017/09/04/corruption-court-to-issue-verdict-for-former-mk-justice.html.
153 Nuno Garoupa and Tom Ginsburg. *Judicial Reputation: A Comparative Theory* (Chicago: The University of Chicago Press, 2015).
154 Ibid., 16.
155 Ibid., 16.
156 *Jakarta Post*. "Jokowi Inaugurates Saldi Isra as New Constitutional Court Justice," (April 11, 2017). Accessed July 11, 2017. http://www.thejakartapost.com/news/2017/04/11/jokowi-inaugurates-saldi-isra-as-new-constitutional-court-justice.html.
157 *Jakarta Post*. "Saldi Isra Hopes to Bring Change as Youngest Constitutional Court Justice," (April 11, 2017). Accessed July 11, 2017. http://www.thejakartapost.com/news/2017/04/11/saldi-isra-hopes-to-bring-change-as-youngest-constitutional-court-justice.html.
158 *Jakarta Post*. "Arief Hidayat Re-elected Constitutional Court Chief Justice," (July 14, 2017). Accessed July 17, 2017. http://www.thejakartapost.com/news/2017/07/14/arief-hidayat-re-elected-constitutional-court-chief-justice.html.
159 *Jakarta Post* "Arief Elected MK Chief for Second Time," (July 14, 2017). Accessed July 17, 2017. http://www.thejakartapost.com/news/2017/07/14/arief-elected-mk-chief-for-second-time.html.

Part IV

Conclusions

9 Conclusion

The "heroic judicial leadership" and "second-generation decline" in comparative perspective

This chapter draws some comparative conclusions from the development of the Indonesian Constitutional Court. It is impossible to understand the development of the Indonesian Constitutional Court without comparing it to the experiences of constitutional courts in other countries. Is the unique heroic leadership of Chief Justice Asshiddiqie and the movement toward a less heroic court specific to Indonesia? To answer this question, we need to look at the experience of different constitutional courts to detect whether the prudential-minimalist model of judicial leadership is a good thing for new democracies and whether there is a real trend of second-generation decline. This chapter explores how the issue of judicial leadership and the trend of second-generation decline have evolved in other constitutional courts.

"The heroic judicial leadership" in comparative perspective

Nathan Brown and Julian Waller argue that courts in newer democracies are likely to play an interventionist role when they develop a constitutional vision and that vision is coupled with a clear political agenda in the court's institutional interest.[1] Brown and Waller further argue that several factors facilitate the courts in newer democracies to craft a constitutional vision: (1) institutional centrality; (2) strong personalities of leadership; and (3) deep division and rivalries among state apparatus.[2] It is beyond the scope of this book to analyze the first and third factors, but the second factor, strong leadership, is very relevant to this book. In a nutshell, Brown and Waller argue that the presence of strong and ambitious court leadership is one of the primary sources of the rise of the interventionist court.[3] The bottom line is that strong leaders are better in articulating clear visions and setting the priorities of the court that they lead. Moreover, if a chief justice thinks of himself as a political actor, then he will lead his court to engage in political matters.

Brown and Waller's thesis relied heavily on the model of the bold, aggressive type of judicial hero. As explained in Chapter 1, the character of Laszlo Solymon, the founding chief justice of Constitutional Court of Hungary, is the epitome of the bold, aggressive, heroic chief justice. Similarly, Chief Justice Valery Zorkin of the Russian Constitutional Court took a forthright and aggressive political stance during his first tenure as chief justice (1991–1993). Moreover, these ambitious court leaders saw themselves as political actors, and they did not hesitate to lead the Court to intervene heroically during the turbulent transitional period in their countries. For instance, Solyom led the Hungarian Constitutional Court to intervene during the welfare cut crisis by striking down the government's economic plan.[4] In Russia, Zorkin attempted to play the role as a broker in the major political dispute between President Yeltsin and Supreme Soviet Chairman Ruslan Khasbulatov.[5] Chief Justice Zorkin, however, went further to enter the political brawls when he sided with Khasbulatov against Yeltsin's proposed referendum on the constitution.[6]

Misleading pictures of bold, aggressive, heroic judges

The scholarship of comparative judicial politics in the last two decades have highlighted the role of many bold, aggressive, heroic chief justices like Laszlo Solyom, Valery Zorkin, Aharon Barak, and Manuel José Cepeda Espinosa. Nevertheless, the stories of these chief justices may give students of comparative constitutional law a misleading picture of heroic chief justices. These bold, aggressive, heroic chief justices might only come once in their country's history. In fact, there are relatively few such chief justices.

By definition, these bold, aggressive chief justices are extraordinary figures. Laszlo Solyom was a towering legal scholar before his appointment as chief justice of Hungary. He held two doctoral degrees: the first doctorate in civil law from the Friedrich Schiller University of Jena (German Democratic Republic), and the second doctorate (Habilitation) from the Hungarian Academy of Sciences.[7] Solyom's involvement in politics began in the 1980s when he served as legal advisor to the environmental organization Duna Kör (Danube Circle), a group opposed to the damming of the Danube River.[8] He also began working in the area of constitutional rights and jurisdiction. He focused on the right to privacy and helped to introduce the concept of data protection in Hungary.[9] Solyom was one of the members of the democratic opposition involved in the Hungarian National Roundtable of 1989, which helped Hungary transition to democracy in the late 1980s.[10] In 1989, the Hungarian parliament appointed Solyom to the newly established Constitutional Court, and he became president of the Court a year later.

Similarly, Manuel José Cepeda Espinosa of the Colombian Constitutional Court was a towering figure before his appointment to the bench. He graduated Magna Cum Laude from Universidad de Los Andes in 1986 and received his Master of Law from Harvard Law School in 1987.[11] He served as Dean of the Universidad de Los Andes Law School from 1996 to 2000. From 1987 to 1990, he served as a presidential advisor for legal affairs to Colombian president Virgilio Barco Vargas. From 1990 to 1991, he was an advisor to Colombian president César Gaviria Trujillo for the Constituent Assembly of Colombia. During the deliberations of the Constituent Assembly, Cepeda was widely credited with helping design key specific constitutional changes, including the creation of a new form of concrete review jurisdiction on the part of the Constitutional Court—that is, the *tutela* action.[12] Later, he served as a justice on the Constitutional Court of Colombia from 2001 to 2009 and was president of the Court from June 2005 to April 2006.

Figures like Solyom and Manuel Cepeda, however, do not come along very often in history and one cannot expect there will be a parade of bold, aggressive, heroic chief justices across the globe. Moreover, there are also misleading pictures of bold, aggressive, heroic judges because of the concept of a "global community of judges." Anne-Marie Slaughter postulates the idea of a "global community of judges," arguing that high court judges frequently talk across the jurisdiction.[13] The global community of judges then tries to influence domestic courts to take distinct approaches.[14] But the fact of the matter is that only bold, aggressive judges participate in these global networks, and this may give students of comparative law a false picture of heroic judges.

Indeed, a bold, heroic judge like Manuel Cepeda is also a comparative constitutional law scholar who engaged with the global community. He gave many international lectures,[15] wrote scholarly works that are available in Western academia,[16] and is currently serving as the president of the International Association of Constitutional Law.[17] But most of the judges who served with Manuel Cepeda did not actively participate in the "global community of judges." Therefore, the world does not know how many of those judges were also bold, aggressive judges like Manuel Cepeda.

The limits of bold, aggressive heroic judges

The courts of bold, aggressive, chief justices like Solyom, Zorkin, or Cepeda are more likely to exercise a strong form of judicial review, which has a tendency to result in the invalidation of legislations. Stephen Gardbaum, in his argument against strong-form review, postulates that strong-form review is more likely to put the independent judiciary under stress because it has a tendency to result in the politicization of the courts.[18] Whenever a court has the authority to invalidate legislation, it will serve as a useful check on politics, but it will also trigger political attacks that threaten judicial independence.[19] Furthermore, because of the power that courts exercise to invalidate legislation, there will be a growing demand that judges should be given democratic accountability. Consequently, judicial appointment to these courts will become political appointments based on political reasons.[20]

Based on Gardbaum's criticism against strong-form review, I argue that bold, aggressive, heroic chief justices are more likely to create unnecessary conflicts and tension between the courts and the elected branches of government. Bold, aggressive chief justices will inevitably become political actors, and the elected politicians will see these heroic chief justices as political opponents or rivals who lack a political mandate. As a result, the elected politicians will put pressure on courts and find a way to remove their political opponents. At this stage, the term length of the judges becomes a crucial issue; life tenure or a long, fixed tenure will give greater leeway for heroic chief justices to exercise bold, aggressive leadership, but it will leave courts under protracted pressures and strains. A short fixed or short nonrenewable term will restrict bold, aggressive chief justices because it makes them concerned about their reappointment. For elected politicians, the short nonrenewable term will give them an opportunity to fill court vacancies with their supporters.

In sum, courts under the leadership of bold, aggressive chief justices tend to have limited life spans and legitimacy problems. In Hungary, a court under the leadership of a bold, aggressive chief justice embodies the legitimacy problem, in which the government easily accused an unelected Constitutional Court of lacking a mandate to invalidate legislation.[21] Bruce Ackerman once warned that the heroic Hungarian Constitutional Court under the leadership of Chief Justice Solyom was untenable in light of its "soft constitutional background."[22] Apparently, after the Court's decision on the social welfare package, the government signaled that it could weaken the Court through its intervention in the selection process of the Constitutional Court justices.[23] When Chief Justice Solyom's term was scheduled to end in November 1998, the government and parliament decided not to renew his term. Consequently, he had to leave the Court and disappeared from public life for a time.[24]

Similarly, Chief Justice Zorkin began his fall from power when he became involved in a major political dispute between the executive and the legislative branches.[25] Chief Justice Zorkin suffered significant humiliation when other members of the Court rebelled against his political endeavors. With his brethren arrayed against him, Zorkin stepped down as the chief justice, and President Yeltsin issued a decree that suspended the Constitutional Court. Bold, aggressive chief justices like Zorkin and Solyzom are like sprinters who fade over long distances.[26]

Heroic prudential-minimalist leadership

Brown and Waller, however, were quite dismissive of a model of judicial leadership that takes a go-slow, persevering, willingness-to-strategically-retreat approach. In their view, courts that lack an aggressive personality at the helm preclude intervention into politics.[27] Chief Justice Arthur Chaskalson of the Constitutional Court of South Africa falls under Brown and Waller's category of a weak leader. In their view, Chaskalson was a great leader with limited political ambition.[28] Chaskalson displayed excellent leadership in upholding human rights in the post-apartheid regime, but he was never interested in leading the Court to delve into the messy political landscape of South Africa.

To be sure, the portrayal of Chaskalson as an unheroic chief justice also provides a misleading picture to students of comparative law. For reasons rooted in the sociology of academia, scholars are not interested in studying less heroic judges.[29] Therefore, students of comparative constitutional law only hear about bold, aggressive, heroic chief justices. A figure like Chaskalson is the antithesis of the bold, aggressive model of judicial heroism. Chaskalson was an effective leader because, under his leadership, the Court was able to survive without any debilitating attacks to its independence. Chaskalson was a prudential-minimalist heroic chief justice who knew how to enhance the Court's authority by engaging in rights-based discourse while also fortifying the Court's status by playing a minimalist role in some policy areas.[30]

Contrary perhaps to an idealized notion of bold, aggressive heroes, this book's findings show a cautious leadership approach to be the most effective. This book holds that the success of the first-generation court under the presidency of Jimly Asshiddiqie was due to his prudential-minimalist heroic leadership. In Chapter 3, I illustrated how the intellectual leadership of Chief Justice Asshiddiqie shaped the Court's jurisprudence. Led by Asshiddiqie, the Court struck down many governmental policies. It pushed the government to respect the protection of civil and political rights, and it even reviewed some important governmental policies on economy. Asshiddiqie continued to enhance the Court's authority through his strategy related to administrative agency, which filled an existing doctrinal gap on the role of the regulatory agency. Indeed, Asshiddiqie was an ambitious chief justice who wanted to dive into messy political terrain. Nevertheless, Asshiddiqie knew how to avoid pressures and strains from elected politicians by mitigating the remedial measures of the Court's bold decisions.

Chapter 4 maps out the prudential-minimalist character of Asshiddiqie's heroism, in which he relied on his seemingly unheroic approach to insulate the impact of the Court's bold decisions. Asshiddiqie led the Court to adopt several techniques that can be considered to represent quasi-weak-form review. The Court frequently issued a "conditionally constitutional" ruling, in which it allowed the law to remain valid as long as it was applied or implemented in the way the Court interpreted it. In some instances, the Court asked the government to interpret the statute in a certain way or prescribed some directives to help the government implement the law. Furthermore, the Court issued weak remedies in two forms: first, "suspended declarations," in which the remedy would only be applied within a specified period; and second, "progressive realization," which allows the government to fulfill the remedy incrementally. By minimizing the impact of its decision, the Court would not upset the lawmaker, but at the same time, the Court proved itself as an independent institution that could issue a particular judicial resolution.

Chapter 5 illustrates that social leadership was another feature of Asshiddiqie's heroism. Asshiddiqie continued to enhance the Court's authority through his strategy related to questions of judicial standing, which filled an existing doctrinal gap with a broad vision of who may bring a case before the judiciary. His expansive views on standing allowed plaintiffs to file petitions as taxpayers or consumers and even bestowed standing on nongovernmental organizations (NGOs). But again, although Asshiddiqie was instrumental in setting the Court's ambitious agenda, he knew when to take a more moderate approach. As a consensus builder, he tried to absorb the voices of the proponent of strict standing who wanted to limit the access to the Court. Moreover, Asshiddiqie successfully promoted a culture of collegiality, in which the justices were not to disagree strongly with their brethren, especially on the issue of standing. Asshiddiqie himself made a choice not to express his dissent, and often he sided with the justices who did not support this ambitious agenda for the sake of maintaining the culture of collegiality.

I have identified in Chapter 1 that the prudential-minimalist approach may take different forms. The first model is explicit judicial deferral, which focuses on mitigating the remedial measures that a judge orders for constitutional violations such as suspended declarations, progressive realization, or prospective ruling. The second model is implicit deferral, which takes place in the form of a combination of a "soft" confrontation with the elected branches of government and avoidance or delay of legal remedies or the effect of a ruling. As I have explained in Chapter 1, the oldest form of the implicit deferral is the *Marbury* strategy, in which Chief Justice John Marshall proclaimed powers of judicial review but deferred the legal and political effect of this reasoning by holding that it lacked jurisdiction to grant an order for mandamus.

Chief Justice Asshiddiqie led the first-generation Court to employ both the explicit and implicit models of deferral. As explained in Chapters 3 and 4, the Court frequently applied explicit deferral by ordering suspended declarations, progressive realization, or prospective remedial measures. Asshiddiqie was acutely aware that the first-generation Court lacked the political and legal support necessary to deliver bold decisions, and therefore, he also often employed the *Marbury* strategy. An apt example is the *Electricity Law* case, in which the Court struck down the legislation authorizing the privatization of electricity industry, but it stated that all of the contract and business permits in the electricity sector that were signed under the law should remain valid until they expired. Asshiddiqie personally considered the *Electricity Law* case as Indonesia's *Marbury v. Madison*.[31] Moreover, Asshiddiqie said that he drew inspiration from John Marshall, as he said, "If John Marshall had the courage to set a cornerstone for judicial review in the American legal history, I could also do the same thing for my country."[32]

In sum, this book argues that the success of the first-generation Indonesian Constitutional Court was due to Asshiddiqie's heroic prudential-minimalist leadership. During his tenure, Asshiddiqie employed the combination of ambitious constitutional interpretations of the Constitution—by striking down many governmental policies—with quasi-weak-form review, which includes the willingness to recognize the merits of deferring to political judgments about the Constitution.

Potential benefits of prudential-minimalist approach

I argued in Chapter 1 that the prudential-minimalist approach is different than judicial self-restraint or passive virtues. Judicial self-restraint usually leads courts to decide only "safe" or routine cases or to issue cautious judgments rather than robust rulings. The prudential-minimalist approach, however, permits courts to engage in risky cases and to issue robust decisions. Chapter 3 and 4 illustrate how Asshiddiqie led the Court to decide on many risky cases, but at the same time, he employed brilliant techniques to reduce the tension between the Court and elected branches of government.

During his tenure as chief justice, Asshiddiqie successfully lessened the tension with other political branches of government and lowered the risk of direct political attacks. By employing quasi-weak-form review, the Court was still able to check legislative and executive power, but it showed that the Court has no absolute power and that the other branches of governments have the final authority to make laws. Of course, this approach will not eliminate the tension and risk of political attacks, but it may help to reduce the tension between the Court and government and lower the risks of provoking governmental attack on the Court, which is possible with a strong form of review.

Under the presidency of Asshiddiqie, the Court was able to survive without any enfeebling attacks on its independence. Nevertheless, the ouster of Asshiddiqie at the end of his 5year term raised speculation that the executive power intervened upon the Court's independence. I argued in Chapter 6 that there is no substantial evidence to support the claim of government intervention in the ouster of Asshiddiqie. First, the House of Representatives (DPR) re-appointed Asshiddiqie for his second term and, in fact, the House Judiciary Committee gave Asshiddiqie special treatment by waiving the requirement of the confirmation hearing. Second, although the Executive power may have been unhappy with Asshiddiqie's leadership style, the president had no direct power to remove the chief justice. Moreover, the Executive power did not have sufficient vote to oust Asshiddiqie, considering that it had only three appointees. I do not deny the Executive's attempt to dethrone Asshiddiqie, but it was a proximate cause rather than the ultimate reason for the ouster of Asshiddiqie.

The ultimate cause of the ouster of Asshiddiqie was the internal power struggle within the Court, especially after the departure of many first-generation justices. The new Constitutional Court Justices under the leadership of Muhammad Mahfud were the ones who orchestrated the removal of Asshiddiqie from the position of chief justice. This scenario was possible because of the short-term tenure for associate justices (5 years) and chief justices (2.5 years). Short fixed-term tenure in the Indonesian Constitutional Court became the weakest institutional feature of the Court, which signifies a lack in the Court's stability and institutional cohesion. With the quick turnover of justices every 5 years, and 2.5 years for chief justices, there is always room to maneuver the justices. Moreover, the short term gives elected branches of government opportunities to fill court vacancies with their supporters.

Should the prudential-minimalist approach be considered a temporary or a permanent strategy? Stephen Gardbaum argues that weak-form review, in general, should be regarded as a temporary approach—especially during the democratic transition—rather than a permanent institutional feature.[33] Rosalind Dixon and Samuel Issacharoff make a distinction between spans of applicability of the remedial measure of weak-form review. The explicit judicial deferral, which includes "progressive realization" and "suspended declaration," can be a permanent feature and can be applied in any case as long as the Court endures.[34] The implicit judicial deferral, which is known as the *Marbury* strategy, is a temporary feature that is relevant as long as courts lack the political support to deliver robust decisions, but once there is stable support for the courts, then courts must issue a more robust decision and ultimately abandon the *Marbury* strategy.[35]

The experience of the Indonesian Constitutional Court suggests that political stability is somewhat fluid as it may increase or decrease over time. By the end of his first term, Asshiddiqie had made a strategic mistake by striking down the national education budget. While Asshiddiqie thought there was stability between the elected branches of government, there was still some fragility. When the Court intervenes too decisively, it risks retaliation. In the end, I believe that the *Marbury* strategy should not be limited to the early days of a Court's operations. Even in a stable democracy, courts may continue to employ the *Marbury* strategy in different contexts.

"Second-generation decline" in comparative perspective

Having analyzed the unique nature of the heroic leadership of Chief Justice Asshiddiqie from a comparative perspective, now I will turn to the second task of this book, which is to assess whether there is a trend of second- or third-generation decline in constitutional courts. The transition from the first-generation courts to second-generation courts has usually been accompanied by direct political attacks by the government against the courts. As explained earlier, in Hungary, the government tried to weaken the Court through its intervention in the selection process of the Constitutional Court justices. When Chief Justice Solyom's term was scheduled to end in November 1998, the government and parliament decided not to renew his term.[36] Similarly, after Chief Justice Zorkin of the Russian Constitutional Court began to get involved in a tug-of-war between the executive and the legislative branches, he had to face pressure from within and outside the Court; Zorkin stepped down, and President Yeltsin issued a decree that suspended the Constitutional Court.[37]

The trend of diminishment and retreat

The tumultuous transition to second-generation court has typically been followed by the pattern of diminishment, decline, or retreat. Herman Schwartz noted that the second generation of the Russian Constitutional Court was "overly cautious substantively."[38] Under the new chairmanship of Vladimir Tumanov, the Russian Constitutional Court tried to stay out of politics, and its productivity fell sharply.[39] When Marat Baglai was elevated to the chief justice position after Tumanov's retirement, he continued to keep the Court out of political controversies.[40] Similarly, the second Hungarian Constitutional Court under the chairmanship of Jason Nemeth chose a retreat mode and showed a strong tendency to defer to the government.[41]

The sign of diminishment and direct political attack also continued in the third-generation court in Hungary. In 2012, the Fidesz government launched a constitutional reform that curtailed the authority of the Hungarian Constitutional Court through the combination of court-packing, jurisdictional stripping, and changing the rule of access to the Court.[42] In 2015, the Hungarian parliament appointed a pro-Fidesz judge, Barnabás Lenkovics, as the new chief justice, so that the government had a reliable ally in the Court president's office.[43]

But not every court has to experience a dramatic transition and a steep decline. The transition in the South African Constitutional Court from the chairmanship of Arthur Chaskalson to that of Chief Justice Pius Langa was normal and uneventful. Langa worked closely with Chaskalson once he took over the deputy presidency of the Court in 1997.[44] As he was approaching his retirement in 2005, Chaskalson decided to take a sabbatical abroad, exposing his probable successor to the full responsibilities of leadership.[45] Thus, these two men carefully coordinated the handover, and the transition went smoothly.

Under the chairmanship of Pius Langa, the Court remained committed to upholding the positions staked out by the previous Court. For instance, the Court issued a bold ruling in the area of socio-economic rights.[46] Chief Justice Langa also continued to articulate the need for the highest court to support the interests of the most disadvantaged members of South African society.[47] Nevertheless, by the end of Langa's term in office, the Court was under enormous pressure from the Executive, and it chose to employ judicial restraint in some major sensitive political issues.[48]

The transition from the second-generation Court to the third-generation Court in South Africa, however, was more eventful. In 2009, the South African president, Jacob Zuma, nominated Justice Sandile Ngcobo to become the successor to Chief Justice Pius Langa. The nomination was quite controversial for several reasons. First, Justice Ngcobo was close to retirement due to the fixed term. The South African Constitution stipulates that a Constitutional Court judge holds office for a nonrenewable term of 12 years, or until he or she attains the age of 70.[49] President Nelson Mandela appointed Ngcobo as a constitutional court judge in 1999, and his term on the Constitutional Court had to come to an end in 2011 because of the term allowed under the Constitution. Second, President Zuma overlooked the deputy chief justice, Dikgang Moseneke, who had been originally touted for the position of chief justice and had received the backing of Chief Justice Langa.[50]

When Chief Justice Ngcobo reached the maximum term limit in 2011, President Zuma tried to extend Ngcobo's term to 5 years. The Constitution allows an Act of Parliament to extend the term of a judge of the Court,[51] and therefore, the Cabinet approved a bill amending the Judges' Remuneration and Conditions of Employment Act. Nevertheless, Chief Justice Ngcobo did not accept an extension of his current term of office and stepped down immediately. President Zuma then appointed Associate Justice Mogoeng Mogoeng to be the new chief justice, again bypassing Deputy Chief Justice Dikgang Moseneke.

The elevation of Mogoeng to the position of chief justice was controversial because of his lack of experience when compared to Deputy Chief Justice Moseneke. Mogoeng was appointed a Constitutional Court judge in 2009, while

Moseneke was appointed in 2002 and became deputy chief justice in 2005. Zuma, however, made it clear that he would not make Justice Moseneke chief justice because of Moseneke's critical comments to the ANC leadership, and apparently, President Zuma was concerned that the deputy chief justice was playing politics.[52]

Moreover, the Court's decision in the *Glenister II* case[53] was not helpful for Justice Moseneke. In 2008, the Court decided the *Glenister I* case, which involved a challenge brought by a private citizen, Hugh Glenister, seeking to bar the Cabinet from initiating legislation to move the Directorate of Special Operations (known as the "Scorpions") from the National Prosecuting Authority to the South African Police Service.[54] The Court, however, declined to intervene in Parliament's consideration of the proposed legislation.

In 2011, Glenister brought the second case, which directly challenged the statute that disbanded the Scorpions unit. In this case, by a 5–4 vote, the Court held that the statute was unconstitutional. Deputy Chief Justice Moseneke and Justice Edwin Cameron wrote the majority judgment, in which they developed the argument for a constitutional duty to fight corruption.[55] From this decision, it can be perceived that Justice Moseneke considered himself a political rival to President Zuma.

Extraordinary versus ordinary chief justices

This book begins with an Aristotelean theoretical approach, which compares two characters of Homeric heroes: Achilles of the *Iliad* as exemplar of *andreia* (courage or manliness) and Odysseus of the *Odyssey* as exemplar of *sophrosune* (temperance). But both Achilles and Odysseus are extraordinary figures. Both were generals endowed with unique qualities: princely birth, good physique, strength, skill in athletics and battle, energy, and eloquence. Achilles is regularly called *Aristos Akhaion*, "the best of the Achaeans"; as a warrior, he surpassed all Achaean heroes with his furious valor, strength, and aggressiveness; his overwhelming presence; and his forcefulness in combat. Odysseus was known as a distinguished warrior, but for reasons different than Achilles. His strength and courage were sufficient to earn him a heroic status, but it was his cleverness and his unique capacity to endure hardship and trial that place him in high regard. In short, heroic characters like Achilles and Odysseus are a rare breed.

The heroic natures of Odysseus and Achilles are helpful to explain the "trend" of second-generation decline. Many first-generation chief justices like Laszlo Solyom, Valery Zorkin, and Arthur Chaskalson were extraordinary figures. Their successors, however, were more ordinary chief justices. Based on this view, the first-generation heroic Court is untypical, but the successors are typical. Therefore, what needs explaining is not the retreat from judicial heroism under political pressure, but rather the first-generation Court's untypical judicial heroism.[56]

By definition, the founding chief justice of the Indonesian Constitutional Court, Jimly Asshiddiqie, is an extraordinary figure. He had been a prominent constitutional law professor before he was thrust into the role of chief justice. He was heavily involved in the constitutional reform process during the democratic transition. With his political experience, Asshiddiqie established a vast political network before he came to the bench. By the time the government established the Constitutional Court in 2003, Asshiddiqie had developed a reputation as an expert in constitutional law and a skillful politician. Perhaps it would have been scandalous if a man like Asshiddiqie were not appointed to the Court.[57]

Chapter 7 explains the emergence of a different type of chief justice in the second-generation Court. Mohammad Mahfud was also, in some ways, an extraordinary figure. He was a constitutional law professor with a decorated political career before he came to the Court. Nevertheless, Mahfud displayed a bold type of heroism with his aggressive and arrogant approach toward the Executive and Legislature. While Asshiddiqie was also ambitious in his constitutional interpretation, at least he relied more on a combination of maximalist and minimalist approaches to minimize the impact of the Court's bold decisions. Mahfud, however, transformed quasi-weak-form review into a tool to issue strong remedies, without giving substantial deference to the legislature. Moreover, Mahfud consistently posited the notion of "substantive justice" and "progressive law" in deciding a case, in which the Court emphasized fidelity to the substantive aims of the law instead of compliance to rigid rules. In the name of substantive justice, then, Mahfud led the Court to issue many ambitious constitutional interpretations.

The transition from the presidency of Asshiddiqie to that of Mahfud was not marked by a sharp decline but rather by a different leadership style. While Asshiddiqie displayed a prudential-minimalist style of leadership, Mahfud's leadership was the embodiment of robust, aggressive leadership, typical of many other heroic justices. Mahfud's aggressive style, however, provoked retaliation from the elected branches of government through the 2011 Amendment to the Constitutional Court Law.

Chief justices with the forceful personalities of Asshiddiqie and Mahfud do not appear often, and they may only come once in the history of their country. If Asshiddiqie and Mahfud were extraordinary figures, their successors were more ordinary chief justices, which explains why there is usually a sudden shift from a heroic court to a less heroic one. Chapter 8 shows that Chief Justice Akil Mochtar was a mediocre chief justice who did not understand his role as the guardian of the legacy of his predecessors. After 6 months in office, Akil Mochtar was arrested by the Anti-Corruption Commission for alleged bribery. The arrest of Akil Mochtar unraveled the hard work of his predecessors to build the Court as a functioning and transparent institution. Mochtar's immediate successor, Hamdan Zoelva, was also an ordinary chief justice. During his brief tenure, Zoelva led the Court to pursue a path of retreat, underscoring the Court's weakness in relation to other branches of government. But the fact of the matter is that the Court did not retreat under pressure; it was rather because Zoelva chose not to issue bold decisions as his earlier predecessors did. Chapter 8 considers the leadership of Chief Justice Arief Hidayat. Hidayat was a typical judicial solider who was out of his depth in politics and preferred a compromised solution rather than defending the Constitutional Court's interest against the other branches of government.

The last three chapters show that ordinary chief justices are those who typically lead the Court. The extraordinary heroic chief justices are an exception. Therefore, even without political backlash, second or third-generation Courts will become less heroic. Obviously, the issue is not about second or third-generation decline, but rather the unique characteristics of the first-generation heroic court.

Conclusion

The Indonesian Constitutional Court is at a critical point in history, having transitioned from a heroic court to a less heroic one. The challenge ahead is how to maintain a constitutional democracy with mediocre judges. The last three chapters of this book show that there is still a large gap to be filled by second-generation and third-generation courts. For instance, many complex cases that involved judicial review of the electoral process arose in the second and third-generation Court. Considering that most judges are mediocre and that the Court will be staffed by many mediocre judges, in the long run, the Indonesian Constitutional Court has no other choice than to rely on these mediocre judges to guard constitutional values. In this context, quasi-weak-form review could become a potentially useful model to help mediocre judges play their role. The Court needs move back to the prudential-minimalist stance under the leadership of Asshiddiqie, which recognizes the merits of deferring to political judgments about the Constitution, while at the same time still interpreting the constitution in a robust manner.

Notes

1 Nathan Brown and Julian G. Waller. "Constitutional Courts and Political Uncertainty: Constitutional Ruptures and The Rule of Judges," 14(4) *Int J Constitutional Law* 817–850, 821 (2016).
2 Ibid., 821.
3 Ibid., 823.
4 See the Constitutional Court of Hungary, Summary Decision No. 43 of 1995 on Social Security Benefit.
5 See Carla Thorson. *Politics, Judicial Review and the Russian Constitutional Court* (Basingstoke: Palgrave Macmillan, 2012), 105–106.
6 Ibid., 106–108. After the legislatures had rejected his constitutional referendum proposal, Yeltsin retaliated by announcing a decree by which he would assume total responsibility for the conduct of affairs in Russia. Zorkin joined Khasbulatov to denounce the speech, and moreover, Zorkin convened an emergency session of the Constitutional Court to evaluate the constitutionality of Yeltsin's speech without waiting for a formal petition.
7 Kim Lane Scheppele. "Guardians of the Constitution: Constitutional Court Presidents and the Struggle for the Rule of Law in Post-Soviet Europe," 154 *U. Pa. L. Rev.* 1757, 1774 (2006).
8 Andras Bozoki (ed). *The Roundtable Talks of 1989: The Genesis of Hungarian Democracy* (Budapest: Central European University Press, 2002), 404.
9 Since Solyom left office, his official biography in the office of the President is no longer available, so for his biography, I rely on *Encyclopaedia Britannica*, available at https://www.britannica.com/biography/Laszlo-Solyom.

10 Andras Bozoki and Gergely Karacsony. "The Making of a Political Elite: Participants in the Hungarian Roundtable Talks of 1989." In *The Roundtable Talks of 1989: The Genesis of Hungarian Democracy*, edited by Andras Bozoki (2002), 85–86.
11 See "Manuel José Cepeda Espinosa." Oxford Law Faculty, (March 16, 2017). Accessed July 06, 2017. https://www.law.ox.ac.uk/content/manuel-jos%C3%A9-cepeda-espinosa.
12 Justice Manuel José Cepeda Espinosa. "Judicial Activism in a Violent Context: The Origin, Role, and Impact of the Colombian Constitutional Court," 3 *Wash. U. Glob. Stud. L. Rev.* 529 (2004); Rodrigo M. Nunes. "Ideational Origins of Progressive Judicial Activism: The Colombian Constitutional Court and the Right to Health," 52 *L. Am. Pol. & Soc.* 67, 77 (2010).
13 Anne-Marie Slaughter. "A Global Community of Courts," 44 *Harv. Int'l L. J.* 191 (2003).
14 For an excellent scholarship on court-on-court encounters as the basis of constitutional convergence, please see Paul B. Stephan. "Courts on Courts: Contracting for Engagement and Indifference in International Judicial Encounters," 100 *Va. L. Rev* 17 (2014).
15 See, for instance, Manuel José Cepeda Espinoza. *Social and Economic Rights and the Colombian Constitutional Court*, Remarks at the Texas Law Review Symposium, Latin American Constitutionalism, Social and Economic Rights Panel (March 4, 2011).
16 See Manuel José Cepeda Espinosa. *Judicial Activism in a Violent Context* (2004); Manuel José Cepeda Espinosa. "Privacy." In *The Oxford Handbook of Comparative Constitutional Law*, edited by Michel Rosenfeld and András Sajo (Oxford, UK: Oxford University Press, 2012); Manuel José Cepeda Espinosa and David E. Landau. *Colombian Constitutional Law: Leading Cases* (New York, NY: Oxford University Press, 2017).
17 Manuel Cepeda is serving as the president of International Association of Constitutional Law for the term of 2014–2018. Please see http://www.iacl-aidc.org/en/about-the-iacl/organs-of-the-iacl.
18 Stephen Gardbaum. "Are Strong Constitutional Courts Always a Good Thing for New Democracies?" 53 *Colum. J. Transnat'l L.* 285, 306 (2015).
19 Ibid., 306.
20 Ibid., 307.
21 Andrew Arato and Zoltan Miklosi. "Constitution Making and Transitional Politics in Hungary." In *Framing the State in Times of Transition Case Studies in Constitution Making*, edited by Laurel Miller and Louis Aucoin (Washington, DC: United States Institute of Peace Press, 2010), 382.
22 Bruce Ackerman. *Future of Liberal Revolution* (Yale University Press, 2008).
23 Scheppele. *Guardians of the Constitution*, 1783.
24 Ibid., 1785. He took up a guest professorship at the University of Cologne but later returned to Budapest to teach at the new private Catholic law school, Peter Pazmany University. Nevertheless, Solyom remained popular in the public mind, and when the term of the Hungarian president was up in summer 2005, Solyom ran for presidential election and was elected by the parliament as the Hungarian president. He took office on August 5, 2005, and finished his term as president in August 2010.
25 See Alexei Trochev. *Judging Russia: Constitutional Court in Russian Politics, 1990–2006*. (Cambridge: Cambridge University Press, 2008), 193–195.
26 The Colombian Constitutional Court did not experience a steep decline in Hungary or Russia. David Landau argues that Colombia's dysfunctional party politics has been the primary factor behind the Court's unusually broad and enduring policy-making role. See David Landau. "Political Institutions and

Judicial Role in Comparative Constitutional Law," 51 *Harvard International Law Journal* 319 (2010).

27 Brown and Waller. *Constitutional Courts and Political Uncertainty*, 837.

28 Ibid., 837.

29 See Mark Tushnet. *Studying "Second Generation" Constitutional Courts: After the Heroes Have Left*, presentation at the Annual Meeting of Law and Society Association, New Orleans, June 2–5, 2016.

30 For a discussion of the cautious approach of the Court in its early years, see Theunis Roux. *The Politics of Principle: The First South African Constitutional Court, 1995–2005* (Cambridge: Cambridge University Press, 2013); see also Lynn Berat. "The Constitutional Court of South Africa and Jurisdictional Questions: In the Interest of Justice," 3 *Int'l J. Const. L.* 39 (2005).

31 Interview with Jimly Asshiddiqie, chief justice of the Indonesian Constitutional Court, in Jakarta, Indonesia. (July 31, 2006).

32 Ibid.

33 Gardbaum. *Are Strong Constitutional Courts Always a Good Thing for New Democracies?*, 318.

34 Rosalind Dixon and Samuel Issacharoff. "Living to Fight Another Day: Judicial Deferral in Defense of Democracy," 2016 *Wis. L. Rev.* 683, 723 (2016).

35 Ibid., 723.

36 Scheppele. *Guardians of the Constitution*, 1785.

37 See Trochev. *Judging Russia*, 193–195.

38 Herman Schwartz, *The Struggle for Constitutional Justice in Post-Communist Europe* (Chicago: University of Chicago Press, 2000), 159.

39 Carla Thorson. *Politics, Judicial Review and the Russian Constitutional Court* (Basingstoke: Palgrave Macmillan, 2012), 121–122. The docket shifted away from separation of powers and high profile jurisdictional disputes toward civil rights issues. While the Zorkin Court found more than two-thirds of the challenged laws unconstitutional, the Tumanoz court decided that little more than half the challenged laws were unconstitutional.

40 Ibid., 145.

41 Kim Lane Scheppele. "The New Hungarian Constitutional Court," 8 *E. Eur. Const. Rev.* 81 (1999).

42 See Kim Lane Scheppele. "How to Evade the Constitution: The Case of the Hungarian Constitutional Court's Decision on the Judicial Retirement Age." *Eutopialaw*, August 8, 2012. Accessed January 17, 2017. https://eutopialaw.com/2012/08/08/how-to-evade-the-constitution-the-case-of-the-hungarian-constitutional-courts-decision-on-the-judicial-retirement-age/; see also Kim Lane Scheppele. "Hungary's Constitutional Revolution." In Paul Krugman's blog of *The New York Times*, December 19, 2011. Accessed January 17, 2017. http://krugman.blogs.nytimes.com/2011/12/19/hungarys-constitutional-revolution/.

43 *Budapest Beacon*. "Pro-Fidesz Justice to Head Hungary's Constitutional Court," January 2, 2015. Accessed January 17, 2017. http://budapestbeacon.com/public-policy/pro-fidesz-justice-to-head-hungarys-constitutional-court/15720.

44 Langa was one of the first 11 justices appointed by President Mandela to the Constitutional Court led by Chaskalson, and so he had been working in the Court since its inception. See the official biography of Chief Justice Pius Langa at http://www.constitutionalcourt.org.za/site/judges/justicepiuslanga/index1.html.

45 Johann Krieger. "Chief Justice Pius Nkonzo Langa," *Advocate*, August 2005. www.sabar.co.za/law-journals/2005/august/2005-august-vol018-no2-pp33-35.pdf.

46 Dennis M. Davis. "Socioeconomic Rights: Do They Deliver the Goods?" 6(4) *Int J Constitutional Law* 687 (2008).

47 Pius Langa. "Transformative Constitutionalism," 17 *Stellenbosch L. Rev.* 351, 354–358 (2006).
48 See Stephen Ellmann. "The Struggle for the Rule of Law in South Africa," 60 *N.Y.L. Sch. L. Rev.* 57 (2015). The Court decision in *Glenister v President of the Republic of South Africa and Others*, 2009 (1) SA 287 (CC) (*Glenister I*) is notable as an instance of judicial restraint.
49 The 1996 Constitution of South Africa, Art. 176 (1).
50 *Enca.com*. "Moseneke Speaks on Being Overlooked for Chief Justice Position," May 21, 2016. Accessed July 10, 2017. http://www.enca.com/south-africa/moseneke-speaks-on-being-overlooked-for-chiefs-justice-position.
51 Nickolaus Bauer. "Chief Justice Sandile Ngcobo Hangs Up His Gavel." *The M&G Online*, July 27, 2011. Accessed July 10, 2017. https://mg.co.za/article/2011-07-27-chief-justice-sandile-ngcobo-to-step-down.
52 " *Sunday Independent*. "Moseneke in New Clash with Zuma," May 14, 2012. Accessed July 10, 2017. http://www.iol.co.za/sundayindependent/moseneke-in-new-clash-with-zuma-1296282.
53 *Glenister v. President of the Republic of South Africa and Others,* 2011 (3) SA 347 (CC) (*Glenister II*).
54 *Glenister v President of the Republic of South Africa and Others,* 2009 (1) SA 287 (CC) (*Glenister I*).
55 *Glenister II*, 88–89.
56 This argument was originally developed by Mark Tushnet, see Tushnet. *Studying "Second Generation" Constitutional Courts.*
57 Ibid.

References

Ackerman, Bruce. *Future of Liberal Revolution*. New Haven, CT: Yale University Press, 2008.

Aditjondro, George J. *Dari Soeharto ke Habibie: Guru Kencing Berdiri, Murid Kencing Berlari; Kedua Puncak Korupsi, Kolusi, dan Nepotisme Rezim Orde Baru*. Jakarta: Masyarakat Indonesia Untuk Kemanusiaan, 1998.

Aep, Zaenal Abidin and Lisa Suroso, *Setengah Abad Jimly Asshiddiqie, Konstitusi dan Semangat Kebangsaan*. Jakarta: Perhimpunan Indonesia Tionghoa & Majelis Tinggi Agama Khonghucu Indonesia, 2006.

Akbar, Patrialis. *Hubungan Lembaga Kepresidenan dengan Dewan Perwakilan Rakyat dan Veto Presiden*. Yogyakarta: Total Media, 2013.

Alberst, Susan et al., "Democratization and Countermajoritarian Institutions: The Role of Power and Constitutional Design in Self-enforcing Democracy." In *Comparative Constitutional Design*, edited by Tom Ginsburg. New York: Cambridge University Press, 2014.

Amar, Akhil Reed. "Hugo Black and the Hall of Fame," 53 *Ala L. Rev*. 1221 (2002).

Anderson, Benedict. "Impunity and Reenactment: Reflections on the 1965 Massacre in Indonesia and its Legacy," 11(15) *The Asia-Pacific Journal* 1 (April 15, 2013).

Anderson IV, Robert. "Measuring Meta-Doctrine: An American Assessment of Judicial Minimalism in the Supreme Court," 32 *Harv. J.L. & Pub. Pol'y* 1045 (2009).

Arato, Andrew and Zoltan Miklosi, "Constitution Making and Transitional Politics in Hungary." In *Framing the State in Times of Transition: Case Studies in Constitution Making*, edited by Laurel Miller and Louis Aucoin. Washington, DC: United States Institute of Peace Press, 2010.

Aristotle. In *The Basic Works of Aristotle*, edited by Richard Mckeon. New York: Random House, 1941.

Asshiddiqie, Jimly. *Gagasan Kedaulatan Rakyat dalam Konstitusi dan Pelaksanaannya di Indonesia: Pergeseran Keseimbangan antara Individualisme dan Kolektivisme dalam Kebijakan Demokrasi Politik dan Demokrasi Ekonomi selama tiga masa demokrasi, 1945–1980-an*. Jakarta: Ichtiar Baru Van Hoeve, 1994.

Asshiddiqie, Jimly. *Format Kelembagaan Negara Dan Pergeseran Kekuasaan Dalam UUD 45*. Yogyakarta: FH UII Press, 2004.

Asshiddiqie, Jimly. "Setahun Mahkamah Konstitusi: Refleksi, Gagasan Dan Penyelenggaraan, Serta Setangkup Harapan." In *Menjaga Denyut Konstitusi: Refleksi Satu Tahun Mahkamah Konstitusi*, edited by Refly Harun, Zainal A.M. Husein, and Bisariyadi. Jakarta: Konstitusi Press, 2004.

Asshiddiqie, Jimly. "Pidato Refleksi Akhir Tahun 2004: Agenda Konsolidasi dan Rekonstrusi Nasional Mengisi Paruh Kedua Era Transisi." [The 2004 End of Year Reflection: Agenda for National Consolidation and Reconstruction to fulfil the Second Stage of Transition] (Speech at the Constitutional Court of Indonesia, Jakarta, December 29, 2004).

Asshiddiqie, Jimly. *Hukum Tata Negara dan Pilar—Pilar Demokrasi: Serpihan Pemikiran Hukum, Media dan HAM.* Jakarta: Konstitusi Press, 2005.

Asshiddiqie, Jimly. *Model—Model Pengujian Konstitusional di Berbagai Negara.* Jakarta: Konstitusi Press, 2005.

Asshiddiqie, Jimly. *Sengketa Kewenangan Antarlembaga Negara.* Jakarta: Konstitusi Press, 2005.

Asshiddiqie, Jimly. *Hukum Acara Pengujian Undang—Undang.* Jakarta: Sekretariat Jenderal Mahkamah Konstitusi, 2006.

Asshiddiqie, Jimly. *Konstitusi dan Konstitutionalism Indonesia.* Jakarta: Sekretariat Jenderal Mahkamah Konstitusi, 2006.

Asshiddiqie, Jimly. Pembangunan Hukum dan Penegakan Hukum di Indonesia. Paper prepared for the 55th anniversary of Faculty of Law, Gadjah Mada University, February 5, 2006.

Asshiddiqie, Jimly. *Pokok—Pokok Hukum Tata Negara Indonesia Pasca Reformasi.* Jakarta: Bhuana Ilmu Populer, 2007.

Asshiddiqie, Jimly. Address at the Opening Plenary Workshop on "Constitutional Court and Democracy in Indonesia: Judging the First Decade," University of New South Wales, December 11, 2014.

Asshiddiqie, Jimly. "Islam, Democracy, and the Future of the Death Penalty." Public Lecture presented by the Centre for Indonesian Law, Islam and Society, the Asian Law Centre and the Melbourne Law School, University of Melbourne, August 11, 2015a.

Asshiddiqie, Jimly. "Missing History?: Interview with Jimly Asshiddiqie on the Death Penalty in Indonesia." By Tim Mann. *Indonesia at Melbourne.* (August 11, 2015b).

Asrun, Muhammad. *Krisis Peradilan: Mahkamah Agung di Bawah Soeharto.* Jakarta: ELSAM, 2004.

Barak Ahron. "A Judge on Judging: The Role of a Supreme Court in a Democracy," 116 *Harv. L. Rev.* 16 (November, 2002).

Barak, Ahron. *The Judge in a Democracy.* Princeton, New Jersey: Princeton University Press, 2006.

Barnouw, Jeffrey. *Odysseus, Hero of Practical Intelligence: Deliberation and Signs in Homer's Odyssey.* Lanham, MD: University Press of America, 2004.

Bedner, Adriaan W. *Administrative Court in Indonesia, A Socio-Legal Study.* Doctoral Dissertation, Rijkuniversiteit Leiden, 2000.

Belknap, Michael R. "Earl Warren Professorship Acceptance Speech," 39 *Cal W. Int'l L.J.* 366 (2009).

Berat, Lynn. "The Constitutional Court of South Africa and Jurisdictional Questions: In the Interest of Justice," 3 *Int'l J. Const. L.* 39 (2005).

Bloch, Susan L. "The Marbury Mystery: Why Did William Marbury Sue in the Supreme Court?" 18 *Const. Commentary* 607 (2001).

Bolt, Robert. *A Man for All Seasons: A Play in Two Acts.* New York: Random House, 1962.

Bourchier, David. "Law, Crime, and State Authority in Indonesia." In *State and Civil Society in Indonesia*, edited by Arief Budiman. Clayton, Victoria: Centre for South-east Asian Studies, Monash University, 1990.

Bourchier, David. *Illiberal Democracy in Indonesia: The Ideology of the Family-State.* New York: Routledge, 2015.

Bozoki, Andras, ed. *The Roundtable Talks of 1989: The Genesis of Hungarian Democracy.* Budapest: Central European University Press, 2002.

Bozoki, Andras and Gergely Karacsony. "The Making of a Political Elite: Participants in the Hungarian Roundtable Talks of 1989." In *The Roundtable Talks of 1989: The Genesis of Hungarian Democracy,*edited by Andras Bozoki. Budapest: Central European University Press, 2002.

Brown, Nathan and Julian G. Waller, "Constitutional Courts and Political Uncertainty: Constitutional Ruptures and the Rule of Judges," 14 *Int J Constitutional Law,* 817–850 (2016).

Budiarti, Rita. *On the Record: Mahfud M.D. di Balik Putusan Mahkamah Konstitusi.* Jakarta: Murai Kencana, Konstitusi Press, 2010.

Budiarti, Rita. *Biografi Mahfud MD: Terus Mengalir.* Jakarta: Konstitusi Press, 2013.

Budiarti, Rita. *Kontroversi Mahfud: Di Balik Putusan Mahkamah Konstitusi Jilid 2.* Jakarta: Konstitusi Press, 2013.

Butt, Simon. "Judicial Review in Indonesia: Between Civil Law and Accountability? A Study of Constitutional Court Decisions 2003–2005." Unpublished PhD dissertation, University of Melbourne, 2006.

Butt, Simon. *Corruption and Law in Indonesia.* London: Routledge, 2012.

Butt, Simon."Indonesia's Constitutional Court: Conservative Activist or Strategic Operator?" In *The Judicialization of Politics in Asia,* edited by Bjorn Dressel. London: Routledge, 2012.

Butt, Simon. *The Constitutional Court and Democracy in Indonesia.* Leiden, the Netherlands: Brill, Nijhoff, 2015.

Butt, Simon and David Hansell, "The Masykur Abdul Kadir Case: Indonesian Constitutional Court Decision No. 013/PUU-I/2003," (6)2 *Australian Journal of Asian Law* 176 (2004).

Butt, Simon and Tim Lindsey, *The Constitution of Indonesia: A Contextual Analysis.* Oxford: Hart Publishing, 2012.

Butt, Simon and Fritz E. Siregar. "State Control over Natural Resources in Indonesia: Implications of the Oil and Natural Gas Law Case of 2012," 31(2) *Journal of Energy & Natural Resources of Law* 107 (2013).

Brenner, Saul, and Harold J. Spaeth. "Majority Opinion Assignments and the Maintenance of the Original Coalition on the Warren Court," 32 *American Journal of Political Science* 72–81 (1988).

Brown, Nathan J. *The Rule of Law in the Arab World: Courts in Egypt and the Gulf.* Cambridge: Cambridge University Press, 1997.

Brown, Nathan J. *Constitutions in a Nonconstitutional World: Arab Basic Laws and the Prospects for Accountable Government.* Albany, NY: State University of New York, 2002.

Brown, Nathan J. "Reason, Interest, Rationality, and Passion in Constitution Drafting." 6(4) *Perspectives on Politics* 675–689 (2008).

Cammack, Mark, Lawrence Young, and Tim B. Heaton, "Legislating Social Change in an Islamic Society: Indonesia's Marriage Law," 44(1) *American Journal of Comparative Law* 45 (1996).

Cammack, Mark. "Indonesia's 1989 Religious Judicature Act: Islamization of Indonesia or Indonesianization of Islam?" 63 *Indonesia* 143–168 (1997).

Cammack, Mark E. and R. Michael Feener, "The Islamic Legal System in Indonesia," 21 *Pac. Rim L. & Pol'y J.* 13 (2012).

Cappelletti, Mauro. *The Judicial Process in Comparative Perspective.* Oxford; New York: Clarendon Press, 1989.

Cepeda Espinosa, Manuel José. "Judicial Activism in a Violent Context: The Origin, Role, and Impact of the Colombian Constitutional Court," 3 *Wash. U. Glob. Stud. L. Rev.* 529 (2004).

Cepeda Espinosa, Manuel José. "Social and Economic Rights and the Colombian Constitutional Court," Remarks at the Texas Law Review Symposium, Latin American Constitutionalism, Social and Economic Rights Panel (March 4, 2011).

Cepeda Espinosa, Manuel José. "Privacy." In *The Oxford Handbook of Comparative Constitutional Law*, edited by Michel Rosenfeld and András Sajó. Oxford: Oxford University Press, 2012.

Cepeda Espinosa, Manuel José, and David E. Landau. *Colombian Constitutional Law: Leading Cases.* New York, NY: Oxford University Press, 2017.

Chaskalson, Arthur. "From Wickedness to Equality: The Moral Transformation of South African Law," 1(4) *Int J Constitutional Law* 590 (2003).

Cha, Dongwook. "The Role of the Korean Constitutional Court in the Democratization of South Korea." Unpublished PhD dissertation, University of Southern California, 2005.

Cheema, Moeen H. "The 'Chaudry Court': Deconstructing the 'Judicialization of Politics' in Pakistan," 25 *Washington International Law Journal* 448 (2016).

Chemerinsky, Erwin. *Constitutional Law: Principles and Policies.* New York: Aspen Law & Business, 2011.

Couso, Javier, Alexandra Huneeus, and Rachel Sieder. *Cultures of Legality Judicialization and Political Activism in Latin America.* Cambridge, UK: Cambridge University Press, 2010.

Croissant, Aurel. "Provisions, Practices and Performances of Constitutional Review in Democratizing East Asia," 23(5) *The Pacific Review* 548–578 (2010).

Crouch Harold A. *The Army and Politics in Indonesia.* Ithaca: Cornell University Press, 1988.

Crouch, Melissa A. "Law and Religion in Indonesia: The Constitutional Court and the Blasphemy Law," 7(1) *Asian J. Comp. L.* 1–45 (2012).

Crouch, Melissa. *Law and Religion in Indonesia: Conflict and the Courts in West Java.* London and New York: Routledge, 2014.

D'Amour, Donald Henry. "Aristotle on Heroes." Unpublished Ph.D. Dissertation, University of Notre Dame, 1971.

Danelski, David J. "The Influence of the Chief Justice in the Decisional Process." In *Courts, Judges, & Politics: An Introduction to the Judicial Process*, edited by Walter F. Murphy, C. Herman Pritchett, and Lee Epstein. Boston: McGraw-Hill, 5th ed. 2002.

Davis, Dennis M. "Socioeconomic Rights: Do They Deliver the Goods?" 6(4) *Int J Constitutional Law* 687 (2008).

Davis, Sue. "The Chief Justice and Judicial Decision-Making: The Institutional Basis for Leadership on the Supreme Court." In *Supreme Court Decision-Making*, edited by Cornell Clayton and Howard Gillman. Chicago: University of Chicago Press, 1999.

Deneen, Patrick J. *The Odyssey of Political Theory: The Politics of Departure and Return.* Lanham: Rowman & Littlefield Publishers, 2000.

Dhakidae, Daniel. *Cendekiawan dan Kekuasaan dalam Negara Orde Baru.* Jakarta: Gramedia Pustaka Utama, 2003.

Dixon, Rosalind and Eric Posner. "The Limits of Constitutional Convergence," 11 *Chi. J. Int'l L.* 399 (2011).

Dixon, Rosalind and Tom Ginsburg, "Deciding Not to Decide: Deferral in Constitutional Design," 9(3–4) *Int'l J. Const. L.* 636 (2011).

Dixon, Rosalind and Samuel Issacharoff, "Living to Fight Another Day: Judicial Deferral in Defense of Democracy," *Wis. L. Rev.* 683 (2016).

Dworkin, Ronald. *Law's Empire.* Cambridge, MA: Belknap Press, 1986.

Edelamn, Paul H. and Jim Chen, "The Most Dangerous Justice: The Supreme Court at the Bar of Mathematics," 70 S. *Cal. L. Rev.* 63 (1996).

Edelman, Paul H. and Jim Chen, "The Most Dangerous Justice Rides Again: Revisiting the Power Pageant of the Justices," 86 *Minn. L. Rev.* 131 (2001).

Effendy, Bachtiar. *Islam and the State in Indonesia.* Singapore: Institute of Southeast Asian Studies, 2003.

Elkins, Zachary. "Constitutional Networks." In *Networked Politics: Agency, Power, and Governance*, edited by M. Kahler. Ithaca, NY: Cornell University Press, 2009.

Ellis, Andrew. "The Indonesian Constitutional Transition: Conservatism or Fundamental Change?" 6 *Sing. J. Int'l & Comp. L.* 116 (2002).

Ellmann, Stephen. "The Struggle for the Rule of Law in South Africa," 60 *N.Y.L. Sch. L. Rev.* 57 (2015).

Elster, Jon. *Ulysses and the Sirens: Studies in Rationality and Irrationality.* Cambridge, UK: Cambridge University Press, 1979.

Elster, Jon. *Ulysses Unbound: Studies in Rationality, Precommitment, and Constraints.* Cambridge; New York: Cambridge University Press, 2000.

Elster, Jon. "Don't Burn Your Bridge before You Come to It: Some Ambiguities and Complexities of Precommitment," 81 *Tex. L. Rev.* 1751 (2003).

Elster, Jon, Claus Offe, and Ulrich Klaus Preuss. *Institutional Design in Post-communist Societies: Rebuilding the Ship at Sea.* Cambridge, UK: Cambridge University Press, 1998.

Epstein, Lee and Thomas G. Walker. "The Role of the Supreme Court in American Society: Playing the Reconstruction Game." In *Contemplating Courts*, edited by Lee Epstein. Washington DC: CQ Press, 1995.

Erdos, David O. *Delegating Rights Protection: The Rise of Bills of Rights in the Westminster World.* Oxford: Oxford University Press, 2010.

Fadjar, Abdul Mukthie. *Hukum Konstitusi & Mahkamah Konstitusi.* Jakarta: Konstitusi Press; & Yogyakarta: Citra Media, 2006.

Fadjar, Abdul Mukthie. *2037 Hari Mengawal Konstitusi.* Malang, Indonesia: In-Trans Publishing, 2010.

Fenwick, Stewart. *Blasphemy, Islam and the State: Pluralism and Liberalism in Indonesia.* New York: Routledge, 2017.

Ferejohn, John and Pasquale Pasquino. "Constitutional Adjudication: Lessons from Europe," 82 *Tex. L. Rev.* 1671 (2004).

Finkel, Jodi. *Judicial Reform as Political Insurance: Argentina, Peru, and Mexico in the 1990s.* Notre Dame, Ind.: University of Notre Dame Press, 2008.

Finkelberg, Margalit. "Odysseus and the Genus 'Hero'," 42(1) *Greece and Rome* (Second Series) 1–14 (1995).

Fiss, Owen. *Pillars of Justice: Lawyers and the Liberal Tradition.* Cambridge, Massachusetts: Harvard University Press, 2017.

Fontana, David. "The Rise and Fall of Comparative Constitutional Law in the Postwar Era," 36 *Yale J. Int'l L.* 1 (2011).

Formichi, Chiara and R. Michael Feener. *Shi'ism in Southeast Asia: 'Alid Piety and Sectarian Constructions.* Oxford; New York, NY: Oxford University Press, 2015.

Gaffar, Affan. *Javanese Voters: A Case Study of Election under a Hegemonic Party System.* Yogyakarta, Indonesia: Gadjah Mada University Press, 1992.

Gardbaum, Stephen. *The New Commonwealth Model of Constitutionalism: Theory and Practice.* Cambridge: Cambridge University Press, 2013.

Gardbaum, Stephen. "Are Strong Constitutional Courts Always a Good Thing for New Democracies?" 53 *Colum. J. Transnat'l L.* 285, 309 (2015).

Garoupa, Nuno and Tom Ginsburg. *Judicial Reputation: A Comparative Theory.* Chicago; London: The University of Chicago Press, 2015.

Gava, John. "The Rise of the Hero Judge," 24 *University of New South Wales Law Journal* 747 (2001).

George, Tracey E. and Albert H. Yoon, "Chief Judges: The Limits of Attitudinal Theory and Possible Paradox of Managerial Judging," 61 *Vand. L. Rev.* 1 (2008).

Gewirtz, Paul. "A Lawyer's Death," 100 *Harv. L. Rev.* 2053 (1987).

Ghias, Shoaib A. "Miscarriage of Chief Justice: Judicial Power and the Legal Complex in Pakistan under Musharraf," 35(4) *Law & Soc. Inquiry* 985 (2010).

Ginsburg, Tom. "Economic Analysis and the Design of Constitutional Courts," 3(1) *Theoretical Inquiries L.* 49 (January, 2002).

Ginsburg, Tom. *Judicial Review in New Democracies: Constitutional Courts in Asian Cases.* Cambridge, MA: Cambridge University Press, 2003.

Ginsburg, Tom and Zachary Elkins, "Designing a Judiciary: Ancillary Powers of Constitutional Courts," 87 *Tex. L. Rev.* 1431 (June, 2009).

Ginsburg, Tom and Mila Versteeg, "Why Do Countries Adopt Constitutional Review?" 30(3) *The Journal of Law, Economics and Organization*, 587–682 (2013).

Glendon, Mary Ann. *Abortion and Divorce in Western Law.* Cambridge, MA: Harvard University Press, 1987.

Goldstein, Joel K. "Leading the Court: Studies in Influence as Chief Justice," 40 *Stetson L. Rev.* 717 (2011).

Gordon, Sarah Barringer. "The Creation of a Usable Judicial Past: Max Lerner, Class Conflict, and the Propagation of Judicial Titans," 70 *N.Y.U. L. REV.* 622 (1995).

Griffin, J. *Homer on Life and Death.* Oxford: Clarendon Press, 1980.

Habibie, Bacharuddin Jusuf. *Decisive Moments: Indonesia's Long Road to Democracy.* Jakarta: Ilthabi Rekatama, 2006.

Harman, Benny K. "Perkembangan Pemikiran Mengenai Perlunya Pengujian UU Terhadap UUD Dalam Sejarah Ketatanegaraan Indonesia (1945–2004)." Unpublished PhD dissertation, University of Indonesia, 2006.

Harris, J. W. "Unger's Critique of Formalism in Legal Reasoning: Hero, Hercules, and Humdrum," 52(1) *Mod. L. Rev.* 42 (1989).

Hasen, Richard L. "Constitutional Avoidance and Anti-Avoidance by the Roberts Court," *Sup. Ct. Rev.* 181 (2009).

Hendrianto, Stefanus. "From Humble Beginning to a Functioning Court: The Indonesian Constitutional Court, 2003–2008." Unpublished doctoral dissertation, University of Washington, 2008.

Hendrianto, Stefanus. "Institutional Choice and the New Indonesia Constitutional Court." In *New Courts in Asia*, edited by Andrew Harding and Penelope Nicholson. London; New York: Routledge Taylor & Francis Group, 2011.

Hendrianto, Stefanus. "The Indonesian General Election and the 'Weak' Constitutional Court," *I-CONnect*: Blog of the *Int'l J. Const. L.* June 4, 2014.

Hendrianto, Stefanus. "The Indonesian Constitutional Court in Crisis over the Chief Justice's Term Limit," *Int'l J. Const. L.* Blog, Feb. 5, 2015.

Hendrianto, Stefanus. "The Rise and Fall of Heroic Chief Justices: Constitutional Politics and Judicial Leadership in Indonesia," 25 *Washington International Law Journal*, 489–563, (June, 2016).

Hendrianto, Stefanus. "A Curious Case of Weak-Form-Review: On Judicial Review of Electoral Process in Indonesia." In *Judicial Review of Elections in Asia*, edited by Yap Po Jen. London: Routledge, 2016.

Hendrianto, Stefanus. "The Divergence of a Wandering Court: Socio-Economic Rights in the Indonesian Constitutional Court," 16(2) *The Australian Journal of Asian Law* Article 5, (2016).

Hendrianto, Stefanus. "Judicial Power and Strategic Communication in Indonesia." In *Justices and Journalists: Global Perspective*, edited by Richard Davis. Cambridge: Cambridge University Press, 2017.

Heryanto, Ariel. *State Terrorism and Political Identity in Indonesia: Fatally Belonging*. London; New York: Routledge, 2006.

Hidayat, Arief. *Kebebasan Berserikat di Indonesia: Suatu Analisis Pengaruh Perubahan Sistem Politik Terhadap Penafsiran Hukum*. Semarang: Badan Penerbit Universitas Diponegoro, 2006.

Hicks, Jacqueline. "The Missing Link: Explaining the Political Mobilization of Islam in Indonesia," 42(1) *Journal of Contemporary Asia* 46 (2012).

Higgins, Benjamin. *Economic Development: Problems, Principles, and Policies*. New York: W. W. Norton, 1968.

Hirschl, Ran. *Towards Juristocracy: The Origins and Consequence of the New Constitutionalism*. Cambridge, MA: Harvard University Press, 2004.

Homer. *The Odyssey*. Translated by Martin Hammond. London: Duckworth, 2000.

Horowitz, Donald L. *Constitutional Change and Democracy in Indonesia*. Cambridge UK: Cambridge University Press, 2013.

Hosen, Nadisryah. "The Constitutional Court and 'Islamic' Judges in Indonesia," 16(2) *Australian Journal of Asian Law* Article 4 (2016).

Indrayana, Denny. *Indonesian Constitutional Reform 1999–2002: An Evaluation of Constitutional Making in Transition*. Jakarta: Kompas Book Publishing, 2008.

Irawan, Aguk. *Biografi Mahfud: Cahayamu Tak Bisa Kutawar*. Yogyakarta: Ar-Ruzz Media, 2014.

Irons, Peter. *Brennan vs. Rehnquist: The Battle for the Constitution*. New York: Knopf, 1994.

Issacharoff, Samuel. "The Enabling Role of Democratic Constitutionalism: Fixed Rules and Some Implications for Contested Presidential Elections," 81 *Tex. L. Rev.* 1985 (2002).

Johnson, Herbert Alan. *The Chief Justiceship of John Marshall, 1801–1835*. Columbia, SC: University of South Carolina Press, 1998.

Kagan, Robert A. "On Responsive Law." In *Legality and Community: On the Intellectual Legacy of Philip Selznick*, edited by Robert A. Kagan, Martin Krygier, and Kenneth I. Winston. Lanham, MD: Rowman & Littlefield, 2002.

Kahin, George. *Nationalism and Revolution in Indonesia*. Cornell University: Ithaca, New York, 1952.

Kahn, Paul. "Owen Fiss: Heroism in the Law," 58 *U. Miami L. Rev.* 103 (2003).

Kapiszewski, Diana. *High Courts and Economic Governance in Argentina and Brazil*. Cambridge: Cambridge University Press, 2012.

Kapiszewski, Diana, Gordon Silverstein and Robert A. Kagan. "On Judicial Ships and Winds of Change." In *Consequential Courts: Judicial Roles in Global Perspective*, edited by Diana Kapiszewski, Gordon Silverstein and Robert A. Kagan. New York: Cambridge University Press, 2013.

Kassim, Yang Razali. *Transition Politics in Southeast Asia: Dynamics of Leadership Change and Succession in Indonesia and Malaysia*. Singapore; New York: Marshall Cavendish Academic, 2005.

Kay, Richard S. "Standing to Raise Constitutional Issues: A Comparative Analysis." In *Standing to Raise Constitutional Issues: Comparative Perspectives*, edited by Richard S. Kay. Bruxelles: Bruylant, 2005.

Kelsen, Hans. "Judicial Review of Legislation," 4(2) *The Journal of Politics* 183–200 (May, 1942).

Kempton, Kate and Malcolm MacLaren. "The Protection of Human Rights in South Africa: A Conversation with Justice Arthur Chaskalson, President of the Constitutional Court of South Africa," 56 *U.T. Fac. L. Rev.* 161 (1998).

Kenawas, Yoes Chandra. "The Rise of Political Dynasties in Decentralized Indonesia." Unpublished Master's Thesis, Rajaratnam School of International Studies, 2013.

Kende, Mark S. *Constitutional Rights in Two Worlds: South Africa and the United States*. Cambridge, UK: Cambridge University Press, 2009.

Kennedy, Charles. "The Judicialization of Politics in Pakistan." In *The Judicialization of Politics in Asia*, edited by Bjorn Dressel. London: Routledge, 2012.

King, Blair. "Empowering the Presidency: Interests and Perceptions in Indonesia's Constitutional Reforms, 1999–2002." Unpublished PhD dissertation, the Ohio State University, 2004.

Klingsberg, Ethan. "Judicial Review and Hungary's Transition from Communism to Democracy: The Constitutional Court, The Continuity of Law, and the Redefinition of Property Rights," 1992(1) *B.Y.U. L. Rev.* 41, 78–81 (1992).

Klingsberg, Ethan. "Contextualizing the Calculus of Consent: Judicial Review of Legislative Wealth Transfers in a Transition to Democracy and Beyond," 27 *Cornell Int'l L.J.* 303 (1994).

Klug, Heinz. "Constitutional Authority and Judicial Pragmatism: Politics and Law in the Evolution of South Africa Constitutional Court." In *Consequential Courts: Judicial Roles in Global Perspective*, edited by Diana Kapiszewski, Gordon Silverstein and Robert A. Kagan. New York: Cambridge University Press, 2013.

Knight, Jack and Lee Epstein. "On the Struggle for Judicial Supremacy," 30 *Law and Society Review* 87 (1996).

Kobylka, Joseph F. "Leadership on the Supreme Court of the United States: Chief Justice Burger and the Establishment Clause," 42(4) *Western Political Quarterly* 545–568 (1989).

Kohen, Ari. *Untangling Heroism: Classical Philosophy and the Concept of the Hero*. New York: Routledge, 2014.

Kommers, Donald P. *The Constitutional Jurisprudence of the Federal Republic of Germany*. Durham, NC: Duke University Press, 1997.

Krieger, Johann. "Chief Justice Pius Nkonzo Langa," *Advocate* (August 2005).

Landau, David. "Political Institutions and Judicial Role in Comparative Constitutional Law," 51 *Harv. Int'l L.J.* 319, 329 (2010).

Landau, David. "A Dynamic Theory of Judicial Role," 55 *B.C. L. Rev.* 1501 (2014).

Langa, Pius. "Transformative Constitutionalism," 17 *Stellenbosch L. Rev.* 351 (2006).
Law, David. "The Evolution and Ideology of Global Constitutionalism," 99 Calif. L. Rev. 1163 (2011).
Law, David. "Judicial Comparativism and Judicial Diplomacy," 163 *U. Pa. L. Rev.* 927 (2015).
Lee, Randy, "Legal Ethics for Government Lawyers: Straight Talk for Tough Times: Robert Bolt's *A Man for All Seasons* and the Art of Discerning Integrity," 9 *Widener J. Pub. L.* 305 (2000).
Lev, Daniel S. *The Transition to Guided Democracy: Indonesian Politics, 1957–1959.* Ithaca, N.Y: Modern Indonesia Project, Southeast Asia Program, Dept. of Asian Studies, Cornell University, 1983.
Lev, Daniel S. *Legal Evolution and Political Authority in Indonesia: Selected Essays.* The Hague: Kluwer Law International, 2000.
Liddle, R. William. "Year One of the Yudhoyono—Kalla Duumvirate," 41(3) *Bulletin of Indonesian Economic Studies* 325–340 (2005).
Lin, Chien-Chih. *The Judicialization of Politics in New Democracies.* Unpublished doctoral dissertation, University of Chicago, 2015.
Lin, Chien-Chih. "Pace of Constitutional Transition Matters: The Judicialization of Politics in Indonesia and Korea," 20 *UCLA J Int'L & For. Aff.* 275 (Fall, 2016).
Lindberg, Todd. *The Heroic Heart: Greatness Ancient and Modern.* New York: Encounter Books, 2015.
Lindsey, Timothy. "Indonesian Constitutional Reform: Muddling Towards Democracy," 6 *Sing. J. Int'l & Comp. L.* 244 (2002).
Linnan, David K. "Indonesian Law Reform, or Once More unto the Breach: A Brief Institutional History," 1(1) *Australian Journal of Asian Law* 1 (1999).
Logan, Donal. *Excommunication and the Secular Arm in Medieval England: A Study in Legal Procedure from the Thirteenth to the Sixteenth Century.* Toronto: Political Institute of Mediaeval Studies, 1968.
MacIntyre, Andrew. *The Power of Institutions: Political Architecture and Governance.* Ithaca, New York: Cornell University Press, 2003.
Mahfud MD, Mohammad. *Politik Hukum di Indonesia.* Jakarta: LP3ES, 1998.
Mahfud MD, Mohammad. *Konstitusi dan Hukum Dalam Kontroversi Isu.* Jakarta: Rajawali Pers, 2009.
Mahkamah Konstitusi. *Sejarah Pembangunan Gedung Mahkamah Konstitusi.* Jakarta: Sekretariat Jenderal Mahkamah Konstitusi, 2007.
Mahkmah Konstitusi. *Upholding the Constitutional Democratic State: The 2011 Annual Report of the Indonesian Constitutional Court.* Jakarta: Sekretariat Jendral Mahkamah Konstitusi, 2011.
Makarim, Nono Anwar. "Press Freedom in Indonesia: A Case of Draconian Laws, Statutory Misinterpretation, but Still One of the Freest in Southeast Asia," 3 *J. Civ. L. Stud.* 131 (2010).
Mallarangeng, Rizal. "Liberalizing New Order Indonesia: Ideas, Epistemic Community, and Economic Policy Change, 1986–1992." Unpublished Dissertation, Ohio State University, 2000.
Mallarangeng, Rizal. *Mendobrak sentralisme ekonomi Indonesia, 1986–1992.* Jakarta: Kepustakaan Populer Gramedia, 2002.
Maltzman, Forrest and Paul J. Wahlbeck. "May it Please the Chief? Opinion Assignments in the Rehnquist Court," *American Journal of Political Science* 421–443 (1996).

Marginson, Simon and Erlenawati Sawir. "University Leaders' Strategies in the Global Environment: A Comparative Study of Universitas Indonesia and the Australian National University," 52(2) *Higher Education* 343–373 (2006).

Marin, Pamela. *Blood in the Forum: The Struggle for the Roman Republic*. London: Continuum, 2009.

Marzuki, Laica. *Berjalan Jalan di Ranah Hukum: Pikiran-Pikiran Lepas Laica Marzuki*. Jakarta: Konstitusi Pers, 2005.

Maveety, Nancy. *Queen's Court: Judicial Power in the Rehnquist Era*. Lawrence, Kansas: University Press of Kansas, 2008.

Mercer, Peter P. "The Citizen's Right to Sue in the Public Interest: The Roman Actio Popularis Revisited," 21 *U.W. Ont. L. Rev.* 89 (1983).

Merrill, Thomas. "The Making of the Second Rehnquist Court: A Preliminary Analysis," 47 *St. Louis U.L.J.* 569 (2003).

Michelman, Frank, I. "Foreword: Traces of Self-Government," 100 *Harv. L. Rev.* 4 (1986).

Mietzner, Marcus. "Political Conflict Resolution and Democratic Consolidation in Indonesia: The Role of the Constitutional Court," 10(3) *Journal of East Asian Studies* 397 (2010).

Mirrow, M. C. "Marbury in Mexico: Judicial Review's Precocious Southern Migration," 35 *Hastings Const. L.Q.* 41 (2007).

Mochtar, Akil. *Pembalikan Beban Pembuktian Tindak Pidana Korupsi*. Jakarta: Sekretariat Jenderal dan Kepaniteraan, Mahkamah Konstitusi, 2009.

Morris, Robert J. "China's Marbury: Qi Yuling v. Chen Xiaoqi—The Once and Future Trial of Both Education & Constitutionalization," 2 *Tsinghua China L. Rev.* 273 (2010).

Moustafa, Tamir. *The Struggle for Constitutional Power: Law, Politics, and Economic Development in Egypt*. New York: Cambridge University Press, 2007.

Murphy, Walter F. "Marshaling the Court: Leadership, Bargaining, and the Judicial Process," 29 *U. Chi. L. Rev.* 640 (1962).

Nasution, Adnan Buyung. "Towards Constitutional Democracy in Indonesia," Inaugural Professorial Lecture, University of Melbourne, October 20, 2010.

Newmyer, R. K. *John Marshall and the Heroic Age of the Supreme Court*. Baton Rouge: LSU Press, 2001.

Nonet, Philippe and Philip Selznick. *Law and Society in Transition: Toward Responsive Law*. New York: Octagon Books, 1978.

Nugroho, Heru. "The Political Economy of Higher Education: The University as An Arena for the Struggle for Power." In *Social Science and Power in Indonesia*, edited by Vedi R. Hadiz and Daniel Dhakidae. Jakarta: Equinox Publishing, 2005.

Nunes, Rodrigo M. "Ideational Origins of Progressive Judicial Activism: The Colombian Constitutional Court and the Right to Health," 52 *L. Am. Pol. & Soc.* 67 (2010).

Okoth-Ogendo, H. W. O. "Constitutions Without Constitutionalism: Reflections on an African Political Paradox." In *Constitutionalism and Democracy: Transitions in the Contemporary World*, edited by Douglas Greenberg. New York: Oxford University Press, 1993.

Palguna, I Dewa Gede. *Mahkamah Konstitusi, Judicial Review, dan Welfare State: Kumpulan Pemikiran*. Jakarta: Sekretariat Jenderal dan Kepaniteraan, Mahkamah Konstitusi, Republik Indonesia, 2008a.

Palguna, I Dewa Gede. *Jalan panjang hingga ke Medan Merdeka Barat: Perjalanan & Pemikiran Hukum I Dewa Gede Palguna (Hakim Konstitusi periode 2003–2008).* Jakarta: Sekretariat Jenderal dan Kepaniteraan, Mahkamah Konstitusi, 2008b.

Palguna, I Dewa Gede. *Nasionalisme, Identitas, dan Kegelisahan: Kumpulan Orasi I Dewa Gede Palguna, Hakim Konstitusi Periode 2003–2008.* Jakarta: Sekretariat Jenderal dan Kepaniteraan, Mahkamah Konstitusi, 2008c.

Palguna, I Dewa Gede. *Saya Sungguh Mencemaskan Bali: Sebuah Kumpulan Tulisan.* Jakarta: Sekretariat Jenderal dan Kepaniteraan, Mahkamah Konstitusi, 2008d.

Palguna. I Dewa Gede. *Pengaduan Konstitusional: Upaya Hukum Terhadap Pelanggaran Hak-hak Konstitusional Warga Negara.* Jakarta : Penerbit Sinar Grafika, 2013.

Park, Jonghyun. "The Judicialization of Politics in Korea," 10 *Asian-Pacific L. & Pol'y J.* 62 (2008).

Patapan, Haig. "Leadership, Law and Legitimacy: Reflections on the Changing Nature of Judicial Politics in Asia." In *The Judicialization of Politics in Asia*, edited by Bjorn Dressel. London: Routledge, 2012.

Pausacker, Helen. "Presidents as Punakawan: Portrayal of national leaders as clown-servants in Central Javanese Wayang." 35(2) *Journal of Southeast Asian Studies* 213–233 (2004).

Peerenboom, R. P. "A Coup D'Etat in Law's Empire: Dworkin's Hercules Meets Atlas," 9 *Law & Phil.* 95 (1990).

Pepinsky, Thomas. *Economic Crises and the Breakdown of Authoritarian Regimes: Indonesia and Malaysia in Comparative Perspective.* Cambridge: Cambridge University Press, 2009.

Perry, H. W. *Deciding to Decide: Agenda Setting in the United States Supreme Court.* Cambridge, MA: Harvard University Press, 1991.

Platzdasch, Bernhard. *Islamism in Indonesia: Politics in the Emerging Democracy.* Singapore: Institute of Southeast Asian Studies (2009).

Polavarapu, Aparna. "Expanding Standing to Develop Democracy: Third-Party Public Interest Standing as a Tool for Emerging Democracies," 41 *Yale J. Int'l L.* 105 (2016).

Pompe, Sebastiaan. "'Absen dari Reformasi': The Indonesian Judiciary in the Face of History," 1 *Indonesian Law and Administration Review* 73–81 (1999).

Pompe, Sebastiaan. *The Indonesian Supreme Court: A Study of Institutional Collapse.* Ithaca, NY: Southeast Asia Program, Cornell University, 2005.

Posner, Richard. "Judicial Biography," 70 *N.Y.U. L. Rev.* 502, 512 (1995).

Prempeh, H. K. "Marbury in Africa: Judicial Review and the Challenge of Constitutionalism in Contemporary Africa," 80 *Tul. L. Rev.* 1239 (2006).

Pribadi, Yanwar. "Religious Networks in Madura: Pesantren, Nahdatul Ulama, and Kiai as the Core of Santri Culture," 51(1) *J. Islamic Stud., Al-Jami'ah* 14 (2013).

Purwadi. *Pendekar Konstitusi Jimly Asshiddiqie.* Yogyakarta: Hanan Pustaka, 2006.

Qureshi, Taiyyaba A. "State of Emergency: General Pervez Musharraf's Executive Assault on Judicial Independence in Pakistan," 35 *N.C.J. Int'L. & Com. Reg.* 485 (2010).

Rahardjo, Satjipto. "Hukum Progresif, Hukum Yang Membebaskan." 1(1) *Jurnal Hukum Progresif* 1–24 (2005).

Rahardjo, Satjipto. *Membedah Hukum Progresif.* Jakarta: Penerbit Buku Kompas, 2006.

Rahardjo, Satjipto. "Tribut Untuk Mahkamah Konstitusi," in Satjipto Rahardjo, *Penegakan Hukum Progresif.* Jakarta: Penerbit Buku Kompas, 2010.

Rathjen, Gregory J. "Policy Goals, Strategic Choice, and Majority Opinion Assignments in the US Supreme Court: A Replication," *American Journal of Political Science* 713–724 (1974).

Reid, John Philip. "Beneath the Titans," 70 *N.Y.U. L. Rev.* 653 (1995).

Resnick, Judith. "Managerial Judges," 96 *Harv. L. Rev.* 376 (1982).

Rhodes, Charles W. "Rocky". "What Conservative Constitutional Revolution? Moderating Five Degrees of Judicial Conservatism After Six Years of the Roberts Court," 64 *Rutgers L. Rev.* 1 (2011).

Robinson, Geoffrey. "Rawan Is as Rawan Does." In *Violence and the State in Soeharto's Indonesia*, edited by Benedict R. O'G. Anderson. Ithaca, N.Y.: Southeast Asia Program Publications, Southeast Asia Program, Cornell University, 2001.

Robison, Kathryn Robison. *Gender, Islam and Democracy in Indonesia.* London: Routledge, 2015.

Robison, Richard. *Indonesia: The Rise of Capital.* North Sydney, NSW, Australia: Allen & Unwin, 1986.

Robison, Richard and Vedi R. Hadiz, *Reorganising Power in Indonesia: The Politics of Oligarchy in an Age of Markets.* London; New York: Routledge, 2004.

Roestandi, Achmad. *Mahkamah Konstitusi Dalam Tanya Jawab.* Jakarta: Sekretariat Jenderal Mahkamah Konstitusi, 2006.

Rohde, David W. "Policy Goals, Strategic, Choice and Majority Opinion Assignments in the US Supreme Court," *Midwest Journal of Political Science* (1972): 652–682.

Roosa, John. *Pretext for Mass Murder: The September 30th Movement and Soeharto's Coup D'Etat in Indonesia.* Madison, WI: University of Wisconsin Press, 2006.

Rosen, Jeffery. "Class Legislation, Public Choice, and the Structural Constitution," 21 *Harv. J.L. & Pub. Pol'Y* 179 (1997).

Roux, Theunis. *The Politics of Principle: The First South African Constitutional Court, 1995–2005.* Cambridge: Cambridge University Press, 2013.

Roux, Theunis. "American Ideas Abroad: Comparative Implications of US Supreme Court Decision-making Models," 13(1) *Int J Constitutional Law* 90 (2015).

Roux, Theunis and Fritz Edward Siregar, "Trajectories of Curial Power: The Rise, Fall and Partial Rehabilitation of the Indonesian Constitutional Court," 16 (2) *Australian Journal of Asian Law* Article 2 (2016).

Royan, Naomita. "Increasing Press Freedom in Indonesia: The Abolition of the Lèse Majesté and 'Hate-Sowing' Provisions," 10(2) *Australian Journal of Asian Law* 290 (2008).

Rubenfeld, Jed. *Freedom and Time: A Theory of Constitutional Self-Government.* New Haven: Yale University Press, 2001.

Rubin, Alfred P. "Actio Popularis, Jus Cogens, and Offenses Erga Omnes?" 35 *New Eng. L. Rev.* 265, 268 (2001).

Satriawan, Iwan, Helmi Kasim, Siswantana Putri Rachmatika, and Alia Harumdani Widjaja. *Studi Efektifitas Penyelesaian Sengketa Hasil Pemilukada oleh Mahkamah Konstitusi* (Study on the Effectiveness of the Settlement of Regional Election Dispute by the Constitutional Court). Jakarta: Sekretariat Jendral Mahkamah Konstitusi, 2012.

Scheppele, Kim Lane. "The New Hungarian Constitutional Court," 8 *E. Eur. Const. Rev.* 81 (1999).

Scheppele, Kim Lane. "Guardians of the Constitution: Constitutional Court Presidents and the Struggle for the Rule of Law in Post-Soviet Europe," 154 *U. Pa. L. Rev.* 1757 (June, 2006).

Scheppele, Kim Lane. "Hungary's Constitutional Revolution." Paul Krugman's Blog. *The New York Times*. December 19, 2011. http://krugman.blogs.nytimes.com/2011/12/19/hungarys-constitutional-revolution/.

Scheppele, Kim Lane. "How to Evade the Constitution: The Case of the Hungarian Constitutional Court's Decision on the Judicial Retirement Age," *Eutopialaw*, August 8, 2012.

Scheppele, Kim Lane. "Not Your Father's Authoritarianism: The Creation of the 'Frankenstate'," *American Political Science Association European Politics & Society Newsletter* 5 (2013).

Schiff, Damien. "Nothing New Under the Sun: The Minimalism of Chief Justice Roberts and the Supreme Court's Recent Environmental Law Jurisprudence," 15 *Mo. Envtl. L. & Pol'y Rev.* 1 (2007).

Schwartz, Bernard. "The Judicial Ten: America's Greatest Justices," 4 *S. Ill. U. L.J.* 405 (1979).

Schwartz, Herman. *The Struggle for Constitutional Justice in Post Communist Europe*. Chicago : University of Chicago Press, 2000.

Schwarz, Adam. *A Nation in Waiting: Indonesia's Search for Stability*. Colorado: Westview Press, 2000.

Schotland, Roy. "Remembering a Constitutional Hero," 43 *N.Y.L. Sch. L. Rev.* 13 (1999).

Sears, Laurie J. *Shadows of Empire: Colonial Discourse and Javanese Tales*. Durham, NC: Duke University Press, 1996.

Segal, Jeffrey and Harold J. Spaeth. *The Supreme Court and the Attitudinal Model Revisited*. Cambridge, UK: Cambridge University Press, 2002.

Shapiro, Martin. "The Success of Judicial Review." In *Constitutional Dialogues in Comparative Perspective*, edited by Sally J. Kenney, William M Reisinger, and John C Reitz. New York: St. Martin's Press, 1999.

Shevory, Thomas C. *John Marshall's Law: Interpretation, Ideology, and Interest*. Westport, CT: Greenwood Press, 1994.

Sieder, Rachel, Line Schjolden, and Alan Angell. "Introduction." In *The Judicialization of Politics in Latin America*, edited by Rachel Sieder et al. New York: Palgrave Macmillan, 2005.

Simandjuntak, Marsilam. *Pandangan Negara Integralistik: Sumber, Unsur dan Riwayatnya dalam Persiapan UUD 1945*. Jakarta, Indonesia: Pustaka Utama Grafiti, 1994.

Siregar, Fritz Edward. "Indonesian Constitutional Politics, 2003–2013." Unpublished SJD Thesis, University of New South Wales, 2016.

Sitompul, Manahan. "Penyelesaian Sengketa Utang-Piutang Perusahaan Dengan Perdamaian Di Dalam atau Di Luar Proses Kepailitan: Studi Mengenai Lembaga Penundaaan Kewajiban Pembayaran Utang." Unpublished doctoral dissertation, North Sumatera University, 2009.

Slaughter, Anne-Marie. "A Global Community of Courts," 44 *Harv. Int'l L. J.* 191 (2003).

Smith, Jean Edward. *John Marshall: Definer of a Nation*. New York: H. Holt & Co. 1996.

Solyom Laszlo, and Georg Brunner (eds). *Constitutional Judiciary in a New Democracy: The Hungarian Constitutional Court*. Ann Arbor, MI : University of Michigan Press, 2000.

Stanford, W. B. *The Ulysses Theme: A Study in the Adaptability of a Traditional Hero*. Oxford: Blackwell, 1963.

Steinberger, Helmut. "Decisions of the Constitutional Court and Their Effects." In *The Role of the Constitutional Court in the Consolidation of the Rule of Law*, edited by European Commission for Democracy through Law. Strasbourg: Council of Europe Press, 1994.

Stephan, Paul B. "Courts on Courts: Contracting for Engagement and Indifference in International Judicial Encounters," 100 *Va. L. Rev.* 17 (2014).

Stephenson, Jr. Donald Grier. "The Chief Justice as Leader: The Case of Morrison Remick Waite," 14 *Wm & Mary L. Rev.* 899 (1973).

Stephenson, Jr. Donald Grier. "The Waite Court at the Bar of History," 81 *Denv. U.L. Rev.* 449 (2003).

Stephenson, Matthew C. "'When the Devil Turns': The Political Foundation of Independent Judicial Review," 32 *J. Leg. Stud.* 59 (2003).

Stone, Catherine. "The Dual Role of a Chief Justice," 45 *St. Mary's L. J.* 553 (2014).

Stone Sweet, Alec. *Governing with Judges: Constitutional Politics in Europe*. New York: Oxford University Press, 2000.

Suhr, Daniel. "Judicial Cincinnati: The Humble Heroism of Originalist Justices," 5 *FIU L. Rev.* 155 (2009).

Sumadi, Achmad Fadlil. *Pengawasan dan pembinaan pengadilan : Fungsi Manajemen Mahkamah Agung terhadap Pengadilan di Bawahnya setelah Perubahan UUD 1945*. Malang: Setara Press, 2013.

Sunstein, Cass. *One Case at a Time: Judicial Minimalism on the Supreme Court*. Cambridge, MA: Harvard University Press, 1999.

Sunstein, Cass. "Constitutional Personae," *Sup. Ct. Rev.* 433 (2013).

Sunstein, Cass. *Constitutional Personae*. New York, NY: Oxford University Press, 2015.

Sykes, Diane. "Minimalism and Its Limits," *Cato Sup. Ct. Rev.* 17 (2014–2015).

Tanuredjo, Budiman. *Lingah-Pacah: Berjuang Menggapai Keadilan*. Jakarta: Lembaga Studi dan Advokat Masyarakat, 1995.

Tanuredjo, Budiman Tanuredjo, *Akal Akal Akil*. Jakarta: Penerbit Buku Kompas, 2014.

Tate, C. Neal and Torbjorn Vallinder (eds). *The Global Expansion of Judicial Power*. New York: New York University Press, 1995.

Thalib, Abdul Rasyid. *Wewenang Mahkamah Konstitusi dan Implikasinya dalam Sistem Ketatanegaraan Republik Indonesia*. Citra Aditya Bakti, Bandung, Indonesia, 2006.

Thee, Kian Wie. "The Soeharto Era and After: Stability, Development and Crisis, 1996–2000." In *The Emergence of a National Economy: An Economic History of Indonesia*, 1800–2000, edited by Howard Dick, Vincent J. H. Houben, J. Thomas Lindblad, and Kian Wie Thee. New South Wales & Honolulu: Allen & Unwin and University of Hawai'I Press, 2002.

Thorson, Carla. *Politics, Judicial Review and the Russian Constitutional Court*. Palgrave Macmillan: 2012.

Tobias, Carl. "Warren Burger and the Administration of Justice," 41 *Vill. L. Rev.* 505 (1996).

Trochev, Alexei. *Judging Russia: Constitutional Court in Russian Politics, 1990–2006*. Cambridge; New York: Cambridge University Press, 2008.

Tushnet, Mark. "The Possibilities of Comparative Constitutional Law," 108 *Yale L.J.* 1225 (1999).

Tushnet, Mark. "Alternative Forms of Judicial Review," 101 *Mich. L. Rev.* 2781 (August, 2003a).

Tushnet, Mark. "Judging Judicial Review: Marbury in the Modern Era: Alternative Forms of Judicial Review," 101 *Mich. L. Rev.* 2781 (2003b).

Tushnet, Mark. "New Forms of Judicial Review and the Persistence of Rights-and Democracy-Based Worries," 38 *Wake Forest L. Rev.* 813, 814 (2003c).

Tushnet, Mark. "Social Welfare Rights and the Forms of Judicial Review," 82 *Tex. L. Rev.* 1895 (June, 2004b).

Tushnet, Mark. *Weak Courts, Strong Rights Judicial Review and Social Welfare Rights in Comparative Constitutional Law*. Princeton, NJ: Princeton University Press, 2008.

Tushnet, Mark. "The Rise of Weak-Form Judicial Review." In *Comparative Constitutional Law*, edited by Tom Ginsburg and Rosalind Dixon. Cheltenham, UK; Northampton, MA: Edward Elgar, 2011.

Tushnet, Mark. "Studying Second Generation Constitutional Courts: After the Heroes Have Left," paper presented at the Annual Meeting of Law and Society Association, New Orleans, June 2–5, 2016.

Tushnet, Mark and Rosalind Dixon, "Weak-form Review and its Constitutional Relatives: An Asian Perspective." In *Comparative Constitutional Law in Asia*, edited by Rosalind Dixon and Tom Ginsburg. Cheltenham, UK; Northampton, MA: Edward Elgar, 2014.

Vinning, Joseph. *Legal Identity: The Coming of Age of Public Law*. New Haven, Yale University Press, 1978.

Walker, Thomas, Lee Epstein, and William J. Dixon. "On the Mysterious Demise of Consensual Norms in the United States Supreme Court," 50(2) *Journal of Politics* 361–89 (1988).

Widner, Jennifer A. *Building the Rule of Law: Francis Nyalali and the Road to Judicial Independence in Africa*. New York: W.W. Norton & Company, Inc., 2001.

Wolfe, Christopher. *The Rise of Modern Judicial Review: From Constitutional Interpretation to Judge-Made Law*. Lanham, MD: Rowman & Littlefield, 1994.

Yamin, Muhammad, *Naskah Persiapan Undang—Undang Dasar 1945*. Jakarta: Yayasan Prapanca, 1959.

Yap, Po Jen. *Constitutional Dialogue in Common Law Asia*. Oxford, UK: Oxford University Press, 2015.

Zanibar, Zen. "Perkembangan Ketatanegaraan Dalam Pandangan Jimly Asshiddiqie yang Tercecer" [The Forgotten Thought of Jimly Asshiddiqie]. In *Konstitusi dan Ketatanegaraan Indonesia Kontemporer: Pemikiran Jimly Asshiddiqie and Para Pakar Hukum* [Constitution and Constitutionalism in Contemporary Indonesia: The Thought of Jimly Asshiddiqie and Other Legal Scholars], edited by Rofiqul-Umam Ahmad, M. Ali Safa'at, and Rafiuddin Munis Tamar. Jakarta: The Biography Institute, 2007.

Zerial, Natalie. "Decision No. 2-3/PUU-V/2007 [2007] (Indonesian Constitutional Court)," 14 *Austl. Int'l LJ* 217 (2007).

Ziegenhain, Patrick. *The Indonesian Parliament and Democratization*. Singapore: Institute of Southeast Asian Studies, 2008.

Zoelva, Hamdan. *Pemakzulan Presiden di Indonesia*. Jakarta: Sinar Grafika, 2011.

Index

For Product Safety Concerns and Information please contact our EU
representative GPSR@taylorandfrancis.com
Taylor & Francis Verlag GmbH, Kaufingerstraße 24, 80331 München, Germany

www.ingramcontent.com/pod-product-compliance
Ingram Content Group UK Ltd.
Pitfield, Milton Keynes, MK11 3LW, UK
UKHW022012180926
475701UK00003B/325

* 9 7 8 0 3 6 7 5 9 1 7 4 8 *